SOCIAL CONTROL UNDER STALIN AND KHRUSHCHEV

Social Control under Stalin and Khrushchev

The Phantom of a Well-Ordered State

EDITED BY IMMO REBITSCHEK AND
AARON B. RETISH

UNIVERSITY OF TORONTO PRESS
Toronto Buffalo London

© University of Toronto Press 2023
Toronto Buffalo London
utorontopress.com

ISBN 978-1-4875-4427-0 (cloth) ISBN 978-1-4875-4431-7 (EPUB)
                                ISBN 978-1-4875-4423-2 (PDF)

Library and Archives Canada Cataloguing in Publication

Title: Social control under Stalin and Khrushchev : the phantom of a well-ordered state / edited by Immo Rebitschek and Aaron B. Retish.
Names: Rebitschek, Immo, editor. | Retish, Aaron B., editor.
Description: Includes bibliographical references and index.
Identifiers: Canadiana (print) 20220486832 | Canadiana (ebook) 20220486972 | ISBN 9781487544270 (cloth) | ISBN 9781487544232 (PDF) | ISBN 9781487544317 (EPUB)
Subjects: LCSH: Stalin, Joseph, 1878–1953 – Influence. | LCSH: Khrushchev, Nikita Sergeevich, 1894–1971 – Influence. | LCSH: Social control – Soviet Union – History. | LCSH: Social norms – Soviet Union – History. | LCSH: Police – Soviet Union – History. | LCSH: Criminal law – Soviet Union – History. | LCSH: Punishment – Soviet Union – History. | LCSH: Soviet Union – Social policy.
Classification: LCC HN523.5 .S63 2023 | DDC 303.3/3094709045 – dc23

Cover design: Heng Wee Tan
Cover image: UC Santa Cruz University Library Digital Collections, Branson DeCou Archive

We wish to acknowledge the land on which the University of Toronto Press operates. This land is the traditional territory of the Wendat, the Anishnaabeg, the Haudenosaunee, the Métis, and the Mississaugas of the Credit First Nation.

University of Toronto Press acknowledges the financial support of the Government of Canada, the Canada Council for the Arts, and the Ontario Arts Council, an agency of the Government of Ontario, for its publishing activities.

Contents

List of Figures and Tables   vii

Acknowledgments   ix

Abbreviations   xi

Note on Terms and Usage   xiii

Introduction   3
AARON B. RETISH AND IMMO REBITSCHEK

Part I: Negotiating Terror and Social Discipline in the 1930s

1 Controlling the Soviet Family through Alimony? Righteous Women, Starving Children, and Bad Fathers, 1925–1939   25
AARON B. RETISH

2 *Nashi/ne Nashi*: Individual Smallholders, Social Control, and the State in Ziuzdinskii District, Kirov Region, 1932–1939   49
SAMANTHA LOMB

3 Social Control in the Workplace: Labour Discipline and Workers' Rights under Stalin   77
MARIA STARUN

4 "Such Was the Music, Such Was the Dance": Understanding the Internal and External Motivations of a Stalinist Perpetrator   107
TIMOTHY K. BLAUVELT

Part II: Forging Society in War and Peace

5 Soviet "Hard Labour," Population Management, and Social Control in the Post-war Gulag   135
ALAN BARENBERG

6 The Protection of Socialist Property and the Voices of "Thieves"   161
JULIETTE CADIOT

7 "They Are Afraid": Medical Surveillance of Reproduction and Illegal Abortions in the Soviet Union, 1944–1953   187
AMANDA McNAIR

Part III: Post Stalin: Trajectories of Social Control

8 From the Street to the Court (and Back): Juvenile Delinquency in the 1950s   213
IMMO REBITSCHEK

9 After the XXth Congress: Liberalization and the Problem of Social Order   237
YORAM GORLIZKI

10 From Mass Terror to Mass Social Control: The Soviet Secret Police's New Roles and Functions in the Early Post-Stalin Era   263
EVGENIA LEZINA

11 Social Control in Post-Stalinist Courts: Housing Disputes and Citizen Demand of Legality   299
DINA MOYAL

12 Soviet Socialisms: From Stalin to Khrushchev   325
DAVID SHEARER

Contributors   345

Index   349

Figures and Tables

Figures

2.1 Schematic map of the grain output in Kirov region, 1937, with Ziuzdinskii highlighted (GASPI KO 1290/1/296/56)   50
5.1 Official mortality vs. transfers to ITKs/prisons for priority camps vs. "convalescence" colonies, 1946–8 (per thousand)   154
10.1 Distribution of different forms of *profilaktika* conducted by the KGB in the Ukrainian SSR, 1960   274

Tables

2.1 Smallholders' income   58
5.1 Population of *katorga* camp sections, 1944–9 (January 1)   139
5.2 *Katorga* convict mortality (reported), 1944–9 (deaths per thousand)   148
5.3 Releases from *katorga* convict sections, 1944–9   150
5.4 Outgoing transfers (total) from *katorga* convict sections, 1944–8   152
10.1 Agents' networks of the KGB of Ukraine during the late Stalinist and Khrushchev periods   271
10.2 "Anti-Soviet" groups disbanded in the Ukrainian SSR, 1954–8   277

Acknowledgments

As with many other recent scholarly endeavours, this volume travelled a long and winding road. It began over beers at the Irish pub in Jena, Germany, and evolved into a conference and then brought more scholars together into this volume. The global pandemic followed by the outbreak of Russia's war against Ukraine have put our capacities and those of our contributors to the test. We owe a special gratitude to all of them. All those who had attended the conference and Peter H. Solomon, Tatiana Borisova, and David Shearer in particular helped to create an exciting atmosphere for the exchange between different generations of scholars. Laird McNeil and Anne Grab did excellent work in editing and formatting the manuscript. We also thank John Angell and John Yates for their prompt and thorough translations. Stephen Shapiro of the University of Toronto Press has supported this volume from the beginning and has patiently fielded our many questions throughout the process. We are particularly grateful to Joachim von Puttkamer, Daniela Gruber, and the Imre Kertész Kolleg Jena for academic and financial support as well as the Fritz Thyssen Foundation, Friedrich-Schiller-University Jena, and the College of Liberal Arts and Sciences of Wayne State University for their generous funding. These institutions made the creation of this volume possible in the first place.

Abbreviations

CPSU	Communist Party of the Soviet Union
DAMO	State Archive of Mykolayiv Region
DPR	Receiver-Distribution Centres
DTVK/L	Corrective labour colonies and camps for underage delinquents
FZO	Factory training school
GAKO	State Archive of Kirov Region
GAPK	State Archive of Perm' Region
GARF	State Archive of the Russian Federation
GASPI Ko	State Archive for Socio-Political History of Kirov Region
GDASBU	State Archive of the State Security Service Ukraine
GULag/Gulag	Chief Administration for Camps
GUM	Chief Administration of the militsiia (civil police)
EKO	Economic Department of the (O)GPU
HPSSS	Harvard Project on the Soviet Social System
IMEL	Institute of Marx-Engels-Lenin
ITK	Corrective labour colony
ITL	Corrective labour camp
KGB	Committee for State Security
Kraikom	Territorial Party Committee
Kolkhoz	Collective Farm
LYA	Latvian Special Archive
MGB	Ministry of State Security
MVD	Ministry for Internal Affairs
Narkomzem	People's Commissariat of Agriculture
NEP	New Economic Policy
NKGB	People's Commissariat of State Security
NKIu	People's Commissariat of Justice

NKVD	People's Commissariat of Internal Affairs
Obkom	Regional Party Committee
OblZU	Regional land management organization
(O)GPU	(Combined) State Political Administration
OSO	Special Board of the NKVD
PermGANI	Perm' State Archive of Contemporary History
POW	Prisoner of War
Raikom/RK	District Party Committee
RaiZO	District land management department
RGAE	Russian State Economic Archive
RGASPI	Russian State Archive for Socio-Political History
RIK	District Executive Committee
RKI	Peasants' Inspection/State inspectorate agency
RKK	Rates and Conflicts Commissions
RSFSR	Russian Soviet Federated Socialist Republic
sak'art'velos šss ark'ivi (I)	Section I of the Archive of the Ministry of Internal Affairs of Georgia
SBU	Security Service of Ukraine
Sovnarkom	Council of People's Commissars
SPO	Secret Political Department of the NKVD
TsANO	Central State Archive of Nizhegorod Region
TsGAMO	Central State Archive of Moscow Region
TsGA Moscow	Central State Archive of Moscow City
TsGASO	Central State Archive of Samara Region
TsGA SPB	Central State Archive of St Petersburg
TsGA UR	Central State Archive of Republic Udmurtia
TsIK/VTsIK	(All-Russian) Central Executive Committee
TsK	Central Committee
TVK/L	Corrective labour colonies and camps
URO/OURZ	Allocation and Distribution Department of the GULAG
USSR	Union of Socialist Soviet Republics (Soviet Union)
VSKHNIT	"Great Sons Willing to Find the Truth of Mysteries"
VTsSPS	All-Union Central Council of Trade Unions

Note on Terms and Usage

We use the Library of Congress system of transliteration for Russian and Georgian except for names commonly known in English (for example, Trotsky instead of Trotskii). Names of cities and regions changed during the period under study, and many have changed since. We use the official names during the period.

Contributors have used archives across several countries with various structures and languages. For simplicity, we cite archival references using /'s that denote: collections/inventories/files/pages.

SOCIAL CONTROL UNDER STALIN AND KHRUSHCHEV

Introduction

AARON B. RETISH AND IMMO REBITSCHEK

People living under Stalinism experienced one of the most repressive regimes in modern history, one that relied on force to transform society and responded to deviant behaviour and suspicious biographies with violence. Joseph Stalin and his ruling circle launched mass police operations as a form of class warfare against what they perceived as "socially dangerous" elements. In fear of social disorder, the regime targeted whole segments of the population. It executed 740,000 people, exiled or deported over 3.5 million peasants and national minorities, and imprisoned those charged with anti-Soviet crimes into a Gulag system that spanned the country, all to try to annihilate potential enemies and control the behaviour of its citizens.[1] The Stalinist state used seemingly unregulated mechanisms of terror to enforce control over its populace. Still, the regime also relied on less brazenly violent mechanisms to discipline, notably the legal and penal system and financial pressure through taxation and fines. Countless citizens appeared in courts as defendants but also as plaintiffs. Punitive payments were used to control the behaviour of peasants. Factory tribunals arbitrated and curbed everyday conflicts between workers. A study of these instruments of social control reveals a complicated administrative structure that did not always work uniformly or smoothly, but that evolved throughout and beyond the reign of Stalin. Moreover, it reveals a new way to spotlight individual agency and to re-examine the evolving relationship between the state and the individual from Stalin to Khrushchev.

Social Control under Stalin and Khrushchev argues that social control in the Soviet Union was not entirely about the monolithic state imposing its vision with violent force. Various divisions within the judiciary and other state organs, from local courts and factory or collective farm councils to the highest officials of the procuracy and prisons, tried to impose their visions of control. They worked through ideology, the laws, messages from the centre, and their own personal ideas of social norms. This book builds on, and challenges, the scholarship on the official responses to social disorder under Joseph Stalin and Nikita Khrushchev by examining social control more broadly. Works that focus on the role of Stalin, the Gulag, or the police show only part of the picture. Social control – that is, enforcing social norms and penalizing deviance from it – was a far more complex process that involved more agents than these studies would suggest.

While most scholars focus on the monolithic nature of a repressive state apparatus, this book explores the issue of agency and widens the focus on the institutions and people that enforced and negotiated these norms. Scholars do not all agree on what constitutes "agency." Debates over its definition are usually wrapped up in a larger controversy about the psychological and philosophical conceptions of human rationality. Our interest is with the physical interaction between individuals and a state machinery and thus we understand agency as the "capacity of human beings to shape the circumstances in which they live."[2] By doing so, we cast a new light on how the Stalinist and the post-Stalinist state tried to discipline and control its citizens, and how people remained resilient to or accommodated and occasionally resisted these attempts. People negotiated their own will and interests with the state and each other in enforcing social norms. The enforcement of social norms and the response to their violations were in the hands of multiple agents, pursuing often competing and even contradicting aims. Social control was not just the objective of a totalitarian state but the result of institutional and individual struggles.

Who set the boundaries and norms for behaviour in a violent dictatorship in the first place? This and other questions marked the starting point for a workshop in 2021 in Jena, Germany. A new generation of international scholars met to discuss the attempts, the ways, and the means to make people manageable in the Stalinist dictatorship. They threw light on the ruptures and continuities of this problem during and after Stalin's lifetime. This volume is the result of these discussions. The contributors put social control in its larger context, looking at the wide network of state mechanisms of law and order and how individual Soviet citizens interacted with them. It is extending the search for individuality into the sphere of social control and thus back to the question of how the state related to and controlled the individual.

The term "social control" has its roots in the field of criminology and has long been equated with legal control. The sociologist James Chriss, however, warns not to narrow social control down to the judiciary and the other "subsystems of policing." Instead, he presents a broader typology that takes into account interpersonal relations and medical interventions as ways to foster individual compliance.[3] Without reproducing this typology, this volume builds on the premise to look beyond conventional policing structures and draws attention to other social (and medical) spheres of human interaction when discussing schemes and limits for individual behaviour. We assume "social control" to be a complex set of processes and means used by institutions and individuals to establish norms of behaviour in a community and to penalize deviance from these norms. While police and courts play an integral part in this set, our focus extends to indirect and less coercive means for regulating social (inter)action. For example, through taxation, housing policies, or welfare provision, modern states incentivize certain behaviours in a society.[4] In a Foucauldian sense, "modern power" is about creating uniformity in social relationships and social practices – less by physical coercion than by regulation and observation.[5] A closer look at these attempts and different means to achieve control helps to understand the relationship between state and individual on a more performative level, and also to place the Soviet Union in the context of modern statehood.

The goal to control society and enforce social norms is a feature of the modern state. Governments across Europe in the nineteenth and twentieth centuries fostered techniques to rationalize their society and influence individual behaviour on a mass scale. Through the expansion of interventionist programs like social welfare and medical programs, they aimed to improve and control their people. Employing the social sciences like economics, sociology, and criminology, they studied their societies and standardized social norms. States also attempted to reshape the environment, from new urban landscapes to forests and agriculture. Controlling the social fabric was not limited to dictatorships.[6] Modern states across the political spectrum tested ways to scientifically guide and shape the social for a grander purpose, but it comes as no surprise that dictatorships in particular took this effort to an unprecedented extreme. Stalin's Soviet Union in particular followed the premise to eradicate the old and foster the new. In the wake of the first Five-Year Plan, the Soviet leadership politicized crime and deviant behaviour. After the forced collectivization of agriculture, Stalin declared victory over the "exploiting class" and the end of class antagonism. Legal violations and outlawed customs were now branded as remnants of capitalism and criminals as "enemies of the people" and thus a threat to the socialist project.[7] Social order in turn meant to cleanse the "proletarian" society from these elements. The "proletarian dictatorship" proved to be an elusive vision. The ideological perception of a classless society collided with social realities and the fluidity and the confusion of social identity.[8] Waging a war against crime put millions into the crosshairs. Nonetheless, the state was willing to create a new society – without the "usual suspects," without chaos – at enormous costs.[9] The ideological claim for this functional social collective remained intact – both under Stalin and Khrushchev. The stakes, the human costs, and the means to attain it, however, changed.

There have been scores of studies on the politics of mass violence under Stalin. Recent scholarship has gone into the interrogation rooms of the secret police and Gulag camps to detail the practices and extent of these policies.[10] We know now more about the cultural and social imprint the political police organs left on Soviet society and how these organs even exported their practices and mindsets into Eastern Europe after the war.[11] However, there are more nuances to explore. Works focusing on the role of the Party leadership, the Gulag, or the police show only one, albeit central, part of the picture of social control under Stalin. Enforcing social norms and penalizing deviance was a far more complex process that involved more agents than these studies would suggest. In the same decade the political police orchestrated purges and random executions, courts, and procurators processed millions of cases.[12] From a law criminalizing abortion to passport regulations, criminal and civil proceedings were as significant for the implementation of social norms as the terror.[13] Legal acts determined the terms of membership in Soviet society.[14] Unlike the police, the justice system was designed to control and not to cleanse society. By enforcing order on the basis of codified norms, legal organs complemented (and often challenged) the police operations and its pre-emptive and unchecked strikes against social target groups.[15] The mechanisms of social policing, the dynamics among police, procuracy, and the judiciary and their respective authority shifted during and after the war and once Stalin was gone.[16] The regime constantly adapted its ways to attain control over society.

The Soviet toolkit of modern governance also included indirect means for encouraging and deterring behaviour. Education and state-run mass media spread ideals and norms. As Vera Dunham spotlighted back in 1976, the Soviet government used nonpunitive forms of social control under late Stalinism, making a deal with the Soviet "middle class" to accommodate their materialistic dreams in exchange for their acquiescence.[17] The Stalinist regime campaigned for social improvement through the advancement of "modern" cultural norms.[18] That included the promise and the provision of welfare (towards children in particular) but also financial incentives that contributed to conditioning, controlling, and transforming the social.[19] Moreover, social control did not just come from above. As scholars have recently argued, throughout Stalin's rule, "Stalinist subjects" themselves made moral and legal claims based on their own social interests. People sued for alimony, divorce, or damages and initiated criminal cases on their own behalf. They petitioned and tested the limits of social concepts by engaging state authorities in an exchange with multiple outcomes.[20] The leeway and the boundaries for individual behaviour were defined by different hands at different times. This volume assembles the latest research on these agents and the variety of ways of policing social and individual behaviour in the Stalinist and post-Stalinist dictatorship.

While individual researchers have been unearthing these nuances for some years now, a comprehensive look at the complex landscape of agency is still missing. There are no English-language books on the broad institutions of Stalinist social control and the popular response to them. Lynne Viola's edited volume on popular resistance was an important step in that regard. It demonstrated the diffuse and multi-layered nature of state power, both horizontal and vertical, reminding us to see state actors in their respective social and cultural contexts and questioning the binary of state and society.[21] While it focused on individual actors and their challenge to bureaucracies, our book highlights the dynamic within the bureaucracies themselves. Rather than the momentum of resistance, we focus on the strategies, means, and failures to attain control over individual and collective behaviour.

Several major strands of research on Soviet bureaucracies have remained unconnected. The historiography of the police rarely relates to the perspective of legal historians and vice versa. Scholars of the 1930s usually focus on either the monolithic nature of a repressive apparatus, or they capture only one particular institutional framework, especially the police. David Shearer and Paul Hagenloh have revealed the inner workings of the political (and the civil) police in the 1930s.[22] However, they only touch upon the court system and the relationship between police, procurators, and judges.[23] A few scholars have also shed light on the role of military courts as complementary tools for the NKVD's operations, while more recent works begin to explore the interagency dynamics (and conflicts) of police, courts, and procuracy in the aftermath of the mass operations.[24] Beyond the 1930s, our knowledge of these interrelationships and the civil police (*militsiia*) in particular and other subdivisions of the Ministry of the Interior is limited to organizational schemes – at least for the period of Stalin's lifetime.[25]

The Soviet legal system holds a prominent position in the historiography, as law and the courts play a significant role in the analysis of state power.[26] This research developed independently from the works on the history of the Soviet police and emphasizes different approaches to Soviet statehood. The history of the law under Stalinism introduced distinct narratives on the functionality of the Soviet state and the means to enforce control. Especially after 1945, the Soviet procuracy and the judiciary coordinated and operated the regime's response towards violations of social norms and thus contributed to a growing Gulag system. Scholars traced the intellectual and structural evolution of legal specialists in the 1930s, yet their relationship with the other ministries as well as their own groundwork and the daily practices of legal and police work could only be speculated on.[27] In fact, the scholarship on the world of courts, procurators, and advocates has remained rather detached from works on the administrative operations of the police and the camp system.[28] In turn, recent scholarship on the Soviet penal system does not include legal or judicial perspectives. Works on the system of "political violence" have not studied the legal dimensions and the practical interdependencies of law enforcement. Links with the judiciary and the procuracy are mostly absent from recent Gulag research as well.[29] Similarly, the research on criminality is fragmented. Recent works cover particular sectors of criminal prosecution (such as war crimes) or particular mass campaigns targeting theft, "hooliganism," corruption, or juvenile delinquency more generally. These works reveal opportunities for individuals to pursue their own interests, and they expose crucial design flaws in the system of criminal law enforcement that demand a more comprehensive approach.[30] In contrast, the field of Soviet civil law has not received much attention since the opening of the archives. The few recent works on property and family conflicts point to how the Soviet state used its laws to construct social roles and enact social control while also showing that everyday citizens used civil law to assert their perceived rights and benefits.[31] Civil law practices constitute a great desideratum in the history of the periods from Stalin and Khrushchev.

This volume provides a far-reaching study of the interplay of law, policing, and punishment under Stalin and Khrushchev and their wake. It explores institutions of social interaction and regulation by focusing on legal, penal, and financial control. It does not claim to be comprehensive, as the Soviet regime provided a complex framework for control. Most notably, the organization of the Communist Party set its own framework of norms, which had a massive influence over the members' behaviour and even the people without Party cards.[32] The book is also limited in its geographical scope. Apart from Timothy Blauvelt's and Amanda McNair's excursus to the Caucasus and Evgenia

Lezina's survey of the activities of the Ukrainian and Latvian KGB, the focal point of this collection lies in Russia. Future research endeavours should feel encouraged to raise and adjust the questions posed here to the entire Soviet space.

While the volume seeks to explore nuances and agency inside the state bureaucracy, it also builds on and connects with research on agency and individuality in Soviet society. Working on Stalinism in particular is a quest for the individual. During the Cold War, this quest challenged the (often quoted) claim of totalitarian control. The political history of Stalinism revolved around the regime's capacities to extend its grip and to forestall resistance. Individuality was perceived as a by-product of a weakening state. Later generations of researchers have then put this claim into its empirical context, highlighting the individual tactics to escape, change, and appropriate political incentives "from above" – within certain limits.[33] Soviet citizens navigated dangers from their peers and from above, and found space to express individual and psychological agency; to express discontent and create their own identity – even in the face of mass repression.[34] As for the time after Stalin, historiography made us aware of the dimensions of "everyday resistance" and non-conformist behaviour.[35] Still, we also read about nuances in the behaviour, thoughts, beliefs, and opinions voiced from a Stalinist society, that was neither atomized nor entirely paralysed.[36] The quest for the Soviet man/woman as an "ideological agent in its own right"[37] must be extended to the structural aspects of human agency. Beyond the question about the legitimacy of this "Stalinist subjectivity," what defined the limits when the thought of individuality turned into action? What constituted and curtailed the practical realm of individuality?

This volume collects glimpses on this realm. It brings together scholars who put social control in its larger context, looking at the wide network of state mechanisms of law and order and how Soviet citizens interacted with them. It explores the issue of agency and widens the focus on the institutions and people that enforced and negotiated these norms – within and beyond the police. By doing so, we cast a new light on how the Soviet state tried to discipline and control its citizens and how people accommodated and occasionally resisted these attempts – during Stalin's lifetime and beyond. In fact, the research on social control has usually been tied to distinct phases of Stalin's reign. *Social Control under Stalin and Khrushchev* opens up perspectives to see both continuities and breaks in the evolution of social control from the late 1920s to the mid-1950s. Each of the chapters can be read separately, but if put together they present the complexity of the institutions of Stalinist social control and the continuities that outlasted Stalin himself. The volume is thus divided chronologically into three sections: "Negotiating Terror and Social Discipline in the 1930s," "Forging a Society in War and Peace," and "Post Stalin: Trajectories of Social Control," which looks at the lasting instruments of social control beyond the death of Stalin in 1953. The underlying question for each of the segments is how various agents envisioned, enforced, and negotiated individual and collective behaviour – amid three major currents in the history of Stalinism.

The first section deals with social control in the age of mass violence, when forced collectivization and the Great Terror set coarse parameters for survival and the behaviour of millions of people. Members of the courts, police, collective farms, as well as citizens navigated within these parameters. Aaron Retish shows that the Soviet state deferred to individual agency to compensate for a porous welfare system. Alimony policies in the 1930s empowered and expected women to stake their claim against domestic exploitation. Unwed mothers and poor women in particular made use of their legal means to force absent fathers back into the scene and to support their children. Even though the state was limited in its capacities to enforce these claims on a broader scale, it encouraged individual agency to assert (domestic) social control. Samantha Lomb in contrast demonstrates how enforcing social control through taxation brought local and regional agency into conflict with Moscow, thus unveiling the limits and different perceptions of policing peasant behaviour within the Party hierarchy. In the mid-1930s, so-called individual smallholders defied collectivization in the Kirov region. The central government sought to integrate them through punitive taxation into larger Soviet social structures (collective farms). In contrast, local and regional Party authorities unilaterally weaponized the tax burden in order to destroy what they perceived as "class alien elements." Ultimately, neither of these approaches succeeded in vanquishing individual peasant practices.

In urban spaces too, different agents projected varying strategies to influence social behaviour. Maria Starun draws the focus on the interplay of different disciplinary and legal structures in enterprises and factories. Here too, social control was not simply about political authorities enforcing their vision of social discipline. Soviet workers engaged with these structures to pursue and protect their interests. Even though Party interventions and administrative disorder undermined the function of this legal framework, many workers appealed to comrades' courts or trade union bodies to impose or challenge social norms within their workplace. Timothy Blauvelt's chapter focuses on a different workplace, examining the internal workings of the Soviet's most notorious policing body: the NKVD. Through mass arrests and executions of the

1930s, the political police were a significant agent for policing society. Blauvelt's focus lays not on the individual interaction with but on the individuality within this institution. Based on case files against former NKVD officials, his paper reveals how the (violent) ways in which social control was exerted were shaped by individual belief and self-interest. The case of Sergo Davlianidze draws our attention to the violent and rather arbitrary spheres of social control in the 1930s. While the state and its people interacted in court proceedings and over taxation policies, individual behaviour was also conditioned by an "ecosystem of violence," in which generational experience, cultural legacies, peer pressure, paranoia, and ideology affected and lent justification for individual action.[38] Still, within this very system the individual could leave an imprint: even as a perpetrator.

The parameters for social control shifted during the war, when the external threat created both violent pressure for effective governance and leeway for individuals and institutions to interpret social norms. This friction lasted through the 1940s and constitutes the framework for the second section. The Gulag was intentionally designed to be an instrument and a distinct system of social control. Alan Barenberg shows how within this system multiple logics and organizing principles were at work, when the camp authorities were controlling and managing the behaviour of convicts. During the war, people sentenced to "hard labour" (*katorga*), were in extremely poor health. Gulag authorities argued over the right course in managing this group of people, labelled as both "dangerous" and incapable of hard labour. Premises of production and productivity came into conflict with penal logics to isolate and exploit the most dangerous convicts. Barenberg illustrates how this tension translated into contradictory practice. There was no single organizational principle to social control in the Gulag.

Juliette Cadiot reverses the perspective on this system. She analyses successful petitions for pardon by Gulag detainees. Once prosecuted for theft, these men and women reflected on their actions and the norms they had violated in the eyes of the regime. Cadiot demonstrates how they underlined their belief and the commitment to the Soviet state. However, the majority of them would question the norms altogether or claim that they did not apply to them in the first place. By labelling them as thieves, the Stalin regime altered the terms of the social contract and thus alienated them from Soviet society and its social norms. This alienation became a significant marker of the Soviet post-war era, and it extended to various spheres of the social. By the end of the Second World War, the Soviet state was not only determined to enforce property legislation, but it enhanced its efforts to extend its reach even deeper into the populace – also by policing women's bodies. Amanda McNair examines how legal and medical structures were mobilized to enforce the ban on abortion and thus its aggressive pronatalist policies. Again, the state deferred to low-level expertise for controlling the behaviour of Soviet citizens. However, procurators and medical personnel did not always comply with the law, sometimes helped others to circumvent it, while scapegoating one another for failing to enforce it. At the same time, the abortion surveillance system did massively constrain women's options to control their bodies and their fate. Procurators, policemen, and physicians established this system of social control, while women sought to maintain their agency in it.

With the Soviet crackdown on theft, abortion, and corruption, legal expertise became increasingly significant to policing the social. This trend started in post-war times and then constituted the basis for political and social reform after 1953. Thus, rather than establishing Stalin's death as a clear breaking point, the volume's third section draws the focus on the larger trajectories of change, when the executive authority over the social shifted from the police to the judiciary, and the legal sphere in general. Already in the late 1940s, the procuracy and the judiciary staked their claim as agents of enforcing and also as a platform for negotiating social norms, advocating not the rule of law but professionalism, precision, and predictability in policing individual behaviour. Immo Rebitschek shows how the procuracy and the courts pushed for scientific and also more reliable methods when investigating and prosecuting juvenile delinquents or supervising juvenile prison and care facilities. After Stalin's death, they finally had the institutional and political leverage to hold the civil police more often accountable for violations of procedural norms. The observance of procedural law and police accountability were part of a larger cultural shift in the 1950s, which shaped ways to assert social control more generally, as Yoram Gorlizki demonstrates. This new system was tied to and often labelled with the re-emergence of "socialist legality." With Stalin gone, the regime called for a stronger commitment to legal norms while it tried to contain arbitrary and extra-legal operations. This premise, however, collided with the social and cultural legacies of Stalin's reign, as the Soviet *militsiia* in particular was ill-equipped to counter the waves of social disorder in the wake of social and economic transformation. Consequently, the regime adjusted its policing tactics by mobilizing the public and developing more prophylactic (and extra-legal) approaches to assert social control.

Evgenia Lezina provides further insights into this adjustment to policing. Lezina examines the mechanics of prophylactic policing by the hands of the secret police (KGB). By the late 1950s and early 1960s, the KGB used more sophisticated, subtle, and complex policing techniques to counter (and to grasp) what they perceived as ever more complex forms of deviancy. Both overt (public) pressure and covert (surveillance) strategies should help to control and possibly compromise the activities of religious groups or alleged nationalist and political "undergrounds." Lezina shows a clear break with the pervasive mass policing techniques of the Stalin era. Still, neither of the subsequently used techniques were entirely new. The KGB rather refined tools of its predecessor and turned networks of agents and trusted persons into the basis of prophylactic policing. While the KGB and the police enforced certain sets of norms and found ways to pressure individuals and groups into submission, Soviet citizens continued to utilize some of the structures to pursue individual interests. Dina Moyal examines how men and women in the USSR claimed their rights over housing disputes in court and thus participated in monitoring and influencing the behaviour of other citizens. Acting on the notion of socialist legality they instilled their own values and norms by using the courts to advance personal needs. Soviet citizens did not simply stand on the receiving end in the Soviet justice system. They successfully sued others and even state institutions. The state in turn relied on these initiatives to supervise its officials.

Soviet state leaders saw social disorder as an existential threat to Soviet power, but social disorder was mostly brought on by their own policies. The Stalinist and post-Stalinist state lurched from crisis to crisis. David Shearer, in his concluding essay, suggests that we see the Stalinist state like an overstretched colonial power trying to control a hostile population. It implemented martial law programs to control society and perceived dangerous populations as disorganized and ad hoc as they were repressive. The Stalinist state intruded on people's lives and their souls, and it became even more invasive in the private sphere after Stalin. That also became a time that the state embraced reform and demilitarization, leaving the colonial system behind. Citizens asserted their civil rights more forcefully, and judicial reformers extended their jurisdiction over the field of social control.

Addressing individual agency and institutional frictions does not turn the Soviet state into a pluralist space. Decisions from the Party leadership and administrative decrees had the power to turn millions of peoples' lives upside down; crushing resistance and leaving no space for appropriation. Executions could not be appealed under Stalin or after. Party members were under their own jurisdiction and had the prerogative to infer with legal decisions. The influence of Party policies on Soviet legal institutions (on all administrative levels) set visible and invisible boundaries for men and women to make use of "their" rights as citizens.[39] Consequently, there is neither cause nor need to reconsider questions about the "rule of law" in the Soviet Union under or after Stalin. The Soviet state and Party leadership actively resisted the idea of a *"pravovoe gosudarstvo"* (law-based state) until the Gorbachev era while measuring themselves against this ideal (especially after 1945). This "hypocrisy"[40] left officials and institutions struggling, but it also left room for agency through legal procedure.

It was also impossible to suffocate individual agency and to streamline decision-making processes in a complex state structure altogether. By pointing to these tensions, this volume is not belabouring the limits of totalitarian rule. It underlines an historical aspect of authoritarian governance that applies to regimes around the globe into the present day. Under the all-encompassing premise of unchecked rule, dictatorships in the twentieth and twenty-first centuries always left pockets of individual agency, enabling citizens to make claims on the regime or to set norms on their own behalf. The boundaries of these spaces varied greatly, and especially in this century authoritarian systems evolved to utilize rather than to suppress civil and legal participation.[41] Even Nazi Germany sustained internal stability because it did not simply eradicate societal segments. The regime enabled citizens to appropriate the repressive rules and mechanisms for their personal gains. This was by no means a smooth interaction of state and society. The social practices of the *Volksgemeinschaft* (people's community) featured individual agency for setting and enforcing social norms – with varying results.[42] Soviet society knew similar dynamics and often the pockets for agency persisted between and within state institutions.

Social Control under Stalin and Khrushchev is a first step to make these pockets visible. It encourages scholars to take a closer look into the various state attempts to control society and into individual agency that both enhanced and undermined this mission. Soviet Party leaders, and Stalin in particular, used the state to transform society, but they feared the social disorder that came with these changes. They utilized and even weaponized the state through law and police authorities to eliminate supposed social threats and to create their vision of a "proletarian state." They spurred the destruction of social structures, but more than any other Russian ruler before, the Soviet regime also hyperbolized the idea to rationalize and structure the behaviour of its people. It carried the early modern idea of a "well-ordered police state"[43] into the age of mass mobilization and still could only fail in its ambition. Soviet leaders were no cameralists. Cameralists imagined the well-ordered state as an institution to foster individual entrepreneurialism to ensure unlimited material growth. The Soviet political elite had different visions. They pinned their hopes on the power of the collective, empowered by an interventionist state. They lived in a world that had long departed from enlightened assumptions about the transformative force of the individual.[44] However, the political traction of this transformation was still valid and pressing to Russian and Soviet elites. The well-ordered state was also about developing administrative and legal means to transform society, to regulate individual behaviour in order to tap society's fullest potential. This promise remained intact. Marc Raeff argues that the imperial Russian state until its very end struggled to deliver on this promise.[45] As we will show, the Stalinist state in turn went much further and employed unprecedented interventionist programs not just to regulate but dictate and also eradicate deviant human behaviour. This endeavour was still in vain.

The idea of this perfect, well-ordered proletarian state was impossible to realize. Individual bureaucrats in the Stalinist state answered to the centre and worked within ideological parameters, but they still made everyday decisions on their own, leaving pockets of individual agency in the state apparatus as well. At the same time the state bureaucracy was limited in its reach and deferred to and relied on citizens to make individual claims on the state and on each other. In this way, the well-ordered state was a phantom. The regime was effective in controlling the fate of millions, while often failing to make the individual compliant. Only after Stalin was gone did it come closer to this objective of a well-ordered state and social control administered at arm's length. Already in the 1940s, the regime adjusted its tactics and favoured legal repression over administrative mass operations. Social control evolved from the violent and crude policies of mass intervention under Stalin to more methodological, predictable, and subtle tools of interference in the 1950s. After Stalin's death, this evolution gained additional traction as the new leaders in the Kremlin chose to invigorate the justice system and to thwart the jurisdiction of the political police. "Socialist legality" was more than a mere rhetorical adjustment. Stalin's successors and Khrushchev in particular decided to control and transform society not through mass repression but more systematic legal pressure (without dispensing with extralegal operations). The new leaders did not abandon their ideological claim to society but reconsidered and adjusted the toolkit to enforce it. In this framework, Soviet citizens increasingly turned to the state to advance their own cause. In short, the Soviet regime enforced social control, but it also enabled people to use the laws and structures to their own ends.

NOTES

1 Oleg V. Khlevniuk, "Archives of the Terror. Developments in the Historiography of Stalin's Purges," *Kritika* 22, no. 2 (Spring 2021): 367–85; David R. Shearer, *Policing Stalin's Socialism: Repression and Social Order in the Soviet Union 1924–1953* (London: Yale University Press, 2009); Paul Hagenloh, *Stalin's Police: Public Order and Mass Repression in the USSR, 1926–1941* (Washington, DC: Woodrow Wilson Center Press and Johns Hopkins University Press, 2009).
2 Mustafa Emirbayer and Ann Mische, "What Is Agency?" *American Journal of Sociology* 103, no. 4 (1998): 965.
3 James J. Chriss, "Social Control Revisited," in *Social Control: Informal, Legal and Medical*, ed. James J. Chriss (Bingley: Emerald, 2010), 1–16.
4 Anthony Ogus, "Nudging and Rectifying: The Use of Fiscal Instruments for Regulatory Purposes," *Legal Studies* 19, no. 2 (1999): 245–66; Frances F. Piven and Richard A. Cloward, *Regulating the Poor: The Functions of Public Welfare* (New York: Vintage Books, 1993).
5 Michel Foucault, *Discipline and Punish: The Birth of the Prison* (London: Penguin Classics, 2020).
6 On the modern state's goal to control society, see James C. Scott, *Seeing Like a State: How Certain Schemes to Improve the Human Condition Have Failed* (New Haven, CT: Yale University Press, 1999); David L. Hoffmann, *Cultivating the Masses: Modern State Practices and Soviet Socialism, 1914–1939* (Ithaca, NY: Cornell University Press, 2011); Stephen Kotkin, *Magnetic Mountain: Stalinism as Civilization* (Berkley and Los Angeles: University of California Press, 1997).
7 Shearer, *Policing*, 5.
8 Christopher R. Browning and Lewis H. Siegelbaum, "Framework for Social Engineering: Stalinist Schemes of Identification and the Nazi Volksgemeinschaft," in *Beyond Totalitarianism: Stalinism and Nazism Compared*, ed. Michael Geyer and Sheila Fitzpatrick (Cambridge: Cambridge University Press, 2009), 231–65.
9 Klaus Gestwa, "Social und Soul Engineering unter Stalin und Chruschtschow, 1928–1954," in *Die Ordnung der Moderne. Social Engineering im 20. Jahrhundert*, ed. Thomas Etzemüller (Bielefeld: Transcript, 2009): 241–77. Sheila Fitzpatrick brought up the term "usual suspects" for the interchangeable categories used by the regime to mark social threats ("socially harmful" groups). Sheila Fitzpatrick, "Ascribing Class. The Construction of Social Identity in Soviet Russia," *The Journal of Modern History* 65, no. 4 (1993): 745–70.
10 Shearer, *Policing*; Hagenloh, *Stalin's Police*; Lynne Viola, *Stalinist Perpetrators on Trial: Scenes from the Great Terror in Soviet Ukraine* (New York: Oxford University Press, 2017); Michael David-Fox, ed., *The Soviet*

Gulag: Evidence, Interpretation, and Comparison (Pittsburgh: University of Pittsburgh Press, 2016); Alan Barenberg and Emily D. Johnson, eds., *Rethinking the Gulag: Identities, Sources, Legacies* (Bloomington: Indiana University Press, 2022).

11 See therefore the special issue on "Culture, Practices, and Secret Policing in the USSR and Eastern Europe," *Kritika* 23, no. 3 (2022). For new insights into the structures, methods, and interplay of the Soviet political police with other institutions, see also Michael David-Fox and Philip Kiffer, eds., *The Secret Police and the Soviet System: New Archival Investigations* (Pittsburgh: Pittsburgh University Press, forthcoming).

12 Peter H. Solomon Jr., *Soviet Criminal Justice under Stalin* (Cambridge and New York: Cambridge University Press, 1996).

13 Mie Nakachi, *Replacing the Dead: The Politics of Reproduction in the Postwar Soviet Union* (New York: Oxford University Press, 2021), 88–122; Albert Baiburin, *Sovetskii pasport: istoriia, struktura, praktiki* (St Petersburg: Izdatel'stvo Evropeiskogo Universiteta v SP, 2017); Wendy Z. Goldman, *Women, the State and Revolution: Soviet Family Policy and Social Life, 1917–1936* (Cambridge: Cambridge University Press, 1995).

14 Golfo Alexopoulos, *Stalin's Outcasts: Aliens, Citizens, and the Soviet State, 1926–1936* (Ithaca, NY: Cornell University Press, 2003).

15 Immo Rebitschek, *Die disziplinierte Diktatur: Stalinismus und Justiz in der sowjetischen Provinz* (Cologne et al.: Boehlau/V&R, 2018); Yoram Gorlizki, "Theft under Stalin: A Property Rights Analysis," *Economic History Review* 69, no. 1 (2016): 288–313.

16 Ibid.; Yoram Gorlizki, De-Stalinization and the Politics of Russian Criminal Justice, 1953–1964 (unpublished diss.) (University of Oxford, 1992); Julie Elkner, "The Changing Face of Repression under Khrushchev," in *Soviet State and Society under Nikita Khrushchev*, ed. Melanie Ilic and Jeremy Smith (London and New York: Routledge, 2009), 142–61; Miriam Dobson, *Khrushchev's Cold Summer: Gulag Returnees, Crime, and the Fate of Reform after Stalin* (Ithaca, NY: Cornell University Press, 2009).

17 Vera Dunham, *In Stalin's Time: Middle Class Values in Soviet Fiction* (Durham, NC: Duke University Press, 1990).

18 David L. Hoffmann, *Stalinist Values: The Cultural Norms of Soviet Modernity* (Ithaca, NY: Cornell University Press, 2003).

19 Maria Galmarini, *The Right to Be Helped: Deviance, Entitlement and the Soviet Moral Order* (Ithaca, NY: Cornell University Press, 2020); Kristy Ironside, *A Full-Value Ruble: The Promise of Prosperity in the Postwar Soviet Union* (Cambridge, MA: Harvard University Press, 2021); Olga Kucherenko, *Soviet Street Children and the Second World War: Welfare and Social Control under Stalin* (London: Bloomsbury, 2016).

18 Social Control under Stalin and Khrushchev

20 Elena Bogdanova, *Complaints to the Authorities in Russia: A Trap between Tradition and Legal Modernization* (London and New York: Routledge, 2021).
21 Lynne Viola, "Introduction," in *Contending with Stalinism: Soviet Power and Popular Resistance in the 1930s*, ed. Lynna Viola (Ithaca, NY: Cornell University Press, 2002), 9–14.
22 Shearer, *Policing*; Hagenloh, *Stalin's Police*; Alexander Vatlin, *Agents of Terror: Ordinary Men and Extraordinary Violence in Stalin's Secret Police* (Madison: University of Wisconsin Press, 2016); Michael Parrish, *The Lesser Terror: Soviet State Security, 1939–1953* (Westport, CT: Praeger, 1996).
23 Oleg Khlevniuk recently emphasized in his article on the Great Terror – it is the "the complex interrelationships of the Party, penal structures, 'the public' and higher authorities [that] require further study," Khlevniuk, "Archives," 382. See also Gábor T. Rittersporn, "Terror and Soviet Legality. Police vs. Judiciary, 1933–1940," in *The Anatomy of Terror: Political Violence under Stalin*, ed. James H. Harris (Oxford: Oxford University Press, 2013), 176–92; Immo Rebitschek, "Lessons from the Terror: Soviet Prosecutors and Police Violence in One Province, 1942 to 1949," *Slavic Review* 78, no. 3 (Fall 2019): 738–57.
24 Nikita Petrov and Marc Jansen, "Mass Terror and the Court: The Military Collegium of the USSR," *Europe-Asia-Studies* 58, no. 4 (2006): 589–602; Viola, *Stalinist Perpetrators*; Lynne Viola, Jeffrey Rossman, Marc Junge, eds., *Chekisty na skam'e podsudimykh: Sbornik statei* (Moskva, Russia: Probel-2000, 2017); Marc Junge, *Stalinistische Modernisierung: Die Strafverfolgung von Akteuren des Staatsterrors in der Ukraine 1939–1941* (Bielefeld, Germany: Transcript Verlag, 2020). For the post-Stalinist period, see Robert Hornsby, *Protest, Reform and Repression in Khrushchev's Soviet Union* (Cambridge: Cambridge University Press, 2013).
25 Louise Shelley wrote the only study on the Soviet civil police (militsia) but it provides only a general institutional overview. Louise Shelley, *Policing Soviet Society: The Evolution of State Control* (New York: Routledge, 1996)
26 Solomon, *Soviet Criminal Justice*; Matthew Rendle, *The State versus the People: Revolutionary Justice in Russia's Civil War, 1917–1922* (Oxford: Oxford University Press, 2020); William E. Pomeranz, *Law and the Russian State: Russia's Legal Evolution from Peter the Great to Vladimir Putin* (London: Bloomsburg, 2019).
27 Eugene Huskey, *Russian Lawyers and the Soviet State: The Origins and Development of the Soviet Bar, 1917–1939* (Princeton, NJ: Princeton University Press, 1986); Eugene Huskey, "Vyshinskii, Krylenko, and the Shaping of the Soviet Legal Order," *Slavic Review* 46, nos. 3–4 (1987): 414–28; Peter H. Solomon Jr., ed., *Reforming Justice in Russia, 1864–1996: Power, Culture, and the Limits of Legal Order* (Armonk, NY: M.E. Sharpe, 1997).

28 Peter Solomon's groundbreaking study on the system of criminal justice does not extend to the workings of the police, the jails, or the Gulag. Solomon, *Soviet Criminal Justice*.

29 Oleg Klevniuk discussed investigations by the procuracy in the camps in the 1930s and highlighted the crucial relationship between procuracy, justice commissariat and NKVD in the aftermath of the mass operations. Oleg Khlevniuk, *The History of the Gulag: From Collectivization to the Great Terror* (New Haven, CT: Yale University Press, 2004), 186–235. Only Jeffrey Hardy addressed the relationship between legal and police structures for the time after Stalin. Jeffrey S. Hardy, *The Gulag after Stalin: Redefining Punishment in Khrushchev's Soviet Union, 1953–1964* (Ithaca, NY: Cornell University Press, 2016). The history of legal infrastructure within the camps (camp courts and procurators) is special desideratum. Galina Ivanova, "Eine unbekannte Seite des GULag: Lagersondergerichte in der UdSSR (1945-1954)," *Jahrbuecher für Geschichte Osteuropas* 53, no. 1 (2005): 25–41. For investigation and the procuracy's supervision in the Gulag, see also Rebitschek, Die *disziplinierte Diktatur*.

30 For research on war crime tribunals, see esp. Francine Hirsch, *Soviet Judgement at Nuremberg: A New History of the International Military Tribunal after World War II* (New York: Oxford University Press, 2020); David M. Crowe, ed., *Stalin's Soviet Justice: "Show Trials," War Crime Trials, and Nuremberg* (London: Bloomsbury, 2019). See the campaign against corruption through the Military Collegium of the Supreme Court. James Heinzen, *The Art of the Bribe: Corruption under Stalin 1943–1953* (London: Yale University Press, 2016), 217–29. For other important accounts on criminality and campaign justice, see Brian LaPierre, *Hooligans in Khrushchev's Russia: Defining, Policing, and Producing Deviance during the Thaw* (Madison: University of Wisconsin Press, 2012); Gorlizki, "Theft under Stalin," 288–313; Martin Kragh, "Soviet Labour Law during the Second World War," *War in History* 18 (2011): 531–46; Andrej S. Berkotov', *Bor'ba s ugolovnoi prestupnosti v Molotovskoi Oblasti v poslevoennye gody (1945–1953 gg.)* (Kand. Diss: Perm', 2004). For accounts on juvenile crime and policing strategies, see Olga Kucherenko, *Soviet Street Children and the Second World War: Welfare and Social Control under Stalin* (London: Bloomsbury, 2016); Catriona Kelly, *Children's World: Growing up in Russia, 1890–1991* (New Haven, CT: Yale University Press, 2007). See also the references in Immo Rebitschek's contribution to this volume.

31 Scott Newton, *Law and the Making of the Soviet World: The Red Demiurge* (London: Routledge, 2016); Albert Boiter; "Social Courts in the USSR," (unpublished PhD diss., Columbia University, 1965). A comment on civil law codes in the USSR provides W.E. Butler, *Soviet Law*, 2nd ed. (London: Butterworths, 1988), 175–7. See also Ger P. van den Berg, *The Soviet System*

of Justice: Figures and Policy (Dordrecht: Martinus Nijhoff Publishers, 1985). Marcie K. Cowley, "The Right of Inheritance of the Stalin Revolution," *Kritika* 15, no. 1 (2014): 103–23.

32 See most recently and especially Yoram Gorlizki and Oleg Khlevniuk, *Substate Dictatorship: Networks, Loyalty & Institutional Changes in the Soviet Union* (New Haven and London: Yale University Press, 2020).

33 Mark Edele, *Stalinist Society* (Oxford: Oxford University Press, 2019), 5. See the comprehensive account on individual agency under Stalinism by Brigitte Studer and Heiko Haumann, eds., *Stalinist Subjects: Individual and System in the Soviet Union and the ComIntern 1929–1953* (Zurich: Chronos, 2006); For a condensed overview on the different research paradigms on Stalinism, see Mark Edele, *Debates on Stalinism* (Manchester: Manchester University Press, 2020), 176–204.

34 See, e.g., Sheila Fitzpatrick, *Tear of the Masks! Identity and Imposture in Twentieth Century Russia* (Princeton, NJ: Princeton University Press, 2005); Jochen Hellbeck, *Revolution on My Mind: Writing a Diary under Stalin* (Cambridge, MA: Harvard University Press, 2006). More recently: Jonathan Waterlow, *It's Only a Joke, Comrade! Humour, Trust and Everyday Life under Stalin (1928–1941)* (Oxford: CreateSpace Independent Publishing Platform, 2018).

35 Vladimir A. Kozlov, Sheila Fitzpatrick, and Sergei V. Mironenko, eds., *Sedition: Everyday Resistance in the Soviet Union under Khrushchev and Brezhnev* (New Haven, CT: Yale University Press, 2011).

36 See especially Lynne Viola, ed., *Contending with Stalinism: Soviet Power and Popular Resistance in the 1930s* (Ithaca, NY: Cornell University Press, 2002); Samantha Lomb, *Stalin's Constitution: Soviet Participatory Politics and the Discussion of the 1936 Draft Constitution* (Abingdon: Routledge, 2018); Olga Velikanova, *Mass Political Culture under Stalinism: Popular Discussion of the Soviet Constitution of 1936* (Cham: Palgrave MacMillan, 2018). "Totalitarian control may have been an ambition of Stalinism, but the dark aim of atomization of an impotent, obedient, terrified people was never achieved," Ronald Suny, *Red Flag Wounded: Stalinism and the Fate of the Soviet Experiment* (La Vergne, TN: Verso, 2020), 57.

37 Igal Halfin and Jochen Hellbeck, "Rethinking the Stalinist Subject: Stephen Kotkin's 'Magnetic Mountain' and the State of Soviet Historical Studies," *Jahrbücher für Geschichte Osteuropas* 44, no. 3 (1996): 457.

38 Lynne Viola, "The Question of the Perpetrator in Soviet History," *Slavic Review* 72, no. 1 (2013): 10.

39 Butler, *Soviet Law*, 171; Alexopoulos, *Stalin's Outcasts*; Juliette Cadiot, "Equal before the Law? Soviet Justice, Criminal Proceedings against Communist Party Members, and the Legal Landscape in the USSR from 1945 to 1953," *Jahrbücher für Geschichte Osteuropas* 61, no. 2 (2013): 249–69.

40 Eugene Huskey, "Form Legal Nihilism to Pravovoe Gosudarstvo: Soviet Legal Development, 1917–1990," in *Toward the Rule of Law in Russia? Political and Legal Reform in the Transition Period*, ed. Donald D. Barry (Armonk, NY: M.E. Sharpe, 1992), 23–42.
41 See, e.g., Rebecca Tapscott, *Arbitrary States: Social Control and Modern Authoritarianism in Museveni's Uganda* (Oxford: Oxford University Press, 2021), 3; Kim Lane Scheppele, "Autocratic Legalism," *University of Chicago Law Review* 85, no. 2 (2018): 545–84.
42 Michael Wildt, *Die Ambivalenz des Volkes: Der Nationalsozialismus als Gesellschaftsgeschichte* (Berlin: suhrkamp, 2019), 41. Denunciations are a well-known example for individuals appropriating the terms and the means of the regime (without emancipating themselves from them). See Christoph Thonfeld, *Sozialkontrolle und Eigensinn: Denunziation am Beispiel Thüringen 1933 bis 1949* (Cologne: Boehlau, 2003), 359.
43 Marc Raeff, *The Well-Ordered Police State: Social and Institutional Change through Law in the Germanies and Russia, 1600–1800* (New Haven, CT: Yale University Press, 1983).
44 Ibid., 253.
45 Ibid., 255.

PART I

Negotiating Terror and Social Discipline in the 1930s

1 Controlling the Soviet Family through Alimony? Righteous Women, Starving Children, and Bad Fathers, 1925–1939

AARON B. RETISH

In 1938, at the height of the Terror, the NKVD tracked down the peasant N.P. Vereshchagin in rural Kirov. He had been hiding, not because of his class status or political associations, but because he owed his second wife back payments in support of their child. Since 1937, the judiciary had employed the NKVD to track down fathers to appear at hearings on alimony suits or when they had skipped out on paying their dues. In this case, the NKVD found that Vereshchagin had three wives spread out across the villages of the region, none of whom he had divorced. His case went to the district procurator who supported charges of providing false information on the registration of civil acts (Article 88). The people's court sentenced him to three months of forced labour and made sure to garnish 25 per cent of his pay in support of his child.[1]

The struggle to get men like Vereshchagin to support their children was a central concern for the Soviet state in the 1930s. In part, this came from a fear of social disorder – that children would be ignored by their parents and become hooligans or be cast to the street to lead a life of crime, joining the seven million street urchins that the Soviet state tried to control at the beginning of NEP but remained a persistent problem of child homelessness and a reminder of the poverty in the Soviet Union.[2] Alimony also supported women whose labour could not sustain them and without support would risk becoming deviant outcasts of socialist society.[3] Child support, then, was supposed to serve as a prophylactic against social disorder by keeping order in the home so it wouldn't spill out to the streets. Alimony was also intimately tied to the promotion of social norms. Stalinist subjects made legal claims to support based on their social status and their own social interests. They drew on the officially produced image of the Soviet state as defending the rights of the oppressed – the proletariat, women, children, and poor peasants – to fight for what they claimed as theirs. The image of the peasant mother who toils without complaint, though, had a mirror image in the press and in judicial records of a woman who used her kids for profit and took advantage of the state to avoid work.

The Soviet state promised to emancipate women from traditional domestic roles and to provide for their children. The especially progressive programs to support women and children began with the introduction of civil divorce in December 1917. The 1918 and 1926 Family Codes that followed reconceived marriage as a voluntary partnership that would one day fade away under socialism and communal care. In the meantime, alimony (*aliment*) would protect women and provide child support.[4] While divorces and children outside of marriage quickly became a part of life, especially in the cities but in the countryside as well, alimony "signified the persistence of the family as the primary form of social organization and security." Even if the family, as one Soviet jurist argued, was legally based on descent and not on marriage, alimony, as support of a mother and her children, was a reminder of the financial dependence of women on men.[5] The Revolution's promised emancipation of women did not undo dominant gendered visions of society, with women remaining in the homes and main caretakers of children. This remained the case in the June 1936 Decree, which glorified motherhood, prohibited abortion, restricted divorce, and strengthened alimony settlements.[6] The pronatalist Stalinist leadership also saw alimony, along with the outlawing of abortion, as central to its major occupation to raise birthrates across the country.

This chapter will study alimony cases in the people's courts in the countryside from the 1926 Family Code through the implementation of the 1936 Law. Alimony was the main reason why peasants brought suits to the courts. In 1927, when the RSFSR Code on Marriage, Family, and Guardianship came into force, alimony claims skyrocketed. They accounted for over half of all civil suits among individuals, far more than any other type of dispute.[7] I will first examine how litigants asserted their claims to entitlements as Soviet citizens by making their domestic lives public in court. I will then focus on the changes to how alimony was handled in the courts in the 1930s, looking first at the strengthening of alimony settlements in the early 1930s and how the administration of alimony through the collectivized farm both helped and complicated the system. The June 1936 Law, and the campaign that followed, highlighted the importance that the state put on alimony in protecting the financial well-being of women and children and in stabilizing Soviet society. I end with the widespread criticism levelled both by peasants and the press that men and women were exploiting or evading welfare policies. State-imposed alimony allowed the state, through the courts, to intervene in domestic affairs to try to assert control of gender relations inside the home.

The story of the hunt for Vereshchagin shows the extent that courts and the NKVD pursued deadbeat fathers to fulfil their economic obligations to their children, but it also shows the limits of the state through the 1930s. The NKVD found Vereshchagin and the court prosecuted him, but not before he had spent years doing as he pleased, marrying and then abandoning his families. Men like Vereshchagin used the under-patrolled countryside to evade court-imposed settlements. The state's success of having men support their children was circumscribed by its own weaknesses to enforce its laws. At times those very laws on alimony constricted the state from doing more. That meant that if they set their minds to it, deadbeat dads could remain deadbeats. Indeed, the very reliance on alimony acknowledged that the state's patchy social insurance system in the countryside was not strong enough to support children and mothers. The state hoped for and often promised welfare support for peasants; it delegated financial responsibilities to local soviets, Committees for Peasants' Mutual Social Assistance (KKOV), and collective farms and empowered the courts to ensure that individuals pay what the state could not.[8]

Claims to What Is Mine

In September 1929, Maria Vlasova petitioned her local people's court in Nizhegorod district (*raion*), Nizhegorod region (*oblast'*). She had been married to her husband Ivan for seven years, and they had three young children. Two years earlier, he left his family in the village to go work in the factory and she had not heard from him in six months. Maria stated, "he impregnated me and since then his children and I have received no support from him ... not one kopek." "We are surviving," she continued, "thanks to my mother Anna who also suffers from desperate poverty." She demanded alimony from her husband "because he is away, and we are starving." The people's court decreed that Ivan had to pay ten rubles a month.[9] Peasant women like Vlasova crafted their personal struggle in language that appealed to the Soviet court and drew on rights to entitlements. To make these claims, women had to invite the state into their homes and adopt the language of the Soviet state.

Peasant women had turned to the *volost'* courts in the pre-revolutionary era as a matter of last resort to help resolve domestic troubles.[10] They pleaded for material help in the courts and from those in power using ritualized language. The language of lament, of starvation and desperate poverty, continued in the Soviet-era legal arena, as seen in

Vlasova's case.[11] It referenced a moral economy of providing for the people when they were starving. Mothers' pleas that they could not feed their children reminded judges of the larger problem of child homelessness across the Soviet Union and, especially in the provinces of the Lower Volga Region, about the recent famine.[12] Soviet courts in the countryside had always preferred keeping children in homes in the community (including facilitating adoption by relatives even when it was prohibited) and in 1926 the Soviet state instituted this practice when it brought back legal adoption.[13] Highlighting poverty was just the most obvious of many strategies that claimants used, and laments were only rarely tied to complete helplessness.

Peasant women also asserted their claims to entitlement and commonly used the refrain of fighting for what was theirs.[14] The Soviet justice system through propaganda campaigns and local lectures and consultations encouraged women to use the courts to defend these rights. These calls extended to property divisions that could coincide with alimony claims. In 1927, Tat'iana Mukhortova asserted her rights as "a fully equal member of the household" to reclaim "what is rightly mine" when divorcing her husband of four months. The court granted her ownership of her fur coat and boots, as well as thirty-eight rubles and fifty kopeks for other items.[15]

Claims rested in part on the mobilization of their membership of a social class – village poor, mothers, widows, or soldiers' wives, especially to contrast with their male opponents in court. As Anna Rodinova of Gigor'evko village in Samara wrote in her petition to the court, "the defendant is a son of a priest from a well-connected family in the village and I don't have a home or livestock."[16] Others, though, argued that as impoverished and socially oppressed citizens, they should be taken care of by law in the Soviet system.

Unmarried women also claimed alimony support for their children. The 1926 RSFSR Code on Marriage, Family, and Guardianship, reinforced that children born outside of a registered marriage should receive the same entitlements to those born in a registered one.[17] That meant supporting poor, illiterate, and young single mothers like the eighteen-year-old Ur'iana Porokhina, who filed a statement claiming Semen Naskov fathered her child. Naskov was a miller and already married with children. She claimed that their secret relationship started when Naskov gave her grain when she was by the mill. He sweet-talked her and came to her home one night. Porokhina brought witnesses who claimed seeing the two of them by the mill and nine months before the baby was born. Naskov countered with witnesses attesting to his upstanding character, but the court still found in Porokhina's favour and forced him to pay alimony because he could only produce witnesses from his family.[18]

Some peasants lived together and had children without being married, which was a growing phenomenon supported by the early Soviet state's move away from formal marriage and increasingly accepted in areas with large out-migration.[19] For example, Dariia Alekseeva brought suit against her former partner Vasilii Lukianov. They had lived together and had a son, Sergei, in March 1927. Vasilii signed a certificate that May documenting that he was indeed the father and promised to pay fifteen rubles a month in support. He did for a year, but then they split and he stopped paying. Dariia drew on the power of the written record, showing the court the stamped promissory note signed by the chair of the sel'sovet and witnessed by fellow villagers. At the court, Vasilii pleaded that he was going into the military and could not pay. The two resolved in front of the court to drop the case and Vasilii would make sure that his child would receive the support.[20]

The language of claimants remained largely the same through the 1936 law, even if the terms of the alimony settlement changed, as will be discussed below. For example, Raisa Komsova emphasized her poverty and inability to work when she brought suit to the people's court in the spring of 1939 against Viktor Komsov, her recently divorced spouse. They were married for six years and had a son, but two months after their divorce he was living with another woman. "Up to now he has paid me no support [*soderzhanie*] and he does not want to pay anything. I am down in the dumps. I have been sick for a year and a half and not able to do any work." Raisa moved in with her daughter-in-law and her three young children. Witnesses and the court inspector supported her claims and noted that her daughter-in-law's economic status was "unenviable." The court made Viktor pay a quarter of his earnings to Raisa as alimony and another thirty rubles a month while she couldn't work. Viktor protested the decision with his own plea of poverty – he was living with four other people. Moreover, he didn't demand a division (*razdel*) of the household and even left the dishes to his wife. He did not win his appeal.[21] While emphasizing her poverty and poor health, the claimant drew on her entitlement for support of her and her child as a citizen of the Soviet Union. Her statement was on the mark, for the court also focused on her economic status and need for economic aid.

Claimants fashioned themselves as natural class allies of the Soviet state and demanded entitlements as citizens. They also emphasized their roles as mothers. These broad self-descriptions remained stable across the 1920s and 1930s and were successful in the courts because they matched judges' ideas of peasant women. As Lisa Granik has shown, gender myths were so built into the law that it established formal inequality in the name of equality. Leaders of the Soviet state saw women as passive, needing protection, and essentialized them as mothers, even while they proclaimed equality between men and women and Soviet law.[22] At the same time, women benefitted from their characterization in the press as hardworking and willing to sacrifice.[23]

Alimony Settlements in the Collectivized Countryside

Speaking to female shock workers of sugar beets in 1935, Joseph Stalin proclaimed that rural women had already been freed from oppressive peasant traditionalism through their work on collective farms. "Only life on the collective farm could eliminate inequality and put a woman on her feet." Now that labour was done collectively, rural women no longer needed to marry into a household to survive, and marriage could be based on love and attraction, Stalin said. That meant the new Soviet family could stand as a foundation for society.[24] Women were emancipated since they had found economic liberation through their labour.[25] Stalin's speech overlooked the enduring domestic exploitation of women that alimony and family policy had not solved but pointed to the larger shift since 1928 that emphasized a strengthening of the family and the hope that collectivization would emancipate women.

By the end of the NEP era, the state had already put more responsibility on parents to oversee children. Soviet laws and jurists emphasized children's well-being. In June 1928, the state placed additional regulations on those paying alimony, compelling them to report when they moved to ensure that they continued to pay support. The new laws added a class angle befitting of the move away from NEP, ordering those who paid alimony to report if their wages improved so they could pay more.[26] The state also moved to restore social order by cracking down on juvenile crime and child homelessness, relying increasingly on repression and placing more weight on parental, rather than communal, control of children. That included making parents liable when their children engaged in criminal behaviour and not permitting them to give up their children to orphanages.[27] In the cities, the *militsiia* swept up homeless children and arrested juvenile petty thieves in 1931, but even in the countryside there was greater stress to uphold parents' oversight of their children.

Courts in the early 1930s began increasing child support above the minimal levels seen in the 1920s by accounting for both parties' financial positions.[28] This presented one of the most significant opportunities for economic improvements for peasant women and children in the early Soviet era. In the 1920s, Narkomiust gave individual courts broad authority to set alimony settlements based on the economic conditions and needs in individual cases. Judges often issued starvation-level allowances to mothers, which meant that women's victories in the courts were mostly symbolic, to uphold their honour. People's courts in Omutkinisk district in Viatka province, for example, had often awarded only one ruble per month to mothers, which a judge from the provincial court said was like giving "alms to the poor."[29] In Samara, judges granted small monthly payments, even when the father was a kulak. In the Totskii people's court, for example, the father Tarasenko agreed to pay the mother Aleksandrova three rubles a month, but a court review pointed out that Tarasenko was a kulak with three horses and four cows and Aleksandrova was a *batrak*. "Such a small sum of money means nothing in a kulak house, but for Aleksandrova who needs to take care of herself and the welfare of her baby it means everything."[30]

Jurists encouraged the community and local administration to pressure men to pay alimony. Already in 1927, to speed up the resolution of claims like alimony disputes and minor crimes, Narkomiust introduced lay-led mediation courts (*primiritel'nye kamera*). These local courts became more active after collectivization when they evolved into collective farm (*kolkhoz*) social courts (*sel'skie obshchestvennye sudy*) and *kolkhoz* comrade courts (*kolkhoznye tovarishcheskie sudy*). Like comrade courts in the factories, discussed by Maria Starun, the rural mediation courts resolved local disputes in informal settings guided by the law. Peasant women quickly turned to these institutions to help resolve lingering alimony disputes. In 1932, alimony and property disputes made up 20 per cent of cases before the lay courts in Sorochinskii district in the Middle Volga Region, the largest category of civil claims before these bodies.[31] While people's courts continued to settle most alimony claims, and the number of alimony claims before the people's courts increased annually in the first half of the 1930s, the mediation courts provided another institution for women to get men to pay during this period.[32] Mediation courts heard cases in public at the village or *kolkhoz* administrative office, and they were led by rural Soviet officials and people's assessors from the community. As A. Goraina, a member of the Ural regional (*oblast'*) court, stated in 1930, it had to be up to the public and all local institutions to force the collection of funds from fathers who would not pay otherwise.[33] In this way, those who sat on mediation courts were an essential part of an enlarged network mobilized by the state and the courts. Mediation courts applied administrative sanctions and asserted communal discipline through public shaming and social pressure to get men to fulfil their obligations.

Collectivization facilitated the change to uniform alimony payments in the countryside. Before collectivization, alimony was tied to the household economy, which put peasants and court officials at odds and local judges in the middle. Peasants expressed concern to local jurists and newspaper editors that women could marry into a household and quickly claim part of the property, weakening the household. For the editors of the Narkomiust serial *Ezhenedel'nik sovetskoi iustitsii*, collective responsibility was central to the effectiveness of alimony because it secured children's well-being. As they editorialized, if the household would not support their own children, then "we are leaving the children to their own fate in the village."[34] In the 1920s, people's court judges' smaller alimony settlements kept household economies safe. They also usually denied women's full claims to household property, even though it was supported under the law.

Figuring out alimony payments in the collectivized countryside was complicated. When both the mother and father were members of the *kolkhoz*, payments were to be made in workday credits (*trudodny*), rather than monetary wages, and would be transferred to the mother through the *kolkhoz* administration. This *barshchina*-style payment gave mothers a mix of food and monetary payments, which allowed them more food to feed their children but not usually enough to get them through the winter and tied their alimony payments to the *kolkhoz*, binding them to the farm and putting them at the mercy of their *kolkhoz* to issue support. Men living in a nearby *kolkhoz* were supposed to have their *kolkhoz* make arrangements with the mother's *kolkhoz* to transfer credits or food. However, when women sought alimony from men living on a collective farm far away, she would have to go to him to get payment in foodstuffs. The courts intervened and began issuing monetary payments in these cases.[35] There were still plenty of cases of independent peasants having children with collective farm members, as happened when the kolkhoznik Stepan Perenkin was taken to court by the independent farmer Anna Serygeva for support of their child. Following the court's investigation, Perenikin was ordered to pay thirty rubles a month. He appealed, claiming that Sevygeva did not provide enough evidence to show that he was the father, but lost.[36]

Collectivization did not fully resolve the issue of how much the peasant household (*dvor*) should be given to the support of the child. Membership to the collective farm was based on the individual and not the household, but courts still could not figure out what to do with shared property inside the home. The debate shifted from the focus on the sustainability of the peasant household in the 1920s to who owned what property inside the hut in the 1930s, without a firm resolution. In

Georgia, courts went after all of the property in a household, from livestock to teapots, but in Russia and many other republics, courts seized only the father's or other custodian's share of the property, and only after it was sold.[37]

In 1935 and early 1936, peasant women regularly brought claims to the people's courts to increase their alimony payments. The claim of Maria Mashoganova in Kirov district (*raion*) against Alksandr Bushkov, the father of her daughter, was typical. In 1930, the court ordered Bushkov to pay eight rubles a month in child support. Five years later, Mashoganova filed suit to have the monthly payments raised to forty rubles. The two engaged in negotiations in the courtroom, where Bushkov agreed to a twenty-three-ruble monthly payment because he received a salary of one hundred rubles a month and Mashoganova received sixty-five rubles. Looking at the financial status of both parties, the court decided that his payment would be increased to thirty-five rubles.[38] That amount was actually higher than what would be demanded in the 1936 law. In another case in the spring of 1936, the court chastised Nikolai Batrukhin for "groundlessly denying" alimony to his former wife because "she earlier had taken all of the goods in the household," but the court made clear that alimony had to be based on the child's need and the parents' financial status.[39]

Despite the growing number of women bringing alimony suits before the courts and the larger alimony settlements in the first half of the 1930s, in 1935 the Supreme Court of the RSFSR criticized people's courts for how they were handling alimony suits. It stated that courts were not issuing large enough alimony settlements because they did not account for the financial or class status of either party and that too many men were not paying alimony that they were legally responsible for. There needed to be legal changes to ensure that women and children received more support.[40]

The Campaign to Protect the Family against Deadbeat Dads

The June 1936 law turned away from easy divorce and the withering away of the family unit that state leaders feared promoted social disorder and put kids on the streets. Divorces became more expensive and faced bureaucratic hurdles, and marriages became more formalized. It also embraced a pronatalist policy to stem what leaders saw as a plunging birth rate by prohibiting abortion, which accelerated criticism from the 1920s by medics and court officials that abortions hurt a woman's organism and that her decision to have a child was both a personal and social affair.[41] The Soviet state's pronatalist decree simultaneously incentivized motherhood by promoting social welfare for women. Moreover, it promised creches and cafeterias on collective farms to care for and feed children with more beds and medical personnel to care for women and infants using modern medicine.[42] The June 1936 law and the publicity surrounding it essentialized women as mothers and the criminalization of abortion enforced this role. Many women vigorously protested the ban, arguing that they would be forced to have more children even though they did not have the means to support them, even with state promises of aid.[43] The new family policy was presented as a way to protect children's rights to have love and support from their parents, but it also signalled the limits of the welfare state.[44] State-publicized support for wards and cafeterias, especially in the countryside, usually did not materialize. Alimony, with the state as the intermediary, remained the main way for women who needed support to get it. The newly strengthened alimony system placed more of the financial burden on fathers, making them responsible for a quarter of the wages for their first child, a third for the second, and half of the wages for a third. The court garnished wages and punished those who did not pay to up to two years in jail. The support of peasant women as mothers, mostly through forced alimony payments from men, happened while millions left the village to find work in the factories, and those in the collective farms were expected to be productive workers.[45]

The court system launched a campaign to promote alimony and support of women's and children's rights with the 1936 Family Code. Like campaigns against hooliganism, juvenile crime, and even with hints of the all-out campaign for collectivization, judges were supposed to put everything aside in the months following the decree to show their support of mothers and were urged on by their superiors and from the press to do even more to support children and mothers.[46] The campaign in 1936–7 consumed the courts at a time when they were already under stress from mass reviews in preparation for an expected popular election of judges promised in the new Constitution and the larger return to legality.[47] People's courts struggled to handle so many claims. In the two months after the June decree, people's courts were flooded with alimony cases. A report from Leningrad city and region found that nearly 50 per cent of all civil cases concerned alimony claims during this period, increasing 56 per cent after the June decree, and 35 per cent of these claims were from people using the court for the first time. These numbers matched the increases across Soviet Russia. In Kirov region, alimony claims went up 57 per cent and in Orenburg they increased by 60 per cent.[48] Nevertheless, in the first few months most of the claims were new.

Judges were expected to promote the protection of children and mothers. Propaganda surrounding the decree encouraged women to stake out their rights to defend their children. People's court judges gave lectures before collective farms on women's rights to alimony, alongside doctors who spoke of the evils of abortion. Judges also wrote articles in local newspapers about how they recently punished several deadbeat "wicked fathers" who tried to skip out on paying alimony.[49] People's courts faced pressure from above to help women litigate their claims, such as helping them find needed records of the child's birth and documentation of the father's salary. One of the problems that the courts faced was finding and interrogating witnesses to support claims or tracking down the defendant. As mentioned at the beginning of this chapter, courts could issue a search by the NKVD for the defendant. Once he was dragged to court and agreed to the alimony settlement, he had to pay a one-hundred-ruble fee for the search.[50] The Constitution reiterated that everyone had the right to appear in court, and at first it was mandatory that alimony cases were heard with the defendant present.[51] So many men had fled the village or moved to the city for work that the police and NKVD could hardly find any defendants, which slowed down alimony settlements. In May 1937, the Code for Civil Procedure was amended to allow courts to allow rulings in absentia if there was a valid reason, like not locating the defendant.[52]

The Supreme Court directed judges to view alimony not just as a civil claim but as a central part of a greater struggle for the improvement of Soviet families and judges were eager to comply. Non-payment was a criminal offence, and judges were to put fathers in jail for child endangerment, something that people's courts followed and newspapers publicized. In Stavropol's district of Kuibyshev region, the local newspaper listed men who the court decided to imprison for their "malicious evasion" of paying alimony.[53] Many people's court judges actively backed the new push to make fathers pay support and pushed to be even more assertive than leaders of the Justice Department wanted. In September 1936, one people's court judge wrote into *Sovetskaia iustitsiia* to ask if passports could note if a father had not paid child support. The answer was no – the new Family Laws had increased parental responsibility for the welfare of children but did not change the enforcement of alimony payments or allow passports to document court decisions on alimony.[54] It was up to the courts and provincial authorities to ensure that fathers paid support.

As in other major campaigns, people's court judges issued the harshest judgments they could, which was the safest thing to do, and let their superiors revise if they wished. Regional courts had already received a special secret directive from A. Vinokurov, chair of the Supreme Court of the USSR, to direct their people's court judges to ensure that mothers received alimony, so judges must have understood the pressure to support children and mothers as much as possible.[55] When a judge assessed a 1,000-ruble-a-month payment to a defendant who made 4,000 rubles, that is, the 25 per cent garnishing of wages set in the Code, the cassational court reduced it to 500 rubles because 1,000 rubles exceeded what was really necessary to maintain a child. The court of Sormovsk district in Gorkii region found in favour of the claimant Rumentseva when she sued her in-laws for alimony because the father of her child, their son, was "in hiding." The court assessed them a quarter of the wages of their son. The cassational college of the regional court overturned the ruling because Rementseva was able-bodied and her grandparents were sick and taking care of their own children and could not be charged the wages of their son. A people's court in Kalinin region, citing Article 158 of the Criminal Code and the 1936 Family Law, sentenced Mikhail Babushkin to eighteen months in jail for not paying child support for the daughter of a man he was charged with murdering five years earlier. The regional court overturned the decision.[56] In the first two months after the publication of the Code, the cassational courts overturned nearly a third of the people's courts determinations and left less than half unchanged.[57]

Judges were easily convinced on paternity claims and quickly placed alimony dues on these fathers, intensifying a trend from the 1920s. Paternity was usually determined by close contact between the claimant and defendant.[58] In November 1939, the 6th circuit of Vosnovsk district, Gor'kii region, resolved a suit by Anna Konstantinovna against Aleksei Petrukhin. The plaintiff claimed that from 1936 to 1937, the two had an affair. She drew on her right to identify the father on the birth registry and claim alimony if she was able to show evidence of intimacy. She brought in several witnesses who attested that Anna and Aleksei had "close relations." That was all the evidence the court needed by law to find Aleksei to be the father and ordered him first to give fifty rubles a month to Anna for child support and then increased it after she appealed to a ¼ of all of his wages, as the 1936 decree allowed.[59] Decisions over paternity frustrated the cassational college, which appeared to have a higher bar for evidence than people's courts. In the Udmurt ASSR, for example, paternity cases were upheld only 18 per cent of the time, even if the people's courts ruled in favour of the mothers and children, as state leaders wanted.[60]

Judges rushed through alimony claims when they could not find the father, but they were also criticized in court reviews through 1937 and

1938 for holding hearings too quickly, before he could be found. *Sovetskaia iustitsiia* pointed its finger at the people's court judge Labazina of Alekseevsk district in Orenburg region, who decided twenty-five of forty alimony cases without the defendant, including one who was living in Dnepropetrovsk and only learned that he was due in court on the day of the hearing.[61] At the same time, courts did not hear alimony cases fast enough for their superiors. People's courts across Kuibyshev region, for example, heard 2,148 alimony claims in July 1936 alone, but that still left 1,086 cases left for review, which was unacceptable to court superiors.[62] Yet, court leaders also wanted them to spend time on each alimony suit. In 1937, Aleksei Lisitsyn, chair of the Civil College of the Supreme Court of the RSFSR, for example, complained that people's courts in Kalinin region spent only five minutes on each alimony case, which was not enough time to instil the social significance of alimony.[63]

Alimony remained an important and contentious issue for the population through the 1930s. Citizens' frustration with the courts boiled over. Even before the campaign, in the early 1930s, the People's Commissariat of the Workers' and Peasants' Inspection (RKI) issued a printed form for citizens to fill out for "the most malicious bureaucratism" (*samoi zlastoi volokity*) of people's courts, and the most common complaint was that the court did not make their spouse pay their court-issued alimony payments.[64] In 1937–8, when people's court judges came under attack at a series of public meetings, and many were then reviewed and purged, one of the main complaints by local peasants was their failure to act correctly on alimony. In July 1937, for example, the newspaper *Krasnoiarskii rabochii* reported that public meetings showed how the judge Mesiats of Uraiskii district had turned into a horrible bureaucrat. It cited the worst of his failings – it took him five months to move on the citizen Ovsianikova's suit to compel her husband to pay alimony to support her children.[65] Mikhail Reikhel' of the Supreme Court of the RSFSR cited his colleague's criticisms of the Kalinin region people's courts' handling of alimony in condemning their "red tape and formalism that disregard the living people" who come before the court and called for further reviews of judges to rectify the problem.[66] In 1938, these judges were then accused of being under the influence of "counter-revolutionary theory by the enemy of the people Pashukanis, Dotsenko, and others" for how they handled alimony cases.[67]

People's courts acted aggressively to increase payments to mothers through the 1930s. They read the political rhetoric in the newspapers from Moscow and they overfulfilled their perceived duties to ensure alimony. Judges' liberal rulings were a headache for the higher courts who wanted more adherence to the letter of the law and more detailed evidence to support decisions. Despite the extraordinary criticism of judges for their handling of alimony cases after the 1936 law, in 1938 a commentator noted that 83 per cent of all alimony cases were resolved in a month and almost all (97 per cent) were ruled in favour of the plaintiff (read, the mother).[68] Judges, though, were not the only people attacked for the failures of the alimony system to support women. The press and peasants themselves criticized women who received support and men who refused to give it. In gendered language, they pointed to the people as the problem, but in their criticism they alluded to the weakness of the state to implement its policies.

The Irresponsible or Clever Muzhik: Evading Alimony and the Limits of State Control

Justice officials complained that men were evading their obligations to pay alimony, and for good reason. In 1928, bailiffs and the office of social security in Viatka province had to follow up on over 90 per cent of alimony settlements to get men to pay.[69] Jurists blamed both natural male laziness/irresponsibility and the backwardness and patriarchy of village culture for these problems.[70] These ideas were part of the debates over family policy in the 1920s, both in the centre and in the provinces. In July 1928, the Buzuluksk *okruzhnhyi* court in Samara stated that, "In a majority of cases men attempted to prove their right to dominate women ... When a man has to pay alimony, he completely denies his duty to pay on the grounds that if the mother gives birth to a child, then it is her obligation to feed it."[71] In the early 1930s, jurists added deceit to the peasant male tendencies when they eluded alimony payments. Stories described how men "were resorting to all sorts of tricks" to evade paying alimony, like staying on the move or selling most of their personal property to reduce their obligations.[72] In 1935, over 35 per cent of those responsible for alimony either were not paying or were paying support irregularly.[73] Restrictions on divorce and the strengthening of marriage in 1936 were supposed to stop the problem of abandoned mothers, and the need for alimony, but state officials and peasants continued to complain that fathers were failing to live up to their responsibilities, which undercut the state's mission to support women and children.

There were in fact many legal ways for fathers to lower their obligations, and they quickly figured out how to dilute alimony payments. Officials acknowledged that many peasants on the collective farm easily found ways to circumvent paying much in alimony by reducing the hours that they worked on the *kolkhoz* and earning more money on the side in handicraft production *kustar'* or other money-earning schemes because how much someone earned was really only known by the individual. Income from personal plots in collective farms could also not be legally calculated in alimony settlements since the plots were part of the collective farm. Courts were supposed to determine alimony for independent peasants, who did not earn wages, by estimating past income based on their taxes, which was an imperfect science and could lower men's obligations. Men easily changed how they earned money to reduce alimony payments; changes that were within their rights and were supported by socialist law on labour and property.

Alimony could be severely reduced for men who had more than three children or children with multiple women, as a father was not supposed to pay more than 50 per cent of his income to alimony. As explained in one legal publication, if a mother had three children with a man and sued him for alimony but he had to support two other children in another household who also sued for support (which could be done even if he was not divorced), then the first claimant could only get 30 per cent of his total wages, rather than getting 50 per cent, with 10 per cent of his wages going to each child.[74] Even when judges pushed for alimony payments, there were many escape routes for the defendant, all of which lowered the amount of financial support for mothers.

With so many loopholes in the law, men could evade the backbreaking alimony that letter writers complained about. Men did not have to "hide out," which was a common refrain in the court records, to escape alimony. Income earned beyond the gaze of the state and the legal idea that all land in the collective farm was public property, and not private, undercut the support of mothers. At the same time, the understanding that personal property in the household remained only clouded the determination of the level of alimony payments. The 1936 law also straightjacketed judges from accounting for the income of both parties for support of children, as they had done in the early 1930s.[75]

Throughout the 1920s and 1930s, newspapers and booklets aimed at the public labelled men who did not pay alimony support as "irresponsible" and "antisocial elements who violate the rights of children."[76] However, internal court reports and articles in judicial series dwelled on the failures of the judicial system for failing to coerce men to pay alimony. They highlighted the courts' red tape and misunderstanding of proper procedures for the problems in issuing alimony or problems with bailiffs who issued compromises with fathers who were not meeting their legal financial obligation. In this way, judicial officials apologized for male irresponsibility and placed the continued failure to collect alimony on local state officials.

Fears of Unrighteous Women and State Weakness

We know that many peasants frowned upon the liberal divorce laws of the 1920s as promoting sexual immorality and the demise of the family. People also complained that alimony across the 1920s and 1930s supported loose women who took advantage of men and the state. As Lauren Kaminsky has shown, in unpublished letters to newspapers and journals, everyday citizens complained that the alimony laws were empowering single women to take advantage of honest men. A letter writer named Fedovota wrote of the problem in the 1930s of the "alimony hunter," "a woman who violates the rights of family men, whose personal life is supported by the healthy family and the unknowing state, who does not wish for her own holy of holies, femininity and morality." In this case, the problem was the woman who took advantage of unknowing men by seducing and entrapping them. Women in these letters were seen as backward or scheming to undo masculinity to take advantage of the state that did not know any better. They embodied the opposite of the petitioner in the courts – dishonourable, wealthy, masked class enemies who were in control of their domestic lives without a thought to their children. According to Fedovota, bachelors were weighed down with alimony payments and avoided women, lest they get sued for alimony and a life of impoverishment. Letters also complained that the alimony laws were destroying men's self-worth.[77] Letter writers saw women as taking advantage of the unknowing state and the men around them.

If people's court judges publicly proclaimed their support of women as custodians of children, they had privately expressed ideas similar to the letters above since the 1920s. In 1929, judges of Samara during a closed session with the Commissar of Justice, Nikolai Ianson, demanded changes to the alimony laws because "now many women see alimony as a living." Others complained that alimony was a calculated scheme to use children to make fathers pay off their mothers.[78] As seen in the cases above, judges were less likely to support women's claims if the defendant went against conservative norms of sexual behaviour. This happened in Kineshemski district, Ivanovo region, when the people's court supported a man's defence that he was not the father of a baby because his witnesses "showed that the defendant was promiscuous."[79] There are also hints that by 1939 that some judges were ready to turn away from the alimony campaign. For example, Anastasiia Zubareva filed suit in December 1939 against Aleksei Virkov, the father of her child. In 1933, they had come to an agreement before the people's court that he would pay twenty-five rubles a month in child support, but now Zubareva argued "that amount was not enough for her baby." She asked for alimony to be raised to a quarter of his wages and for 1,800 rubles in alimony dating back to the June 1936 code. The people's court had enough. They granted the increase in alimony but found, three years after the campaign for alimony, that "the documentation that she provides is too old" to show that they were suffering.[80] Courts continued to support women's claims to support their children and to hold fathers to fulfil their responsibility to their children and alimony disputes would remain a staple of people's courts. However, the urgency to fulfil the 1936 Family Laws died down, as happened with other Soviet campaigns, and people's court judges and newspaper editors turned their attention elsewhere.

Conclusion

Alimony is an imperfect system for an imperfect world. For Soviet leaders, and for many concerned Soviet citizens, it enabled too many women and men with so-called bourgeois, backward, or dishonest tendencies to take advantage of the system, which threatened Soviet society as a whole. Alimony also acknowledged the persistent inequalities in Soviet society and gaping holes in its state welfare system, especially in the countryside, a problem that persisted through the 1930s. At the same time, the fight for support of women and children was part of a larger campaign in the mid-1930s to intervene in domestic relations by banning abortion but also by having the police and courts focus more on domestic violence and publicize these trials in the press. As Amanda McNair shows, the 1936 criminalization of medical abortions increased state surveillance of women's bodies and took away their individual autonomy. Even while the state used coercion and pleas to change domestic relations and individual actions, it had limited abilities to change family relations.

The progressive alimony policies of the Soviet state still empowered peasant women to stake claims to entitlements as a right in court by employing their social group. There were significant individual victories, especially for previously marginalized people, like unwed mothers and poor women, and alimony payments were strengthened in the 1930s. However, alimony never fully resolved the domestic exploitation of women. Even after 1936 and a mass campaign to promote alimony, it was clear that the Soviet system, including its court system and laws, was too weak to compel fathers to pay alimony to give women enough material support to raise their children.

Court-issued alimony was part of a larger imperfect system of social control. The court system ruled on alimony settlements that obligated fathers to support their children. Rural soviets, *kolkhoz* administrators, police, the NKVD, social welfare offices, and lay courts all helped to enforce these rulings. For all the institutional attention on alimony, though, the Soviet state was limited in how much it could control the behaviour of fathers, or even its own state agents. Judges did not establish alimony settlements that would grant women freedom from economic exploitation. The courts, police, and NKVD could not keep tabs on all the bad fathers across the countryside. Soviet laws on personal property and on how to calculate alimony undercut the state's own goal of increasing child support and easing the financial burden on mothers. Alimony by design and in practice could only improve the lives of women and children by degrees, it could not change social realities and only reinforced gender relations in the Soviet countryside.

NOTES

1 Gosudarstvennyi arkhiv Kirovskoi oblasti (GAKO) R-1989/1/214/3ob–16.
2 Alan M. Ball, *And Now My Soul Is Hardened: Abandoned Children in Soviet Russia, 1918–1930* (Berkeley and Los Angeles: University of California Press, 1994), 1; David Shearer, *Policing Stalin's Socialism: Repression and Social Order in the Soviet Union, 1924–1953* (New Haven, CT: Yale University Press, 2009), esp. ch. 7. As Immo Rebitschek shows later in this volume, this problem continued through the post-war period.
3 Maria Galmarini-Kabala, *The Right to be Helped: Deviance, Entitlement, and the Soviet Moral Order* (DeKalb, IL: Northern Illinois University Press, 2016), 66.
4 The term alimony (*aliment*) meant support for mothers and children; it was not limited to support of former spouses. At the heart of Soviet alimony was child support. The term *aliment* was used in legal publications and in court rulings but not in decrees on the family before 1928, which favoured phrases like "material support" and "support of maintenance" instead. This changed in the 1930s, when laws and decrees used alimony more frequently and featured it prominently in the 1936 Family Law, as alimony became defined and directly linked to wages. I discuss alimony settlements and property divisions at length in my manuscript "In the People's Courts: Judges, Peasants, and Soviet Justice in the Rural Courtroom, 1917–1939."
5 Wendy Goldman, *Women, the State and Revolution: Soviet Family Policy and Social Life, 1917–1936* (New York: Cambridge University Press, 1993), 133,

194. On changes to the rural family, see Sheila Fitzpatrick, *Stalin's Peasants: Resistance and Survival in the Russian Village after Collectivization* (New York: Oxford University Press, 1994), 221–3.
6 On the parallel story of largely urban domestic servants, see Alissa Klots, "The Kitchen Maid as Revolutionary Symbol: Paid Domestic Labour and the Emancipation of Soviet Women, 1917–1941," in *The Palgrave Handbook on Women and Gender in Twentieth-Century Russia and the Soviet Union*, ed. Melanie Ilic (Basingstoke: Palgrave Macmillan, 2018), 83–100; David Hoffmann, *Stalinist Values: The Cultural Norms of Soviet Modernity, 1917–1941* (Ithaca, NY: Cornell University Press, 2003), 88–9. The decree has been explained by Nicholas S. Timashoff in *The Great Retreat: The Growth and Decline of Communism in Russia* (New York: E.P. Dutton and Co, 1946) as part of a retreat to the traditional family structure. Hoffmann argues that the Stalinist leadership instead both accelerated policies from the revolution and NEP and promoted a new type of family that could be mobilized and controlled by the state.
7 Krinkin, "Dela alimentnye (iz prakitki narodnykh sudov Viatskoi gubernii)," *Ezhenedel ' nik* 49–50 (24 December 1928): 1245. People's courts in Viatka province heard 2,875 alimony suits in 1926 and 3,867 in 1927, a 34.5 per cent increase. B. N. Khlebnikov, *Sudebnaia statistika* (Moscow: Iuridicheskoe izdatel ' stvo NKIu SSR, 1939), 99–100. Disputes over living quarters was a distant second at 10.3 per cent. M. Granovskii, "Ispolnenie sudebnykh reshenii – vazhneishii uchastok sudebnoi raboty," *Sovetskaia iustitsiia* 2–3 (20 February 1938): 21. This chapter will focus on the RSFSR. From 1927 (if not before), Soviet courts were more interventionist in Muslim family dynamics in Central Asia, as they led the assault on gender inequality and female seclusion, especially of minors, in favour of European-style women's liberation as proscribed in new laws. See Douglas L. Northrup, "Subaltern Dialogues: Subversion and Resistance in Soviet Uzbek Family Law," *Slavic Review* 60, no. 1 (2001): 115–40.
8 The Sovnarkom created the Peasant Mutual Social Assistance (*Krest'ianskie Komitety Obshchestvennoi Vzaimopomoshchi* or KKOV) in 1921 to provide material assistance to workers, poor peasants, and families of Red Army soldiers in need. KKOV offered social insurance programs and later loans to small landholders but were perennially underfunded and peasants and officials widely criticized them for their ineffectiveness and inactivity. It was disbanded during collectivization, and the collective farms assumed the KKOV's responsibilities. I.I. Klimin, *Rossiiskoe krest'ianstvo v gody novoi ekonomicheskoi politiki (1921–1927), chast' pervaia* (St Petersburg: Izdatel'stvo Politechnicheskogo Universiteta, 2007), 242–56.
9 Tsentral'nyi arkhiv Nizhegorodskoi oblasti (TsANO) R-2055/1/53/3–11. Quotes on l. 3. He challenged the ruling on the grounds that he had been

paying for the children's upbringing and could not afford to pay alimony on top of that. The cassational court upheld the people's court's ruling.
10 See Jane Burbank, *Russian Peasants Go to Court: Legal Culture in the Countryside, 1905–1917* (Bloomington: Indiana University Press, 2004).
11 Golfo Alexopolous, *Stalin's Outcasts: Aliens, Citizens, and the Soviet State, 1926–1936* (Ithaca, NY: Cornell University Press, 2003) and "The Ritual Lament: A Narrative of Appeal in the 1920s and 1930s," *Russian History/ Histoire Russe* 24, nos. 1–2 (1997): 117–29; Daniel Newman, "Criminal Strategies and Institutional Concerns in the Soviet Legal System: An Analysis of Criminal Appeals in Moscow Province, 1921–1928," (PhD thesis, UCLA, 2013).
12 Ball, *And Now My Soul Is Hardened*.
13 Tsentral'nyi gosudarstvennyi arkhiv Udmurtskoi Respubliki (TGA UR) R-876/1/1,5; R-1013/1/2; Tsentral'nyi gosudarstvennyi arkhiv Moskovskoi oblasti (TsGAMO) 3966/1/268/1ob–18; Goldman, *Women, the State and Revolution*, 98.
14 Galmarini-Kabala, *The Right to Be Helped*, esp. ch. 1.
15 Tsentral'nyi arkhiv Samarskoi oblasti (TsGASO) R-349/2/428/1ob–16.
16 TsGASO R-357/47/2/81.
17 "Kodeks zakonov o brake, sem'e i opeke," in *Postanovleniia III sessiia Vserossiiskogo Tsentral'nogo Ispolnitel'nogo Komiteta XII sozyva* (Moscow: VTsIK, 1926), 124–44.
18 GAKO R-2757/1/65.
19 On regional variations of villagers' support of extra-marital relationships in the pre-revolutionary era, see Christine Worobec, *Peasant Russia: Family and Community in the Post-Emancipation Period* (DeKalb, IL: Northern Illinois University Press, 1995), 144–6.
20 GAKO R-2126/1/1182/ 2–7.
21 TsANO R-5505/1/360/1–24. Quote on l.1.
22 Lisa Granik, "The Trials of the *Proletarka*: Sexual Harassment Claims in the 1920s," in *Reforming Justice in Russia, 1864–1994: Power, Culture and the Limits of Legal Order*, ed. Peter H. Solomon (New York: Routledge, 1996), 131–67.
23 Sheila Fitzpatrick, *Everyday Stalinism: Ordinary Life in Extraordinary Times: Soviet Russia in the 1930s* (New York: Oxford University Press, 1999), 139–43.
24 Quoted in M. O. Reikhel', *Dela ob alimentakh* (Moscow: Iuridicheskoe izdatel'stvo NKIu SSSR, 1939), 4.
25 A point made by Granik, "The Trials of the *Proletarka*," 131–67.
26 L. Azov, "Alimenty v derevne," *Krest'ianskii iurist* 13 (15 July 1928): 8–10.
27 Goldman, *Women, the State, and Revolution*, 308–10; Hoffmann, *Stalinist Values*, 106.

28 Goldman, *Women, the State, and Revolution*, 296–310. On the subjective nature of need in rulings on alimony, see Mark Ellman, "The Theory of Alimony," *California Law Review* 77 (1989): 3–74.
29 Krinkin, "Dela alimentnye," 1245–6.
30 TsGASO R-1061/3/1/8ob–8.
31 TsGASO R-637/2/117/15.
32 S.E. Kopelianskaia, *Zashchita prav rebenka v sovtskom sude: Prakticheskoe posobie* (Moscow: Sovetskoe zakonodatel'stvo, 1936), 46.
33 A. Goraina, "Vzyskanie alimentov i obshchestvennost'," *Sovetskaia iustitsiia* 7–8 (March 1930): 37–8.
34 V.M. "Otvetstvennost' dvora po vyplaste alimentov," *Ezhendel'nik* 10 (14 March 1926): 293–4. Ia. Brandenburgskii, "K predstoiashchei sessii VTsIK. (Krest'ianskii dvor i aliminety)," *Ezhendel'nik* 31 (8 August 1926): 937–8. Ukraine's courts encouraged alimony to be settled in foodstuff or their equivalent costs.
35 Anikeev, "Za formoi pogliadeli sut," *Sovetskaia iustitsiia* 2–3 (20 February 1938): 71–2. Courts in the 1920s experimented with payments in kind, but those were not paid through the state.
36 GAKO R-1991/1/112/57–60.
37 Reikhel, *Dela ob alimentakh*, 33–4.
38 GAKO R-1991/1/112/34ob–34. For an instance where the court under the judge turned down a father's petition to lower payment, also in December 1935, see GAKO R-1991/1/112/85.
39 GAKO R-1991/1/112/103ob–4. Quote on l. 104ob–104.
40 As reported in Kopelianskaia, *Zashchita prav rebenka v sovtskom sude*, 46.
41 See Fitzpatrick, *Everyday Stalinism*, 142–3; Goldman, *Women, the State, and Revolution*.
42 "O zapreshchenii abortov, uvlichenii material'noi pomoshchi rozhenitsam…," *Izvestiia*, 28 June 1936: 1.
43 David Hoffmann, *Cultivating the Masses: Modern State Practices and Soviet Socialism, 1914–1939* (Ithaca, NY: Cornell University Press, 2011), 110. Sarah Davies, *Popular Opinion in Stalin's Russia: Terror, Propaganda and Dissent, 1934–1991* (Cambridge: Cambridge University Press, 1997), 66–7.
44 The reportage of the 1936 decree also broke from the previous codes by emphasizing emotion, especially parental love of children, just as alimony became more regimented, without emotional investment in the amount of support to be ordered by the court.
45 Lisa Kirschenbaum, *Small Comrades: Revolutionizing Childhood in Soviet Russia, 1917–1932* (New York: Routledge, 2000), 141–6; Hoffmann, *Cultivating the Masses*, 152.
46 S. Benenson and S. Zilov, "Dela ob alimentakh v narodnykh sudakh Moskovskoi oblasti," *Sovetskaia iustitsiia* 10–11 (15 June 1937): 78. On

campaign justice for collectivization, see Peter H. Solomon, *Soviet Criminal Justice under Stalin* (New York: Cambridge University Press, 1996), ch. 3.
47 Solomon, *Soviet Criminal Justice*, ch. 5.
48 A. Lisytsyn, "Zakon 27 iiunia 1936 g. i sudebnaia praktika," 15; E. Bornina, "Alimentnye dela," *Sovetskaia iustitsiia* 34 (5 December 1936): 12. Alimony could be settled between the two parties, but still needed to be registered and approved by the people's court.
49 "Po narodnym sudam," *Sovetskaia iustitsiia* 3 (15 February 1937): 29.
50 Reikhel, *Dela ob alimentakh*, 38.
51 L. Otmar-Shtein, "O rebenke, kak priamoi 'ulike' i pozhiznennykh alimentakh," *Sovetskaia iustitsiia* 1 (15 January 1937): 15.
52 S. Benenson and S. Zilov, "Dela ob alimentakh," 42.
53 GARF R-9492/1/20/179; "V sudebnykh i sledstvennykh organakh," *Bol'shevistskaia tribuna* (Stavropol', Kuibyshevskaia oblast'), 25 February 1939, 4.
54 "Pochtovyi iashchik," 27 *Sovetskaia iustitsiia* (25 September 1936): 22.
55 GARF R-9474/16/92/19ob–19.
56 "Pri vzyskanii na soderzhanie detei s deda i babki," "Postanovlenie prezidiuma Verkhovnogo suda RSFSR ot 10 oktiabria 1937 g.," *Sovetskaia iustitsiia* 1 (12 January 1938): 61, 62. The case eventually found its way to the Supreme Court of the RSFSR, which upheld the original decision, citing the 1928 Supreme Court explication that not only relatives were responsible for supporting minors.
57 E. Bornina, "Alimentnye dela," *Sovetskaia iustitsiia* 34 (5 December 1936): 12.
58 GAKO R-1991/1/1/1–8. For a similar case, see f. R-1991/1/112/57–60.
59 TsANO R-5505/1/314/119–20. The 1918 code had required unwed women to identify the father three months before birth. In 1926, that right was extended to after birth as well. The father was given a year to dispute parentage before the court ordered alimony. A similar case happened in Sosnovsk district in Gor'kii in which the newly deemed father had to pay a quarter of his wages for the rest of his life and an additional thirty rubles a month for a year to account for the mother's lost wages while she did not work to take care of her child. TsANO R-5505/1/314/30. In December 1935, a people's court in Kirov district supported Sofiia Markova's claim that Aleksandr Bakin fathered her child when they both worked in the village. The key questions for the court were where could they have had sex and was Markova promiscuous. Bakin defended himself by showing that he had stayed with the chair of the sel'sovet while she had a room in the policeman's home and then with another man. He brought in a witness who testified that after the baby was born, Markova said that she would just write in Bakin as the father since he receives a nice monthly salary of

250 rubles from the kolkhoz. However, Markova got a witness to testify that she did live with Bakin, which was enough for the court to rule that Bakin was most likely the father and ordered that he pay fifty rubles a month in child support, just under 25 per cent of his salary.

60 N. Lagovier, "Dela grazhdanskie," *Sovetskaia iustitsiia* 8 (March 1936): 8–9.
61 "Sobliudat' trebovaniia grazhdanskgoo protsessual'nogo kodeksa o vyzove v sud storon," *Sovetskaia iustitsiia* 2–3 (20 February 1938): 69.
62 A. Lisitsyn, "Zakon 27 iiunia 1936 g. i sudebnaia praktika," *Sovetskaia iustitsiia* 1 (1937): 14–15.
63 "Rech' prokurara soiuza SSR t. A. Ia Vyshinskogo," *Sotsialisticheskaia zakonnost* 2 (1937): 105.
64 TsGASO R-3499/1/841/206–28.
65 "Po soiuznym respublikam: Otchety narodnykh sudei po dannym mestnoi pechati," *Sovetskaia iustitsiia* 18 (20 September 1937): 32; The village correspondent in Luinsk district in Kuibyshev reported dozens of kolkhoz women coming to court during market days to check on their alimony cases. "Some cry while others are indignant and they return a few weeks later and don't hear an answer again." Timonin, "Korespondentsii chitatelei," *Sovetskaia iustitsiia* 6 (20 March 1938): 41–2.
66 "Rech' prokurara soiuza SSR t. A. Ia Vyshinskogo," 108. Both Reikhel' and Lisityn would both be arrested and executed the following year.
67 S. Orlov, "Alimentnye dela v praktike narodnykh sudov Opochetskogo okruga Kalininskoi oblasti," *Sovetskaia iustitsiia* 8 (20 April 1938): 41.
68 Ia Shumiatskii, "Alimenty v sudebnoi praktike," *Sovetskaia iustitsiia* 12 (20 June 1938): 10–11.
69 Krinkin, "Dela alimentnye," 1246. The Soviet state was surprisingly effective in 1928 and only failed to get any support from men 12 per cent of the time.
70 For more on state conceptions of peasant backwardness and the role of the state to modernize the village, see Tracy McDonald, *Face to the Village: The Riazan Countryside under Soviet Rule, 1921–1930* (Toronto: University of Toronto Press, 2011).
71 TsGASO R-357/48/63/6. In fact, men had to divide property acquired during the marriage equally after a divorce.
72 A. Goraina, "Vzyskanie alimentov," 37.
73 Kopelianskaia, *Zashchita rebenka*, 47–8.
74 Reikhel, *Dela ob alimentakh*, 16–20. As laid out in Article 28 of the 1936 Code: "O zapreshchenii abortov"; Hoffmann, *Cultivating the Masses*, 150–80.
75 Income and savings of both parties were taken into account for disabled children who needed to be provided for over age eighteen.
76 S.E. Kopelianskaia, *Zashchita prav rebenka v sovtskom sude*, 6.

77 Quoted in Lauren Kaminsky, "Utopian Visions of Soviet Life in the Stalin-Era Soviet Union," *Central European History* 44 (2011): 75–6.
78 TsGASO R-637/2/42/15ob–16.
79 A. Lisytsyn, "Zakon 27 iiunia 1936 g. i sudebnaia praktika," *Sovetskaia iustitsiia* 1 (15 January 1937): 15.
80 GAKO R-1989/1/596a/5.

2 *Nashi/ne Nashi*: Individual Smallholders, Social Control, and the State in Ziuzdinskii District, Kirov Region, 1932–1939

SAMANTHA LOMB

This chapter uses a micro-historical approach to examine how various levels of government exercised social control over individual smallholders in Ziuzdniskii district (*raion*) of the Kirov region (*oblast'*) through taxation. In his discussion of micro-history as a method of historical analysis, Giovanni Levi asserts that "the unifying principle of all micro-historical research is the belief that microscopic observation will reveal factors previously unobserved."[1] This micro-historical study of Ziuzdinskii district allows the reader to see how local and personal factors were often the driving forces behind decisions and power struggles that on a macro level may seem driven by communist rhetoric and policies originating in Moscow.

Zuizdinskii district (highlighted in dark grey in Figure 2.1) is located in the northeastern part of Kirov region.[2] This district was heavily forested and *khutor* agriculture (small-scale independent farmsteads created under Stolypin) dominated.[3] As such, Ziuzdinskii district is representative of the northern areas of the RSFSR and provides a counterpoint to discussions of the Black Earth region and Ukraine that dominate discussions of collectivization. Additionally, a micro-historical look at Ziuzdinskii district "reveals factors previously unobserved."[4] By examining state interactions with individual smallholders in this specific district we can see how key categories, in this case citizens to be integrated into the collective economy or class enemies, were defined at various levels of government and how taxation was used to enforce state policies aimed at these specific categories.[5] States have long used taxation as a way to promote behaviours they found advantageous and to discourage behaviours they found harmful. An example is the "sin tax," which increases taxation on items deemed harmful to health or healthy social behaviour, such as alcohol, cigarettes, and sugary drinks.[6] In this case, the Soviet government was using taxes to encourage peasants to join collective farms through

Figure 2.1 Schematic map of the grain output in Kirov region, 1937, with Ziuzdinskii highlighted (GASPI KO 1290/1/296/56)

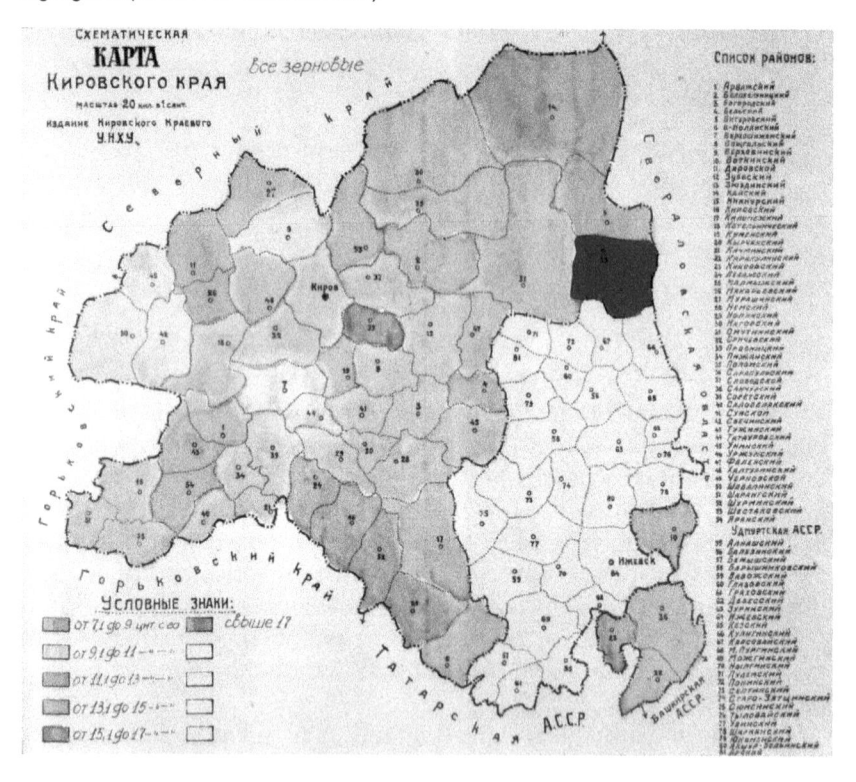

higher taxes on individual smallholders and offering tax breaks for collectivized households. In this way, taxation serves as a nexus where basic categories meet and reshape each other and a way to express and negotiate the tensions of a modern regime.[7]

During the drive to collective agriculture, the Soviet state began to organize among and exert pressure on uncollectivized peasants to encourage them to join collective farms. These uncollectivized peasants, excluding those the state defined as kulaks, were referred to as individual smallholders. The Soviet state wanted to minimize the number of individual smallholders because individual smallholdings in an otherwise collectivized village complicated land allocation, crop rotation, and other aspects of agricultural planning, as well as undermining state collectivization goals. As a result of various enticements and coercive policies, the overall number of individual smallholders in the countryside fell rapidly in the 1930s. In 1932, 39 per cent of peasants in the Soviet Union were still individual smallholders. But with each passing year, the proportion of uncollectivized peasants declined, falling to 17 per cent in 1935 and to 7 per cent in 1937.[8] In Kirov region, the number of individual smallholder households shrank by almost half, from 67,133 in 1935 to 37,933 in 1936. This was due in part to them joining the collective farms, but also to them becoming industrial workers, white-collar workers, or leaving the region.[9] At the end of 1937, Kirov's individual smallholders farmed almost 6 per cent of all farmsteads, but they only occupied 1 per cent of the area's cultivated land.[10] However, these numbers do not reflect the considerable district-level variation in collectivization rates. In industrialized and agriculturally well-developed districts, and districts that were closer to the centre of the region, the number of individual smallholders decreased rapidly.[11] But individual smallholders remained an influential presence in many districts, such as Kotel'nicheskii, Arbazhskii, Sanchurskii, and Ziuzdinskii districts, up through 1938, when punitive taxes on horse ownership forced most smallholders to join collective farms or move into industry.[12]

Much of the current historiography on individual smallholders focuses on their disintegration from mainstream society. Indeed, individual smallholders faced a number of discriminatory policies, including high levels of taxation and loss of land. The historian Sheila Fitzpatrick has asserted that the state's objective was to squeeze the individual smallholders until there was nothing more to get out of them and they were forced to join the collective farms. As a result, she emphasized, they were often given plans and quotas that were intentionally unrealistically high.[13]

While Fitzpatrick's work has enhanced our understanding of the fiscal pressures imposed on smallholders, what she does not address is the conflict between state, regional, and local officials over how much tax should be levied and what the goal of the taxes were. Central officials pushed to integrate individual smallholders into society, even forbidding collective farms from rejecting them. Regional and local officials, on the other hand, were interested in removing the individual smallholders from their regions and districts because many viewed them as class alien, disruptive elements. Pressed as regional and local officials were for financial resources, they also wanted to squeeze them to fulfil financial and procurement plans. As a result, even when the People's Commissariat of Agriculture (Narkomzem) introduced higher taxes, regional and local officials objected that these taxes were not high enough; in some cases, they unilaterally adjusted the taxes higher.

Such efforts brought them into direct conflict with the central state. This conflict became particularly sharp in 1937 as the newly ratified 1936 Constitution and changes in tax law protected the rights of individual smallholders and district officials' seizure of property for tax arrears violated these rights. When these violations were investigated in Ziuzdinskii district, local officials were removed from office for these infractions. These realities, which are discussed below, offer a significant challenge to the views found in the current literature.

Additionally, the current historiography ignores the fact that while there was conflict between smallholders on the one hand, and the government and some collective farms on the other, other smallholders lived in harmony with collective farmers. Independent smallholders often farmed collective farmland and held positions on collective farms, much to the chagrin of the government officials eager to levy taxes and seize property.[14] This was the case in Ziuzdniskii district. These everyday accommodations undermined the centre's intentions to exert social control in the countryside.

Rural soviet officials tended to leave such practices unchallenged. The district-level officials, in particular district committee (*raikom*) secretary Viacheslav Batyrev and district executive committee (*raion ispolkom*, or RIK) chairman Arkhip Chadaev, viewed individual smallholders as a dangerous class that needed to be crushed. They set about doing so through the levying of punitive taxes. The Kirov regional administration tacitly approved these actions and put pressure on the district to stop the practice of allowing individual smallholders to use collective farmland. However, the punitive tax campaign brought the district-level power structure into conflict with Moscow, particularly after 1936, when the new constitution explicitly guaranteed protection from unlawful search and seizure, and the 1937 tax code restricted the types of property that could be confiscated and sold for back taxes. Moscow pressured the regional procurator to deal with the issue, and in 1938 many of the top district leaders were arrested (but none were ever convicted) for excesses and violations of smallholders' constitutional rights. As the case of Ziuzdinskii district makes clear, the relationship between individual smallholders, collective farmers, and the government was multifaceted and far more complex than previously believed.

Official Policy towards Individual Smallholders

The Soviet state employed "carrot and stick" policies aimed at encouraging individual smallholders into collective farms. They did this by offering smallholders incentives to join and blocking attempts to keep them out or alienate them from the collective farms. At the 16th Party Congress (1930), local and regional officials were warned "not to persecute individual smallholders, but rather to offer them help and try, in every possible way, to attract them into the collective farms."[15] At the same time, the Soviet government used ever-increasing tax pressure to stimulate individual peasants to join collective farms.

The tax burden on individual smallholding households was significantly higher than on collective farm households but siginficantly less than the punitive taxes levelled on kulaks.[16] And this tax burden increased over the years as the state pushed for total (*sploshnaia*) collectivization. For example, in 1931, individual smallholders were taxed based on a graduated agricultural tax scale which charged four kopeks in tax for the first twenty-five rubles of recorded annual income and seven kopeks per each subsequent ruble. In 1932, taxes increased with the implementation a flat tax of seven rubles for all households that earned under one hundred rubles. Households with incomes over one hundred rubles were taxed according to a graduated tax scale.[17] Furthermore, in 1931, income from the sale of agricultural products at market prices began to be taken into account when calculating individual smallholders' agricultural tax.[18] In 1932, the rates of calculated profitability for taxable objects like vegetable gardens were increased by one and a half times.[19]

However, contrary to expectation, the Soviet state applied a class lens to the individual smallholders as a group, rather than simply viewing them all antagonistically.[20] This meant that poor households either paid no tax or a siginficantly smaller amount compared to weathier households. For example, in 1931, households whose tax obligations were less than one ruble paid no agricultural tax. In 1932, changes in tax code removed this exemption, instead granting the rural tax commission the ability to grant a full or partial tax exemption to "individual low-power (*malomoshchnye*) households." This policy change resulted in a significant decrease in individual smallholding households exempted from agricultural taxes.[21] Seemingly conflicting policies which often served to ameliorate state-imposed burdens was characteristic of the Soviet approach towards individual smallholders in the 1930s.

Nevertheless, in addition to agricultural taxes, individual smallholders had to pay cultural and self-taxes, the amount of which was determined by how much they paid in agricultural tax. A household exempt from agricultural taxes was not exempt from cultural or self-taxation. Such households paid five rubles in cultural taxes in 1931 and from six to ten rubles in self-taxation. In 1932, the cultural tax for poor households increased to eight to sixteen rubles, and self-tax increased to eight to twelve rubles. Households that paid agricultural taxes also saw their cultural and self-tax rates increase from 1931 to 1932.[22] Furthermore, in 1932, individual peasants were also subject to one-time taxation, designed to push middle peasant households into collective farms.[23]

Tax pressure on individual smallholders continued to increase in 1933 as the fixed agricultural tax rate for poorer housholds increased to fifteen rubles and the tax amount for households taxed on the progressive scale also increased. The share of non-agricultural earnings included in the taxable base decreased, but this did not lead to a reduction in the tax burden. In contrast, more complete accounting for non-agricultural incomes, combined with the abovementioned higher tax rates, caused a significant increase in the level of taxation.[24] In addition, the maximum amount of self-taxation for individual smallholders taxed at a fixed rate increased from eighteen to twenty rubles in 1933.[25] The increase in taxes levied on individual smallholders reflected not only an increase in the level of taxation, but also a slight improvement in their economic situation. Individual smallholders had adapted to the pressures the state had exerted on them during the intial collectivization drive, and many of them began to gradually increase their wealth.[26]

The agricultural tax of 1934 reflected the state's renewed focus on using taxes to push individual smallholders onto collective farms.[27] The annual fixed tax rate for the agricultural tax jumped from fifteen to twenty-five rubles for individual smallholders with taxable income of less than 200 rubles, and the taxation scale for farms with higher incomes also increased. Self-taxation of individual smallholders also increased, as did the cultural tax cap for individual smallholders taxed at a fixed rate.[28] The tax regulations also provided for a significant increase in the rates of imputed profitability of crop production and in the amount of handicraft earnings that could be taxed.[29]

Additionally, at the end of September 1934, the Central Executive Committee and the Council of People's Commissars of the USSR decided to introduce an additional, one-time, monetary tax on individual smallholders. Households with market incomes or draft animals (that is, those that could most successfully thrive outside of collective farms) were specifically targeted.[30] To force the peasants to pay the old and new taxes on time and in full, the list of individual smallholder property subject to confiscation to pay off arrears was radically revised to include all property, except for the house, fuel for its heating, and household items.[31]

Despite this increased tax burden, many provincial Party officials viewed individual smallholders as disruptive elements and petitioned Moscow to take even greater repressive measures against them. On 7

September 1934, the Gor'kii regional Party committee (*kraikom*)[32] wrote a letter to Kaganovich, Molotov, Chernov, and Zhdanov. In it, the *kraikom* listed the measures that they thought needed to be taken against individual smallholders.[33] The Gor'kii *kraikom* suggested increasing taxes and grain quotas, which were only 10–15 per cent greater than collective farmers' quotas in 1934, as well as outlawing or restricting alternative forms of income such as trade or growing produce on their garden plots. The regional Party committee recommended that individual smallholders' quotas be 30 per cent larger than collective farmers' quotas. It urged the state to allow the regions the discretion to adjust this rate, upward or downward in specific districts, as long as they maintained the 30 per cent difference overall. They also wanted to change the Central Executive Committee (TsIK) decision that gave poor or disabled individual smallholders a break on agricultural taxes and to impose grain taxes on individual smallholders in the mountains and the forest. Finally, the regional Party committee wanted to revise the governmental law of 1929, which established a minimum amount of household goods that could not be auctioned (*ne podlezhashchii k prodazhe s torgov*). The *kraikom* believed that it was necessary to decrease this minimum because "the individual peasant has adapted to this minimum so much so that almost nothing can be inventoried, and nothing can be sold [for back taxes]."[34]

The regional Party committee also wanted to promulgate a law about individual smallholders' obligatory participation in labour and cultural duties. The *kraikom* wanted the right to deprive individual smallholders of their garden plots in cases where individual smallholders sabotaged sowing and did not work their fields.[35] They wanted to mandate individual smallholder participation in timber harvesting and transport, as "currently only the collective farmers work in the forest. The collective farmers are very offended by this and it is considered to be one of the reasons for the weak growth of collectivization in forested districts."[36] Similarly, collective farmers and individual smallholders were required to provide the state a fixed number of unpaid labour days a year, under the corvée laws introduced at the beginning of the 1930s.[37] These labour days were spent on projects such as the construction of schools, clubs, hospitals, roads, and fire prevention measures. However, individual smallholders frequently refused to participate, and the burden usually fell to the collective farmers, an obvious source of irritation for the collective farmers. The regional Party committee responded by urging the state to pass a special law demanding that individual smallholders participate on equal terms with collective farms.[38] The *kraikom*'s demands resulted from an array of local concerns and greivances, but also conveyed a sense of the region's moral economy. Individual smallholders shirking these social obligations was not only a persistent irritant, it was also perceived as unfair. As late as 1938, collective farmers were complaining about individual smallholders avoiding communal responsibilities.[39]

In the face of this resentment towards individual smallholders, People's Commissar of Agriculture Iakov Iakovlev reminded his audience at the Second Congress of Outstanding Collective Farmers in February 1935 that it was the government's goal to enrol all the peasantry in collective farms. He chastised collective farm activists for making individual smallholders suffer for their earlier opposition to collectivization by holding up their admission until they had made payments equivalent to the full value of any animal or equipment that they had sold off prior to joining the collective farm. Highlighting the central state's goal of enrolling all peasants in collective farms, the New Model Collective Farm Charter, promulgated at this congress, stated that collective farms had no right to refuse individual smallholders entry. However, the charter did allow collective farms to demand compensation from applicants who had disposed of horses and seed in the past two years, though the sum could be paid in instalments over the course of several years. Activists who had contributed to the collective farm economy were deeply unsatisfied with this provision, but it exemplifies the state's efforts to attract rather than isolate smallholders.[40]

At the same time the state paved the way for easy entry into collective farms, it increased pressure on those who resisted joining. In the mid- to late 1930s, the central state began targeting the remaining individual smallholders with punitive taxes and sowing plans reminiscent of the "fixed plans" given out to kulaks several years earlier. For example, in 1935, *narkomzem* gave individual smallholders in Kirov region sowing plans one and a half to two times greater than was really possible to fulfil.[41] In July 1936, individual smallholder Leukhin wrote a letter to the newspaper *Kirovskaia pravda* to complain. He had 2.52 hectares in winter crops, but was given a quota for three hectares, which was more than the land he had. When he had complained to local authorities, the rural soviet and the procurement committee representative said that nothing could be done.[42] Collective farms were reluctant to accept individual smallholders who had such plans as members because the collective farm had to fulfil the grain deliveries for these individual smallholders, which could be up to two and a half times more grain than the average collective farm household was responsible for.[43]

In addition, the 1935 agricultural tax on individual smallholders had been completely overhauled. The rates of calculated returns, particularly from horses and cows, significantly increased and the age of the horses subject to taxation decreased from four to three years. Income from handicrafts was also included in the taxable base in the amount of 50–100 per cent of the earnings received minus basic production costs. As for the income from the sale of agricultural products at market prices, they ceased to be correlated with income from other types of activities and were included in the taxable base in the amount of from 50 to 75 per cent of the recorded indicators. Additionally, a number of changes were made to the procedure for granting benefits and discounts to individual smallholders. Agricultural taxes were reduced by 10 per cent for households that had three disbaled members if they had no more than two able-bodied people, and by 20 per cent if there were four or more disabled people (in 1934, these discounts were respectively 20 and 30 per cent). "Low-powered" families that did not have a single able-bodied member or any cattle were fully or partially exempted from paying the agricultural tax.[44] For individual smallholders paying agricultural tax, the self-tax in 1935 was set at 40–60 per cent of their income.[45]

Like the agricultural tax, the 1935 cultural tax also took into account not only draft animals and market income, but also non-agricultural occupations, which led to the tax being significantly higher than in 1934.[46] It increased again in 1936 when the cultural tax was from 75 to 100 per cent of the amount of agricultural tax for the previous year for individual farmers without draft livestock, market, and non-agricultural income and from 100 to 175 per cent for individual farmers with draft animals, market, or non-agricultural income.[47] The increased taxes reduced the number of individual smallholders, as many joined collective farms to avoid the tax burden. Those individual smallholders that remained became poorer and often hopelessly in arrears.[48]

However, in 1937, the administrative procedure for imposing fines on individual smallholders and other taxpayers and confiscating their property was abolished, and the list of property that was not subject to confiscation to cover arrears was expanded. The mandatory deadlines for paying the agricultural tax were also extended and the penalties for late payments decreased to 0.1 per cent per day.[49] Self-taxation began to be carried out at fixed rates, rather than being determined based on the agricultural tax paid. The maximum amount for households without field crops and draft animals was forty rubles; for households with crop fields and draft animals it was seventy-five rubles. Individual smallholders who were disabled due to their advanced age (sixty years or more) and did not have other able-bodied members in their families were exempted from paying monetary taxes and fees.[50]

However, district officials often ignored central state guidelines and unilaterally increased these taxes. In 1936–7, the regional committee (*oblastnoi komitet* or *obkom*) instructor Akimov noted that local officials in Sanchurskii district sometimes increased the taxes levied on individual smallholders. In some cases, they did so by adjusting the smallholders' reported income upwards to account for non-agricultural income. According to Akimov, in Zimnicheskii rural soviet, former head of the raion land organization Skladnev or tax inspector Korchagin (later the head of the district land organization) personally verified individual smallholders' income. They increased individual smallholders' reported income to compensate for what they felt was unreported income earned from making valenki (*pimokatstva*), as demonstrated below:

Table 2.1. Smallholders' Income

Name	Income confirmed by the Council of People's Commisars	Unilaterally increased Income
Aleksei Geraimovich Laptev	900	1,400
Vasillii Mikhailovich Krylov	1,800	2,400
Petr Semenovich Filonov	400	800
Nikolai Ignat'evich Filonov	400	700
Vasilii Ignat'evich Filonov	1,200	2,100
Vasilii Fedorovich Paklanov	600	1,100
Nikolai Vladimirovich Pakulin	600	1,100

In Aktainskii rural soviet, Akimov noted that it was the rural soviet, not the district officials, who increased the reported incomes. Rural soviet chairman Ukhov deemed incomes, which had been confirmed by the district tax commission, underreported and he personally corrected the numbers upward.[51] *Obkom* instructor Korepanov noted that individual smallholders in Ziuzdinskii district also faced arbitrary tax increases to compensate for unreported non-agricultural income. These increased taxes were difficult for smallholders to pay, and this resulted in large numbers of asset seizures. For example, in the village of Kir'ian, Karakulinskii rural soviet, all of the twenty-three individual smallholding households had property seized for taxes.[52] While the impact was substantial, the evidence does not allow one to say that the levies were arbitrary or incorrect. One thing is certain, local authorities were often harsher on their neighbours than were central authorities.

The central state as represented by Narkomzem and Iakovlev consistently reminded collective farm activists and rural officials that the goal was to get all the peasants on the collective farms. Even when punitive taxes were introduced, they were designed to force the remaining individual smallholders onto collective farms and fulfil the central goal of complete collectivization. Regional and district authorities, by contrast, primarily viewed smallholders as troublesome people who avoided paying their share of taxes and shouldering their share of collective work. As a result, at various times regional and district officials sought to increase the burden on the individual smallholders either by appealing to central authorities or by taking action on their own. Their goal, as we shall see, was to destroy individual smallholders as a class.

Ziuzdinskii District

Understanding the context in which the district officials were operating while attempting to assert social control is key to understanding why they resorted to harsh treatment of individual smallholders. Harsh or repressive measures were the last resort of state organs that did not have the means to govern effectively. And the Ziuzdinskii district Party and state organizations lacked the funds, infrastructure, personnel, and support from the regional and central state and Party apparatus to effectively implement state policies and maintain social control in the district. They also on occasion faced violent resistance to Soviet rule.

Ziuzdinskii district was a poor, grain-importing district that focused on flax production and animal husbandry.[53] As a result, many of Ziuzdinskii's inhabitants had to have a source of supplementary income, primarily labour outside the area (*otkhod*) or handicraft production.[54] The educational level of the population was low (65 per cent of the population was semi-literate) and the inhabitants were classified as very religious.[55] The population at large had suffered from serious health problems, and as a result many were so disabled that they were unable to work and hence required some sort of state support.[56]

Ziuzdinskii district had been on the front lines of the Civil War.[57] As a result, there were a lot of hidden weapons scattered about. This created a powder keg of violence, as those who opposed Soviet power remained in isolated *khutory* and small settlements and had access to weapons. In 1929–30, the Zuizdinskii countryside, particularly in Ezzhinskii and Kuvakushkii rural soviets, were home to two bands of bandits,[58] both about one hundred strong. The bandits lived in the forest, where they conducted military drills and from which they shot at local officials. The problem became so dire that in the autumn of 1930, a military unit from Viatka was dispatched to crush the bandits.[59]

However, this did not end the life-or-death encounters between those disenfranchised by or dissatisfied with Soviet power and Soviet workers. In 1931–2, there were a series of so-called white-terrorist acts aimed particularly at communists, such as the murder of the Zakultanskii rural soviet chairman by a "kulak-bandit" who ambushed him. Similarly, in 1931, two communists were murdered at a meeting in the village of Ozhegino, and in March 1932 the chairman of Savinskii collective farm, E.M. Chernaev, was shot at.[60] In the spring of 1932, activist and Komsomol rural soviet chairman Varankin was murdered in what was ruled an act of kulak terror.[61]

With the Party and state not able to ensure the safety of its own people, violence was an effective tool to intimidate peasants and keep them from joining collective farms. In the spring of 1931, a group of bandits, formed from fleeing kulaks, terrorized the Savinskii collective farm administration.[62] In Zakulanskii rural soviet, bandits threatened to beat or murder people joining collective farms so only fifty households in the rural soviet had been collectivized. The village of Ragozy in Kytmanovskii rural soviet, where the Red commander Soboleva was killed in 1918, had anti-Soviet attitudes that persisted into the early 1930s. As a result, only twelve households of the total seventy-five had joined the collective farm by 1932.[63]

The violence continued into 1934. At the 25 July Party meeting, Party members argued that the *raikom* was blind to the political significance of the murder of activists despite the fact that in the last eight months there had been eight terrorist attacks.[64] The continued violence aimed at state and Party representatives had a chilling effect on finding cadres willing to go to the countryside. Six days after the meeting discussing terrorist attacks, which included the murder of a brigadier, Party member Luchnikov was appointed to be the new collective farm chairman on the farm where the brigadier was killed. Despite being threatened with being stripped of his Party card if he didn't take up the post, he absolutely refused to go. He was expelled from the Party and a fellow named Varankin (different from the Komsomol member murdered in 1932) was sent to do the job.[65]

Violent incidents were rarer in the later part of the decade, but they still occurred, usually in connection with frustration at illegal searches and seizures or as part of expanded constitutional rights for former class enemies. For example, on the Stalin collective farm in 1937, V.A. Porubov and O.A. Porubov (probably brothers) beat up rural soviet member Matren Porubov in the collective farm club because he had written up a property inventory.[66] Though most of this violence took place before Batyrev and Chadaev came to Ziuzdinskii in the fall of

1935 and early 1936, respectively, RaiZO head Shishkin lived through these attacks, and no doubt these incidents of violence were fresh in the collective memory of the district Party and soviet organizations. These recollections of class enemy violence, which exemplified a lack of social control at the district level, fuelled district officials' harsh attitudes towards individual smallholders, who they viewed as antagonistic to soviet power. These "ecosystems of violence" are further discussed in Tim Blauvelt's chapter.

In addition to facing violent threats, more mundane problems also plagued Ziuzdinskii district's leadership. The district was chronically underdeveloped, understaffed, and underfunded, with district workers often being owed several months of back pay. The size of the district, the lack of a transportation infrastructure, its forested landscape, and the distance between collective farms and isolated homesteads made it virtually impossible for a small group of people to govern effectively. In 1932, there were only seventeen Party cells and 221 Party members to cover 42 rural soviets. The district Party and executive organs were mostly staffed by communists, who preferred to live in the district centre Afanas'evo, rather than in the countryside for both safety and convenience.[67]

In March 1935, the district became smaller as Biserovskii district, the northern third of the district, was calved off to form its own district.[68] What remained was divided into twenty-six rural soviets, which were home to 118 collective farms and four forest product combines, some of which were located as many as sixty-five kilometres (forty miles) from the district centre of Afanas'evo across bad roads. Even though the district had become smaller, this distance still made it quite difficult for district officials to regularly visit these far-flung farms and combines and for citizens to visit the district centre for health care, education, and cultural events.[69]

Like much of the Soviet countryside, the communists in Zuizdinskii district were often overwhelmed by the scope of the tasks that faced them.[70] An article from the Zuizdinskii district newspaper *Zuizdinskii kolkhoznik* criticized the *raikom* Party cell for not regularly holding meetings (going two months without one in the spring of 1936) and for mixing Party and *raikom* business.[71] *Obkom* Agricultural Sector inspector Korepanov, who visited in September 1937, likewise noted the disorganization in the Party. He claimed that at the beginning of 1937 there was absolutely no information in the *raikom* on who the members of *raikom* were and what reports they made at collective farm meetings. He complained that political agitation on collective farms was carried out on an *ad hoc* basis and no one checked the work of the agitators.[72]

Local Party officials, however, frequently complained they were not receiving any support from the regional organizations. At the 23 April 1937 Party meeting Lotov, the deputy head of the district land organization, expressed great frustration with shortages of iron and other materials which were illegally sold by warehouse managers for vodka, butter, and the like. He claimed that he wrote to Stoliar, the *obkom* first secretary, three times about this issue and got no answer. He also complained that the regional authorities didn't listen to the district workers. Poroshin, the deputy secretary of the RK seconded this, stating that the *oblast'* pays no attention to them. Kharin, a collective farm chairman, also grumbled about the fact that the regional authorities ruled via paper, but he claimed the new Kirov regional administration was better than the old Gor'kii administration. RaiZO head Shishkin complained that the regional land management organization (OblZU) had sent him telegrams telling him to plow the fields with ten centimetres of snow on the ground and the ground frozen to a depth of sixteen centimetres.[73] The small number of reliable people with which to staff various administrative bodies as well as disorganization at the local level and a lack of support from the region seriously limited the control Party and state organs could exercise over the far-flung settlements of Ziuzdinskii district.

The lack of control the Ziuzdinskii district Party and state organizations could exercise over the countryside was evident in the way collectivization was implemented. In Ziuzdinskii district collectivization did not progress smoothly in part because of banditry and residual anti-Soviet enclaves left over from the Civil War. The scattered *khutor* settlements also impeded collectivization. In the spring of 1935 Shishkin reported that the *khutor* system was slowing the implementation of correct crop rotation on the collective farms that still had private land holdings in breaking up their fields.[74] Local officials claimed that the presence of *khutory* greatly slowed down productive work on the collective farms and in several cases became a breeding ground for bandits. They continued to ask the regional authorities for help to resettle some of the population.[75] In the Kirov region overall, collectivization rose 90.3 per cent by October 1935,[76] but the overall rate of collectivization in Zuizdinskii district remained low, 79.8 per cent, due to the number of *khutory* and the persistence of individual smallholding.[77] As late as 1939 there were still 334 *khutory* (one to two household settlements) in the district waiting to be resettled.[78]

Even when *khutory* were liquidated, individual smallholders co-existed amicably alongside collective farms in Ziuzdniskii district. *Obkom* Agricultural Sector inspector Korepanov, who visited Ziuzdinskii district in September 1937 to investigate violations of the collective farm charters noted individual smallholders being allowed to plant on collective farmland was commonplace. For example, in Buznazhovskii rural soviet, individual smallholder M.F. Makarov cleared and sowed three hectares, of which one and a half hectares belonged to the Molotov collective farm.[79] Similarly, individual smallholder V.N. Kytmanov illegally plowed 0.07 hectares of the Nal'shchevskaia agricultural artel's land adjacent to his garden.[80]

Often the collective farm administration knew about such incidents and took no action. In Kolychevskii rural soviet, former kulak and individual smallholder Bulychyev sowed winter crops on 0.5 hectares of "The Seventh Congress of Soviets" collective farm's land in 1937. The collective farm's management knew he was using collective farmland, but did not take any action.[81] Likewise, individual smallholder Varvara Vasil'eva sowed 0.3 hectares of potatoes on the V. Kolych collective farm's land in the spring of 1937. When Korepanov visited Ziuzdinskii district, she was harvesting these potatoes. He claimed that collective farm administration and the chairman of the rural soviet knew about her illegal planting, but again did nothing.[82] Even worse from Korepanov's perspective was that some collective farms actually allocated land to individual smallholders. In the spring of 1937, the Novoselovskii collective farm administration allocated up to 0.5 hectares of land for individual smallholder Medvedev to sow with spring crops.[83] Korepanov also alleged that in Kytmanovskii rural soviet, the Stalin collective farm's administration and its chairman, the communist Porubov, gave several female individual smallholders permission to sow up to 0.12 hectares of collective farm land with flax in the spring of 1937.[84] This everyday accommodation of individual smallholders undermined the Soviet state's social control over the rural population.

Ziuzdinskii district officials faced a number of challenges: continuing violence from anti-Soviet elements, poor infrastructure, a lack of reliable cadres and a lack of support from regional authorities. They also faced a district whose geography frustrated the collectivization goals thrust upon them and allowed individual smallholding to persist. So, when the 1936 Constitution extended rights to politically suspect people, the district officials, who had tenuous control over their district at best, reacted negatively and implemented a campaign to crush individual smallholders through harsh tax assessments.

The Return of Class Enemies

The 1936 Stalin Constitution restored full citizenship rights to former kulaks, religious figures, and others who had been deprived of voting rights.[85] Article 9 of the Stalin Constitution also provided for the continued existence of individual farming in the USSR. Article 128 guaranteed the inviolability of the home, which tax collectors frequently violated, breaking in to inventory and then seizing and selling home goods for back taxes. Local officials were not pleased with the new rights given to individual smallholders in the draft constitution. They claimed that these rights were being used to undermine the already embattled and overstretched local communists. In at least one rural soviet in Ziuzdinskii district a former kulak became rural soviet chairman and created his own "family circle" of supporters around him. He promoted the development of the individual smallholding economy, stating "now we will develop individual small holding quickly and the harvest will be far greater than on the collective farms."[86] Others in Ziuzdniskii district likewise used the Stalin Constitution to support individual smallholders' interests. In particular, many individual smallholders used the constitution to justify their refusal to pay what they viewed as discriminatory taxes. For instance, some of the individual smallholders of Kharinskii rural soviet categorically refused to fulfil any state obligation, arguing that the constitution guaranteed the equal rights of all citizens so they didn't have to fulfil the discriminatory quotas.[87] Rural soviet chairman Buzmakov reported in February 1937 that kulaks were agitating among the individual smallholders. One, Luchinkov, cited Article 9 of the constitution to avoid meeting his state obligations and payments and said the collective farmers have similar rights.[88] Others used the constitution to justify shirking the hated labour obligations. The individual smallholder Nekrasov, from the village Grigor'evskaia in Dan'kovskii rural soviet, said, "I will not go to the forest now [to fulfil his timbering obligation], the new constitution has freed us and it will be law and you never come to us [speaking to a member of the rural soviet] don't give us orders, it is enough now and we will do what we want."[89]

More worrying for the district leadership was when individual smallholders' criticism shifted away from specific aspects of the Soviet system to challenging fundamental policies like collectivization. At the 13 May 1937 Party meeting, Party organizer Evlampii Cheranev reported that individual smallholders were conducting anti-Soviet agitation, spreading rumours that collective farms were entering their final year and were singing anti-Soviet *chastushki* (mocking or irreverent songs). Evlampii also alleged that smallholders were trying to destroy the authority of the collective farm chairman E.N. Cheranev on the First of May collective farm, Moskovskii rural soviet.[90] In Afanas'evskii rural soviet, one Rotkanov, identified as a formerly disenfranchised White bandit, allegedly gathered former kulaks, monks, and individual smallholders and conducted counter-revolutionary agitation among them, stating "that the red night has come in which the communists will be physically beaten, collective farmers and individual smallholders must save themselves."[91] Given the history of violence directed towards low-level state and Party officials in Ziuzdinskii district, it is likely such threats were taken seriously. And violence against state actors was reported. The deputy editor of the district newspaper, candidate Party member Vasilii Samsonov noted at a 13 May 1937 Party meeting that in the district wall newspapers were torn up or destroyed and sel'kory were beaten.[92] Such incidents posed threats to local administrators' efforts to keep order in the countryside. The communists in Zuizdinskii district responded with a campaign to seize individual smallholder property for tax arrears.

That action came back to haunt them. *Raikom* secretary Batyrev, RIK chairman Chadaev and several other Ziuzdniskii district officials were investigated for gross perversions of revolutionary legality and excesses in 1937. Their colleagues testified that Batyrev, Chadev, and head of the district financial organization Fedor Cheranev, had ordered the illegal seizures of smallholder property and the liquidation of smallholder households because they viewed them as class enemies. The chairman of the Afanas'evskii rural soviet testified that Batyrev told him that it was necessary "to finish off the individual smallholders."[93] Chadaev's replacement as head of the RIK, Poroshin, said Batyrev spoke up at meetings urging "not to yield [their] position to the class enemies."[94] The chairman of the Kytmenovskii rural soviet reported that Cheranev gave orders, saying, "when collecting arrears, pay attention to property, take everything down to the last log (*okladnogo brevna*), strike the individual smallholder so that his brain flies out [figuratively speaking: *chtoby mozgi vyleteli*], and in particular adopt harsher measures with kulak households, sell the house and chase them into the banya."[95]

In addition to trying to crush class enemies in Ziuzdinskii district, budgetary shortfalls and pressure to fulfil financial and state procurement plans also caused the district officials to squeeze the individual smallholders. Rural soviet chairman Iuferev testified to the pressure that Chadaev put on district workers to fulfil the financial plan. He noted that in the first days of January 1937, at a meeting of the rural soviet chairmen, discussing the financial plan, he said "if you do not make a breakthrough in fulfilling the financial plan, then some of you will be victims."[96] Rural soviet chairman Cheranev testified that Chadaev's RIK presidium "gave me a reprimand because I was being liberal with the individual small holders and conducted few inventories and seizures of property."⁹⁷ The chairman of the Ezzhinskii rural soviet, P.I. Siuzev, testified that Batyrev called him on the telephone in the winter of 1936 and was interested in how the rural soviet was fulfilling the flax procurement and financial plans. When Siuzev told him he was behind, Batyrev supposedly replied, "you are nannying the individual smallholder, let go of the reins." Siuzev claimed that later in the *raikom* building, before a meeting, Batyrev said to him, "you have fulfilled the flax procurement and financial plans very poorly, today I will lay into you (*ia na tebia naliaaguiu*)." He asserted that Batyrev spoke up at the meeting and cursed him out (*rugal mne krepko*) and "from his speech it was possible to understand that I was a lazy ass (*bezdel'nik*) I didn't do anything and did not fulfill plans. Then [Batyrev] brought up a number of rural soviet chairmen who were working well, who committed perversions and distorted revolutionary legality [by seizing and selling property] as examples."⁹⁸ Siuzev additionally testified that Chadaev gave him directions to strengthen repression in connection with the individual smallholders, up to seizing the last hut from them for arrears. He claimed Chadaev told him that Bobkov had said, "squeeze the tax press (*zhim nalogovym pressom*) on the individual smallholders and kulaks because you will get nothing else from them."⁹⁹ It is quite likely that Bobkov was Aleksandr Bobkov, chairman of the Regional Executive Committee in 1937, implying that Chadaev's actions were in accordance with at least unofficial policy targeting individual smallholders.¹⁰⁰

This pressure produced results. The deputy regional procurator, Libert', noted that in November and December of 1936 Batyrev had illegally sanctioned a fivefold increase in mass fines of individual smallholding households. As a result, from 10 November to 10 December, eighteen individual smallholding households were fined a total of 5,885 rubles, with the median fine being 312 rubles a household.¹⁰¹ He claimed that during the fulfilment of the financial plan, sixty-six houses, seventy cages, sixty-one stables, eighty-eight other structures, were seized and sold.¹⁰²

On 10 and 11 May 1937, the authorized representative of the Kirov *oblast'* procurator, Durynichev, personally verified the tax assessments in Kuvakushskii and V. Kolychevskii rural soviets in Ziuzdinskii district. He uncovered mass arbitrary administrative inventorying and seizure of individual smallholder property, including home goods. He described it as a method of dekulakization and wanted a special commission set up to investigate and return illegally seized property. On 13 May 1937, the RIK agreed with Durynichev's recommendations, though it is unclear if the property was returned.¹⁰³

Individual smallholders were often treated harshly by local- and district-level officials who tended to view them much in the same way they had viewed kulaks. District officials and local officials saw them as a group to be exploited to fulfil plans to be drained and crushed. It appears that at least tacitly some in the regional organization also agreed. These actions directly countermanded Moscow's views by violating the individual smallholders' constitutional rights and various Narkomzem orders. As a result of their actions against the individual smallholders, which violated their newfound constitutional rights, Batyrev and Chadaev faced criminal charges.

Conclusion

The charges Batyrev and Chadaev faced in 1938 were very serious. The regional procurator Postnikov alleged that in 1935, 1936, and 1937 they had allowed and abetted gross perversions of revolutionary legality, mass excesses, and illegal seizures of property and the liquidation of households.[104] RaiZO head Prokopii Shishkin was added at the end of the indictment due to his role in the land-allotment planning.

In a separate indictment, Deputy Regional procurator, Libert, wrote the *obkom* asking permission to charge Batyrev under Article 58 points 7 and 11 of the criminal code of the RSFSR. He asserted that Batyrev had connections with the enemies of the people, headed up counter-revolutionary Right–Trotskyist wrecking activity designed to disrupt Party and state land management, in particular during the distribution of the state acts on eternal use of land. Batyrev was accused of discrediting the process and creating dissatisfaction and resentment among the labourers of the district by improperly distributing land. He was also accused of wrecking while fulfilling state quotas for flax and disrupting the economic might of the collective farms, as well as malfeasance in the sphere of financial and tax policies and the cynical distortion of revolutionary legality, in the corruption of the Party and soviet *aktiv*, and the weakening of the financial state of the district.[105] Despite filing indictments, the procurator's charges did not stick. It was likely a result of a Central Committee resolution condemning excesses in denouncing communists from the January 1938 Plenum. Charges against all three men were dropped and they returned to leadership roles.[106]

Ironically for people like Batyrev, Shiskin, and Chadaev, in April 1938, the Central Committee and the Council of People's Commissars adopted a resolution in which local authorities pledged to put an end to the "anti-state and anti-collective farm practice of permissiveness towards individual smallholders and strictly monitor the exact fulfillment of all state tax obligations by individual smallholding households, grain rates, meat supplies, etc."[107] In August 1938, the Supreme Soviet of the USSR introduced a special tax on horses belonging to individual smallholders, "in view of the fact that, according to the testimony of collective farmers, horses in individual peasant farms are usually used not for agricultural work in their own households, but for the purpose of speculative profit."[108] These policies, combined with Sovnarkom and TsK's 19 April 1938 ban on expelling members from collective farms represented the final push to integrate individual smallholders into collective farms. However, the implementation of such policies of social control left much to be desired. Collective farms continued to expel members in spite of the ban and individual smallholders continued to either live side by side with collective farmers, or collective farmers engaged in individual farming practices by sowing personal crops on collective farm land (often with permission from the administration), keeping garden plots that exceeded the prescribed norms and focusing much of their attention on growing crops for market.[109] Many even kept their horses in their yard, under the pretense that there were no collective stables or purchased horses (illegally) for their own use.[110]

As we can see, the central state, like the district leaders, had difficulties enforcing its social control over the peasantry. Even in the face of outright bans on behaviours (like expelling collective farmers) traditional peasant practices continued. But the way the central state viewed and interacted with individual smallholding peasants differed greatly from the way district officials viewed and interacted with them and tried to exert control. The central authorities in Moscow viewed individual smallholders as citizens, to be taxed and integrated into larger Soviet social structures. Local (and regional) authorities conversely viewed them as class alien elements, fundamentally dangerous and incapable of being integrated into Soviet life. This perception was likely a result of firsthand experiences with violence from individual smallholders, their resistance to Soviet rule and the difficulties district and regional officials experienced in trying to govern large, underdeveloped territories. As a result, in direct defiance of Moscow's integrationist policies, they pursued the destruction of individual smallholders through punitive taxes. This approach brought the leadership of Ziuzdinskii district into direct conflict with Moscow, which resulted in their removal from power and charges filed against them.[111] However, ultimately Moscow needed all the cadres it could find to administer the country and so charges were dropped and Ziuzdinskii district's former leaders returned to positions of authority. So at all levels of governance social control was often elusive and only possible through the use of repressive violence, which was not a sustainable long-term solution.

NOTES

1 Giovanni Levi, "On Microhistory," in *New Perspectives on Historical Writing*, 2nd ed., ed. Peter Burke (University Park: Pennsylvania State University Press, 2001), 101.
2 Now called Afanas'evskii district.
3 As of spring 1932, there were 808 khutory, 251 two-family settlements, 178 three-family settlements, 110 four-family settlements, and 92 five-family settlements in Zuizdinskii district, of which 1,115 households were to be resettled in collectivized villages. Resettlement was an expensive and time-consuming process, which meant of the 1,115 households earmarked for resettlement only 705 were resettled by 1934, with 410 waiting to be resettled. In Afansovskii rural soviet, where the district seat of Afanasovo was located only 38 per cent of khutory had been resettled and only 20 per cent in Chashcherskii rural soviet. Gosudarstvynni arkhiv sotsial'no-politicheskoi istorii Kirovskoi oblasti (GASPI KO) 1255/1/3/3, GASPI KO 632/1/71/41. As of 1939 there were still 334 khutory (1–2-household settlements) in the district waiting to be resettled, GASPI KO 632/2/2/92.
4 Levi, "On Microhistory," 101.
5 Yanni Kotsonis, *States of Obligation: Taxes and Citizenship in the Russian Empire and Early Soviet Republic* (Toronto: University of Toronto Press, 2014), 26.
6 Aurelio Miracolo, Marisa Sophiea, Mackenzie Mills, and Panos Kanavos, "Sin Taxes and Their Effect on Consumption, Revenue Generation and Health Improvement: A Systematic Literature Review in Latin America," *Health Policy and Planning* 36, no. 5 (June 2021): 790–810.
7 Kotsonis, *States of Obligation*, 26.
8 Sheila Fitzpatrick, *Stalin's Peasants: Resistance and Survival in the Russian Village after Collectivization* (New York: Oxford University Press, 1994), 106, 153.
9 GASPI KO 1290/1/296/66.
10 G.G. Zagvozdkin, "Triumf i tragediia 30-kh godov," in *Entsiklopediia zemli Viatskoi, Vol. 4. Istoriia* (Kirov: Gosudarstvennoe izdatel'sko-poligraficheskoe predpriiatie "Viatka," 1995), 380.
11 Between 1934 and 1935 the number of individual smallholders in Orichevskii district decreased precipitously from 2,170 households in 1934 to 926 in 1935, and of those 926 households, 300 were landless. As of 1 January 1936, 98.2 per cent of all households in Omutninskii district,

where there were large-scale metallurgical enterprises, were collectivized, GASPI KO 1255/2/345/98. The Kirov district, directly adjacent to the regional capital, was 96.3 per cent collectivized (471 individual smallholding households compared to 12,515 collective farm households) as of 1 January 1937. It reached 97.2 per cent collectivized (356 individual smallholding households compared to 12,407 collective farm households) as of 1 January 1938, and 98.7 per cent collectivized (162 individual smallholding households compared to 13,008 collectivized households) as of 1 October 1938, GASPI KO 1290/2/350/46.
12 Other districts also had several hundred individual smallholders in 1938. Kichminskii district was home to 387 individual smallholding households, GASPI KO 1290/359/176, and Salobeliakskii district had 711 remaining individual smallholders, GASPI KO 1290/2/361/33.
13 Fitzpatrick, *Stalin's Peasants*, 154–5.
14 In some villages, the line between collective farms and smallholders was not always stark. In Kotel'nicheskii district in 1938, regional investigators found individual smallholders happily integrated into collective farms, even holding leadership positions on the farms, much to their dismay. On the "Armored Car" (Bronevik) collective farm in Sibirskii rural soviet, the chairman, bookkeeper, and head groom were all individual smallholders. They earned up to fifty work days a month (the chairman, Shabalin, received 55, 37, and 35 work days in three months, respectively). The local officials pressured the collective farm "to rectify" the situation. As a result, the chairman and the head groom joined the collective farm and the bookkeeper was let go. Similarly, on the Krasnyi Putilovets collective farm, individual smallholder S. Baev was elected as a brigadier, which allegedly resulted in a disruption of sowing, GASPI KO 1290/2/348/22. Several individual smallholders also worked on the Gruzovik artel', GASPI KO 1290/2/348/23. In Sanchurshkii district, an individual smallholder was employed on Zhdanovskii collective farm from September 1936 till February 1937 as a stable hand, with a salary of two poods of grain a month from the invalid and elderly's help fund, GASPI KO 1290/1/296/125. Sometimes the local officials were even complicit in sending individual smallholders to work on collective farms. For example, the Kotel'nicheskii RaiZO sent the individual farmer Afanasii Mikhailovich Kozlov from the village (poselok) of Makarenki to be the chairman of the "Far East" collective farm. Kozlov was a formerly disenfranchised, fixed quota, dekulakized person, GASPI KO 1290/2/348/21.
15 GASPI KO 931/1/96/42.
16 V.A. Il'inykh, *Nalogovo-podatnoe oblozhenie sibirskoi derevni. Konets 1920-kh – nachalo 1950 gg.* (Novosibirsk: OIIFF RAN, 2004), 38.
17 Ibid., 37.

18 There were, however, restrictions on how much of the market income could be taxed. In 1931, the amount of market earnings included in individual smallholders' annual taxable base was not supposed to exceed taxable income from other types of activities by more than 75 per cent. In the regulations on the agricultural tax for 1932, this limit was increased to 100 per cent. Ibid.
19 Ibid.
20 Progressive policies that took into consideration the applicant's class status, economic abilities, and disability status were also applied in other spheres of soviet socio-economic policy, such as the allotment of alimony. For more information, see Aaron Retish's contribution to this volume.
21 Il'inykh, *Nalogovo-podatnoe*, 36. In addition, individual smallholders could no longer claim a preliminary deduction of twenty rubles of income per person or deductions for large families but could get a reduced tax rate if there were more than two disabled members in the household. Ibid., 37.
22 Ibid., 38.
23 Households that were taxed at progressive rates paid 100–75 per cent of the agricultural tax in one-time taxes. Ibid.
24 Ibid.
25 Ibid.
26 Ibid., 39.
27 Ibid., 39–40.
28 Ibid., 40, 38.
29 Ibid., 39.
30 Ibid., 40–1.
31 Ibid., 41.
32 Ziuzdinskii district was part of Gor'kii Krai until December 1934 when the Kirov region was formed. In December 1936 the Kirov region was transformed from a *krai* to an *oblast'*.
33 Fitzpatrick, *Stalin's Peasants*, 155.
34 GASPI KO 1255/1/3/4.
35 GASPI KO 1255/1/3/4.
36 GASPI KO 1255/1/3/4.
37 Fitzpatrick, *Stalin's Peasants*, 179.
38 GASPI KO 1255/1/3/4.
39 GASPI KO 1290/2/348/22.
40 Fitzpatrick, *Stalin's Peasants*, 113, 125.
41 In comparison the fall sowing plan per collective farm household was 2.2 hectares, GASPI KO 1225/1/642/13.
42 GASPI KO 6777/3/50/230. Fitzpatrick has noted that individual smallholders became notorious for refusing to sow, leaving their allotments uncultivated and supporting themselves by carting or black

market trade, *Stalin's Peasants*, 154. While this did occur on occasion in the Kirov region, as noted above, it seems more common for individual smallholders to request land to try and fulfil the plan rather than refusing to sow. This might have been because removing themselves out of the agricultural economy did not in fact stop overzealous local officials from expropriating smallholders for back taxes. A report from regional procurator Postnikov noted that from June to August 1936, only thirty-eight cases were brought against individual smallholders for refusal to sow seeds, harvest crops, and fulfil grain procurements, GASPI KO 1225/1/642/55.
43 GASPI KO 1225/1/642/13. In addition, such high sowing and procurement quotas deprived individual smallholders of seed or fodder reserves. This also made collective farms less willing to take individual smallholders as members, because they could not bring any assets to the collective farm. The collective farmers of the Pliusninskaia artel' in Darovskoi district wrote to the political department at the machine tractor station in 1934 and asked if there would be any sort of assistance to collective farms who admitted individual smallholders who did not have seeds or forage and who did not fulfil part of their grain deliveries to the state (for which the farm would then be liable), GASPI KO 2083/1/19/224.
44 Il'inykh, *Nalogovo-podatnoe*, 42.
45 Ibid.
46 Ibid., 41.
47 Ibid., 42.
48 Ibid., 43.
49 Twenty per cent of the tax amount had to be paid by 1 September, 20 per cent by 1 October, 35 per cent by 15 November, and 25 per cent by 15 December. Ibid.
50 Ibid.
51 GASPI KO 1290/1/296/113.
52 GASPI KO 1290/2/44/12.
53 GASPI KO 632/1/44/7.
54 In April 1932 about 10 per cent of able-bodied men in the district engaged in otkhod in the forest regions. Otmuntninskii district and the large forest products combined in Biserovskii district, where up to 300 people worked, were the primary destinations. Ziuzdinskii district was also home to numerous small furniture and carpentry artels, as well as bookmaking, bread baking, and sewing artels, GASPI KO 632/1/44/6.
55 GASPI KO 632/1/44/8. Religious in this context referred to being Orthodox Christians but not sectarian or schismatic Christians.
56 An estimated 10 per cent of the population had some type of infectious disease, such as typhus, smallpox, rubella, or typhoid fever; another 10 per

cent were plagued by TB or chronic bronchitis. Almost a third (30 per cent) suffered from some sort of digestive problems, such as catarrhal gastritis. GASPI KO 632/1/44/9.
57 Aaron B. Retish, *Russia's Peasants in Revolution and Civil War: Citizenship, Identity, and the Creation of the Soviet State, 1914–1922* (Cambridge: Cambridge University Press, 2008), 204–12.
58 While the term "bandit" here is indeed a Soviet term, I agree with its usage, as these were groups of men who would lay in wait in the forest and attack passersby, which is most certainly banditry. Some may have been dissatisfied or displaced by collectivization, but there were also certainly criminal elements in these groups as well.
59 See the entry "Rovsnik veka – Vasilii Iakovlevich Lozhkin (1904–1988)," *Viatskie zapiski* no. 23, http://www.herzenlib.ru/almanac/number/detail.php?NUMBER=number23&ELEMENT=gerzenka23_6_1 (accessed 23 March 2022).
60 GASPI KO 632/1/44/12–14.
61 GASPI KO 632/1/43/112.
62 GASPI KO 632/1/44/2–14.
63 GASPI KO 632/1/44/12–14.
64 GASPI KO 632/1/71/95.
65 GASPI KO 632/1/71/101.
66 GASPI KO 1290/I/72/34.
67 The rural Soviets (52 per cent) were non-Party as a result, GASPI KO 632/1/44/9–10.
68 It merged again with Ziuzdinskii raion in 1955, GAKO R–1373/5/13/56.
69 GAKO R-1373/5/13/46–7.
70 Roberta Manning also describes the over-extension of communists and their tendency to cluster in the safer and more prestigious district centres in "Government in the Soviet Countryside in the Stalinist Thirties: The Case of Belyi Raion in 1937," The Carl Beck Papers in Russian and East European Studies [S.l.], no. 301 (January 1984); Sean Guillory, "Profiles in Exhaustion and Pomposity: the Everyday Life of Komsomol Cadres in the 1920s," The Carl Beck Papers in Russian and East European Studies [S.l.], no. 2303 (March 2014).
71 GASPI KO 641/1/1/14.
72 GASPI KO 1290/1/291/35.
73 Given how far north they are and the fact that the city of Kirov, which is farther south, can see snow as late as June, it is probably true, GASPI KO 632/1/138/ 26, 37, 30.
74 GAKO R-1373/5/13/57.
75 A report from the period of 1 January–1 March 1937 noted that until recently there were 228 khutory, and of them 137 were collective farm households and 91 were individual smallholders, GASPI KO 1290/1/72/29.

76 GASPI KO 1225/1/642/6.
77 GASPI KO 1255/1/3/4.
78 GASPI KO 632/2/2/92.
79 GASPI KO 1290/1/291/34.
80 GASPI KO 1290/1/291/31.
81 GASPI KO 1290/1/291/33.
82 GASPI KO 1290/1/291/33.
83 GASPI KO 1290/1/291/33.
84 GASPI KO 1290/1/291/32.
85 The Stalin Constitution and 1936 laws on abortion and the Family Code signalled a larger shift toward more conservative social policies. See Retish's contribution to this volume.
86 GASPI KO 1290/1,/72 l. 33; Samantha Lomb, *Stalin's Constitution: Soviet Participatory Politics and the Discussion of the 1936 Draft Constitution* (London: Routledge, 2018), 132.
87 Lomb, *Stalin's Constitution*, 130; GASPI KO 1290/1/56/120–1.
88 GASPI KO 632/1/138/2.
89 GASPI KO 632/1/141/7.
90 It is not clear how exactly they were undermining his authority, GASPI KO 641/1/2/26.
91 GASPI KO 1290/1/72 l. 33.
92 GASPI KO 641/1/2/26.
93 GASPI KO 641/1/2/36.
94 GASPI KO 641/1/2/36.
95 GASPI KO 1290/2/44/36.
96 GASPI KO 1290/2/44/13.
97 GASPI KO 1290/2/44/13.
98 GASPI KO 1290/2/44/35.
99 GASPI KO 1290/2/44/13.
100 GASPI KO 1290/2/44/35–6.
101 GASPI KO 1290/2/44/33–4.
102 GASPI KO 641/1/2/35.
103 GAKO R-1373/5/17/88, 89–92.
104 GASPI KO 1290/2/44/12.
105 GASPI KO 1290/2/44/32, 38.
106 Batyrev moved to the city of Gor'kii in Nizhnii Novgorod region and worked as the deputy director and head of the cadres department for the Gor'kii medical institute from 1938 to 1941. He served in the war and was awarded a medal "For Valorous Work in the Great Patriotic War." He was part of the UNKVD in 1943–4 and died at an unknown time after the war; his last job was head of the Sport and Gormebsoiuz artels in 1951. E.N. Chudinovskikh, ed., *Politicheskie lidery Viatskogo Kraiia- Biograficheskii*

spravochnik (Kirov: GASPI KO, 2009), 124–5. Chadaev became the head of the cadres department of the Omutninsk metallurgical factory from 1938 to 1940, and from 1940 he was deputy head of the Omutninskii district health department. Later he worked as deputy chairman of the Board of Factory Livestock Breeding. He died in 1958. Ibid., 492. Shishkin worked as a master at the Kirov Chrome factory from 1938. Ibid., 516.

107 Il'inykh, *Nalogovo-podatnoe*, 44.
108 Ibid.
109 Lomb, "Moscow Is Far Away: Peasant Communal Traditions in the Expulsion of Collective Farm Members in the Vyatka–Kirov Region 1932–1939," *Europe-Asia Studies* (July 2021).
110 GASPI KO 1290/1/292/94, repeated in GASPI KO 1290/1/296/62.
111 The pursuit of "incorrect" tax policies would also be charges levelled against several other *raikom* first secretaries, including Aleksandr Skorobogatov of Salobeliakskii district who was accused, among other things, of knowingly disrupting the tax policies of Soviet power and the illegal seizure of property for debts, etc. GASPI KO 6799/ 1/ SU-499, t.1/26. Under interrogation, Skorobogatov confessed to receiving orders "to distort the tax policy in order to arouse discontent with the tax pressure on the peasants of the district," GASPI KO 6799/ 1 /SU-499, t.1/32. Skorobogatov's co-defendant, Feodor Grishin, the first secretary of the Iaranskii RK, was also accused of "violating the laws on property seizures for back taxes taking property from middle and poor peasant individual smallholders down to work clothes, bed clothes and other household goods." The indictment against him also alleged he had ignored those engaging in buying and selling (i.e, speculation), and that in 1936–7 the leaders of the Iarnask district organizations had specifically targeted Marii rural soviets for reassessing (adjusting upwards) agricultural taxes. In 1937, 26,155 rubles had to be returned for illegal taxes in 1936–7, GASPI KO 6799/1/SU-499, t.5/38. Like Batyrev, the charges against both Skorobogatov and Grishin were eventually dismissed and both men freed to return to Soviet service.

3 Social Control in the Workplace: Labour Discipline and Workers' Rights under Stalin

MARIA STARUN

Introduction

During the Stalinist industrialization drive that began in 1928, the Soviet Union proclaimed itself to be a proletarian state, despite ever-growing demands on workers and their subordination to one-man management (*edinonachalie*).[1] The Soviet state promoted the idea of the common good and conceived of industrialization as both industrial and civil progress in which every worker thrives despite huge sacrifices and stiffening discipline. Tightening discipline was not new to the Soviet worker, however, as more and more institutions had appeared throughout the 1920s to regulate it. Workers were equipped with a vast array of such institutions in the workplace – comrades' courts, rates and conflicts commissions (*rastsenochno-konfliktnye komissii* or RKKs), trade union committee plenaries, and others. During the 1920s, the Komsomol, the Party, management, and trade unions had all established themselves in factories and created institutions both for them to impose discipline, and for workers to negotiate their legal rights. Taken together, these institutions formed a complex space of social control within factories and enterprises that was distinct from the civil court system.

During the first Five-Year Plan, the main function of the space was disciplinary control of workers to fulfil planned objectives. Soviet experts understood discipline and law as a historical category. Hence, every new social order necessitated a new disciplinary order.[2] The Five-Year Plan's new disciplinary order, which was pragmatic and entirely economic in outlook, relegated workers' rights behind the effective and efficient organization of production. However, as I argue here, the profusion of both disciplinary and low-level legal institutions in the workplace at that time demonstrates the extensive opportunities for the authorities to establish control and for ordinary workers to protect their interests. Moreover, all these structures can be said to be concerned with both discipline and rights.[3] Workers could resolve disputes and contest disciplinary sanctions via formal complaints. That is, by asserting a right (*pravo*).[4] Such procedures enabled Soviet citizens, first, to exercise collective participation in and control over discipline and, second, to express agency in the struggle for their rights (*prava*).

I discuss the various workplace institutions within the industrial system of discipline and rights. I focus on comrades' courts and rates and conflicts commissions. Comrades' courts were mass-membership collective bodies, while rates and conflicts commissions settled individual disputes. I also consider proceedings in less institutionalized forums, like workers' and trade union assemblies and works committee meetings. Their interactions illustrate both the dispersion and the integration of all the parts of the system.

Labour discipline and workers' rights in the Soviet Union have not received sufficient attention from historians, although social historians have been more interested in this subject than legal scholars.[5] The legal historian Harold J. Berman emphasized that Soviet experts expected the plan to replace statutory law and individual rights would be swallowed by collectivism.[6] More recently, the legal scholar Scott Newton has argued that law undergirded the massive machinery of the Soviet state economy. In his view, law (*pravo*) supplied the language of command and control by which the Soviet authorities launched and carried through the most brutal program of directed industrialization in economic history.[7] But his focus is the functioning of the state, not its local exponents in the workplace.

The industrial workplace, despite the state's attempts to control it, stands out by its degree of autonomy with its own legal order. This cuts across the idea of socialist legality as monolithic and universal. It suggests there was some juridical decentralization and flexibility even while the principle of one-man management held sway.[8] The Stalinist workplace appealed to collectivist forms of cooperation and was located in the particular material environment of the factory shops, machines, and tools in which the functioning of the factory's machines mattered more than the rights of its workers.[9]

The building of communism was supposed to bring the withering away of the state and along with it the judicial hegemony of the legal system. Therefore, instructions at the beginning of the first Five-Year Plan were sometimes vague and undefined and allowed for a broad interpretation of their meaning. Overall, the Soviet judicial system was not adequately equipped to resolve complicated domestic and individual conflicts.[10] However, these were the very matters that the system of discipline and rights in the workplace was meant to address. In his chapter in this volume Aaron Retish discusses the imperfect Soviet alimony system. The state also delegated legal functions in the Soviet countryside to the lay-led mediation courts (*primiritel'nye kamery*), the rural analogue of comrades' courts.

Rules and instructions only tell part of the story of social control in enterprises under Stalinism. We need to study the practices and procedures of social control in the workplace (as well as negotiations over rights in the workplace), for they reveal the interplay of rules, norms, and customs.[11] As the anthropologist Mary Douglas has shown, social control is a collective product.[12] I describe institutions of social control from the point of view of both state interest and the workers who were equal participants in it. I examine the nature of social control to show how this juridically decentralized space operated, where managers were surrounded by local organizations of social control that either helped or opposed them.

The difficulty of studying the institutions of social control is that the cases dealt with at the workplace were often ephemeral and left almost no trace in the archives. However, Elektrozavod in Moscow has one of the most complete archives and contains several years of comrades' court records, statistical data and surveys on RKKs, and legal consultations. But there is nothing in the sources about, say, the number of reprimands handed down by informal proceedings on trade union assemblies. That lively and comradely form of control largely remains out of reach to researchers. The records we do have show some of the mechanisms by which social control was exercised. Comrades' courts and RKKs were institutionalized in the justice system, which both made them an important conduit for the state's legal policies at the local level and more visible in the archival sources than other disciplinary bodies.

This chapter investigates how and by what measures social control was implemented at enterprises during the first Five-Year Plan. I describe a complex legal system which did not always proceed as the law or the rules intended. By showing how different actors (workers, managers, the Party, and state institutions) endeavoured to secure their interests in the framework of a hierarchy of workplace rights and discipline authorities, I demonstrate how this particular space of socialist discipline and legality functioned.

Comrades' Courts

Comrades' courts were established by an All-Russian Central Executive Committee (VTsIK) resolution of 27 August 1928. They were set up under the supervision of the People's Commissariat of Justice in consultation with the All-Union Central Council of Trade Unions (VTsSPS) as a pilot project at factories in the major industrial centres of Moscow, Leningrad, and Ivanovo. The expression "pilot project" is misleading. Comrades' courts were nothing new for Soviet power. They had originated in the proletarian milieu and were in existence at the time of the Revolution and the Civil War.[13] They were a means of dealing with disciplinary and ethical offences by work colleagues. At first, judges were democratically elected from among the workers. After November 1919, when comrades' courts were incorporated as quasi-judicial bodies in the state justice system, it became mandatory for management to be represented too. At the beginning of the New Economic Policy, comrades' courts were abolished as superfluous in the era of vertical hierarchy of one-man management.[14]

During NEP, Soviet leaders paid special attention to formalizing and codifying the law. The state also took over discipline from workers and authorized their superiors to impose it. Nevertheless, in the 1920s there was not much discussion of bringing back comrades' courts. There was some suggestion that workers should suffer less than the full force of the criminal law for, say, pilfering from work. In 1928 the trade unions even opposed comrades' courts on the grounds that new powers to intervene in "quarrels" would "undermine the unions' authority. Their job was to defend members' interests, not sit in judgment on them."[15] Comrades' courts were brought back on the initiative of bureaucrats in the Ministry of Justice who were keen to unburden the people's courts of minor matters, which made up 30 per cent of all criminal cases.[16] The idea of reform emerged as early as 1927 and so the establishment of comrades' courts and conciliation chambers belongs not to the years of industrialization but to the NEP era when the state aimed to make official courts more efficient and to bring justice closer to the people.[17] Robert Sharlet describes this period as the era of the "revolution of law," which preceded the cultural revolution.[18] The reform was not intended to promote discipline, though discipline played a growing role in the work of the courts as the first Five-Year Plan gradually unfolded.

Indeed, comrades' courts were not called disciplinary bodies. They were social organs (*obshchestvennye organy*) where elected lay judges handled conflicts. The courts' purpose was "to settle private charge cases such as offensive language or behaviour arising chiefly from outdated forms of culture and living as well as other minor cases."[19] People's courts were, as the reformers saw it, clogged with such cases. Therefore, justice officials set about decriminalizing certain offences, like minor theft, and transferring some civil cases, notably private charges, to lay courts, including the rural conciliation chambers set up in parallel with the industrial courts.[20] The reformers' thinking was that such cases ought not to claim all society's attention or require the mobilization of the entire panoply of Soviet justice, which, like much else in those years, needed to find drastic savings.[21] Moreover the program of the Party provided that almost every Soviet citizen should have a part in running the country; comrades' courts were an instance of that. Justice – and the state as such in this Communist vision – would wither away as the law gradually turned away from repressive means of affecting behaviour towards preventative moral suasion and education.[22]

Supporters of reform emphasized comrades' courts' accessibility. Workers saved time by not going to the people's courts. With comrades' courts they could get cases handled almost without leaving their workstations. Critics of reform in 1929 regretted the courts' limited area of responsibility. Because comrades' courts were confined to the workplace, many everyday issues that did not have a direct connection to the workplace, like marital infidelity, swearing, or general uncouthness, did not receive any attention from the community. Other critics argued that the comrades' courts were superfluous. G.K. Moskalenko, an expert on labour law, said in 1929 that name-calling among workers was rare because in conditions of labour discipline there was no room for domestic conflict, and therefore there would not be very many such cases in the comrades' courts. Others declared that proletarians had never made up the majority of parties in private charges anyway, and therefore such courts were entirely unnecessary for them.

The press applauded comrades' courts' useful duality. They were a judicial body with a specific area of responsibility and imposed binding sanctions on specific matters. At the same time, they were "not really courts" so much as a "means for the labour collective to have an educative influence on certain of its members in the event of socially harmful acts."[23] Therefore, it was argued, they should not get tied up in "procedural formalism." Comrades' courts were not meant to bother with paperwork beyond brief minutes. In fact, the archives are all but devoid of records on the comrades' courts in this period. This laxity in record-keeping means that the early days of the comrades' courts is best traced through Soviet press reports.

The press, eager to give the impression that life was ahead of the law, portrayed comrades' courts as the fruit of the creativity of the masses who demanded such an institution of social control.[24] Indeed, at some enterprises comrades' courts were set up on the initiative of the Party collective even before their legal introduction.[25] Even after the promulgation of the resolution, comrades' courts somehow emerged as if by "spontaneous insistence of the workers." The journal *Sud idet*, reporting on the establishment of the first comrades' court in Leningad at the Proletarskii works, insisted that the idea came entirely from the workers. "The thought was born, unprompted and spontaneous, of judgments being given by their own comrades' court." The piece describes the workers mobilizing in response to a shop chief being "assaulted with a brick." It does not really explain how the assault came to be deemed worthy of public condemnation, only that the workers were angry and outraged: "The workers cannot tolerate a situation where, when all forces are focused on our socialist construction, certain groups of individuals like Masal'skii damage it." The damage to socialist construction consisted in subversion of the principle of one-man management, specifically "confidence in administrative technical personnel."[26] As a result, the intention of justice officials to transfer low-level cases to comrades' courts collided with a demand for disciplinary control from below, with comrades' courts popping up locally entirely in connection with disciplinary problems.

It was hoped that clearing up personal cases would also help avoid pressure on management, who felt such matters were no concern of theirs. Here was also an important corporate aim: "By eradicating the degradation of the personality of workers by treating offenders with comradely action, comrades' courts create the healthy business-like atmosphere at enterprises and in establishments that is necessary for the amicable collaborative work of the labour collective."[27]

In their first year, the courts were indeed brought closer to the workers and their personal interests. In a case of hooliganism and offensive language, the court chairman asked the accused: "How can you demand respect for yourself if you don't respect another?"[28] The *Sud idet* piece referred to comrades' courts as the "highest form of evaluation of the person and his behaviour," covering defendants' working, cultural-lifestyle, and social identities.[29] People took insults to their name, and public censures printed in the local press, seriously. Workers were outraged when they read revelations about themselves in wall newspapers, and they quickly tore the papers down.[30]

The format proved particularly helpful to female workers suffering from harassment at work or violence at home. Family cases were not formally the responsibility of comrades' courts until a special resolution of December 1929.[31] But, as the courts were not bound by codified law, sometimes they took them up anyway. Thus, women's interests initiated social control for the benefit of female employees rather than the employer. Women brought complaints about beatings or harassment and obtained the public condemnation of the offenders.[32]

At the same time, female honour was a double-edged sword that could also be used against women. One female worker in 1929, for example, overhearing another describe colleagues as prostitutes was disgusted that women had to put up with such insults at work. Likewise, a frequent claim before the court was the spread of an offensive rumour that a woman had an abortion. Collectivist visions of sexual morality in the 1930s corresponded with the state's pronatalism when such rumours were considered as insults even before the official criminalization of abortion. After the criminalization of abortion in 1936, as Amanda McNair shows in her chapter, women faced medical and judicial intrusion, policing, and prosecution of their reproduction as well as popular collective condemnation. Female honour as a collective value and state interest was always grist to the comrades' courts' mill.

Private charges also touched on what at first glance appear to be more acutely political matters. Terms like "kulak" and "enemy" (*vrag*) became common insults to one's honour. A worker at the Volodarskii printworks, for example, filed a complaint against another for calling him a kulak and an idler (*lodyr*). Witnesses described the complainant as both the son of a poor family and a hard worker. The plaintiff, meanwhile, had been heard threatening revenge on Soviet power for his two brothers who had been shot. None of the evidence led to any serious investigation or sanction. The defendant was found guilty of engaging in a petty squabble by spreading false rumours and making false accusations, for which he was punished by public censure via the local newspaper.[33] The rhetoric of accusation that was characteristic of public discourse had permeated into the workplace but not yet taken a fatal turn.[34]

Accusations of class delinquency were perceived by workers themselves as offensive to their dignity. Comrades' courts did not necessarily go looking for political guilt. Nor did the reports of commentators and worker correspondents see anything suspicious in that. Even where a court found that a worker was an alien to the proletariat, the finding did not lead to further political scrutiny. At the first session of the comrades' court at the Metallicheskii works, one of the accused was described like this: "Baryshev is different. Both his physical appearance of a pointy beard and sullen frown and his persistent references to 'enemy scheming' provoke hostility towards him."[35] Note that Baryshev's suspicions and questions from first glance should have demonstrated his loyalty to the regime but instead it provoked questions about him. In the course of proceedings, it emerged that Baryshev was in fact an "alien to the factory" and had previously been earning on the side. Here was a comrades' court performing the function of establishing the "class essence of an offence" to "straighten out the offender."[36] In this respect, comrades' courts differed from other workplace disciplinary bodies which were only concerned with determining the nature of any wrongdoing. But irrespective of the discussion in the court and the discovery of a certain class lability, the only sentence passed on any party to the dispute was public censure, though the court did also criticize Party and trade union organizations for not having attended to the re-education of the workers in their care.

The VTsSPS worries that workers might get carried away with frivolous litigation was not justified according to statistics compiled by the People's Commissariat of Justice. On average, a comrades' court heard only two to three cases during the spring of 1929. At Elektrozavod, for example, the comrades' court met around thirteen times between August 1929 and the end of the year. Most of the cases were about slander, i.e. they were private charges.[37] Only two concerned labour discipline. Nevertheless, comrades' courts in general took on cases beyond their jurisdiction, involving people who did not work in the same enterprise. Reports complained that they were too enthusiastic about fining people. Sentences of fines were passed in 45 cases out of 118 in Moscow. The courts were also criticized for favouring repression. They were said to be giving in to the "mood among certain of the workers who saw repression as the only weapon available."[38]

The jurisdiction of comrades' courts was expanded in 1929. Comrades' courts could now consider disputes between workers from different enterprises. They also could award up to twenty-five rubles' compensation for damage to property. The trade unions were still not happy with comrades' courts or their expanded role. On 22 March the newspaper *Trud* published a VTsSPS official directive prohibiting the setting up of any new comrades' courts.[39] The Urals regional trade union council and the Smolensk provincial trade union council also expressed objections.[40]

In 1930, after reviewing the results of the first year of industrialization, the Soviet state's focus on labour discipline gave comrades' courts a new purpose. From this point on, the VTsSPS became involved in the comrades' courts. It also published a statement castigating the "wreckers of socialist competition" among whom were counted not only "the bureaucrat and actual workplace wreckers," but also absentees, bums, drunkards, hooligans, grabbers, self-seekers (*rvachi*), and the like. The best way to combat such violators was acknowledged by the comrades' courts. They would inform and focus factory-floor opinion and become a pillar of the struggle for iron labour discipline.[41]

As the state began its campaign for labour discipline, comrades' courts were "rearmed." Rather than just relieve the people's courts of private charges, they were now to facilitate a shock assault to fulfil the Industrial and Financial Plan (Promfinplan). The reason was the government's disquiet at the slow growth of output in the early months of the first Five-Year Plan. A Council of People's Commissars (Sovnarkom) resolution stated: "One of the main causes impeding the growth of our industry and the economy as a whole is the slackening of labour discipline among certain workers in industrial and transportation enterprises."[42]

Everyone was called on to improve discipline – workers' organizations, judicial bodies, and managerial and technical staff. Labour discipline took on new importance. Factory medical rooms were told not to issue sick notes for minor injuries.[43] At this time labour discipline, in accordance with Lenin's old strictures, came to be given "wide social significance."[44]

Things changed abruptly following the Sixteenth Party Congress in summer 1930 and an appeal from the Central Committee. The press began writing that comrades' courts should be "reoriented to the struggle for the basic collective interests of the great socialist construction."[45] This quote characterizes the turn-around in relation to the individual and the protection of individual rights: "It is more dangerous and disgraceful to steal the product of workers' labour than to thieve someone's hat from a tool cupboard; a blow to the factory output and finance plan hurts more than beatings; the shame of a production breakdown is worse than any personal hurt or insult…. More important than the individual is the 'person' of the works or factory."[46]

The VTsSPS issued a new resolution on comrades' courts on 8 September 1930. The resolution had the effect of creating two types of workplace courts – comrades' courts under the auspices of the People's Commissariat of Justice and industrial (*proizvodstvennye*) comrades' courts under the auspices of the trade unions. Although the latter were supposed to deal only with disciplinary offences, they could take up cases on their own initiative. They could even dismiss a worker without consulting management, to whom they therefore became a considerable counterweight. This ability of courts to dismiss workers was against the Labour Code of 1922 and ensued further confusion with the courts' jurisdiction.[47] Consequently it was decided that there should be only one type of court –

industrial comrades' courts – to act against breaches of labour discipline and domestic or workplace offences undermining discipline.

Another new resolution on reform of comrades' courts was published in 1931, which reconfigured comrades' courts to prioritize labour discipline.[48] Whereas labour discipline had not even been mentioned in the 1929 resolution on comrades' courts, disciplinary offences were at the top of the list of types of cases to be handled by the new comrades' courts. The only true crimes were now crimes against the Five-Year Plan. Honour was still to be protected, but now it was primarily the honour of production and participation in socialist construction, not personal honour. Comrades' courts sat to consider and discuss not mere guilt but "guilt before socialist construction."[49] Still, private charges did not disappear from the comrades' courts. Statistics show that they accounted for nearly a majority of cases.[50] However, their social significance declined. The lengthy, ideologically relevant disciplinary cases were sent to the Central Union committees from the regions, while personal cases were usually resolved in a single session, so all attention at the central level was devoted to the demonstration of order and discipline. Moreover, management and other bodies became involved in the courts' activity. Under the new reform, comrades' courts could also not take up cases unless management approved.

At the same time, discipline became a shared endeavour for both workers and management in which all were held accountable for insufficient vigilance.[51] It was commonly argued in cases of spoilage, wastage, and defective products (*brak*), for example, that Soviet organization of labour was not capitalist but socialist. Therefore, defective products "could not be sold to anyone afterwards" except comrades in socialist construction.[52] Whatever was produced was the responsibility of all the workers. A product was even deemed to be an element of a worker's personality. The mistake of any comrade was seen as affecting everyone in the context of overall socialist ownership and the purported absence of alienation of labour.

Reports from trade union officials in 1932 contain frequent complaints that workers were reluctant to initiate cases in courts, and most cases were started by management or trade union organizations. Organizations still preferred to deal with matters internally anyway, but there were exceptions. At the Izhora plant, workers frequently brought cases against the management even though the rules did not technically allow them to. Management and factory-floor organizations asserted workers' claims diminished their authority and went against the principle of one-man management, but the Izhora courts replied that they treated all equally irrespective of position.[53] The 1931 VTsSPS resolution did not specify whether management was bound by the jurisdiction of comrades' courts, and this loophole was exploited by active courts like the one in Izhora. For them, comrades' court proceedings were not only a way to try individual offenders but also a tool to start broad investigations into faults in the organization of production. From these it often emerged that management, at some level or another, was in the wrong. A chair of Izhora court reported to the trade union that according to the rules, the head of the work brigade and his assistant were not answerable to the court but the industrial court had issued them a severe reprimand because it was their fault that the common endeavour was spoilt.

One example of how the Izhora courts handled this industrial hierarchy was the exposing of a workshop chairman who "was determined to find wrecking" when a worker's machine broke. The worker was a member of the Komsomol and the son of a proletarian, and there was no suggestion that the machine had been damaged deliberately. He was reinstated after a meeting of the comrades' court. Comrades' courts did not just follow political trends even while a campaign of self-criticism, which encouraged it, was underway. They instead stuck to their instructions, which did not encourage them to engage in such political rhetoric.

The comrades' court at the Izhora plant may have bent the rules, but it was run by the factory committee under the leadership of local Party officials, who blessed its actions. The court's success was the result of the trade union's efforts to get control of the courts while also securing wide powers for the court to initiate cases and creating a body of "enthusiast" judges.[54] Until this moment in 1932, the comrades' court at Izhora still experienced the usual problems shared by other comrades' courts of a lack of mass support, no means of enforcing decisions, overreliance on fines, and defendants failing to appear. The Izhora court, like other comrades' courts also issued sanctions beyond their powers, such as ordering compulsory work, imposing fines over ten rubles, and applying multiple sanctions at once.

The terms of reference of the Izhora comrades' courts said that "For the proper settlement of cases the court must investigate and study the overall production situation in the factory and examine facts that may not appear to have any direct bearing on the case at hand."[55] If there was a problem with waste or defective products (*brak*), the important thing was not to pin all of the blame on an individual, but to identify shortcomings in organization and production, issues in technology, labour problems, poor instructions, supply difficulties, and so on. Thus, comrades' courts simultaneously fought to fulfil the Industrial and Financial Plan, and blurred responsibility of individual workers accused of offences and mistakes and focused instead on the whole structure of a factory made up of workers, supervisors, and machines.[56]

Comrades' courts regularly issued rulings that placed blame on mistakes not on the worker, but on managers, and sometimes the whole plant. "The *brak* are the fault not only of the individual worker who made them but chiefly of the commanders in charge of the sector."[57] "The comrades' court found a breakdown of work in the sector and waste by production commanders." The effect was that the amount of faulty product was indeed reduced, at least in the official statistics. Whereas in May 1933 the overall percentage of breakages was 8.6 per cent, by October it was down to 2.9 percent, and in the third quarter of the year there were only two instances.[58] Courts pointed to deficiencies in equipment or factory organization, and thereby fairness, and cleared the professional reputation of the accused and maintained the viability of the team of workers. The idea of socialist construction as a shared endeavour converted individual condemnation into individual re-inclusion, allowing the collective to resolve whatever technical problem the particular case had exposed. Thus, in the comrades' court the collective reflected on itself, revealing the tension between needing to separate an errant member from the collective and wanting to keep a comrade in. The all-seeing eye of the collective was not turned on the individual alone: the collective put itself on trial. If anyone is late, all must feel the shame, because they allowed this to happen and failed to change their comrade. So, the comrades' court enabled the collective to continue functioning and engaging in a shared endeavour. The battle with material disorder became the basis of universal solidarity.

The same idea of a shared endeavour also served to mitigate some of the punishments provided by Stalin's harsh legislation accompanying a new campaign for discipline at work towards the end of the first Five-Year Plan. Following a TsIK and Sovnarkom joint resolution of 15 November 1932, management could dismiss a worker for a single day's absence.[59] Similar sanctions were available under the law of 7 August 1932 on theft from work. Indeed, between 1932 and 1933 the percentage of minor theft cases related to the total number of cases in comrades' courts rose from 11 per cent to 19 per cent.[60]

Participants at the First All-Union Meeting of Industrial Relations of Comrades' Courts even asked the People's Commissariat of Justice and the VTsSPS to allow comrades' courts to consider cases of thefts from enterprises of up to one hundred rubles. The proposers added, thoughtfully, that any theft committed by someone who was also found to be a class enemy should be referred to the judicial authorities. The request was not granted. If anything, the subsequent resolution of 27 February 1932 on comrades' courts reduced their area of responsibility. Now the only thefts they could deal with were first offences. In practice, the resolution did nothing to ensure that comrades' courts would actually stop handling theft cases.

Not all comrades' courts were lenient in their sentences, nor were court decisions dictated by the accused's comrades. Imposed sanctions were often a compromise, allowing the defendant to be retained as a member of the collective as a useful worker in the shared endeavour of socialist construction.[61] However, that does not mean that each individual worker aspired to follow this prescribed role of a socialist constructor and be satisfied with this compromise.

Instructions for the comrades' courts, drawn up by the judiciary and trade unions, limited the possibility of them imposing arbitrary sanctions. Besides, the value of comrades' courts was not supposed to be in the sanctions they might impose. Rather it was the comradely talk during which the whole collective would "give the member a hearing, explain his errors and missteps to him, and demonstrate why his actions were unacceptable and harmful to the working class."[62] The hearing implied sanctions. Most of the RSFSR citizens convicted in comrades' courts in 1935 were punished by a fine (26 per cent) or public censure (39 per cent). Nine per cent were threatened with dismissal – which is not to say they were actually dismissed, but made the worker's routine more challenging.[63]

For all the attention from the state and society, disciplinary cases were never actually the comrades' courts' main business. In 1933, only 25 per cent of comrades' courts' cases were infractions of labour discipline.[64] The percentage remained roughly the same in 1935, when only 30 per cent of 88,000 cases involved labour discipline infractions. The proportion of labour discipline cases was greatest in 1932, towards the end of the first Five-Year Plan, when there was a policy of tougher employment legislation and control of discipline.[65] Note that private charges did not vanish from the comrades' courts. They made up about a quarter of all cases in the republics, except for the Ukrainian SSR where they were 40 per cent.[66] The impression that all comrades' courts became solely disciplinary bodies is therefore incorrect. Certainly, discipline was the focus of attention for state and Party. It was argued over constantly in union central committees and in the press, little attention going to the private charges that remained important to the workers.

Comrades' courts came into being because the state wanted to unburden people's courts and bring justice closer to the people during NEP.

At first they were a means of settling domestic or workplace disputes and some workers used the opportunity to defend their "personal dignity."[67] As comrades' courts turned more towards disciplinary cases they became a place where the collective maintained discipline and discussed matters requiring public condemnation for the sake of not labour discipline only but also the members of the collective – as in cases of harassment, for example, where the victim had a personal interest in securing the comrades' condemnation of the harasser. Yet the successful defence of individual interests in this body of social control was the exception rather than the rule.

Comrades' courts show that comrades' discipline, which had been a proletarian value since the early twentieth century, was of concern to the workers themselves as a community and not just bureaucrats.[68] In a Soviet enterprise, doing work well could earn various rewards, so discipline was internalized as a personal interest of each community member. Ideology created an image of the shared endeavour and collective responsibility for socialist construction. The worker was responsible for and had an interest in the smooth operation of the collective, avoiding absences, drunkenness, staff turnover, etc. Social control therefore not only served the fulfilment of the Five-Year Plans but also ensured stable working conditions despite wrongdoers who might undermine the factory's plan and depress wages and bonuses there.

Despite all these collective benefits, management got more and more say over comrades' courts as discipline gained in salience. Comrades' courts' effectiveness was largely dependent on the initiative of local activists. Some courts, like the one at the Izhora plant, were busy. Others existed only on paper. The business of comrades' courts was subject to frequent changes due to the state's campaigns for more labour discipline. Nonetheless, at the local level there was considerable latitude to interpret instructions from above, making it possible to avoid the harsh strictures of legislation and contain some offences within the four walls of the enterprise.

Rates and Conflicts Commissions

Rates and Conflicts Commissions (RKKs) were another important body for discipline in the workplace. They considered employment disputes involving individuals and groups. They were established by a Sovnarkom resolution of 18 January 1922, in the beginning of the NEP when compulsory work service had been discontinued and freedom of contract in employment had been restored.[69] RKKs were responsible for overseeing the application of collective contracts and tariff agreements and settling any disputes arising from collective or employment contracts.[70]

RKKs were based on parity between management and workers. They had equal representation and number of votes in decisions. The management was appointed by the factory administration, and the workers' side was elected by the factory committee or a workers' assembly. Some experts in the trade unions criticized these elections by a workers' assembly because RKKs were not mass membership bodies and their meetings were not meant to be the public's concern. They were open to experts, complainants, or witnesses, but neither were they a free-for-all: "To implement that view in practice would quite simply make the RKK's job harder and create such a charged atmosphere at meetings that it would be impossible to discuss matters in a calm and business-like manner."[71]

It was thought that RKKs handled matters of such complexity that they required a perfectly calm atmosphere, which "of course cannot happen if there are 50–100 or even 200 people in attendance, many of them with an interest in settling the matter one way or another." Thus, the workforce's opportunities to take part in RKKs were limited, which makes an interesting contrast with the comrades' courts, where mass participation was welcomed. Disputes with management were not meant to come before comrades' courts, which were at first asked to deal with disagreements and arguments between individuals only.

In RKK minutes, management's proposals always had to appear above the workers' proposals so the format of the minutes reflected the principle of one-man management.[72] Seemingly workers would be keen to use RKKs, where they had parity with managers, to assert their rights and obtain favourable interpretations of collective contracts. Things did not quite work like that on Stalinist enterprises.

In matters of new or amended terms of employment, or if a case could not be resolved by consensus in an RKK, it could be referred to a conciliation chamber and, if no agreement could be reached there either, the case moved to an arbitration tribunal. All these bodies provided conciliation and arbitration, but only RKKs were a standing body at the workplace. An alternative was to go to the people's courts. Workers and employers could take work disputes to the labour session of people's courts. The snag was that a certain number of matters were subject to mandatory prior investigation by RKKs.[73] Therefore employment disputes took much longer than other civil cases. Workers were at a disadvantage, as legal action cost them more in time and resources if they needed to get clearance from the RKK first before the people's court.

In 1937, the lawyer B. Borisov proposed to the Plenum of the Supreme Court that the RKKs' jurisdiction be reduced to allow workers to litigate more in courts of general jurisdiction. He criticized the dual process when the complainant had to go through all the committees at the workplace before having their case considered by the court of general jurisdiction. The RKK should continue to deal with cases of dismissal for unfitness, which directly affected production, but any charge punishable by a fine of any amount should go directly to the courts.[74] He also said labour inspectors were too easily persuaded by complainants to rescind RKK decisions, increasing the burden on the courts to resolve disputes. He proposed ending such trade union oversight. Cases would go directly to the regular courts.

How did the RKKs, which existed ostensibly to protect rights, fit with the notion of discipline? Disciplinary sanctions and dismissals for particular offences caused disputes between employer and worker. Workers could always (except in cases of minor theft) appeal a punishment from management to an RKK. In the early 1930s, with the state campaign for discipline, RKKs also came to be regarded as an important means of mobilizing an enterprise's workforce on state and Party targets to increase productivity, improve workers' material conditions, and combat issues of poor labour discipline, such as absenteeism and being self-serving (*rvachestvo*).[75]

The VTsSPS also published a resolution in April 1932 proposing that RKKs should concentrate on workplace cases. However, after the November 1932 decree against truancy was issued, one could be fired for just one violation, so RKKs also received instructions that they were not under any circumstance to take any cases of absenteeism. The state regulated the field of social control and gradually limited the jurisdiction of the RKK over discipline.

If we look at specific examples, we see that the Elektrozavod RKK was set up only in March 1928 and by August had already met sixty-one times. It heard 241 individual cases and 64 collective cases (in the terminology of the authors of the report), involving a total of 708 people. The RKK decided cases in favour of and against management about in roughly equal proportions (150 to 117), but when part of these decisions appeared on appeal to the civil courts a greater proportion of rulings (21 to 5) went in favour of the workers.[76] In the first half of 1929 the Elektrozavod RKK handled 128 complaints. Sergei Zhuravlev, citing statistics showing a decline in applications to the Elektrozavod RKK, concludes that by 1930 it had forfeited its authority in the eyes of the workers.[77] But another statistic from the same archival collection shows that in 1931 the number of complaints increased.[78]

Even if RKKs were active, workers believed that they favoured management. They complained that if they went to an RKK to protest against dismissal, they were met by the very people who had dismissed them, i.e. their own bosses.[79] On major issues like dismissal or reprimand, 73.1 per cent of complaints were resolved in favour of management. At Elektrosila in Leningrad in 1932 the picture was even worse. Of 440 cases, 109 were resolved in favour of the workers, 297 in favour of management and 34 partially in favour of management. A People's Commissariat of Labour survey of RKKs reported: "The RKKs were under the influence of management and were entirely ignorant of their rights and existing laws (owing to illiteracy of its members)."[80]

Officially workers' representatives on RKKs were supposed to defend interests and just demands of workers, which it then had to reconcile with the interests of the enterprise.[81] The workers' side was not supposed to make proposals that were worse for the workers than for management. One woman's protest against dismissal read: "Is it right for me to be fired by the manager of the trust when I got back from maternity leave? I think firing me because I've got a small baby is completely wrong and not what the article on Protection of Maternity and Babies says and therefore I request that you make an appropriate resolution."[82]

In this case, childcare was not accepted as a valid reason for absence. Women were placed, whether by disregard or some exigency of the plan, in an especially vulnerable position. The aim was to keep tabs on excessive workforce mobility[83] and increase labour discipline among all workers despite gender differences and neglecting the state's pronatalist goals. This complaint was submitted in December 1934 but dealt with only in March of the following year. Management offered the complainant another job, but the workers' side insisted the dismissal had been against the law and therefore she should be reinstated in her old position.

The workers' representatives in the RKKs could apply various arguments to meet their comrades' demands or to mitigate sanctions against them. These representatives' arguments were ridiculed by trade union officials when workers' side, for example, demanded a worker be uprated because he was studying in the Workers' Faculty; or not be dismissed because he was a shock worker, had experience in the job, or was an authority figure; or a reprimand for absenteeism be rescinded because it was the first offence.[84] RKKs were also more constrained by codified laws and due process than comrades' courts, so they were less flexible in imposing sanctions.

The parity structure of RKKs also challenged the principle of one-man management. The workers' side of RKKs was thought to be supplanting management, especially in dismissal cases. Therefore, the workers' side sometimes sought more compromises in decisions. In one case of absenteeism by a shock worker, management maintained that the sanction of the loss of a bonus should be justified, so the workers' side proposed a more institutional decision – that the works committee should make a special case and waive the rule for shock workers.[85]

If the RKKs were mistrusted, it was not only because they were seen as under the control of the management. That so many cases were settled in management's favour or without reaching the RKK is because workers often sent in complaints without even an obvious purpose, like demanding a pay rise. Sometimes workers had not had the relevant legislation properly explained to them by their trade union representatives and so they insisted on going to RKKs with unfounded complaints, considering it sufficient. The RKKs had their own problems fulfilling their mission. Complaints were continually held up; members failed to perform their duty; and commission decisions were sometimes not implemented. RKKs were said to represent some "special class" instead of the working class. Workers' perceptions that RKKs should operate only for their benefit was not only their idea. According to the comments of the staff of VTsPS, as far back as 1929, the RKK was conceived of as a body designed primarily to protect workers.[86] The lack of care for the needs of workers in 1930 was described straightforwardly – by one head of a local cell at a meeting of the electricians' central committee – as "*Nikolaevshchina*," implying that decisions depended on whether "the worker makes himself agreeable or not."[87] The law of the workplace, which was semi-detached from the justice system of the state, left too much up to individual likes and dislikes of individual judges. Disciplinary and conciliation bodies acted in the framework of established workplace relationships and were constrained by them. It does not seem as though by and large the parity of the sides made much difference.

Even where cases were fairly decided, there was no guarantee that management would comply with the decision. They used a simple enough ruse: first accept the RKK's decision and then send letters saying, on second thought, it was unlawful because they were bound to follow instructions from their director only.[88] In theory, workers could force management to comply with an RKK decision by simply sending them an enforcement notice, whereupon the decision would be executed. In practice, management could resist if it did not want to pay severance,[89] reinstate a worker,[90] or grant a pay rise.

What use were RKKs, beyond as a mechanism to dispute disciplinary sanctions? RKKs could award compensation for property stolen at work or for the non-issue of protective clothing, neither of which was possible in the comrades' courts. However, such an option was limited by a shortage of resources and stubbornness by management. A worker at the Liubertsy works was awarded forty-two rubles' compensation for a coat stolen from her at work. The management side accepted the award but paid out only twelve rubles on the grounds that the thief from whom the money could be recovered had not been found.[91]

Although RKKs had less room to manoeuvre than comrades' courts, judicial power was so decentralized that they too were sometimes able to go beyond their formal powers. At Skorokhod, for example, "democracy"[92] (as a contrast to the principle of one-man management) went so far that it was the RKK that approved the pay of the factory director, the deputy director, and the managerial and technical staff.[93] Private charges also turned up in RKKs, even though they were not set up to handle them.[94] For example, one insulted worker made a complaint not to the comrades' court but to the secret section of the factory committee, which referred it to the RKK. The RKK, which was not empowered to hand down reprimands, gave the abuser one anyway.

Although workers sometimes submitted patently ill-considered complaints to the RKKs, it is clear they were at least aware that justice had to be fought for. The Elektrozavod statistics show that most (65 per cent) of those involved in disputes were workers who had only recently been taken on.[95] Perhaps workers aware of their rights tended to change jobs more often, looking for better conditions. Newly hired workers may have also demanded more out of ignorance of local rules and customs to which older workers were already accustomed. Thus, complaints to RKKs, like those to comrades' courts, show workers seeking to defend their honour and rights, even though some of them lacked the weapons and the discursive knowhow for the fight.

The worst that could happen to a worker at an RKK was to get called a *rvach* – a grabber, a self-seeker, and one who advances himself by any means. What distinguished a *rvach* from an unjustly treated worker? The difference was hard to grasp. Anyone applying to RKKs about tariffs, compensation, payments, or incorrect rations could be branded a self-seeker to extract maximum personal benefit from his work to the detriment of the common cause.[96] Managers sometimes attempted to dismiss disputes in just such terms, describing them as "wrecking." At Elektrozavod meetings were held where the workers were told to desist from taking any complaints to the RKK. There were even special examinations to find out who was a real *rvach*. Two workers at the Izhora plant artificially reduced their productivity to force management to increase the salary for the job. They asked the RKK to give them either a higher wage or else move them to a new job. Their claim was tested by putting another worker on the same job, who overfulfilled the norm and did it better. The pair were declared enemies of socialist production and the case was transferred to the comrades' court, where further discreditable details about them came to light.[97]

Workers' complaints, even unfounded ones, had the important effect of pointing out larger problems in the factory, such as workers being badly organized on the shop floor, and norms unfairly set. In that, RKKs were similar to comrades' courts. If there was an "unhealthy workshop atmosphere," they revealed it. The Izhora plant provides another good example. A group of machine operators had not been paid for overtime. Their shop RKK gathered evidence and upheld the complaints but found that the problem had been caused by the "foreman's bureaucratic attitude to the workers' interests."[98] Urged on by the workers, the RKK referred charges of red tape and bureaucratism against him to the comrades' court. The comrades' court convicted both the foreman and the deputy foreman and launched a large-scale campaign against bureaucratism around their case. Both were sentenced to a severe reprimand, to be published in the press. The RKK and comrades' court had cooperated to give broad application to an ordinary dispute.

Yet broadening the context demonstrated that the rights of workers were secondary to the efficiency of production. All complaints from workers about downgrading, loss of pay, or infringement of individual rights had to be treated by the RKK as if they were complaints about incorrect management and misuse of labour on the factory floor.[99] Trade union officials said that whenever a worker was "hurt" by a collective contract, production came to harm at the same time.[100] In effect, RKKs existed and considered workers' complaints and requests because someone had to address the scientific, technical, and organizational problems that were held to be the basis of employment justice at the local level. So RKKs display the same economism in the discourse of rights that was perceptible in all workplace bodies from the early 1930s on.

For all the plans made for them, RKKs never became "one of the main and principal forms of protection of workers' material interests."[101] Officials in local trade-unions spoke more about complying with directives than about defending workers' rights. The latter was also a rare topic for discussions in Moscow. In the 1930s RKKs received far less attention from the state than comrades' courts. Tens of volumes of instructions for RKKs were published in the second half of the 1920s; only the odd few texts appeared in the early 1930s.

Conclusion

Rates and conflicts commissions and comrades' courts were gradually subsumed to the control of labour discipline, even though both were set up in the era of the NEP and were originally intended to deal with individual disputes. RKKs were meant to settle disputes with management. Comrades' courts were meant to handle disputes between workers at the same enterprise. RKKs were mainly concerned with determining the nature of offences. Comrades' courts, as mass-membership bodies, provided means for workers' communities to process and publicly discuss offences. The two bodies were therefore complementary. Each reacted differently to the transformation wrought by the first Five-Year Plan and campaigns to improve discipline. Comrades' courts, far less constrained by employment legislation, took the disciplinary route and were given greater powers. Meanwhile, RKKs never became a popular vehicle for the defence of workers' rights. Each had its role, but their purpose in conjunction was to discover deficiencies in technological or organizational order at enterprises.

Therefore, workers' rights were often treated as secondary to production, no more than a warning flag about a bigger problem. They could be enjoyed only in the context of the "common cause." Discipline became the over-riding consideration in both RKKs and comrades' courts, but not the only one. Even in the comrades' courts there were opportunities to assert individual rights by way of collective or individual cases against overwork, poor working conditions, workplace harassment, domestic violence, etc. That was only one of the trends, however. The effectiveness of different bodies at the local level depended on the initiative of the activists – the members of comrades' courts in drumming up cases against administration, or the workers' side of RKKs in making the most of their ability to disagree with management.

Comrades' courts and RKKs, which both acted under the auspices of government departments, were not alone in control of discipline in factories and enterprises. They interacted with other workplace organizations, including trade union and Party cells, each with their own means of social control. At the request of the party and the state, trade unions became increasingly involved in social control during the Five-Year Plan. Their main task was to create the context for a common cause, "to inculcate in the consciousness of the broadest working masses the idea 'that the workers work not for capitalists but for a state that belongs to them and for their own class – that consciousness is a great driving force for the development and enhancement of our industry.'"[102]

Primary Party organizations were also tasked with mobilizing the masses to fulfil production plans, reinforce labour discipline, and promote shock work. They were concerned by broadly the same offences as the dispute-resolution bodies. If Party members offended there was, in the words of the minutes of the Party cell at Elektrozavod, "no point in dragging them to the RKK then we need to rigorously sort them out here."[103] Party members preferred to go to their own Party cell. Cells themselves intervened on behalf of injured comrades. They might, for example, oppose the publication of a defamatory piece in the local newspaper.

Different Party bodies also dealt with a similar range of cases. Proceedings might be conducted at a Party committee plenary, a local Party commission, a Party cell bureau, or even an open Party assembly in the factory. Management could also orchestrate the Party assembly's support for dismissal of a recalcitrant worker by selecting speakers critical of the defendant.[104]

However, at most enterprises there was no system for transferring cases from one forum to another. The rules were interpreted case by case. Mostly, the local trade union works committee allocated cases to a comrades' court, RKK, or people's court. The same offence might be handled by several bodies at once and sanctioned by changes in work, social, and Party status. Comrades' courts respectfully notified Party cells of their cases. Then the Komsomol and Party could issue additional punishment according to their own rules. They might issue reprimands, impose correctional measures, or throw offenders out. All the sanctions could only manipulate the status that their organization provided. Such sanctions could be contested beyond the proceedings by appealing to district or municipal dispute commissions, whose function was to settle internal Party and Komsomol disputes.[105] There was a risk there. It was possible for further discreditable personal details to emerge – meetings missed, membership subscriptions not paid, etc.

Comrades' courts and conflicts commissions were unique spaces to assert social control because they acted largely independently of other bodies and had their own ways of asserting discipline. At Soviet enterprises, workers found themselves in a difficult situation, when discipline was simultaneously monitored by management, social organizations, and comrades' collectives. The parties' interests were represented in various combinations. Each body had its own agenda and ways of discussing and a certain set of sanctions available. That such things differed from one enterprise to another shows the relative independence of the workplace as a space of discipline and legality.

On the one hand, workers' individual rights were determined by the material reality of socialist construction. To protect workers' interests was to improve the structure, organization, processes, and theory of production. Workers' grievances were seen as warning flags about deficiencies that needed fixing. Workers could exploit the disciplinary rules in their own interest and the common cause of socialist construction helped involve them in proceedings at different levels. On the other hand, the Soviet worker's individual agency was subject to many limitations. First, how well workers could do was influenced by political campaigns (for discipline or against *brak,* or absenteeism) in which Party or workplace bodies had an interest in achieving particular outcomes or meeting statistical targets. Second, many decisions by disciplinary bodies were simply not implemented because the system of social control was so disorganized. The bodies that dealt with discipline and rights in the workplace are notable for having no clear hierarchy and no consistency in decision-making. They formed a sprawling, multi-layered system overseen by the comrades, the workplace supervisors, the trade union, and Party officials all at the same time. Workers had plenty of options, but success in asserting individual rights was difficult.

Yet the workplace was only the first level of the workers' struggle for their interests. Beyond the disciplinary and rights domain of the workplace, Soviet citizens were able to bring grievances and complaints to the trade unions and the People's Commissariat of Labour; they might even go all the way to the Supreme Court in the struggle to assert their employment and civil rights.[106]

NOTES

1 The special directive of the Central Committee of VKP (b) was published only in September 1929, but as a governing principle, one-man management was proclaimed during the Civil War by Lenin and other important Bolsheviks, like major trade union official Mikhail Tomsky. One-man management continued to be a guiding principle during the New Economic Policy. M. Tomskii, "Novye zadachi soiuzov," *Vestnik truda* 1 (1922): 4; Jane Burbank, "Lenin and the Law in Revolutionary Russia," *Slavic Review* 54, no. 1 (1995): 23–44.
2 Z. Grishin, *Sotsialisticheskaia organizatsiia i distsiplina truda i voprosy sovetskogo trudovogo prava* (Moscow: Sovetskoe zakonodatel'stvo, 1934), 9.
3 By discipline I primarily mean labour discipline, although in Soviet ideology, where the measure of a man was his attitude to work, the term took on a general social meaning. The internalization of labour discipline

was actively promoted during the first Five-Year Plan. In *The State and Revolution* Lenin writes that discipline will be established by the state power of the workers, leading to an order in which control and accounting will be performed by the hands of the workers themselves and not bureaucrats belonging to a special section of the population. This view of the individual as both agent and object of discipline matches Michel Foucault's thinking and was evident in the Soviet regime, when even workplace discipline included not only offences against internal rules but also breaches of ethics affecting workers' moral character.

4 A. Petrov, *Zashchita trudovykh prav: istoriia, teoriia, praktika* (Moscow: Iurait, 2021), 53.

5 Lewis H. Siegelbaum, *Stakhanovism and the Politics of Productivity in the USSR, 1935–1941* (Cambridge: Cambridge University Press, 1990); Donald Filtzer, *Soviet Workers and Stalinist Industrialization: The Formation of Modern Soviet Production Relations, 1928–1941* (Armonk, NY: M.E. Sharpe Incorporated, 1986); H. Kuromiya, *Stalin's Industrial Revolution. Politics and Workers, 1928–1932* (Cambridge: Cambridge University Press, 1988); Lewis H. Siegelbaum and Ronald G. Suny, eds., *Making Workers Soviet: Power, Class, and Identity* (Ithaca, NY: Cornell University Press, 1994); S.M. Schwarz, *Labor in the Soviet Union* (New York: Praeger, 1951); W.G. Rosenberg and Lews H. Siegelbaum, eds., *Social Dimensions of Soviet Industrialization* (Bloomington: Indiana University Press, 1993); K.M. Straus, *Factory and Community in Stalin's Russia: The Making of an Industrial Working Class* (Pittsburgh: University of Pittsburgh Press, 1997).

6 Harold J. Berman, *Justice in the U.S.S.R.* (Cambridge, MA: Harvard University Press, 1968), 39.

7 Scott Newton, *Law and the Making of the Soviet World: The Red Demiurge* (Abingdon: Routledge, 2014), 4.

8 Newton proposes "factory state" to describe the Soviet Union. Ibid., 158.

9 Not enough historical research has been done on the bodies controlling discipline in the workplace. There have been detailed studies of "active form" labour disputes, meaning strikes and protests by workers in open opposition to the state; these are of interest to students of the relationship between state and society. *Trudovye konflikty v SSSR, 1930–1991* (Moscow: Institut rossiiskoi istorii, 2006). Another possible approach was to look separately at trade union or workplace bodies at particular enterprises where the rules on how they operated and interacted with other bodies were not clear, yet they are concluded to be ineffective. L.V. Borisova, *Sovetskie profsoiuzy i trudovye konflikty v period NEPa* (Moscow: IRI RAN, 2018); S.V. Zhuravlev and M.M. Mukhin, *"Krepost' sotsializma": Povsednevnost' i motivatsiia truda na sovetskom predpriiatii, 1928–1938 gg.* (Moscow: ROSSPEN, 2004).

10. Laura Nader and Harry F. Todd, Jr., eds., *The Disputing Process: Law in Ten Societies* (New York: Columbia University Press, 1978), 312.
11. John M. Conley and William M. O'Barr, "Back to the Trobriands: The Enduring Influence of Malinowski's *Crime and Custom in Savage Society*," *Law & Social Inquiry* 27, no. 4 (2002): 847–74.
12. Mary Douglas, *How Institutions Think* (Syracuse, NY: Syracuse University Press, 1986).
13. Comrades' courts existed prior to 1917 in education too. They were introduced at the district level in the 1850s, but closed down because the state saw them as too liberal. Nevertheless, comrades' courts continued to be introduced at the initiative of some schools. For more details, see Nikolai Pirogov, *Izbrannye pedagogicheskie sochineniia* (Moscow: Izdatel'stvo Akademicheskii pedagogicheskikh nauk, 1953); Aleksei Butovskii, *O shkol'nom tovarishcheskom sude* (St. Petersburg: tip. im. Stasiulevicha, 1907); Nikifor Il'in, *O vospitanii obshchestvennosti v shkole* (Moscow: tip. Mosk. gor. uchilicha glukhonemykh, 1916); Ia. Karas', "Shkol'noe tovarishchestvo. Iz zapisok narodnogo uchitelia," *Russkaia shkola* 3 (1897): 100–16. Workers' comrades' courts, however, were the direct antecedents of comrades' courts at the workplace.
14. For more detail, see Maria Starun, "'Natsionalizatsiia' obobshchestvlennoi distsipliny: Tovarishcheskie sudy v Sovetskoi Rossii v 1917–1922 gg.," *Cahiers du monde russe* 62, no. 4 (2021): 553–80.
15. Gosudarstvennyi arkhiv Rossiiskoi Federatsii (GARF) 1235/74/391/69.
16. GARF 1235/74/391/69v.
17. Mihail Kozhevnikov, *Istoriia sovetskogo suda* (Moscow: Iurid. izd-vo, 1948), 196–7; E.Ia. Vol'dman, *Tovarishcheskie sudy na predpriiatiiakh, v uchrezhdeniiakh i organizatsiiakh*, Cand. Hist. Sci. diss. (Moscow, 1969), 108; Pavel Polianskii, "Obsledovanie Rabkrinom sudebno-sledstvennoi sistemy i sozdanie tovarishcheskikh sudov," *Vestnik Moskovskogo universiteta. Seria 11. Pravo* 5 (2020): 19–36.
18. Robert Sharlet, "Pashukanis and the Withering Away of Law in the USSR," in *Cultural Revolution in Russia 1928–32*, ed. Sheila Fitzpatrick (Bloomington: Indiana University Press, 1978), 169–88.
19. In 1928–9 comrades' courts were referred to in this way by both print journalists and reformers themselves, among whom was the People's Commissar of Justice N.M. Ianson. *Sud idet* 1 (1929): 4.
20. Peter H. Solomon, "Criminalization and Decriminalization in Soviet Criminal Policy, 1917–1941," *Law and Society Review* 16 (1981): 9–43.
21. G.K. Moskalenko and M.E. Timofeev, *Tovarishcheskie sudy. Posobie dlia tovarishcheskikh sudov na fabrichno-zavodskikh predpriiatiiakh, v gosudarstvennykh i obshchestvennykh uchrezhdeniiakh, dlia fabzavmestkomov i sudebnykh rabotnikov* (Moscow: Iuridicheskoe izdatel'stvo NKIu RSFSR, 1929).

22 Ibid., 3–5.
23 *Sud idet* 1 (1929).
24 Soviet historians also saw comrades' courts from the revolutionary era as being created by the masses. E.Ia. Vol'dman, *Tovarishcheskie sudy na predpriiatiiakh, v uchrezhdeniiakh i organizatsiiakh*: Cand. Hist. Sci. diss. (Moscow, 1969); P.I. Ikorskii, *Organizatsiia i deiatel'nost' tovarishcheskikh sudov v pervye gody sovetskoi vlasti (1917–1922 gg.)*: Cand. Hist. Sci. diss. (Voronezh, 1966); E.Ia. Vol'dman, "Tovarishcheskie sudy v Rossii do Velikoi oktiabr'skoi sotsialisticheskoi revoliutsii," *Nauchnye trudy Omskoi Vysshei shkoly militsii* 10 (1972): 174–91.
25 *Sud idet* 21 (1928).
26 *Sud idet* 6 (1929), 319–22.
27 Moskalenko and Timofeev, *Tovarishcheskie sudy*, 14.
28 *Sud idet* 2 (1930), 11.
29 Ibid., 13.
30 *Sud idet* 21 (1929).
31 VTsIK RSFSR, Sovnarkom resolution of 30 December 1929, "O tovarishcheskikh sudakh na fabrichno-zavodskikh predpriiatiiakh, v gosudarstvennykh i obshchestvennykh uchrezhdeniiakh i predpriiatiiakh," *Sobranie uzakonenii RSFSR (SU RSFSR)* 4 (1930).
32 *Sud idet* 21 (1929), 1257–8.
33 *Sud idet* 17 (1929), 1031.
34 Ibid., 1032.
35 *Sud idet* 12 (1929), 637.
36 Ibid., 639.
37 Tsentral'nyi gosudarstvennyi arkhiv goroda Moskva (TsGA Moscow) 2090/1/361.
38 GARF 1235/74/391/71.
39 *Trud*, 22 May 1929.
40 GARF 1235/74/391/68v.
41 *Sud idet* 10 (1930), 3.
42 *Sud idet* 7 (1929), 344.
43 TsGA Moscow R-2090/1/306/15.
44 Ibid., l. 26.
45 *Sud idet* 23–4 (1930), 28.
46 Ibid.
47 Vol'dman, *Tovarishcheskie sudy na predpriiatiiakh, v uchrezhdeniiakh i organizatsiiakh*, 140.
48 *SU RSFSR* 14 (1931), 160.
49 *Sud idet* 11 (1929), 635.
50 See notes 68–70.
51 *Sud idet* 7 (1929), 358.

52 GARF R-7676/1/679a. "Sud nad brakodelami tsentral'noi remontnoi masterskoi zavoda 'Krasnyi putilovets,'" 19.
53 GARF R-7676/1/679. "Slet rabotnikov tovarishcheskikh sudov mashinostroitel'nykh predpriiatii g. Leningrada," 1933, 9.
54 V. Epifanovich, *Tovarishcheskim sudam – opyt izhortsev* (Moscow and Leningrad: Izd. i tip. Profizdata, 1934).
55 Ibid., 24.
56 Yiannis Kokosalakis shows how in the first Five-Year Plan, Communists used workplace meetings, workers' assemblies, and other gatherings to find problems in the manufacturing process and industry organization. Comrades' courts cannot with confidence be called Party organs, even though most of the membership was generally Communist and so the demand for this sort of critique of process should be attributed not to the Communists only, but the entire workforce. "Bolshevik Bargaining in Soviet Industry: Communists between State and Society in the Interwar Soviet Union," *Journal of Modern History* 93, no. 2 (2021): 324–62.
57 Epifanovich, *Tovarishcheskim sudam – opyt izhortsev*, 48.
58 Ibid., 59. The issue here is reducing breakages as a proportion of total output rather than cutting the number of faulty products in comrades' court cases. Reducing defects at the Izhora plant was also the subject of a report to the assembly of production engineering workers of machine building enterprises in Leningrad. Other enterprises reported a similar trend, but it is impossible to prove that this was due solely to the activities of the comrades' courts. See GARF R-7676/1/679.
59 Z. Grishin, *Sovetskoe trudovoe pravo* (Moscow: Sovetskoe zakonodatel'stvo, 1936), 144.
60 Vol'dman, *Tovarishcheskie sudy na predpriiatiiakh, v uchrezhdeniiakh i organizatsiiakh*, 164. Tsentral'nyi gosudarstvennyi arkhiv Sankt-Peterburga (TsGA SPB), 6284/1/19/37; Peter H. Solomon, *Soviet Criminal Justice under Stalin* (Cambridge: Cambridge University Press, 1996).
61 GARF R-7709/1/50/11.
62 Epifanovich, *Tovarishcheskim sudam – opyt izhortsev*.
63 GARF R-9492/1/813/2.
64 Ibid., 31.
65 Vol'dman, *Tovarishcheskie sudy na predpriiatiiakh, v uchrezhdeniiakh i organizatsiiakh*, 186.
66 In the document they were called regular (*bytovye*). But the statistics do not contain any data on who initiated the cases. GARF R-9492/1/813/4.
67 Wording from the RSFSR Criminal Code of 1926.
68 Mark D. Steinberg, *Moral Communities: The Culture of Class Relations in the Russian Printing Industry, 1867–1907* (Berkeley and Los Angeles: University of California Press, 1992); P.I. Ikorskii, *Organizatsiia i deiatel'nost'*

tovarishcheskikh sudov v pervye gody sovetskoi vlasti (1917–1922 gg.). Diss. Kand. Ist. Nauk.
69 D.I. Khlebnikov, *RKK. Rastsenochno-konfliktnye komissii* (Moscow: Izd-vo MGSPS "Trud i kniga," 1927), 15.
70 A. Raniets, *Chto nuzhno znat' fabzavmestkomu i administratsii v rabote RKK* (Moscow: Trud i kniga, 1930), 8. More detail on the legislation governing RKKs: B.N. Kazantsev, "Nekotorye problemy regulirovaniia trudovykh otnoshenii i ulazhivaniia konfliktov na proizvodstve v zakonakh i zakonoproektakh o trude SSSR. 1928–1980e gody," in *Trudovye konflikty v SSSR, 1930–1991*, ed. Andrei Zakharov (Moscow: IRI RAN, 2006), 85–7, 91.
71 V.F. Buianov, *Kak dolzhna rabotat' rastsenochno-konfliktnaia komissiia. Rukovodstvo dlia rabotnikov RKK* (Moscow: VTsSPS, 1929), 13–14.
72 Khlebnikov, *RKK*, 44–5.
73 *Rastsenochno-konfliktnye komissii i trudovye konflikty. Zakonodatel'stvo s izmeneniiami po 20 iiunia 1931 g.* (Moscow: Sovetskoe zakonodatel'stvo, 1931), 4.
74 B. Borisov, "Sud i prokuratura na strazhe garantirovannogo Stalinskoi Konstitutsiei prava na trud," *Sotsialisticheskaia zakonnost'* 1 (1938): 34.
75 GARF R-7676/7/302/22–3.
76 TsGAM "Otchet RKK zavkoma," R-2090/1/170/21–2.
77 S.V. Zhuravlev and M.M. Mukhin, *Krepost' sotsializma: Povsednevnost' i motivatsiia truda na sovetskom predpriiatii, 1928–1938 gg.* (Moscow: ROSSPEN, 2004).
78 TsGAM 2090/1/533/18.
79 GARF R-5515/20/162. "Materialy po rassledovaniiu prichin nepravil'nogo uvol'neniia s raboty," 1933, p. 58.
80 GARF R-5515/20/129. "Perepiska s Narodnymi Komissariatami truda soyuznyh respublik po zaiavleniiam raznykh lits o rassledovanii prichin nepravil'nogo uvol'neniia s raboty," 1932, pp. 20–1.
81 Raniets, *Chto nuzhno znat' fabzavmestkomu i administratsii v rabote RKK*, 78
82 GARF R-7860/4/130/10.
83 The Russian word is *letunstvo,* meaning workers frequently changing jobs in search of better conditions.
84 Raniets, *Chto nuzhno znat' fabzavmestkomu i administratsii v rabote RKK*, 48.
85 GARF R-7690/1/169/133.
86 GARF R-5451/13/379/1.
87 Nikolaevshchina referred to the tsarist era's deprivation of workers' rights. GARF R-7690/1/169/29, 31.
88 GARF R-7676/7/302.
89 *Trud*, 27 July 1935.
90 GARF R-1005/1a/968.
91 GARF R-7676/7/302/2.

92 Quotation marks in the original.
93 GARF R-5451/13/379.
94 Raniets, *Chto nuzhno znat' fabzavmestkomu i administratsii v rabote RKK*, 160.
95 TsGAM R-2090/1/306/50v.
96 TsGAM R-2090/1/314/"Protokoly obshchikh sobranii rabochikh i sluzhashchikh vol'framovogo otdela," 1929, p. 17.
97 Epifanovich, *Tovarishcheskim sudam – opyt izhortsev*, 47.
98 Ibid., 7.
99 GARF R-7676/1/333/18.
100 Ibid.
101 Ibid., 1.
102 *KPSS v rezoliutsiiakh i resheniiakh s"ezdov, konferentsii i plenumov TsK (1898–1986)*. T. 5. 1929–32 (Moscow: Izd-vo politicheskoi literatura, 1984), 175.
103 TsGAM R-468/1/73. "Protokoly plenuma biuro i sobranii iacheiki VKP(b) vol'framovogo otdela," l. 1.
104 GARF R-5515/20/162/31–59.
105 TsGAM P-635/1/33. "Stenogr. sobraniia sekretarei proizvod. iacheek 26.12.32," l. 24.
106 Maria Starun, "Pohod Alekseia Sidortseva protiv sovetskogo suda: svidetel'stva, argumenty i poisk materialnoi istiny," *The Soviet and Post-Soviet Review* 49, no. 2 (2022): 115–49.

4 "Such Was the Music, Such Was the Dance": Understanding the Internal and External Motivations of a Stalinist Perpetrator

TIMOTHY K. BLAUVELT

Contextualizing the Stalinist Perpetrators[1]

The scale of state-sponsored violence over the past century poses fundamental questions about human nature and about how and under what circumstances people can be induced to behave in seemingly inhuman ways. As in early studies of the Holocaust and of the Nuremburg trials, much of the focus in the Cold War analyses of the Stalinist Great Terror in the USSR focused on the role of Stalin and the top leadership of a totalitarian regime, often regarding the middle-level officials who actually implemented the violence as either "cogs in the machine" or as sadists and psychopaths whose natural criminal proclivities found favourable contexts. While orders from above clearly played a central role in the Terror, and there undoubtedly were psychopaths among the NKVD investigators, such approaches often sidestepped the more nuanced issue of how "ordinary people" became perpetrators and the ways in which the secret police investigators fit into Stalinist society more generally and themselves reflected that society. Several recent projects by historians of the USSR have endeavoured to make use of newly accessible security archive material (particularly from the SBU archives in Ukraine) in order to apply some of the insights from the historiography of Nazi Germany to the Stalinist case.[2] The extensive archival files of the former KGB archive of the Georgian SSR of the trials of Georgian NKVD officials that took place in Tbilisi during the period of "de-Stalinization" following the XXth Party Congress in 1956 provide an additional opportunity to examine the careers, motivations, and outlooks of individual officials, in effect to draw a more differentiated image of the Soviet secret policeman.[3] The vast amount of testimony, commentary, appeals, and personal statements found in these files allows for an examination of the inevitable mosaic of motivations underlying the relationship of the individual and the state machine and the interplay of disposition and situation, of ideology and rationality. Such aspects inevitably influence and mutually reinforce one another: the "ecosystem of violence" of the early Soviet period, including the context, culture, and ideology in the initiation and expansion of violence (the experience of the violence of the First World War, revolution and Civil War during the perpetrators' formative years during 1914–21); the perpetrators' psychology and understanding of legality; the institutional environment of peer pressure, rivalry, empowerment, and demands from superiors within the NKVD; the mass psychology and public ideology (or discourse) of the period in society at large; the viability of alternate discourses or norms to those propagated by the Party and the state; and the way in which individual motivations may have shaped actions.[4] Examining the perpetrators' internalization of the official discourses, and the interactions between belief and self-interest, sheds further light on the ways in which social control in the Stalinist system was exerted not only coercively from above and without, but also from below and within, and not only among the masses, but among the very implementers of state violence who were responsible for assuring control over the masses.

This chapter furthers the effort to "populate the macro historical" through an examination of the case files of the 1957 trial of Sergo Davlianidze, an official in the NKVD in Georgia at the height of the Great Terror who took an active part in the arrests and interrogations of that period. Comprising twenty-four volumes of background documents, depositions, letters and personal appeals, court transcripts and testimony of victims, former colleagues and of Davlianidze himself, the case provides an opportunity to seek a "balance between the micro and macro-historical"[5] and an understanding of how officials of coercive state agencies were able to commit acts of oppression on such a large scale against largely innocent victims.

Biography of a Secret Policeman

Although Sergo Davlianidze would become a high-ranking official, given his background he seems a viable candidate to serve as a mid-level NKVD "everyman" of the Stalin period. At the height of the Great Terror he served as the Deputy Head of the 4th Department of the Georgian NKVD, and from 1938 to 1948 he held other increasingly important positions in the Georgian secret police and railway secret police in the Transcaucasus and the North Caucasus. Davlianidze was born in 1904 in the Kutaisi district in Georgia, in what he claimed was a poor peasant family that later joined a collective farm.[6] Like many of his colleagues, he had a limited educational background, only four years of primary school, though in successive autobiographies he tried to retrospectively improve his educational status from "incomplete lower" to "incomplete middle," and sometimes even to "incomplete higher" (at one point he claimed to have studied for two years in a hydro institute). He was literate in Russian and apparently understood but could not write in Georgian, so despite his rural Georgian origins he functioned primarily in Russian. He claimed to have fought in the Russian Civil War in a Red Army unit in the North Caucasus in 1919, although later assessors observed that this was unlikely as he would have been only fifteen at the time. According to his official files he became a policeman in Tiflis (Tbilisi) from 25 February 1921, at the time that the city fell to the invading 11th Red Army, and joined the Komsomol by the end of that year. In 1923–4 he served for a year in a Georgian Rifle Company of the Red Army in Batumi.[7] Upon completing this service, in April 1924 he was appointed Secretary of the Komsomol District Committee (*raikom*) in Manglisi in rural Georgia, where he worked until October 1925, when he was seconded ("*komandirovan*") to the secret police (then the *Cheka*), in which he would spend most of his working life.

Davlianidze's prosecution files provide us with his own descriptions of his career from his multitude of statements, appeals, and autobiographies, as well as the view from the state and Party examinations and the opinions of his colleagues, rivals, and other witnesses. According to a later review of his file by the Institute of Marx–Engels–Lenin (IMEL), he had been relieved from his position as district Komsomol secretary in Manglisi in June 1925 for incompetence, "lack of leadership," and because of the "many serious defects in Komsomol work in Manglisi." Davlianidze was "not at all familiar with the policy and directives of the Party and Komsomol on work in the countryside," a review commission at the time found.[8] Despite (or perhaps because of) this poor evaluation, he was sent to Tbilisi to work briefly as a secretary of the Economic Department of the Komsomol Central Committee and was then transferred to the Georgian Cheka in October 1925. From this time until 1937 Davlianidze worked in district secret police offices around Georgia (primarily in Chiatura in western Georgia in 1928–31), and in the Economic Department (EKO) or the Georgian secret police (now renamed the GPU) in Tbilisi. Evaluations of his early career in the secret police continued to be noticeably poor: in 1926, while a GPU deputy plenipotentiary in Shoropani, he was evaluated as "childish and lacking authority," and "only fulfilled assignments and showed no initiative, has a limited outlook, is not capable of working on his own and gives good results only under close supervision." And in a criticism that would appear over and over again throughout his career, Davlianidze was held to be a poor team player "who often fights with colleagues."⁹ In a letter of appeal to Lavrenty Beria sent in 1953, Davlianidze described a number of conflicts in which he became embroiled during this period with local Party officials and with secret police colleagues who were apparently aligned with Beria's rival Tite Lordkipanidze: in 1926 with the Manglisi Komsomol Secretary; 1927 in Shoropani against Lordkipanidze's client Mikheil Didziguri; in 1929 with the local *raikom* in Chiatura; in 1930 with Lordkipanidze's client Kavteladze in Chiatura; and in 1930–1 with Dzidziguri, Lordkipanidze, and Georgian Party chief Samsun Mamulia, in which Mamulia accused Davlianidze of "throwing around accusations and exceeding his authority." A Georgian Central Committee review commission found that an "unprincipled struggle" had broken out between Davlianidze in the GPU and the local Party *raikom*, in which Davlianidze "in an entirely unacceptable manner gathered materials (often tendentious) with the help of the GPU apparatus to discredit the leading officials."[10] According to Davlianidze's 1953 letter, in each of these cases Davlianidze appealed directly to Beria, either in person or in written form, and was protected by the latter from negative consequences from these quarrels.[11]

In 1933–4, while in the Economic Department of the Georgian GPU in Tbilisi, Davlianidze became again involved in a conflict with Lordkipanidze. This was simultaneously an institutional one between the Transcaucasian Republic-level OGPU (of which Lordkipanidze was now the head) and the Georgian GPU over the authority of the latter to arrest several respected experts who were supposedly involved in a counter-revolutionary plot, without the permission of the former.[12] As a result of this affair, Davlianidze was arrested and imprisoned in October–November 1934, at which time he again sent a written appeal to Beria (and to Beria's client Solomon Mil'shtein, then deputy head of the Special Section of the Georgian Central Committee). After a month of incarceration, Davlianidze was summoned from his cell to see the head of the Transcaucasus OGPU in November 1934. Expecting to be brought before Lordkipanidze, Davlianidze was surprised to find Beria's client S.A. Goglidze now in that position. Lordkipanidze had been removed from this post and later sent to Crimea (and in 1937 executed as an enemy of the people), thus Goglidze freed Davlianidze and restored him to his position.[13]

For another two years, in 1935–7, Davlianidze was sent back to Chiatura as district NKVD head. Then in July 1937 he was returned to Tbilisi and appointed Deputy Head of the 4th Department of the

Georgian NKVD. Also known as the Secret Political Department (SPO), this was headed by a major Beria client, Bogdan Z. Kobulov, and was responsible for working with informants ("*agenturnye materialy*") and for dealing with "enemy activity," members of "anti-Soviet parties and groups," former White Army members, clergy, and nationalists not tied to foreign nationalist organizations.[14] Given that these areas comprised the primary pretext for accusations against supposed "enemies of the people," the 4th Department became the focal point of the NKVD's activities during the Great Terror. Department Head Kobulov directly supervised the first three of the seven sections, while the 4th, 5th, 6th, and 7th sections, which dealt primarily with the districts of Georgia, were the responsibility of Davlianidze.[15] As deputy department head, Davlianidze had the authority to sign documents and issue orders in place of Kobulov when the latter was out of the office or otherwise occupied. For a part of this period, from December 1937 to February 1938, Kobulov was also acting deputy head of the Georgian NKVD, so Davlianidze often served as the acting head of the department.[16] Davlianidze regularly answered directly to the Georgian NKVD head Goglidze (another major Beria client) and to Georgian Party First Secretary Beria himself.[17]

As a former NKVD colleague later testified, "moving from head of the Chiatura district NKVD to Deputy Head of the 4th Department of the NKVD GSSR in the second half of 1937, at the peak of the repressions, was a huge leap, which could not have happened without the patronage of the leadership of the NKVD, including of Kobulov, and of course without particular activeness on the part of Davlianidze himself."[18] This promotion was materially rewarding as well, as Davlianidze and his family were given a spacious apartment in a prestigious building at No. 5/7 Sadzhaia (now Kiacheli) Street, known as the "Generals' House," home to a number of senior Party, military, and police officials.[19] Davlianidze flourished in this new position, and in August 1938 was promoted to deputy head and then head of the 3rd Department (Counter Intelligence) of the Georgian NKVD. In 1939 he became head of the NKVD Transport Department of the Transcaucasus Railway, and in mid-1941 and again from in 1944 to 1945 he was Deputy Commissar of the Georgian secret police (now called MGB and then NKGB).[20] Also in 1945 he became a candidate member of the Georgian Central Committee and obtained the rank of general-major.

The Terror and the war years seem to have been the apogee of Davlianidze's career. In 1945 he "created a conflict situation in the Georgian NKGB" that spoiled his relations with its head, A.N. Rapava (another Beria appointee),[21] and he was subsequently transferred to

Dzaudzhikau in North Ossetia as head of the MGB Transport Department of the Ordzhonikidze (North Caucasus) Railroad. From this point Davlianidze again began to receive negative evaluations (*kharakteristiki*) of his work. He was accused of "creating an unhealthy and conflictual situation in his department from his very first day there," of "surrounding himself with people chosen not for their professional qualities, but by their family closeness or familiarity from previous work," and of using his clients (who were all Georgians) "for gathering information on the moods and opinions of department staff, causing distrust and fear of one another," and "under the guise of special official business, he often organized trips of his close associates to Tbilisi in order to procure groceries and goods for his family." He was accused of spending 9,317 rubles of "operational funds" on personal items (although he later returned the money), and he "registered his apartment as an official safe-house and paid for it out of state funds." His "arrogance (*kichlivost'*) with his title of General-Major angered his staff," and he unnecessarily showed off by moving around the city accompanied by a special guard detail. During his first eleven months on the job he had 36 per cent of his staff (fifty-one people) arrested and 51 per cent (seventy-two people) transferred without explanation. All of this "served as the cause of poor results of agent operational work for 1946."[22] Upon assuming his position in Dzaukzhikau in August 1946, he soon sent denunciations to the Party leadership about his colleagues in the North Ossetian Autonomous Republic Party committee (*obkom*), and many months later in November 1947, to his chagrin, these complaints were sent back to the North Ossetian *obkom* for consideration. This led to an ugly confrontation with the North Ossetian Party leaders at an *obkom* session, which in turn resulted in a request that Davlianidze receive an official reprimand and that he be removed from his position. This order was confirmed by the central MGB in 1948.

Davlianidze spent the subsequent years sending appeals to high-ranking officials asking to have his case reconsidered and his job, or at least his pension, restored: to Abakumov, then to Beria, and later to Bulganin and Khrushchev. Following his conflict with Rapava in 1945, however, nobody in the Beria group was willing to stand up for him, and his appeals to other elites fell on deaf ears, and even had negative results: in 1951 the half-pension that he had managed to obtain (still a huge sum of 4,350 rubles per month) was cancelled again, and in July 1953 he was stripped of his general-major rank for "behaviour discrediting the high rank of leadership of the MGB."[23] Following the arrest of Beria, Davlianidze was summoned to Moscow to serve as a witness in the trials of Beria, Goglidze, and Kobulov in December 1953, and in that of his formal colleagues K.S. Savitskii, N.A. Krimian, A.S. Khazan, and G.I. Paramanov in May 1954. Several of the accused and also the witnesses in these trials gave testimony that incriminated Davlianidze. In July 1956, while working as the director of a grocery store in Tbilisi, Davlianidze was arrested and a case was brought against him by the procurator's office of the Transcaucasus Military District on charges of counter-revolutionary activity for his actions in the NKVD during the Terror and afterwards.

The Trial

Sergo Davlianidze was brought to trial in Tbilisi in October 1957 on charges of counter-revolution (Articles 58–7 and 58–8). While unlike in several other Soviet republics no trials of NKVD officials took place in the Georgian SSR during the "Beria thaw" in 1939–41 – as Georgia was a centre for Beria's NKVD network, which was the clear beneficiary of this purge of the clientele of the former NKVD head Nikolai Ezhov – several such trials of mid- and lower-level investigators in addition to that of Davlianidze took place in Tbilisi in 1957, following the trials and executions of the more prominent Beria clients in 1954–5. The sessions were held in the theatre of the House of Railway Workers, and while not publicized or reported in the press they were not entirely secret, and seem to have been widely discussed among Tbilisi society. It is not clear how many such trials there were, the case files for several are held in the Georgian KGB archive, but others may have been sent to Moscow. Most likely these trials, like those of 1954–5, were held primarily in order to display the evils of Beria and to demonstratively scapegoat and weed out residual elements of the former Beria network; it is also possible that, like the trials of NKVD officials of 1939–41, these had the symbolic and pedagogical goals of demonstrating to the community of secret police officials themselves that things were now fundamentally different and there would be no return to the methods of the past.[24] The indictment of Davlianidze took more than a year to prepare, and it included twenty-four volumes of supporting documentation and depositions of witnesses. He was accused of undermining the economic power of the Soviet state and terroristic counter-revolutionary activity in the interests of the capitalist countries, in collaboration with the already convicted group of Beria, Kobulov, Goglidze, and their henchmen:

> With the goals of the destruction of cadres who were honest and devoted to the Communist Party and to Soviet power, the plotters, through mass arrests of innocent people, beat and tortured them. Obtaining clearly false

confessions of state crimes and forcing arrestees to denounce other innocent people, the plotters implemented terroristic annihilations of honest Soviet people under the guise of sentencing them for counter-revolutionary activity.... For implementing these criminal schemes against the Soviet state and people, Beria and his henchmen specially recruited from among the hostile elements those individuals and careerists for whom the interests of the people were alien.[25]

In the course of the investigation of this case it has been concluded that: "In carrying out the hostile plots of Beria, Goglidze and Kobulov, those condemned betrayers of the Motherland, flouting and flagrantly violating the laws of the Soviet state, DAVLIANIDZE committed a number of serious crimes against the Soviet people."[26] Nineteen witnesses gave testimony in person during the three-week hearing, including some of Davlianidze's former colleagues and subordinates, as well as some of the victims. He was represented by a lawyer, and both he and his lawyer were allowed to challenge statements of the prosecution and ask questions of the witnesses. A number of other witnesses, including some of Davlianidze's colleagues against whom he had testified and who had already been condemned to death, such as A.S. Khazan, N.A. Krimian, and A.N. Rapava, gave depositions beforehand that were included in the indictment and read out during the trial.

The prosecution went through each of the cases outlined in the indictment and argued that Davlianidze falsified cases, conducted arrests without proper evidence and procedure, used illegal violent means to extract confessions, and signed false indictments that led to the sentencing of 456 people (including 156 Communist Party members), 222 of whom received the death penalty.[27] Davlianidze was painted, in the testimony of Krimian, as an active figure in the purges in Georgia: "In the period 1936–1938 DAVLIANIDZE was one of the cruelest investigators, active, most of all, in regional cases. Wherever in the regions there had been few arrests, usually DAVLIANIDZE turned up to 'introduce order.'"[28] A former secretary in the 4th Department, Milova, testified that: "DAVLIANIDZE, as head of the secret political department (4th) of the NKVD GSSR personally conducted investigations on cases, and also frequently went around to the offices of other investigators where interrogations were going on. And when DAVLIANIDZE participated in an interrogation with other investigators or interrogated arrestees himself in his office, the from all of these rooms where interrogations where taking place one could hear the screams of the arrestees who were subject to repressions."[29]

Davlianidze was held responsible for abuses in cases involving a supposed counter-revolutionary centre among students at the technical university, for the repression of spouses of convicted "enemies of the people," for fabricating cases in the Georgian districts of Gori, Upper and Lower Svaneti, and the village of Mukino, and also during his time in the Transcaucasian and Ordzhonikidze railroads. In nearly all of these cases, Davlianidze signed arrest orders and indictments or wrote resolutions supporting the orders of his subordinates. In several of the cases he was accused of beating arrestees himself or of giving such orders.

The prosecution also characterized Davlianidze as an unprincipled careerist and intriguer who made ample use of his ties to Beria and Beria's clients Kobulov, Goglidze, and Rapava. Davlianidze's former subordinate A.G. Galavanov stated that "DAVLIANIDZE was considered a troublemaker and a schemer (*sklochnik i intrigan*). Therefore we did not much care for him, though he was always on good terms with the leadership."[30] Another colleague testified that Davlianidze "obviously suffered from conceitedness."[31] His former NKVD subordinate, Davit Urushadze, stated that "Davlianidze was quiet and coarse, or maybe it was just his unpleasant face ... many people were afraid of him because he was rude to his staff. He wrote denunciations [*klyauzy*] to Moscow on everybody and through this he aimed for advancement. He was rude with colleagues and was always gloomy, sullen and pretentious, especially when we went to see him in his office."[32] Thus Davlinidze was, the prosecution argued, a conniving careerist who in order to impress his bosses Beria, Kobulov, and Goglidze and thus advance his career misused his position during the Terror to falsify cases and illegally gain confessions and denunciations, resulting in the execution and imprisonment of hundreds of innocent Soviet citizens and Party members.

Questions of Procedure

The Davlianidze case files offer a window into the institutional climate of the Soviet secret police at the height of the Terror. The trial in particular brought to light admissions from Davlianidze and other witnesses about common procedural violations that were rampant. One of these was arrests that were carried out prior to receiving the sanction of the procurator, or of interrogations proceeding before such arrest orders or indictments were filled out.[33] Another was the after-the-fact compiling of interrogation protocols. According to the rules, investigators were to keep a handwritten transcript of the questions and responses, which would then be signed by both the investigator and the arrestee, and then typed and formally signed. When the procurators at Davlianidze's trial inquired as to why there were no originals of the protocols in the archival case files, Davlianidze and other witnesses admitted that during this period, supposedly due to time constraints, investigators would simply take notes (which were later discarded) and dictate the protocols directly to the typists.[34] In reality, investigators often simply prepared the protocols according to their own whims, including accusations against anybody for anything that they wanted.[35] Investigators would then try to beat the arrestees until they agreed to sign the pre-prepared protocols. One former NKVD colleague testified that supposed plots to assassinate Beria and the top NKVD leadership were popular with the leadership, so investigators tried to include such admissions in the protocols as often as possible.[36] As L.F. Tsanava testified in 1953: "Terror against Beria became so fashionable that it was preferred to have admissions by arrestees in every case of preparing a terrorist act against Beria.… The arrestees said what Kobulov wanted them to, and he would summon his assistants, Krimian, Khazan, Savitskii and Paramonov and others, and divide up among them which confessions each arrestee should give and they set to work. They beat the arrestees until they gave the confessions that Kobulov needed."[37]

In many cases, again in violation of procedure, the arrestees were not allowed to read the protocols that they were forced to sign, and in some cases arrestees who did not speak Russian were not provided with translations and were told that what was being written down was "none of your business!"[38] Another, and similar, procedural violation that Davlianidze admitted to during the course of the trial was the inappropriate use of what he called the "album system" of compiling material, in which investigators gathered materials together in forms (*spravki*) listing the accusations and sentencing that were then sent in combined lists to a higher authority for final approval.[39] All of these practices comprised what Davlianidze and others referred to as the "simplified method" of investigation that was used in the NKVD, particularly from 1937.[40] Another violation of procedure that came up several times during the trial was that of "breaking up cases," in which investigators started new cases on individuals arrested or incriminated in other cases, or in so-called group cases.[41] According to Davlianidze's former NKVD subordinate Aslanikashvili, this made it easier for investigators to falsify cases, to increase the amount of testimony, as well as the apparent number of cases that they handled.[42]

The General's Defence

Throughout his testimony in the initial deposition, in responses to questions and challenges during the trial, and in the thirty-two-page handwritten "last word" that he was allowed to read out at the conclusion of the trial and to have included in the official record, Davlianidze, like so many of the defendants at Nuremberg as well as his fellow NKVD perpetrators, claimed to be a cog in the machine who was compelled to blindly follow orders. The core of Davlianidze's defence was that in nearly all of the cases brought up against him he was acting on the instructions of Kobulov, Goglidze, and Beria, that he was unaware of their supposedly counter-revolutionary agenda, that he rarely personally used violence or ordered his subordinates to do so (and in those cases when he did, he was only acting on instructions from above), and that he did not himself fabricate evidence, make the decisions to bring cases, carry out arrests, or have the ability to influence sentencing. He had no intention to cause harm, he argued, and no reason to do so. Those witnesses who testified that he exceeded his authority and used violence were dissembling, motivated by personal animosity towards him. He did not create the system in which he found himself, and even if he had understood at the time the illegality of what he was being ordered to do, he would not have been able to change that system or to refuse to implement those orders:

> I am not to blame for the fact that it fell to me to work in these organs in the period when, for over a quarter of a century, they were headed one after another by those who were exposed of committing every imaginable wrongdoing – Yezhov, Beria, Merkulov, Abakumov and others – whom I recognized as leaders and bosses and who were confirmed in their positions by the leadership of the CPSU and the Soviet government. They had the right to oversee, set up or introduce changes in the system, methods and forms of work in the organs. They had the right to give orders, instructions and commands, and I as an official, dependent in service on them, was bound to fulfill these orders and was subordinate to the arrangement of work that they created in the organs.[43]

Davlianidze steadfastly refused to admit that violence was used by the NKVD in interrogations prior to 1936. Soon after Davlianidze's appointment as 4th Department Deputy Head, Georgian First Secretary Beria held an official session for the NKVD leadership in the building of the Georgian Central Committee in late July or early August 1937 at which "the leadership of the organs introduced into use illegal measures of physical force on arrestees" accused of state crimes, although in Davlianidze's understanding "sanction for the use of illegal measures on arrestees by officials of the organs in each specific case" was required from the Party and NKVD leadership[44]: "The beating of arrestees started in July–August 1937, but not in 1936. I remember at a session of the Georgian Central Committee, where also Khazan, Krimian, Savitskii, and the [NKVD heads] of the autonomous republics were present, Beria read out a directive from the leadership in Moscow on using repression towards arrestees for state crimes. On the basis of this, Goglidze and Kobulov gave written instructions on beating arrestees."[45] Davlianidze based the concluding argument of his trial around these points: "I bear responsibility for the fact that I illegally arrested people, but I thought that I was fulfilling the instructions of the Party and the Government. It was impossible to protest against this order of things, and even members of the government did not say anything about this at the time."[46] Davlianidze's lawyer summed things up in a similar manner: "It is necessary to consider the situation of that time, the criminal situation of conducting investigations. In the defendant's action there was no goal of overthrowing Soviet power, no evidence that he conspired with Beria and his henchmen, and there were no counter-revolutionary motives in his actions."[47] While claiming to be only a "blind instrument" in the illegality of the period, Davlianidze also appealed to the court by claiming that the "unmasking" of Beria in 1953 and the de-Stalinization campaign and critique of the "Cult of Personality" begun in the Party by First Secretary Nikita Khrushchev during the XXth Party Congress in February 1956 had made him understand that the system in the organs during the Stalin period had been unlawful:

> Until the unmasking in 1953 of the provocateur Beria and his henchmen, I did not know anything about [the unlawfulness] and could not have recognized it. The degree of my guilt, as a member of the CPSU and former official of the organs of the NKVD-MGB, I understood only after I became acquainted with the materials of the 20th Party Congress. [During the Stalin period] I did not realize all of this as an implementer, and even if I had understood, I would not have been able to exert any influence, I could not have changed anything. What is more, nobody would have believed me and I would only have become subject to criminal and party responsibility for not fulfilling orders and instructions of the NKVD-MGB and also the decisions of the Central Committee and former leadership of the USSR.[48]

Davlianidze had no previous legal education or preparation prior to his police career, he argued: "In 1952 I started studying law on my own, and from that moment I was floored [*byl podkovannym*] – before this the people in working in the organs did not have a legal education, but were connected with working with informers [*agenturnaia rabota*]."[49]

Stalinist Subjectivity in the NKVD

In addition to his arguments that he merely fulfilled orders from above, was ignorant of the illegality of those orders, and would have been unable to refuse or do anything about the existing system if he had understood this illegality, Davlianidze also made an appeal to the mentality (or "spirit") of the times within the NKVD and in Soviet society in the Stalinist period as a whole, an appeal to what has more recently been characterized as "Stalinist subjectivity."[50] This "subjectivity" approach emphasizes intentions and motivations to action in the historical context of Stalinist society: the ways in which the regime incorporated the population through policies of social identification and mobilization on the one hand, and the ways in which the population "internalized" the discourse of the regime on the other. Scholars of Stalinist subjectivity have emphasized the use of unpublished memoirs and diaries as a means to get at people's inner thoughts, which are obviously very different kinds of sources than transcripts in a trial. Yet even though Davlianidze's statements and appeals were intended for specific audiences and specific (and self-serving) purposes, one nevertheless gets the sense that his belief in the Stalinist discourse of internal and external enemies was both genuine and actually ongoing. Given the exigencies of the time, Davlianidze argued, he believed in the urgency of the struggle with "class enemies" and their agents and that his orders were correct and morally justified:[51]

> As measures dictated by the spirit of the times and its demands, in connection with the critical situation for the USSR both domestically and internationally and the nearness of war of the capitalist country against the USSR, neither I nor others at that time had any basis at all not to believe in the leadership.[52]
>
> I was fulfilling the orders of the Central Committee of the Communist Party of Georgia and of Moscow and the People's Commissar of the Georgian SSR. *Such was the music, so such was the dance* [italics added for emphasis].[53]

The authority of the Party and NKVD leadership, together with the constant and all-embracing campaigns against enemies and wreckers, created a situation in which an average person could not help but subject oneself to the dominant narrative: "Former People's Commissar Ezhov was 2nd Secretary of the Central Committee of the CPSU and we believed in him. There were orders from Ezhov to use force, and I, like everybody else, was under an imaginary psychosis [*pod mnimym psikozom*]. Now, of course, I view everything through different eyes. But then all the instruction manuals, literature, newspapers and articles screamed of counter-revolution, and through this they made us into obedient automatons."[54] The all-encompassing and ceaseless nature of the regime's discourse in this period of danger, external and internal threat, conspiracy, and paranoia suggest that there is more to this for Davlianidze than simply an instrumental argument for self-justification. This discourse seems to have fundamentally shaped Davlianidze's categories of thinking and his view of reality, and that it would have been very difficult, if not impossible, for somebody like Davlianidze in this situation to think outside of the official discourse (no matter how much he was by nature a cynical, self-aggrandizing, and fundamentally corrupt individual). And even though he did make this argument in his own defence in spoken testimony and in written appeals addressed to the authority of the court and the state and Party in a manner that is inherently self-interested, one gets the sense from his statements – such as continuing to refer to rehabilitated victims as enemies and to class background as objective bases for guilt – that his world view at the time of the trial twenty years later was still inherently Stalinist.

Davlianidze's Guilt

While Davlianidze consistently maintained that he was innocent of counter-revolutionary intentions and insisted that he only followed orders from above, during the trial a number of witnesses contradicted his claims to not have beaten arrestees or have given such orders. Some stated that he personally struck, slapped, or pistol whipped them during interrogations.[55] Davlianidze himself admitted to using violence, on orders directly from Moscow, on three Russian engineers arrested in Upper Svaneti,[56] and his former colleague Krimian testified that Davlianidze was "known for particular enthusiasm for beating arrestees."[57] During an interrogation he conducted while serving in the Transport Department the Transcaucasus Railroad, he told the detainee that "As far as you're concerned, I'm the court and the tribunal and I'll do whatever I want with you."[58] Other former colleagues held that Davlianidze had given them oral instructions to beat victims,[59] and one testified that Davlianidze exhorted him, "You haven't beaten [the arrestee] enough, beat him to the end!"[60] Davlianidze admitted at several points to indicating "interrogate robustly" ("*Krepko doprosit'*") in instructions. In his testimony in court, he insisted that to his mind this meant "interrogate thoroughly." Several of his former subordinates (Galavanov and Lazerev) contradicted him, however, and stated that they understood this to mean using violence and that all their colleagues understood it in this way.[61] It did not help Davlianidze's position that in his own deposition prior to the trial, when attributing the phrase to other former investigators, he himself stated that "'to interrogate robustly' meant to beat the arrestee."[62] By the end of the trial, Davlianidze finally admitted using physical force on a number of occasions.[63] More fundamentally, though, Davlianidze was compelled to admit negligence and carelessness in signing dozens of arrest orders and indictments without having sufficient evidence, admitting that "My mistake was that I signed indictments on cases that were not thoroughly investigated,"[64] and "I am guilty of giving consent to the indictment without sufficient incriminating material."[65]

A disagreement emerged during the trial over the role of the NKVD officials who conducted investigations and reported cases to the special tribunals that made the decisions on sentencing, the three-man so-called *troikas*, which usually included a procurator, a Party official, and an NKVD representative. Davlianidze and some of his other former NKVD colleagues argued that these troikas did not consult with the investigators in making their decisions or ask for their opinions about the cases.[66] In the deposition of former Georgian NKVD head A.N. Rapava, however, that was used in Davlianidze's trial (Rapava himself had chaired a number of troikas), it was stated that "First we asked the opinion of the investigator reporting the case, and then one of the members of the troika would suggest something. Sometimes I suggested something first."[67] This directly called into question Davlianidze's assertions of innocence of the final decisions on the hundreds of cases that he had endorsed, and the fact that he had signed so many orders or approvals for arrests and investigations could not have failed to play a role in swaying the opinion of the court and showed that he had much more authority to make decisions in his position than he acknowledged during the trial.

In the end, on 31 October 1957, Davlianidze was found guilty on all counts and sentenced to twenty-five years in the Dubravnyi Corrective Labor Camp with confiscation of property and removal of all state awards and titles. He died nearly ten years later, in August 1967, while incarcerated in the Mordovan Autonomous Republic.

Conclusions

Based on the case documents, the portrait of Davlianidze that emerges is not one of a good person: he comes across as conniving, vain, self-serving, sometimes arrogant, highly suspicious, and often vindictive. He was rude to his subordinates and quick to inform on his colleagues (likely assuming that they would do the same to him). In this way he was perhaps a typical Soviet citizen of the Stalinist period. And while witnesses and colleagues repeatedly characterize him as a schemer and intriguer, they refrained from calling him a sadist or a psychopath, characterizations that frequently came up in connection with Davlianidze's rivals Khazan, Krimian, and Savitskii.[68]

Thresholds to Violence

Although there were cases in which Davlinidze apparently misused his position and exceeded his authority earlier in his career, his exposure to extreme violence seems to have begun only from 1937 during the Great Terror. At various times he claimed to have seen action in the Civil War in 1919 and in putting down the anti-Soviet uprising in August 1924, though this seems rather dubious, and even if true such experiences do not come across as formative. Life in Georgia was comparably peaceful during the period in comparison with other parts of the former Russian Empire. Thus, perhaps unlike his NKVD colleagues in Russia and elsewhere in the USSR, Davlianidze seems to have experienced little or even none of the violence of the period of the Great War, the revolutions of 1917 and the Russian Civil War.[69] Lynne Viola's argument of conditioning in an "ecosystem of violence" seems not to apply in Davlianidze's case. Upon being transferred from his peripheral post in Chiatura to the centre of NKVD activity in the purges in the 4th Department in the summer of 1937, Davlianidze seems to have been unaware (and perhaps even surprised) by the new policy of using violent means of interrogation on detainees to extract confessions and denunciations and using information extracted in this way as the sole basis for convictions and further arrests. He initially denounced his colleagues Khazan, Krimian, and Savitskii to Georgian NKVD head Goglidze for such methods,[70] and only after the address by Beria to the secret police instructing them to use these methods does he understand the "signal" and start using them himself.[71]

What we see here is perhaps the need for this violent behaviour to be "modelled" and thus normalized within the institutional context of the NKVD. In the same way that sociological theories about crowd violence suggest that riots may begin with the actions of a very small number of individuals, gradually through observation and imitation such behaviour becomes normalized and thus more acceptable to more individuals in the group, and the thresholds to previously unacceptable behaviour become reduced. For example, to be the first person in a mob to throw a rock is a very different thing from being the thirty-first. Cases of mass state violence in this sense may resemble the dynamics of crowd violence in slow motion, with the larger number of average perpetrators taking cues from the behaviour modelling from those fewer individuals with far lower thresholds to violence.[72]

Institutional Environment

The environment of the institutions in which state violence takes place is certainly also crucial. Once becoming accustomed to the new situation in the Georgian NKVD in the summer of 1937, Davlianidze seems to have quickly become acculturated and to flourish. His penchant for paranoia, suspicion, and denunciation had found an ideal milieu. The institutional environment within the Georgian NKVD created its own inertia. Protected by patronage ties to the leadership of the "organs" and of the Party and by the authority given by that leadership, the investigators were imbued with a feeling of empowerment together with an absence of any sense of transparency or accountability. The mutual rivalry and suspicion of one another, combined with the fact that such behaviour was the criteria on which they were evaluated, encouraged the investigators to do everything they could to facilitate more and more arrests and obtain more confessions, and to use whatever methods and shortcuts in procedure necessary in doing so. To this must be added the fact that Davlianidze and his contemporaries lacked exposure to conceptions of the "rule of law," even in its interpretation via "socialist legality." As Davlianidze argued during the trial, he and his colleagues had no legal background or education, and it was only later in his life that he began to think about such concepts.[73] Yet while Davlianidze did not shy away from using violent measures, unlike Beria or some of his other colleagues it seems that he did not go out of his way to beat or torture detainees or to take particular pleasure in it, preferring instead to sign orders and assign such tasks to his subordinates. Whether or not these investigators actually suffered from mental illnesses, it does seem that they went out of their way to create reputations for themselves as psychotics and fanatics, perhaps for entirely rational purposes of self-preservation and advancement within the NKVD of the period.[74] Within the rapidly changing institutional context of the Georgian NKVD in 1937 the investigators learned very quickly what behaviour was rewarded and what was sanctioned in a situation of constant mutual suspicion and paranoia. German Einsatzgruppen perpetrators often argued that they had to commit violence lest they become victims themselves. Yet their defence was never able to present any such cases of this happening. In the Stalinist NKVD, however, operatives seem to fear very legitimately that expressions of softness could be grounds for arrest and punishment for subversion and sabotage.

Nevertheless, Davlianidze clearly thrived in this atmosphere, and the period of the Great Terror and the Great Patriotic War were the peak of his career. His performance earlier had been mediocre at best, and his continued denunciations and paranoia about his colleagues and subordinates after 1945, when the political conditions had begun to change, led to the unravelling of his career and his eventual sacking. Those very tendencies that served him so well during the purges became a liability during the period afterwards.[75] Working successfully as an NKVD official brought promotion to the rank of general-major, a slew of medals, and a good apartment at a prestigious address in Tbilisi. Davlianidze, like most of his colleagues in the Georgian NKVD, were outsiders to the Georgian capital, with little education, family connections, prestige, or other forms of social capital and were looked down upon by the urban elite, causing resentment in return. This most dangerous imbalance of great power and low esteem, together with the lack of accountability, most likely also contributed to the zeal with which the NKVD investigators dealt with the formerly high-ranking Georgian Party officials and their spouses and also the university and institute students and faculty that made up a significant proportion of the victims.[76]

Ideology and Stalinist Subjectivity

This sense of suspicion and paranoia prevalent in the Georgian NKVD can only have been reinforced by the "discursive" element, the internalization of the unremittingly propagated ideology of class struggle and the fear and threat of counter-revolutionary enemy activity and wrecking. In 1937, every radio receiver, newspaper headline, and street banner in the USSR screamed relentlessly of the omnipresent danger of wrecking and sabotage and called for vigilance and firmness. As the "sword and shield" of the Party and state, the staff of the NKVD viewed themselves as the last line of defence of society and of the ideals of the Revolution against dehumanized enemies of the people. The investigators seem to have deeply internalized this rhetoric, accepting that these threats were genuine, that the situation was truly critical, and that the conspiracies and crimes to which their victims confessed were all too real. Although Davlianidze claimed at various points in his trial to have come to a new understanding of the illegality of the NKVD's methods, a number of his comments suggest that he still considered many of his victims to be guilty and to have deserved their punishment. He was often contemptuous of them, and at several points during the trial had to be reminded that arrestees whom he referred to as enemies had in fact been formally rehabilitated.[77] He also asserted as a statement of objective fact that the basis for his mutual animosity regarding certain of his colleagues was rooted in class essence (as they came from unreliable class backgrounds).[78]

There are clearly objections to the "subjectivist" argument in its more extreme forms, those holding that the discourse of the party-state created an inescapable world view encompassing all of the Stalinist subjects.[79] Yet the subjectivist approach may be particularly useful in understanding the NKVD perpetrators, who seem to have deeply internalized the official rhetoric, all the more so when that discourse often coincided with the institutional milieu and peer relations among them, and with their own self-interest. The fact of perpetration of violence in itself may add additional impulse to this internalization: once one has committed previously unthinkable acts of violence in the name of particular rhetoric, one has an even greater need to internalize the rhetoric that necessitates and justifies the behaviour.

Ultimately in Davlianidze, perhaps like as with many others of his fellow secret police perpetrators of the Stalin period, we see a combination of motivations: acculturation to the institutional environment in the NKVD; peer pressure, anxiety, and ambition in the competition with his colleagues and rivals to produce the results that brought reward and recognition from the bosses; satisfaction in the power and authority that they derived from their position and power; belief that what they were doing was correct and ultimately morally justified; ignorance of the illegality (and ultimate futility) of the methods they were using and of the concept of legality itself, making it impossible to imagine that they would one day be prosecuted for their actions by the same party-state that ordered and encouraged them to undertake these actions; and an internalization of the regime discourse of ever-present danger of counter-revolutionary subversion and wrecking and the urgent need to act decisively against that threat in order to maintain control over society, a discourse that the investigators needed to internalize all the more strongly once they had begun perpetrating previously unthinkable acts of violence in the name of it. This was likely further amplified by the demands and rewards of the camaraderie among the investigators in the institutional environment of the Georgian NKVD.

The basis of the charges of counter-revolution and anti-Soviet activity brought against Davlianidze and the other NKVD perpetrators in the 1950s trials in Georgia obscured the essential goal of the proceedings. Rather than recognize that that the causes of the crimes of the Great Terror and the Stalin era more generally lay in the authoritarian party-state system and the inherent absence of rule of law, the prosecution had to frame their accusations around the malicious intent and misdeeds of those guilty of perverting the Leninist system, which in post-de-stalinization Georgia meant "the condemned provocateur Beria and his henchmen." Davlianidze and the others were formally charged with counter-revolution by being accomplices in Beria's plots to undermine the Soviet state and economy, yet despite the specific articles of the indictment, the thrust of the prosecution's case was not counter-revolutionary intentions or involvement in conspiracy, but wilful and knowing violation of laws and procedures. Ultimately perhaps what the procurators were seeking to demonstrate was not so much what the perpetrators did, but the zeal with which they did it. There were almost always general or specific orders from superiors (in this case, from Kobulov, Goglidze, and Beria), so therefore the prosecution aimed to demonstrate that the accused was worse than a lawbreaker, he was a bad person and a harmful element, and for this they needed to show vigour, enthusiasm, and viciousness in carrying out those orders. Davlianidze could rightly argue that he was unaware of any conspiracies, that he was not as directly linked to Beria and his network as some of his colleagues had been, and that his intentions had never been counter-revolutionary. One can sense the inevitable frustration of Davlianidze and his fellow perpetrators with the paradox of the situation in which they were being tried and punished for those very crimes that they had earlier been encouraged to commit by that very same authority. In testimony included in the Davlianidze case, Khazan expressed this paradox directly: "[The order to use repressive methods] put me and all of the NKVD personnel into a terrible position. In 1937 the NKVD leadership made it mandatory, as they told us, to beat arrestees on the orders of the higher organs. To refuse this was seen as enemy counter-revolutionary work, and now, after many years, for the implementation of this very directive, you are accused of counter-revolutionary crime."[80]

Finally, though, despite vociferously denying the official changes to the end, Davlianidze was reluctantly forced to admit being guilty of those things for which he was tacitly being prosecuted, of negligence in conducting cases and signing orders, leading to the baseless sentencing and execution of hundreds of innocent people. As with the stories of "ordinary men"[81] among the perpetrators of other acts of mass violence in a variety of different historical settings, the case of Davlianidze hints at an unsettling aspect of human nature. In situations, such as those Davlianidze found himself, where violence is enabled by contextual conditions, encouraged by a lowering of thresholds to violence, and justified by a prevailing ideology, many people, perhaps a majority, seem to go along with such violence and unquestioningly do what they feel is expected of them.

NOTES

1 An earlier and longer version of this chapter was published in Russian as "'Kakova byla muzyka, takov byl i tanets.' Delo Sergo Semenovicha Davlianidze," in *Chekisty na skam'e podsudimykh. Sbornik statei*, ed. Marc Junge, Lynne Viola, and Jeffrey Rossman (Moscow: Probel-2000, 2017), 631–61.
2 Lynne Viola, "The Question of the Perpetrator in Soviet History," *Slavic Review* 72, no. 1 (2013): 1–23; Alexander Vatlin, *Agents of Terror: Ordinary Men and Extraordinary Violence in Stalin's Secret Police* (Madison: University of Wisconsin Press, 2016); Marc Junge, Lynne Viola, and Jeffrey Rossman, eds., *Chekisty na skam'e podsudimykh*; and Lynne Viola, *Stalinist Perpetrators on Trial: Scenes from the Great Terror in Soviet Ukraine* (Oxford: Oxford University Press, 2017). For a recent review of this literature, see Oleg Khlevniuk, "Archives of the Terror: Developments in the Historiography of Stalin's Purges," *Kritika* 22, no. 2 (2021): 367–85. Most of these works focus on the trials of *chekisty* for "violations of socialist legality" that took place in 1939–41 after Beria's elevation to the head of the USSR NKVD. So such trials were held in the Georgian SSR at that time. See also Marc Junge, *Chekisty Stalina: moshch' i bessilie* (Moscow: AIRO-XXI, 2017), 240–5.
3 The archive of the former Georgian KGB is now formerly referred to as sakartvelos shinagan sakmeta saministro (shss) arkivi (I) [Section I of the Archive of the Ministry of Internal Affairs of Georgia], from here on sak'art'velos šss ark'ivi (I).
4 See in particular Viola, "The Question of the Perpetrator," 21.
5 Viola, "The Question of the Perpetrator," 22.
6 sak'art'velos šss ark'ivi (I) 6/4643–58/24/21/244.
7 sak'art'velos šss ark'ivi (I) 6/4643–58/24/1/98.
8 sak'art'velos šss ark'ivi (I) 6/4643–58/24,1/95.
9 sak'art'velos šss ark'ivi (I) 6/4643–58/24/1/206–16.
10 sak'art'velos šss ark'ivi (I) 6/4643–58/24/1/97.

11 sak'art'velos šss ark'ivi (I) 6/4643–58/24/1/228–31.
12 sak'art'velos šss ark'ivi (I) 6/4643–58/24/1/232. Also see S.O. Gazaryan, *Eto ne dolzhno povtorit'sia (Dokumental'naia povest'* (Yerevan: Literaturnaia Armeniia, 1988), 22.
13 For a recent reassessment of this conflict between the Georgian and Transcaucasian NKVD, see Timothy Blauvelt, "Between Modernity and Neo-Tradition: Patronage Politics and Bacteriophage Research in Interwar Soviet Georgia," *Euxeinos. Culture and Governance in the Black Sea Region* 12, no. 34 (2022): 90–114.
14 *Kontrrazvedyvatel'nyi slovar* (Moscow: Feliks Dzherzhinskii Higher School, 1972).
15 sak'art'velos šss ark'ivi (I) 6/4643–58/24/1, 3–7.
16 sak'art'velos šss ark'ivi (I) 6/4643–58/24/18/98; 6/4643–58/24/21/62.
17 For more on Beria's rise from the secret police to the heights of the Party leadership in Georgia and the Transcaucasus, together with a cohort of secret police clients, see Timothy Blauvelt, "March of the Chekists: Beria's Secret Police Patronage Network and Soviet Crypto-Politics," *Communist and Post-Communist Studies* 44, no. 1 (2011): 73–8. The extent of overlap of personnel between the Party and the NKVD in Georgia made the republic rather unique in the USSR during the Stalin period.
18 sak'art'velos šss ark'ivi (I) 6/4643–58/24/18/74.
19 Beria himself lived in this building when he was head of the secret police in Georgia and prior to becoming Party chief there.
20 sak'art'velos šss ark'ivi (I) 6/4643–58/24/1/181.
21 sak'art'velos šss ark'ivi (I) 6/4643–58/24/1/203.
22 sak'art'velos šss ark'ivi (I) 6/4643–58/24/1/201–2.
23 sak'art'velos šss ark'ivi (I) 6/4643–58/24/1/204.
24 On the 1939–41 trials, see Junge, *Chekisty Stalina*, 223–8, and Viola, *Stalinist Perpetrators on Trial*, 166–9; on the 1954–5 trials, see Timothy Blauvelt and Davit Jishkariani, "Contextualizing the Stalinist Perpetrators: The Case of NKVD Investigators Khazan, Savitskii and Krimian," with Davit Jishkariani, in *Political Police and the Soviet System (Kritika Historical Series)*, ed. Michael David-Fox and Philip Kiffer (Pittsburgh: University of Pittsburgh Press, forthcoming 2023).
25 sak'art'velos šss ark'ivi (I) 6/4643–58/24/18/70.
26 sak'art'velos šss ark'ivi (I) 6/4643–58/24/18/71.
27 sak'art'velos šss ark'ivi (I) 6/4643–58/24/18/73.
28 sak'art'velos šss ark'ivi (I) 6/4643–58/24/18/71.
29 sak'art'velos šss ark'ivi (I) 6/4643–58/24/18/72.
30 sak'art'velos šss ark'ivi (I) 6/4643–58/24/18/72.
31 sak'art'velos šss ark'ivi (I) 6/4643–58/24/21/62.
32 sak'art'velos šss ark'ivi (I) 6/4643–58/24/21/98.

33 sak'art'velos šss ark'ivi (I) 6/4643–58/24/21/259; Viola, *Stalinist Perpetrators on Trial*, 54. From July 1937 to November 1938 the requirement for such sanction was suspended on the order of procurator A. Vyshinskii.
34 sak'art'velos šss ark'ivi (I) 6/4643–58/24/21/69.
35 sak'art'velos šss ark'ivi (I) 6/4643–58/24/21/108; 6/4643–58/24/1/12.
36 Testimony of K.S. Savitskii, in "Zapiska R.A. Rudenko v TsK KPSS s prilozheniem obvinitel'nogo zakliucheniia po delu sledovatelei NKVD Gruzinskoi SSR. 25 maia 1954 g.," RGASPI 17, o. 171/474/148–96, published in V.N. Khaustov, ed., *Delo Beriia. Prigobor obzhalovaniiu ne podlezhit* (Moscow: MFD, 2012), 463.
37 Testimony of Tsanava, in "Zapiska R.A. Rudenko v TsK KPSS," 465.
38 sak'art'velos šss ark'ivi (I) 6/4643–58/24/21/38.
39 sak'art'velos šss ark'ivi (I) 6/4643–58/24/1/13. See Marc Junge, Omar Tushurashvili, and Bernd Bonwetsch, eds., *Bol'shevitskii poryadok v Gruzii, tom 1: Bol'shoi terror v malen'koi kavkazskoi respublike* (Moscow, 2014), 26, fn. 48.
40 sak'art'velos šss ark'ivi (I) 6/4643–58/24/21/259, sak'art'velos šss ark'ivi (I) 6/4643-58/24/21/64 and 118.
41 sak'art'velos šss ark'ivi (I) 6/4643–58/24/21/40.
42 sak'art'velos šss ark'ivi (I) 6/4643–58/24/21/66.
43 sak'art'velos šss ark'ivi (I) 6/4643–58/24/21/255.
44 sak'art'velos šss ark'ivi (I) 6/4643–58/24/21/259–60.
45 sak'art'velos šss ark'ivi (I) 6/4643–58/24/21/78.
46 sak'art'velos šss ark'ivi (I) 6/4643–58/24/21/238.
47 sak'art'velos šss ark'ivi (I) 6/4643–58/24/21/239.
48 sak'art'velos šss ark'ivi (I) 6/4643–58/24/21/263.
49 sak'art'velos šss ark'ivi (I) 6/4643–58/24/21/40.
50 Stephen Kotkin, *Magnetic Mountain: Stalinism as Civilization* (Berkeley: University of California Press, 1996), 22–3; Jochen Hellbeck, "Speaking Out: Languages of Affirmation and Dissent," in *The Resistance Debate in Russian and Soviet History*, ed. Michael David-Fox, Peter Holquist, and Marshall Poe (Bloomington, IN: Slavica, 2003), 103–37.
51 sak'art'velos šss ark'ivi (I) 6/4643–58/24/21/254.
52 sak'art'velos šss ark'ivi (I) 6/4643–58/24/21/261.
53 sak'art'velos šss ark'ivi (I) 6/4643–58/24/21/197.
54 sak'art'velos šss ark'ivi (I) 6/4643–58/24/21/226–7. Davlianidze's colleague Khazan made a similar statement in early testimony used in Davlianidze's trial: "In 1937 I was inspired by the directives of the Party on struggle against enemies of the people." (sak'art'velos šss ark'ivi (I) 6/4643–58/24/3/32).
55 sak'art'velos šss ark'ivi (I) 6/4643–58/24/21/73 and 157.
56 sak'art'velos šss ark'ivi (I) 6/4643–58/24/21/158.
57 sak'art'velos šss ark'ivi (I) 6/4643–58/24/18/p. 72.

58 sak'art'velos šss ark'ivi (I) 6/4643–58/24/21/200.
59 sak'art'velos šss ark'ivi (I) 6/4643–58/24/21/171–2.
60 sak'art'velos šss ark'ivi (I) 6/4643–58/24/21/87.
61 sak'art'velos šss ark'ivi (I) 6/4643–58/24/21/64 and 106.
62 sak'art'velos šss ark'ivi (I) 6/4643–58/24/1/7.
63 sak'art'velos šss ark'ivi (I) 6/4643–58/24/21/197 and 226.
64 sak'art'velos šss ark'ivi (I) 6/4643–58/24/1/10.
65 sak'art'velos šss ark'ivi (I) 6/4643–58/24/21/79.
66 sak'art'velos šss ark'ivi (I) 6/4643–58/24/21/258; 6/4643–58/24/21/160.
67 sak'art'velos šss ark'ivi (I) 6/4643–58/24/1/131.
68 For example, sak'art'velos šss ark'ivi (I) 6/4643–58/24/16/30.
69 See M. Chikhradze, "Tbilisis kulturuli tskhovreba 1910–1920-ian tselbshi," *amirani* 3 (2000), 85–105; T. Nikol'skaia *Fantasticheskii gorod. Russkaia kul'turnaia zhiznm v Tbilisi (1917–1921)* (Moscow: Piataia strana, 2000); and Harsh Ram, "Modernism on the Periphery: Literary Life in Postrevolutionary Tbilisi," *Kritika* 5, no. 2 (2004): 367–82.
70 sak'art'velos šss ark'ivi (I) 6/4643–58/24/1/73.
71 Khazan in his testimony said that this "signal" had been given by Beria earlier in the year to those NKVD officials working in Tbilisi, following the February–March Party Plenum in Moscow, and that he began using violence from May of that year. (sak'art'velos šss ark'ivi (I) 6/4643–58/24/3/30).
72 Based on social sciences approaches of the 1970s, such as Mark Granovetter, "Threshold Models of Collective Behavior," *American Journal of Sociology* 83, no. 6 (1978): 1420–43, Malcom Gladwell applied this approach to understand the proliferation of school shootings in the United States in an article in *The New Yorker* ("Thresholds of Violence: How School Shootings Catch On," 12 October 2015).
73 sak'art'velos šss ark'ivi (I) 6/4643–58/24/21/58.
74 For a more detailed discussion of this, see Blauvelt and Jishkariani, "Contextualizing the Stalinist Perpetrators."
75 The Davlianidze case also demonstrates how these same factors – the combination of paranoia, distrust, and ambition – allowed (or even encouraged) the purges to enter the NKVD itself, particularly in the Mukino Village affair and that of the NKVD food section, in which NKVD staff were prosecuted, even in the apparent absence of any political rivalry between factions in the Georgian NKVD.
76 For example, the repression of a group of students accused of forming a "Youth Organization" (sak'art'velos šss ark'ivi (I) 6/4643–58/24/18/75–82), of the Director of the Tbilisi Medical Institute K.V. Tsomaia (who died during interrogation) and his subordinates (sak'art'velos šss ark'ivi (I) 6/4643–58/24/18/85), of students and scientific personnel of the Georgian

Industrial Institute (sak'art'velos šss ark'ivi (I) 6/4643–58/24/18/93–5), and of a group of lawyers (sak'art'velos šss ark'ivi (I) 6/4643–58/24/21/121–9).
77 sak'art'velos šss ark'ivi (I) 6/4643–58/24/21/216. During the trial he said: "Now witnesses are taking advantage of the moment and saying anything they think of ... such babbling [*boltovnia*] can only compromise Soviet power ... the victims are trying to lay it on thick [*stremyatsya sgustit' krasku*]," sak'art'velos šss ark'ivi (I) 6/4643–58/24/21/226.
78 sak'art'velos šss ark'ivi (I) 6/4643–58/24/21/43–4; sak'art'velos šss ark'ivi (I) 6/4643-58/24/21/243.
79 For recent critiques of the "subjectivist" approach, see Mark Edele, *Stalinist Society: 1928–1953* (Oxford: Oxford University Press, 2011), 237–8; and *Debates on Stalinism* (Manchester: Manchester University Press, 2020), chapter 7.
80 sak'art'velos šss ark'ivi (I) 6/4643–58/24/3/30.
81 Christopher R. Browning, *Ordinary Men. Reserve Police Battalion 101 and the Final Solution in Poland* (New York: Harper Perennial, 1993).

PART II

Forging Society in War and Peace

5 Soviet "Hard Labour," Population Management, and Social Control in the Post-war Gulag

ALAN BARENBERG

On 20 May 1945, NKVD chief Lavrenttii Beria's deputy Vasilii Chernyshev sent him a memo regarding a proposal to expand the use of "hard labour" (*katorga*) punishment in the Gulag, the vast Soviet system of prisons, camps, and exile settlements. This proposal, forwarded by Central Committee Secretary Nikita Khrushchev, argued that hard labour sentences of fifteen to twenty years ought to be given to a much larger group of criminals, largely because the existing alternatives were unsuitable. According to the proposal, the pre-war maximum sentence of ten years in a camp was not sufficient punishment for many criminals – yet capital punishment was too harsh, and what was more, resulted in the loss of the productive potential of prisoners. Evaluating this proposal, Chernyshev concluded that "the widespread dissemination of this new heavy type of punishment at the end of the victorious war is hardly advisable." As he argued, *katorga* needed to remain as it was, as a particular punishment for a specific subset of criminals.

Chernyshev's response was based around three central points, all of which emphasized both the nature of *katorga* and how difficult it had been to implement as ordered since its introduction in 1943. First, *katorga* was narrowly defined as a punishment for those who had aided the enemy in carrying out reprisals and violence against the civilian population and Red Army prisoners of war (POWs) during the war. As of May 1945, only about 29,000 had been sentenced to hard labour under these terms. Was it advisable to expand it to other categories of criminals? Second, those convicted of *katorga* were in extraordinarily poor health: of these 29,000 convicts, nearly 10,000 were already permanently disabled and unable to work. Third, *katorga* was virtually impossible to implement in Gulag camps. The stipulation that *katorga* convicts be completely isolated from other prisoners had been particularly difficult to enforce – it was simply impossible to run a camp section without including non-*katorga* specialists (either non-prisoners or prisoners sentenced to other forms of punishment). Citing *katorga*'s implementation in Vorkutlag, the camp holding most of these convicts, Chernyshev concluded that hard labour was inefficient – *katorga* convicts "lost the perspective to survive to the end of their sentence" and received no incentives for productive labour. Chernyshev's sobering (and yet overly optimistic) assessment was that all *katorga* convicts would surely be completely disabled within five to six years.[1]

In Chernyshev's memo and the proposal to which it responded, one can see the manifestation of two different principles of population management and social control at work in the Soviet Gulag. On the one hand, the category of the *katorga* convict and Khrushchev's proposal to expand this method of incarceration fit well with Stephen Barnes's characterization of the Gulag as running according to a "hierarchy of detention" that required "the sorting of prisoners into different levels of isolation according to their perceived level of danger for Soviet society and their perceived chances for release."[2] On the other hand, Chernyshev's response largely matches Golfo Alexopoulos's assertion that the sorting of prisoners in the Gulag was "governed not by the perceived danger of prisoners, but by their health ... with the ultimate goal of maximizing production and exploitation."[3] Examining this memo and the debate of which it was a part, this chapter examines the place of *katorga* convicts within the post-war Gulag to better understand Soviet penal policy and techniques of social control. It argues that debates surrounding *katorga* in the post-war reveal the inner workings of the Gulag system and penal policy in important ways. Although the population of *katorga* convicts was never particularly large (at most, approximately 60,000 out of more than two million inmates in Gulag camps and colonies), population management strategies applied to *katorga* convicts reflect ongoing contradictions among the various missions of the Soviet Gulag: to categorize and isolate, to punish, to rehabilitate, and to exploit.[4]

Turning from high-level policy debates to the implementation and administration of *katorga* in the wartime and post-war camp system, additional contradictions between different principles of population management and social control appear. Gulag officials, from the level of the individual camp section up to the central Gulag administration in Moscow, were evaluated by how well they implemented penal policy, often on the basis of quantitative indicators. Thus, they needed to demonstrate that each overriding function of the Gulag was successfully carried out in their particular jurisdiction. The second half of this chapter uses *katorga* convict population data from the camps to evaluate the interplay between the "hierarchy of detention" and the sorting of prisoners by health and productive capacity. As it demonstrates, population management and social control in the wartime and post-war Gulag involved both efforts to control prisoners' bodies and to shape statistics so that they demonstrated successful management. The place of *katorga* convicts in the "hierarchy of detention" fundamentally shaped the management of the convicts themselves and the potential manipulation of the data that was reported about their mortality.

Chernyshev's memo, which was penned three weeks after the USSR declared victory over Germany and its allies in the Second World War, also hints at a broader debate about the fate of pre-war and wartime practices of social control in the post-war era. The end of the Second World War, and the transition from wartime to peacetime, was an important moment for the reconsideration of institutions of social control across the USSR. On the one hand, the state of war had led to a suspension of many of the usual levers of social control and a devolution of some powers from the centre to the localities. On the other hand, extraordinary measures had been introduced to re-establish social control in territories that had been occupied by Germany and its allies. Instituted in 1943 to punish collaborators, *katorga* was one such measure. What can its fate in the post-war tell us about how techniques of social control fared after Soviet victory?

Soviet *Katorga*: A New Form of Punishment?

Soviet *katorga* was established as a form of punishment by USSR Supreme Soviet decree on 19 April 1943. This decree called for perpetrators of crimes against Soviet civilians and Red Army POWs to be tried by field court-martial and, if found guilty, to be punished by hanging in a public place. Additionally, those who collaborated with these perpetrators in crimes against Soviet civilians and Red Army POWs were to be subject to a new form of punishment, "exile to hard labour [*katorga*] for terms from 15 to 20 years."[5] The formulation itself was remarkable in multiple ways. First, the length of sentences was unusually long – although sentences of up to twenty-five years were theoretically allowed, custodial sentences of over ten years were still uncommon until after the war.[6] Second, *katorga* was a term with significant baggage. It was the Soviet term used to describe the conscription of foreign labourers by Germany during the war. It was also the term for a common punishment of the pre-revolutionary era.[7] Soviet penal theorists and officials had generally been careful to draw an absolute distinction between the Soviet and Tsarist penal systems, so the reuse of a term from Tsarist Russia was highly unusual.[8] Finally, the formulation invoked both a fixed sentence and the notion of exile, seemingly mixing punishment for a fixed term in a Gulag camp with the equally widespread, but very different practice of exile, which was generally not for a fixed length of time.

Katorga was intended to be an entirely new form of carceral punishment that stood alongside a term in a "corrective labour camp" (ITL), "corrective labour colony" (ITK), or prison.[9] Although Beria's initial order for the incarceration of *katorga* convicts was not particularly detailed (it was just over a page in length), the document made it clear that they were to be held in existing camps or prisons. However, *katorga* convicts were to be isolated from ordinary prisoners. These convicts were to be held in separate, locked barracks with bars on their windows, supervised by armed guards, and separated from regular prisoners' barracks by a high fence. When travelling to and from work, they were escorted by armed guards. They were required to wear special clothing of a distinct colour with their personal number sewn on their uniform tops. *Katorga* convicts were subjected to labour that was physically harder than that of regular prisoners. They were to be assigned only to hard physical labour and were given a workday that was one hour longer than that established for regular prisoners. Punishment for regime violations was particularly harsh, and convicts were excluded from many incentives for good behaviour. For example, for the first year of their incarceration, these convicts were forbidden from receiving monetary compensation, corresponding with family members, receiving packages, and reading books and newspapers.[10] The overall intent of these measures is obvious: hard labour convicts were, simply put, supposed to be treated more harshly than normal prisoners. They were supposed to work harder, be guarded more closely, and be completely isolated from the world outside the camp, and indeed from regular prisoners. And they were to be physically marked, distinguishing them visually from other prisoners and from non-prisoners. The fact that these prisoners were required to wear their numbers is notable in that it evoked both Nazi practices of tattooing concentration camp prisoners with their numbers and also Imperial Russian practices of physically marking those convicted of *katorga*. Unlike both of those practices, however, this identifying number was not permanently inscribed on the body. Nevertheless, it was a significant departure from existing practices in the Gulag.

Katorga convicts were never particularly numerous. Table 5.1 shows the population of major *katorga* camps and colonies from 1944 to 1949. At the beginning of January 1944 there were approximately 800 in the camp system. At the beginning of January 1945, this had grown to about

Table 5.1. Population of *katorga* camp sections, 1944–9 (January 1)[11]

	Priority			Non-Priority				"Convalescence"		
							OITK	OITK	OITLK	
Year	Norillag	Sevvostlag	Vorkutlag	Angarlag	Karlag	Siblag	Tomskaia *oblast'*	Vologodskaia *oblast'*	Molotovskaia *oblast'*	Total
1944	0	0	494		345					839
1945	662	2,326	9,036	2,196	221	4,490				12,245
1946	5,452	5,601	18,158	1,383	4,676	4,971	5,387	662		40,422
1947	8,172	6,910	24,663	1,258	4,711	4,712	4,822	852	3,804	60,728
1948	8,857	5,455	26,662	2,170	4,264	4,432	3,458	705	2,712	60,359
1949	8,791	5,225	27,339	1,691	5,311			503	2,323	59,023

Sources: GARF R-9414/1 ch. 2/412, 413, 416, 424, 434, 450; GARF R-9414/1/1231, 1232, 1251, 1252, 1278, 1280, 1282, 1283, 1300, 1317, 1318, 1337, 1338.

12,000 convicts. In January 1946, there were approximately 40,000, and in January 1947 there were 60,000. From that point on, the population size stabilized around 60,000 until after Stalin's death. Thus, the size of the *katorga* convict population grew rapidly in 1944 through the end of 1946. Not surprisingly, 1945 was the year that saw the largest increase of the *katorga* convict population in absolute terms, with nearly 30,000 new convicts sent into the system during a single year. At first, *katorga* convicts were, by and large, confined in one of only a few priority camps in the Gulag, each of which was located above the Arctic Circle and primarily engaged in mining: Vorkutlag in Vorkuta, Norillag in Noril'sk, and Sevvostlag in Kolyma. Initially, prisoners who were unable to work (due to illness, disability, or pregnancy) were sent to Karlag in Kazakhstan, which would later be one of three camps set aside for convicts deemed incapable of hard labour, which I refer to throughout this chapter as non-priority.[12] Later, a third set of penal institutions was set aside for convicts who were more seriously ill or weak, designated specifically for their "convalescence" (see below).[13]

Although they were held in camps and prisons, *katorga* convicts were not, strictly speaking, prisoners (*zakliuchennye*). This was part of a broader wartime trend of using Gulag camps to hold and exploit non-prisoner populations. Although never explicitly stated, the apparent reasons for this were two-fold. First, the Gulag camp population fell dramatically at the beginning of the war due to loss of Soviet territory and the large number of prisoners released to fight at the front. The overall health of the remaining prisoners also deteriorated dramatically, meaning that the Gulag had much less labour at its disposal. Second, the camps provided a convenient location to isolate populations that were considered potentially dangerous in the context of the war. Such inmates included forcibly displaced populations from Eastern Poland that were sent to the Soviet interior in the summer of 1940.[14] These "refugees" were followed by a number of other groups sent to camps to be held indefinitely during the Nazi–Soviet war: Soviet ethnic Germans mobilized for forced labour from their places of exile, former Soviet POWs freed from captivity but then subjected to forced labour in Soviet camps, and also Soviet citizens who lived under enemy occupation and who were subject to "verification and filtration." While it is difficult to estimate how many non-prisoners were sent to the camps during the war, it was likely more than half a million people.[15] Specific rules governing the incarceration of these groups were developed and circulated to the camps that held them.[16] In particular, regulations called for these populations to be held separately from prisoners to prevent potentially dangerous social mixing, especially since prisoners were generally considered to be more dangerous than each of these populations. However, given how poorly such rules tended to work in the Gulag, and wartime shortages of guards and other personnel, this isolation was rarely complete.

Two important characteristics distinguished *katorga* convicts from those other groups of non-prisoners. First, they were the only ones subjected to conditions that were *harsher* than those for regular prisoners. Each of the other populations held in camps was supposed to be subjected to a more lenient regime than regular (non-*katorga*) prisoners, although given the lack of regulations and the very wide range of real conditions on the ground, it is not possible to draw clear conclusions about how this worked in practice. Second, members of the other groups were not sentenced to actual terms of incarceration, and so therefore were held on an indefinite basis. Nearly all of these other groups were released either during or after the war, with the notable exception that those who were being held to be "verified and filtered" were sometimes exiled or convicted of specific crimes as part of the process. *Katorga* convicts, of course, did not have their status changed at the end of the war. Although an individual case appeal might occasionally result in having one's status changed to that of an ordinary prisoner (as was the case, for example, with Vorkutlag convict Elena Markova), the overall status of *katorga* convicts did not change after the war.[17]

Reforming *Katorga*?

The end of the Second World War brought with it a re-examination of institutions of social control and the operations of the Gulag. *Katorga*, as a hastily implemented wartime policy, was one such institution to revisit. Proposed reforms came from two very different directions, as Chernyshev's May 1945 memo above suggests. There were repeated attempts to expand the use of *katorga* as a punishment and to make the camp regime for *katorzhniki* stricter. Thus, a December 1945 draft decree of the Presidium of the USSR Supreme Soviet called for serious crimes committed by *katorga* convicts in the camps (ranging from terrorism to violence against camp officials to labour violations) to be punished with additional terms of *katorga* or execution, either by bullet or hanging. Further, it called for ordinary prisoners found guilty of many of these offenses to be subject to similar punishments.[18] The overall goal of such proposals was to sort more prisoners into the harshest *katorga* category and to render that particular type of punishment more severe. This was an example of what Barnes referred to as the tendency of the Gulag to be organized according to a clear "hierarchy of detention."

However, the general thrust of other proposed reforms was to loosen some of the tightest restrictions on *katorga* convicts, addressing many of the concerns raised in Chernyshev's May 1945 memo. A draft twenty-three-article set of regulations of the regime for *katorzhniki*, "Regulations for *Katorga* Work" (*polozhenie o katorzhnykh rabotakh*), dated December 1945, sought to sort *katorga* convicts into finer categories, both to improve labour incentives and to make the staffing of such camp sections more practical. According to the draft, convicts would be divided into three groups: "probationary" (*ispytuemye*), "correcting" (*ispravliaiushchie*), and "privileged" (*l'gotnoe polozhenie*).[19] The first group, which included all convicts for at least their first year of incarceration, lived in isolation, was forbidden from corresponding with family, and faced greater disciplinary actions for violations of the camp regime. The second group was to be held in barracks with better living conditions, was eligible for qualified work (which would be less dangerous and taxing than "general work"), and was allowed to correspond with family. After three to five years in the second group, convicts could then be shifted into the third group. In this group, convicts would be held separately, could be employed in specializations and in responsible positions such as brigade leader, and were eligible for material rewards. Further, after two to three years in this regime, they even were eligible to be transferred into a regular camp with the approval of the Special Board of the NKVD (OSO). This tiered regime was intended to more clearly define the regime in which *katorga* convicts were held, and also to provide a system of rewards and punishments to encourage good behaviour and higher labour productivity. Further, by allowing more *katorga* convicts to work in their specializations or as brigade leaders, it would have made the requirement of using *katorga* convicts for all positions in their camp sections more practical to implement. These proposed modifications of the *katorga* regime were an example of the logic of a "hierarchy of detention," since they sought to sort *katorga* convicts into finer categories based largely on their behaviour while incarcerated – but on the whole, the general thrust was to improve the labour exploitation of these prisoners by modifying the regime and increasing incentives for high productivity.

Another of Chernyshev's concerns addressed in the proposed regulations was to improve the productivity of *katorga* convicts by sorting them according to health. As Chernyshev had stated, although use in hard labour activities was a requirement for these convicts, a very large proportion of them were too ill or weak to work, thus rendering it irrational to send more to Vorkutlag and other priority camps like it. Thus, the proposed regulations would have excluded the young and old from *katorga*, stipulating that those under eighteen and over fifty-five should not be sentenced to this punishment.[20] Even though Chernyshev had initially dismissed the notion of excluding the seriously ill or disabled from *katorga* convictions entirely, these later discussions nevertheless included proposals that seriously ill and disabled prisoners also be excluded from *katorga* sentencing.[21] Chernyshev noted in a report to Beria dated 6 October 1945 that limiting *katorga* sentences to the healthy and able-bodied was advisable since *katorga* convicts were being sent to Noril'sk, Pechora [sic], and Kolyma, "where sending those unable to work was clearly inappropriate."[22] However, proposals to exclude convicts incapable of hard labour from *katorga* were not included in later drafts of the regulations. Instead, subsequent drafts called for convicts who were too ill or weak to work to be sent to camp sections set aside specifically for this purpose. Thus, instead of excluding weak and disabled prisoners from *katorga* sentences entirely, the remedy proposed was to send such convicts to specific locations with milder climates and where they could be engaged in light labour.

Attempts to create a formal set of regulations for *katorga* convicts in 1945–6 were ultimately unsuccessful, as were attempts to revisit this debate in late 1948 and early 1949.[23] In fact, the only significant formal change to the regime for holding *katorga* convicts adopted during Stalin's lifetime was connected to the establishment of "special camps" in 1948. These special camps exclusively held those considered to be the most dangerous state criminals.[24] Upon the creation of such camps, *katorga* convicts whose crimes fell into the categories established for special camps were also to be transferred out of regular camps, albeit into special sections set aside for *katorga* convicts within the special camps. In such sections, *katorga* convicts would be subject to the overall regime established for special camp prisoners rather than the regulations for *katorga* convicts.[25] This likely had little practical importance, however, since the regulations for special camps were clearly modelled on those for *katorga* convicts in the first place. Further, there were no formally adopted written regulations on the regime in the special camps when they were established in 1948![26] Overall, then, despite debates and proposals, the conflict between sorting prisoners by danger or health status remained unresolved, at least formally.

"Convalescence" Camps for *Katorzhniki*

If we move closer to the situation "on the ground" in the camps, it is nevertheless clear that despite the ostensible failure of reforms to the *katorga* regime, the Gulag began to more carefully sort *katorga* convicts according to their health and ability to work. Although formal regulations still required that *katorzhniki* be sent exclusively to priority camps (with minor exceptions), the distribution of prisoners changed rapidly over the course of 1945–6. At the beginning of 1945, there were only about 12,000 *katorga* convicts in camps – approximately 9,000 in Vorkutlag, 2,300 in Sevvostlag, and 700 in Norillag. Only 221 were held in Karlag, the original camp designated to receive severely ill *katorzhniki*. Thus, virtually all hard labour convicts were indeed being sent to priority camps. But beginning in 1945, convicts whose ability to work was in doubt were no longer sent directly to such camps. While about half of the approximately 20,000 new *katorga* convicts sent to camps in 1945 went directly to Vorkutlag, Norillag, and Sevvostlag, the other half were diverted to Angarlag (a camp also known as Taishetlag, Bratsklag, and *Stroitel'stvo* 601 – for simplicity's sake, I will call it Angarlag throughout), a camp complex near the western terminus of the Baikal-Amur Mainline, a major Gulag railroad construction project. For several months, Angarlag became a key transit point for the sorting of convicts of questionable working capacity. The *katorga* population of the camp reached a peak of over 9,000 in early October, rendering it the second-largest camp for *katorga* convicts after Vorkutlag for a brief period.[27] In October and November 1945, the vast majority of these convicts were transferred to either Karlag in Kazakhstan or Siblag in Western Siberia, with only those who were not healthy enough to survive transportation remaining, a group consisting of some 1,400 prisoners by December 1945.[28] A short-lived section for *katorga* convicts in Kotlasslag, located at a major rail junction in Arkhangel'sk region on the way to Vorkutlag, served much the same function from March to July 1945, although only about 850 convicts were ever officially registered there.[29]

The practice of separating prisoners by camp based on their health status was not unique to *katorga* convicts, nor was it an exclusively wartime/post-war phenomenon. As Golfo Alexopoulos, Dan Healey, Mikhail Nakonechnyi, and others have demonstrated, the Gulag devoted considerable resources to assessing the health and productive capabilities of prisoners.[30] The transfer of prisoners based on health characteristics had been practised since the 1930s, although it became even more common during and after the Second World War. As Alexopoulos has argued, and Nakonechnyi has confirmed in greater detail, this was a way to maximize the exploitation of prisoners by concentrating the healthiest at higher-priority camps. The expectation was that these prisoners would be more productive and less likely to perish. Reporting high productivity rates and low mortality rates was essential for individual camp chiefs and for the Gulag as a whole. The flip side of this strategy was to transfer weak or dying prisoners to lower priority camps, where there was already an expectation of lower productivity and higher mortality. Transfer itself was a useful way to take ill or dying prisoners "off the books," since a prisoner who died during transportation was generally not reported in the mortality statistics of a camp. Further, transferring a prisoner to a lower priority camp was often a prelude to their early release on medical grounds, the process of so-called *aktirovka* or *aktirovanie* – an effective method to lower reported mortality by releasing a prisoner *before* they died to avoid counting such deaths on a camp's balance sheet.[31] Camps that were intended for weak, seriously ill, or disabled prisoners, so-called accumulation spots, came to play an essential role in the Gulag during and after the Second World War.[32]

The transportation of thousands of *katorga* convicts in 1945 was the first stage of a reorganization of camps intended to separate weak, seriously ill, and disabled *katorga* convicts from those sent to the priority camps – largely along the lines that Gulag officials had lobbied unsuccessfully to have included in the 1945 reform. Following the transfer of thousands of prisoners to Angarlag, Siblag, and Karlag in 1945 (non-priority camps), the MVD designated sections in labour colonies for the "convalescence" (*ozdorovlenie*) of *katorzhniki* in 1946–7: OITK Tomskaia *oblast'* (AKA Tomskii ITL, Stroitel'stvo 601), a close neighbor of Siblag in Western Siberia; OITK Vologodskaia *oblast'* (AKA Belozerskii OLP, located in a former monastery), and OITLK Molotovskaia *oblast'* (AKA Ponyshlag).[33] It is noteworthy that these sites were ITKs (colonies) rather than ITLs (camps) – which confirms Golfo Alexopoulos's argument that labour colonies, as the "base of the Gulag pyramid," were frequently used as dumping grounds for weak prisoners from priority camps.[34] The timeline of this reorganization of camps for *katorga* convicts roughly coincided with the creation of a large number of "convalescence" camps and sections throughout the Gulag in 1946. In particular, an MVD order dated 27 May 1946 established a network designed to hold approximately 90,000 prisoners for "convalescence" and established a special ration regime for prisoners held in them.[35] In short, despite the failure of the proposed 1945 reforms to *katorga*, an extensive network of camps for seriously ill and disabled *katorga* convicts was nevertheless created in 1945–7 – now, there were essentially three tiers of camps holding *katorga* convicts, which I refer to as priority, non-priority, and "convalescence." By January 1947, of the approximately 60,700 *katorga* convicts held in the Gulag, over 39,000 were being held in the three priority camps (24,663 in Vorkulag, 8,172 in Norillag, and 6,910 in Sevvostlag), with just over 20,000 held in non-priority and "convalescence" camps. However, one should hardly conclude on the basis of these data that two-thirds of *katorga* convicts were judged to be capable of hard labour. The priority camps also had specific sections set aside for the "convalescence" of seriously ill and disabled prisoners, ostensibly justified by the fact that transfer from these remote camp complexes was not always possible, especially in the winter months.[36]

From the perspective of the Gulag leadership, the practice of sorting convicts by their health status was undoubtedly even more important for *katorga* convicts than was the case with ordinary prisoners, largely due to their position in the "hierarchy of detention." *Katorga* convicts served longer than average sentences and were extremely unlikely to be released for any reason. They were not eligible for early release on medical grounds (*aktirovka*). There was a limited number of other camps and colonies to which an unproductive *katorzhnik* could be transferred. Unhealthy and unproductive *katorga* convicts weighed on the balance sheets of camp directors and Gulag administrators alike who were expected to regularly report on prisoner productivity and health – and unloading the "ballast," which was practised throughout the Gulag, particularly in times of high mortality, was much harder to do. Thus, the creation of a network of non-priority and "convalescence" camps for *katorga* convicts represents another example of how two organizational principles of the Gulag identified by Barnes and Alexopoulos, the "hierarchy of detention" and sorting prisoners according to their health to "maximize exploitation," came into conflict. In the case of *katorga* convicts, their status narrowed the repertoire of strategies that could be used to lower mortality rates, either by shifting deaths "off the books" or by giving seriously ill prisoners the opportunity to recuperate. The imperative that such convicts be held in isolated sections and punished with hard labour thus clearly conflicted with a desire to sort prisoners according to their health, which was intended both to concentrate the most physically healthy prisoners in priority camps and to reduce mortality in such camps, whether through deliberate deception or attempts to help weakened and ill prisoners to recover.

Katorga through the Lens of Gulag Population Statistics

Drilling down to the level of the individual camp, statistical reports kept by the Gulag administration on the camps reveal even more about the reported health of the *katorga* convict population and strategies to improve what was reported. These data, collected by the Gulag's Allocation and Distribution Department (URO/OURZ), must be approached with great care. There are significant gaps in the records, particularly when it comes to the period of 1943–4 when camp sections for *katorga* convicts were first created. Even more importantly, Alexopoulos, Nakonechnyi, and others have demonstrated that there were many efforts to manipulate health data, particularly with an eye towards artificially lowering mortality rates during crisis periods. The data on *katorga* convicts may have been harder to manipulate since the convicts were not eligible for early medical release (*aktirovka*), a common practice that allowed camps to avoid reporting prisoner deaths, but we cannot use these reports as a transparent measure of convict health and mortality. Thus, these data are useful for examining how well strategies to maximize prisoner labour use and minimize apparent mortality worked in the context of *katorga* convicts, but we must be much more careful drawing conclusions about prisoner health.

Official mortality data are the obvious place to begin (see Table 5.2). These data suggest important trends in terms of change over time and the variation between priority, non-priority, and "convalescence" places of incarceration. The first known reported mortality statistics for *katorga* convicts date from January 1944, when there were fewer than 1,000 convicts in the camps: 494 in Vorkutlag and 345 in Karlag. Given that Karlag had been designated for the disabled, seriously ill, and pregnant, this suggests that nearly half of those convicted of *katorga* in 1943 were already seriously ill or disabled after being sentenced. Yearly mortality rates for these camps in 1944 confirm this observation: for Vorkutlag, the rate was 390.4 deaths per 1,000 prisoners, whereas for Karlag it was 905.3 deaths per thousand. Put in other terms, in 1944 nearly one out of every three convicts in Vorkutlag died, whereas nine out of every ten convicts in Karlag died. These are shockingly high death rates, among the highest ever reported in the Gulag.[37] In 1945, a year when the population of *katorga* convicts in the camps increased from approximately 12,200 to over 40,000, death rates remained high in all three of the priority camps designated for *katorga* convicts: 161.5 deaths per thousand in Norillag, 284.8 deaths per thousand in Sevvostlag, and 198 deaths per thousand in Vorkutlag. Mortality rates in Karlag were lower in 1945, at 126.1 deaths per thousand. In each of these four camps, one out of every ten *katorga* convicts perished. However, in the other non-priority camp where *katorga* convicts were held in 1945, Angarlag, the rate was 805.5 per thousand. In other words, in the camp set aside in 1945 for the assessment and sorting of convicts too weak to be transferred directly to a priority camp, an average of eight out of every ten died. This extremely high reported death rate suggests that these *katorga* convicts were in a dire state and that conditions in the camp were absolutely detrimental to their survival.

Table 5.2. *Katorga* convict mortality (reported), 1944–9 (deaths per thousand)

	Priority			Non-priority				"Convalescence"		
Year	Norillag	Sevvostlag	Vorkutlag	Angarlag	Karlag	Siblag	OITK Tomskaia *oblast'*	OITK Vologodskaia *oblast'*	OITLK Molotovskaia *oblast'*
1944	55.9	24.7	390.4		905.3				
1945	161.5	284.8	198	805.6	126.1				
1946	82.1	153.4	40.9	39.2	94	96.5	71.1	150	22.9
1947	55.5	233.9	53.7	28.9	54.8	73.3	86.8	198.8	257.4
1948	36.3	74.36	29.3	18.1	41.9	72.4	53.4	43.3	99.1
1949	16.3	16.4	14.1	19.1	35.2	37.2	37.7	39	34.9

Sources: GARF R-9414/1 ch. 2/412, 413, 416, 424, 434, 450; GARF R-9414/1/1231, 1232, 1251, 1252, 1278, 1280, 1282, 1283, 1300, 1317, 1318, 1337, 1338.

What about official mortality data after the war, particularly after prisoners were sorted into newly created "convalescence" camp sections? The data suggest that prisoner mortality declined overall, but this varied significantly among the camps. In two of the priority camps, Norillag and Vorkutlag, yearly mortality rates declined dramatically after the war: in Norillag, mortality declined from 82.1 per thousand in 1946 to 16.3 per thousand in 1949; in Vorkutlag, mortality declined from 40.9 per thousand in 1946 to 14.1 per thousand in 1949. However, mortality remained very high in Sevvostlag in 1946 at 153.4 deaths per thousand, and actually increased in 1947 to 233.8 deaths per thousand: nearly one out of every four *katorga* convicts! This suggests that Sevvostlag was more severely affected by the post-war famine of 1947–8 than were Vorkutlag and Rechlag. By 1948, however, Sevvostlag's mortality rate had declined considerably to 74.36 per thousand, falling again to 16.7 per thousand in 1949. Overall, the above data suggest that the practice of limiting the intake of the priority camps to healthier prisoners, along with improved conditions in the camps, led to significantly lower reported death rates by 1949.

These data also suggest that mortality was indeed significantly higher in non-priority and "convalescence" camps than it was in priority camps, although it also generally declined over time. Mortality rates in the non-priority camps of Angarlag, Karlag, and Siblag were generally higher than those of the priority camps from 1946 to 1949. By 1949, the reported mortality rates of Karlag and Siblag were approximately double those of the priority camps, whereas Angarlag was in line with the priority camps. In the *katorga* "convalescence" sections that were explicitly set up for the most seriously ill or disabled convicts, which were all in colonies rather than camps, mortality rates jumped from 1946 to 1947, likely due to famine, before beginning to decline thereafter. Overall, the picture presented by the official mortality data shows extremely high mortality in 1944 and 1945, another significant increase in mortality in some camps and colonies in 1947, likely connected with famine, but overall a general decline from 1945 to 1949, with mortality remaining about twice as high in non-priority and "convalescence" sections as it was in the priority camps.

As grim as the official mortality rates are, they cannot be treated as an unproblematic reflection of prisoner health. Alexopoulos and Nakonechnyi have noted that both releases and transfers were used to lower official mortality, so it is important to examine them as well. As Table 5.3 shows, releases of *katorga* convicts were extremely rare. Overall, from 1944 to 1949, fewer than 250 convicts total were released from camps or colonies, from an overall population of *katorga* convicts

Table 5.3. Releases from *katorga* convict sections, 1944–9

	Priority			Non-priority				"Convalescence"		
							OITK	OITK	OITLK	
Year	Norillag	Sevvostlag	Vorkutlag	Angarlag	Karlag	Siblag	Tomskaia *oblast'*	Vologodskaia *oblast'*	Molotovskaia *oblast'*	Total
1944	1	0	20		0					21
1945	4	0	4	12	0					20
1946	6	6	9	9	1	4	58	1	1	95
1947	14	3	19	2	9	12	2	0	3	64
1948	3	0	0	1	5	1	0	0	0	10
1949	3	9	4	0	1	1	0	0	0	18

Sources: GARF R-9414/1 ch. 2/412, 413, 416, 424, 434, 450; GARF R-9414/1/1231, 1232, 1251, 1252, 1278, 1280, 1282, 1283, 1300, 1317, 1318, 1337, 1338.

"Hard Labour," Population Management, and Social Control 151

that reached approximately 60,000. Of the three priority camps, the greatest number were released from Vorkutlag, though it also had by far the largest number of convicts. Releases were generally not higher in non-priority or "convalescence" sections, with the single exception of 58 prisoners being released from OITK Tomskaia *oblast'* in 1946, the year that the section was established. From these data, therefore, we can safely conclude that *aktirovka* or *aktirovanie*, which allowed the early release of prisoners on medical grounds, was not widely practised in the *katorga* sections. *Katorga* convicts were simply not eligible for medical release, and official data confirm that it must have been rarely used in practice. Thus, although "release-to-die" was common among regular prisoners, it clearly was not for *katorga* convicts – thus demonstrating a concrete example of how the "hierarchy of detention" and the principle of sorting to improve reported health and maximize output came into conflict. If we are looking for significant underreporting of *katorzhnik* mortality, we must look elsewhere, as releases were simply not numerous enough to have affected mortality numbers significantly.

Outgoing convict transfers, as shown in Table 5.4, were another possible opportunity to hide mortality. As is immediately apparent, *katorga* convicts were transferred far more often than they were released from 1944 to 1948. What were the reasons for these transfers, and do they represent opportunities to hide prisoner mortality? Based on what we know about this subset of convicts and transfer practices in the Gulag in general, I would hypothesize that they can be explained in one of three ways. First, some convicts were transferred based on their perceived health and labour capability. This was to ensure that the greatest number of convicts capable of heavy labour were in priority camps and, on the flip side, for weaker and less productive convicts to be sent to non-priority or "convalescence" sections. Thus, in 1948, 1,343 convicts were transferred from OITK Tomskaia *oblast'*, 1,317 of them to camps. It is likely that many of these prisoners were being transferred from a "convalescence" section to a higher-priority camp on the basis of improved health. As Nakonechnyi has shown, the Gulag administration used such transfers to priority camps as evidence of their success in efforts to improve the health of ill and weakened prisoners.[38] Presumably, such a transfer of healthy convicts was not an attempt to hide potential mortality. However, transferring prisoners to lower-priority camps or colonies due to poor health was an obvious place to hide mortality. Thus, for example, 926 convicts were transferred from Norillag in 1946, 640 of whom were sent to colonies or prisons, which were lower-priority institutions. If these prisoners were already weak, ill, and/or disabled, this was an opportunity for a high-priority camp to remove "ballast" from

Table 5.4. Outgoing transfers (total) from *katorga* convict sections, 1944–8

	Priority			Non-priority				"Convalescence"		
							OITK	OITK	OITLK	
Year	Norillag	Sevvostlag	Vorkutlag	Angarlag	Karlag	Siblag	Tomskaia *oblast'*	Vologodskaia *oblast'*	Molotovskaia *oblast'*	Total
1944	0	2	28		116					146
1945	276	18	134	7,362	2	0				7,792
1946	926	219	3,525	48	119	826	429	22	37	6,151
1947	246	86	229	824	251	461	480	5	286	2,868
1948	76	69	292	437	59	460	1,343	255	249	3,240

Sources: GARF R-9414/1 ch. 2/412, 413, 416, 424, 434, 450; GARF R-9414/1/1231, 1232, 1251, 1252, 1278, 1280, 1282, 1283, 1300, 1317, 1318, 1337, 1338.

its rolls, and perhaps to lower its official mortality rate. Second, some transfers were efforts to redistribute labour resources between institutions of equal priority, for example between priority camps. According to Table 5.4, 3,525 prisoners were transferred from Vorkutlag in 1946. Gulag records suggest that at least 2,300 of these prisoners were sent to Sevvostlag, another priority camp. This seems like a less likely place to hide excess mortality, since prisoners in poor health were unlikely to have been chosen for transfer to another high-priority camp. Third, some prisoners were transferred for what we might call reasons of managing convict behaviour. For example, informants were transferred for their protection after being uncovered, whereas prisoners involved in violence, attempted escapes, or acts of mass resistance were often transferred as a way to try to avoid further violence and disruption within a particular camp. Therefore, there were three potential reasons for the transfer of *katorga* convicts, and this was likely an opportunity to reduce reported mortality.

Overall, how much did transfers reduce reported mortality of *katorga* convicts in the wartime and post-war Gulag? Following the discussion in the previous paragraph, the most likely way to identify the use of transfers to reduce mortality is to examine transfers of convicts to colonies or prisons, the transfers most likely to have been made on the basis of poor health. For priority camps, these were transfers of severely weak or ill convicts to lower-priority institutions. For "convalescence" sections of colonies, which had already been set aside for the most ill prisoners, there was likely no legitimate purpose for transferring convicts – and so therefore such transfers were likely attempts to get prisoners "off the books" before they died. Figure 5.1 contrasts the official mortality rate (the lower bar) with potential excess mortality hidden through transfers (upper bar) for priority camps and the lowest-priority "convalescence" colonies. While it is difficult to make any sweeping conclusions based on these data, they do suggest two things about the potential use of prisoner transfers to reduce reported mortality in sections that held *katorga* convicts. First, more prisoners were transferred to colonies or prisons from the "convalescence" sections than from the priority camps. Thus, this was more likely to have been used as a strategy to reduce mortality in "convalescence" sections than it was in priority camps. Second, there is no clear trend in the potential use of transfers to reduce reported mortality – instead, we see a few spikes of increased use of transfers, notably in Norillag in 1946 and OITK Vologodskaia *oblast'* in 1948. This suggests that transfers may have been used periodically in particular camps and colonies to hide high mortality among *katorga* convicts in moments of stress and crisis in the post-war rather

Figure 5.1 Official mortality vs. transfers to ITKs/prisons for priority camps vs. "convalescence" colonies, 1946–8 (per thousand)

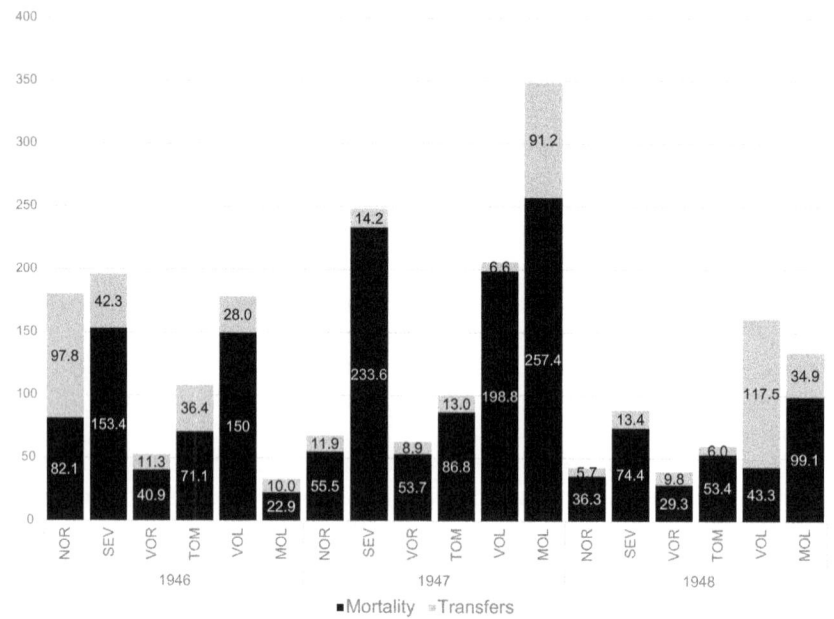

NOR: Norillag TOM: OITK Tomskaia Oblast'
SEV: Sevvostlag VOL: OITK Vologodskaia Oblast'
VOR: Vorkutlag MOL: OITLK Molotovskaia Oblast'

Sources: GARF R-9414/1 ch. 2/412, 413, 416, 424, 434, 450; GARF R-9414/1/1231, 1232, 1251, 1252, 1278, 1280, 1282, 1283, 1300, 1317, 1318, 1337, 1338.

than as a blanket policy to reduce reported mortality. Such findings are consistent with Mikhail Nakonechnyi's argument that attempts to manipulate mortality through releases and transfers were "often the result of ad hoc improvisation," with no apparent "sustained collusion" to lower reported mortality outside of times of great national stress.[39] One should note, however, that even if every outgoing transfer were counted as a death, mortality was still lower than the high levels officially reported in 1944 and 1945 when the *katorga* system was being established, suggesting that conditions had nevertheless improved.

Conclusions

What can the attempt to reform the incarceration of *katorga* convicts during the Second World War and in the immediate post-war tell us, both about *katorga* as a form of punishment and about the Gulag as a whole? Returning to discussions on the reform of *katorga* that played out in the second half of 1945, I would like to highlight a particularly important comment made in the back and forth on the proposed regulations. One report, signed by two NKVD colonels who worked on judicial operations (and who were not connected directly with the Gulag itself), S.N. Sukharev and S.P. Voronkov, explained why there was such a difference of opinion on the reforms within the NKVD ranks.[40] As they wrote, "We must say that the highlight of our discussion with the Gulag leadership was the difference in our positions; the Gulag personnel proceeded, as a rule, from organizational and economic considerations when considering one or another article of the *polozhenie*, but we [proceeded] from considerations of the overall direction of criminal policy and penitentiary practices of our state."[41] In other words, the Gulag leadership was primarily concerned with how to fit *katorga* convicts into the overall Gulag system and exploit their labour most effectively, whereas judicial officials in the NKVD were intent on making sure that the overall principles of criminal justice in the Soviet system were maintained. This statement, in my reading, suggests that the NKVD leadership understood the ongoing conflict between two organizing principles of the Gulag system, as identified by Barnes and Alexopoulos, respectively: the "hierarchy of detention" vs. sorting by "health ... with the ultimate goal of maximizing production and exploitation." Thus, conflicts within the NKVD/MVD administration over the status and treatment of *katorga* convicts reveal the complicated and sometimes contradictory nature of the Gulag's population management and social control strategies and how they were implemented in various contexts. While the personal intervention of top Soviet leaders (especially Stalin and Khrushchev) profoundly shaped Soviet criminal and penal policy, so did debates among officials about the contours and implementation of such policies, as the contributions of Juliette Cadiot, Evgenia Lezina, and Immo Rebitschek to this volume also demonstrate.

Moving beyond policy discussions to the actual implementation of *katorga* as seen through the lens of statistics compiled by the Gulag also demonstrates how the various functions of the Gulag came into conflict with one another, particularly regarding the management of prisoner health and mortality and how it was reported. *Katorga* convicts were assigned a specific place in the prisoner hierarchy, one that called for extreme isolation and punishment/exploitation through the most difficult labour tasks in the Gulag. This was bound to increase their physical exploitation and increase risk of serious illness or death, while at the same time rendering it more difficult for the Gulag leadership to hide mortality, particularly via early medical release. Yet the Gulag leadership nevertheless sought to more rationally (from their perspective) allocate these convicts to improve productivity and minimize official mortality rates. Thus, non-priority and "convalescence" sections for *katorga* convicts were created in 1945–6 to house those *katorga* convicts deemed to be either permanently disabled or too ill/weak for hard labour. Examining prisoner mortality, releases, and transfers suggests that this strategy was surely successful in reducing the official mortality in priority camps after the war, although somewhat unevenly, given that mortality remained extraordinarily high among *katorzhniki* in Kolyma through the end of 1947. Since medical releases were virtually impossible for these convicts, transfer was one of the only strategies that could be used to move dying *katorzhiniki* "off the books," and this article demonstrates that this was likely used by particular camps and colonies to hide short-term crises in prisoner health. Data also suggest that some convicts did have their health somewhat restored in "convalescence" sections to a level that Gulag administrators considered to be adequate to return them to hard labour, although this represented only a small minority of those sent to such sections.

Thus, while *katorga* convicts comprised a relatively narrow (and small) population in the Gulag, an in-depth examination of their place in the wartime and post-war Gulag suggests that we must be careful about attributing a single, totalizing organizational principle to population management and social control in the Gulag. This evidence is helpful for assessing the new interpretive models for understanding Soviet forced labour that have transformed Gulag studies in recent years. Barnes' insistence on seeing the Gulag as an ideological institution that sought to sort prisoners into finer and finer categories, as advanced in *Death and Redemption*, has been enormously influential, especially in how it moved the historiographical conversation away from tired debates about whether the Gulag was a political or economic institution. Similarly, work by Alexopoulos, Healey, and Nakonechnyi has drawn our attention to how assessments of prisoners' health and productive potential fundamentally shaped the Gulag's operations, even if these authors do not necessarily agree on *how* these assessments were used. Yet this look at *katorga* convicts suggests that we cannot understand the operations of the Gulag and their enormous effects on prisoners' lives without recognizing that there were multiple logics animating its operations. As the inmates of the Gulag for whom punishment, isolation, and brutal exploitation were most paramount, *katorga* convicts in fact reveal the limitations of any attempt to view the Gulag through a single explanatory lens. Even for these convicts, whose very sentences required their strict isolation and maximal exploitation exclusively through hard labour, Gulag officials sought to sort them by health status. Overall, it drives home the conclusion that the Gulag must be understood as a system that sought to punish and isolate, re-educate, and exploit for economic ends. Given the broad range of functions it was assigned, we should not be surprised that these functions were not always in harmony, as is the case in many modern penal systems.

NOTES

1 A.I. Kokurin and N.V. Petrov, eds., *Gulag 1918–1960: (glavnoe upravlenie lagerei)* (Moscow: Mezhdunarodnyi fond "Demokratiia", 2000), 132–3.
2 Steven A. Barnes, *Death and Redemption: The Gulag and the Shaping of Soviet Society* (Princeton, NJ: Princeton University Press, 2011), 16–17.
3 Golfo Alexopoulos, *Illness and Inhumanity in Stalin's Gulag* (New Haven, CT: Yale University Press, 2017), 184.
4 By contrast, the number of prisoners in the Gulag convicted of theft had reached half of the total prisoner population by 1953. See Juliette Cadiot's chapter in this volume.
5 On the background behind this order, see Sergey Kudryashov and Vanessa Voisin, "The Early Stages of 'Legal Purges' in Soviet Russia (1941–1945)," *Cahiers du Monde Russe* 49, no. 49/2–3 (20 September 2008): 263–96; Vanessa Voisin, *L'URSS contre ses traîtres: l'épuration soviétique: 1941–1955* (Publications de la Sorbonne, 2015); Aleksandr E. Epifanov, *Organizatsionnye i pravovye osnovy nakazaniia gitlerovskikh voennykh prestupnikov i ikh posobnikov v SSSR 1941–1956 gg.* (Moscow: Uniti-Dana, 2017).
6 According to Peter Solomon, the maximum sentence of twenty-five years was introduced into the Fundamentals of Criminal Legislation of the USSR in 1937 and adopted into the criminal code of the RSFSR in 1938. Peter H. Solomon, *Soviet Criminal Justice under Stalin* (New York: Cambridge University Press, 1996), 227. See also I.T. Goliakov, *Sbornik dokumentov po istorii ugolovnogo zakonodatel'stva SSSR i RSFSR, 1917–1952 gg.* (Moscow: Gos. izd-vo iurid. lit-ry, 1953), 396, 412. Yet such sentences were rare before the war. For example, in January 1939, a mere 3,663 of the 1,289,491 prisoners in Gulag camps were serving sentences of greater than ten years. A.B. Bezborodov and V.M. Khrustalev, eds., *Naselenie Gulaga: chislennost' i usloviia soderzhaniia*, vol. 4, Istoriia stalinskogo Gulaga: konets 1920-kh – pervaia polovina 1950-kh: sobranie dokumentov v semi tomakh (Moscow: ROSSPEN, 2004), 75–8.
7 On *katorga* before the revolution, see Sarah Badcock, *A Prison without Walls? Eastern Siberian Exile in the Last Years of Tsarism* (Oxford: Oxford University Press, 2016); Daniel Beer, *The House of the Dead: Siberian Exile under the Tsars* (New York: Knopf, 2017); Andrew Gentes, *Exile to Siberia, 1590–1822* (London: Palgrave Macmillan, 2008).

8 Soviet officials did occasionally invoke the term *katorga*, however. See, for example, a 1923 letter from Cheka chief Feliks Dzerzhinskii arguing for the Soviet use of "hard labor" for colonization. Letter from F.E. Dzerzhinskii to I.S. Unshlikht, 16 August 1923, https://readymag.com/tassagency/1365024/10/ (accessed 17 January 2023).

9 Epifanov, *Organizatsionnye i pravovye osnovy nakazaniia*, 378–80.

10 N.V. Petrov, ed., *Karatel'naia sistema: struktura i kadry*, vol. 2, Istoriia stalinskogo Gulaga: konets 1920-kh – pervaia polovina 1950-kh: sobranie dokumentov v semi tomakh (Moscow: ROSSPEN, 2004), 220–1.

11 These data come from the *Otdel ucheta i raspredeleniia zakliuchennykh/Spetsial'nyi otdel*, generally under the title of *Kartochiki ucheta dvizheniia zakliuchennykh po…* In some cases, these data are supplemented with numbers from the *Svodki GULAG o chislennosti, dvizhenii i trudovom ispol'zovanii zakliuchennykh i mobilizovannykh kontingentov v ITL NKVD SSSR*. Data for 1948–9 for Karlag, Norillag, Sevvostlag, and Vorkutlag include the populations of their respective special camps (Steplag, Gorlag, Berlag, Rechlag). Data for Angarlag in 1949 includes data for the special camp Ozerlag; 1949 data for OITK Vologodskaia oblast' and OITLK Molotovskaia *oblast'* is incomplete. Data on transfers does not include convicts transferred from regular camps to special camps when they were created in 1948–9. Data for Angarlag in 1945 is for 1 February.

12 Petrov, 2:220–1; Epifanov, *Organizatsionnye i pravovye osnovy nakazaniia*, 404.

13 In separating camps and colonies into three categories, I follow Golfo Alexopoulos's argument that there were higher- and lower-priority camps in the Gulag. Golfo Alexopoulos, *Illness and Inhumanity in Stalin's Gulag* (New Haven, CT: Yale University Press, 2017). Mikhail Nakonechnyi first highlighted the existence of a further category of "convalescence" institutions in the post-war Gulag. Mikhail Nakonechnyi, "'Factory of Invalids': Mortality, Disability, and Early Release on Medical Grounds in GULAG, 1930–1955," (PhD diss., University of Oxford, 2020), 231.

14 Wilson Bell, in his work on Western Siberia during the Second World War, notes that in the summer of 1940 exiles from areas of Poland annexed by the Soviet Union under the terms of the Molotov Ribbentrop pact were confined in Tomasinlag, a forestry camp northeast of Tomsk. In order to make room for the "refugees," prisoners were relocated to other camps in the area. Wilson T. Bell, *Stalin's Gulag at War* (Toronto: University of Toronto Press, 2018), 99–100. Julius Margolin, a Polish Jew deported to the Gulag in 1940 to Belbaltlag, was initially exiled as a "refugee" to a northern logging camp, although he and his fellow deportees were subsequently convicted and sentenced by the OSO. See Julius Margolin, *Journey into the Land of the Zeks and Back: A Memoir of the Gulag*, trans. Stefani Hoffman (New York: Oxford University Press, 2020).

"Hard Labour," Population Management, and Social Control   159

15 Zemskov notes that the mobilized Soviet Germans alone numbered over 400,000. V.N. Zemskov, *Spetsposelentsy v SSSR, 1930–1960* (Moskva: Nauka, 2003), 94–5.
16 See, for example, the regulations on "mobilized" Germans. Kokurin and Petrov, *Gulag 1918–1960*, 129–32.
17 On Elena Markova's resentencing, see Gosudarstvennyi muzei istorii gulaga (GMIG) 5/1/1/1-4.
18 Gosudarstvennyi arkhiv Rossisskoi Federatsii (GARF) R-9414/1/76/51–2.
19 GARF R-9414/1/76/71.
20 GARF R-9414/1/76/60. An analysis of under-eighteens dated 24 September 1945 suggested that there were thirty-five *katorga* convicts under eighteen currently in Soviet prisons. GARF R-9414/1/76/ 37–48.
21 GARF R-9414/1/76/5.
22 GARF R-9414/1/76/15.
23 On the reforms proposed in 1948–9, see GARF R-9414/1/359.
24 On the establishment of the special camps, see Barnes, *Death and Redemption*, 146–63.
25 Petrov, *Istoriia stalinskogo GULaga*, 2, 372–3.
26 A comprehensive set of regulations circulated in draft form in 1950. Kokurin and Petrov, *Gulag 1918–1960*, 555–67.
27 GARF R-9414/1 ch. 2/424/164.
28 GARF R-9414/1 ch. 2/424/201; http://old.memo.ru/history/nkvd/gulag/ entry for Taishetskii ITL UNKVD po Irkutskoi oblasti (accessed 2 April 2022). Epifanov, *Organizatsionnye i pravovye osnovy nakazaniia*, 406. This is also discussed in Alexopoulos, *Illness and Inhumanity in Stalin's Gulag*, 198–203.
29 GARF R-9414/1 ch. 2/424/87. Kotlaslag held *katorga* convicts only very briefly. Julius Margolin encountered them while he was a prisoner in this camp. Margolin, *Journey*, 464.
30 Alexopoulos, *Illness and Inhumanity in Stalin's Gulag*; Dan Healey, "Lives in the Balance: Weak and Disabled Prisoners and the Biopolitics of the Gulag," *Kritika* 16, no. 3 (2015): 527–56; Mikhail Nakonechnyi, "'Factory of Invalids.'"
31 For an in-depth explanation of how *aktirovka* worked as a bureaucratic process, see Mikhail Nakonechnyi, "'They Won't Survive for Long': Soviet Officials on Medical Release Procedures," in *Rethinking the Gulag: Identities, Sources, Legacies*, ed. Alan Barenberg and Emily D. Johnson (Bloomington: Indiana University Press, 2022), 103–28.
32 Nakonechnyi, "'Factory of Invalids,'" 311; 323–4.
33 On the various names for this section, see Bell, *Stalin's Gulag at War*, 154.
34 Alexopoulos, *Illness and Inhumanity in Stalin's Gulag*, 189–94.

160   Alan Barenberg

35 Kokurin and Petrov, *Gulag 1918–1960*, 536–9. Later that year, the status of a number of these camps was switched from "convalescence" to invalid camps, signifying that the prisoners held there were chronically ill and unfit for labour. A.B. Bezborodov and V.M. Khrustalev, eds., *Naselenie Gulaga: chislennost' i usloviia soderzhaniia*, vol. 4, Istoriia stalinskogo Gulaga: konets 1920-kh – pervaia polovina 1950-kh: sobranie dokumentov v semi tomakh (Moscow: ROSSPEN, 2004), 535–6. Thanks to Mikhail Nakonechnyi for bringing these orders to my attention and explaining their significance.
36 For example, in early 1951 the MVD ordered 1,336 "invalids" to be transferred from *ITL i Stroitel'stvo 601* [sic] (a.k.a. Angarlag) to Vorkutlag. Presumably, they were being transferred to a section set aside for "convalescence." Bezborodov and Khrustalev, *Istoriia stalinskogo GULaga*, 4, 122.
37 While the reported rates are significantly lower for Norillag and Sevvostlag, the data only cover November and December and are likely incomplete.
38 Nakonechnyi, "'Factory of Invalids,'" 311. Such transfers have been documented throughout the post-war era, for example in 1951. Petrov, *Istoriia stalinskogo GULaga*, 2, 372–3. A follow up that explains the transfers that took place as a result of this order can be found in Bezborodov and Khrustalev, *Istoriia stalinskogo GULaga*, 4, 122.
39 Nakonechnyi, "'They Won't Survive for Long,'" 122.
40 Voronkov was "officer for special tasks" in the NKVD at this time. "Kto Rukovodil Organami Gosbezopasnosti: 1941–54," http://old.memo.ru/history/nkvd/kto2/ (accessed 13 September 2021). It is unclear what Sukharev's job was at the time, but he led the judicial section of the MVD beginning in March 1947. Aleksandr Kokurin, N.V. Petrov, and R.G. Pikhoia, *Lubianka: VChK-OGPU-NKVD-NKGB-MGB-MVD-KGB: 1917–1960: Spravochnik* (Moscow: Demokratiia, 1997), 116.
41 GARF R-9414/1/76/79.

6 The Protection of Socialist Property and the Voices of "Thieves"

JULIETTE CADIOT

In August 1932, Joseph Stalin decided to impose harsh punishments ranging from ten years' detention in a Gulag camp to the death penalty for the theft of socialist property.[1] The official fight against theft was initially presented as an emergency measure to halt attacks on trains and mills, as well as raids on crops. But this brutal law broke with the traditional tolerance of minor theft since the end of war communism. Indeed, the 1923 Soviet Penal Code viewed stealing as a minor offence, even if theft of public property was more severely punished than theft of private property.[2] To persuade his fellow Politburo members of the importance of these severe measures, Stalin based his arguments on a definition of socialist property as "sacred and inviolable," i.e., as analogous to private property under capitalism.[3] In the 1936 Constitution, in 1940, and particularly in 1947, new decrees asserted the need to punish thieves of socialist property severely, in the last case with sentences ranging from seven to twenty-five years in the Gulag camps. In so doing, the law definitively reversed the standard articles on theft in the Penal Code. By the time of Stalin's death in 1953, over half of the detainees in the Gulag camps had been indicted and sentenced for theft.[4]

From 1932 until the late 1950s, the protection of socialist property became a slogan, an anthem that rang out in juridical discourse and judiciary practices, and in the writing of the law. In the wake of this new policy, the defence of public property gradually came to be presented as protecting state property.[5] These decrees regarding theft, however, were disproportionate, reprehensible, and heartbreaking to enforce especially in periods of hardship and famine as in 1932 and, as seen in cases I study in this chapter, in 1947. Certain judges were accused of attempting to moderate decreed punishments sometimes in light of the misery and despair of the accused.[6]

Terror was a way to impress, and hence to discipline, a starving population. In order to portray the singular legal history, I propose listening to thieves' "voices" and attempting to comprehend how they made sense of their actions and punishment at the end of the 1940s and in the 1950s. Locating samples of their voices was not easy. I know of no available memoirs by convicted thieves of socialist property. Gulag memoirs referred to them as vulnerable victims of Stalin's cruelty or as vicious criminals (*vory*).

This chapter analyses successful petitions for pardons, mostly by impoverished Gulag camp detainees after the Second World War, and the context of their crimes. The narratives of their offences indicate that they had more and less internalized Soviet morality and were awkwardly aware of the obligations that it implied. The letters provide thieves "voices," explanations of their acts and thoughts, and requests for liberation or lightened sentences.

The chapter describes the encounter between new legal norms and the trajectories and psyches of those who violated these new laws and raises the traditional Durkheimian question concerning the adequacy between law and common/shared sentiments of a population.[7] These letters of prisoners recalled their own notions of fairness, their understanding of the social protection they expected of the Soviet regime. This dialogue with the law bound them to a supposed protective, "paternalistic" state.

These letters for pardons make it possible to understand how even inside the Gulag, the poorest Soviet citizens felt and expressed their participation in Soviet society. Writers described a psychological journey in which the new social norm of protecting socialist property was not well understood before their condemnation but taught through harsh punishment. For some individuals, however, living conditions in the Gulag represented a brutal incarceration under appalling conditions, disproportionate sentences, and the deeply violent penitentiary culture of post-war Gulag camps that explicitly rearticulated the bond between the detainee (*zek*) and the regime. They openly criticized the severity and the cruelty of the theft decrees and the disproportionate punishment attached.

Petitions for Pardons, the Tenuous Path to Forgiveness, the Exception Produces the Archive

The laws punishing any violation of socialist property and any theft of state property are part of a long history of the commodification of spaces, objects, and property. Invited by Stalin to draw analogies, we can try to compare them with other historical episodes in which the implementation of new rules of property, a change in the order of qualification of things and their values, met the habits and representations that we could qualify at first, as popular. A historian in search of an analogy might compare these developments with what is known about eighteenth-century English peasants thanks to the work of E.P. Thompson. Thompson considers popular anger expressed through riots and crimes of depredation to be part of a discourse of shared usages and customary rights. He sees the English crowd as moved not only by economic need but by specific ethical values. In other words, Thompson argues that their crimes were morally motivated. In his view, historians can make sense of the rationality that motivated their actions as part of a "moral economy."[8] Without using the term, I apply this analogy to the Soviet case to emphasize that stealing socialist property was not merely an act of survival but also revealed the people's habits and notions of fairness and their own rights. Discourses of refusal of the new economic rules are about customs and habits, occasionally including some that were recently adopted but inscribed in a long history of protection by the mighty.

This study is based on the "voices" of thieves who expressed themselves in successful petitions for pardon. Composed in the camps, the petitions typically begin with a description of social trajectories. Next, the detainees focused on the criminal act, whether a random theft or minor embezzlement, which they presented either as exceptional or as a matter of regret. The letters conclude by narrating their explanations of the infraction of which they had been convicted. To cite Thompson's expression, however, the motives for the thefts remain obscure.[9] Some involve an "ethic of subsistence," as James C. Scott labels it, although framed in a specifically Soviet grammar and lexicon.[10] Convicted thieves undertook a discussion in which a specific "load" was expressed, but their words are generally emotional, distorted or even inaudible, difficult to interpret, and modelled by Soviet rhetoric.

To study the thieves' voices, I draw upon a collection of two hundred files of pardon requests by "thieves of socialist property" who were ultimately pardoned by the Presidium of the USSR Supreme Soviet. These letters were signed by the prisoners themselves, but it's sometimes difficult to know who wrote them since some prisoners were almost analphabets in Russian. Convicts already imprisoned or detained in the camps could adopt a variety of requests for pardon (*pomilovanie*), including shortened sentences (often linked to liberation), conditional release (parole), or deletion of their criminal records (*sniat' sudimosti*).

Pardons were for individuals and took into account the nature of the crime, conduct in the camp, and the convict's personality.[11]

Appeals that resulted in a pardon (and are thus preserved in the archives) constitute only an infinitesimal proportion of the total number of petitions received, processed, and resolved by the auditors of the Supreme Soviets of the fifteen Soviet Republics and the USSR. Confronted by proliferating applications due to exploding numbers of convictions, a bureau of preparation for appeals for pardon was created to sort the files in June 1947. The auditors examined the requests and either denied the pardons (without reporting them to the USSR Presidium secretary or president) or decided to forward them to the USSR Presidium. Only those forwarded had the right to be granted a pardon.

In 1952, over 1.3 million pardon applications were received from across the country, evidence of the bond between Soviet citizens and their leaders, and of citizens' belief in the protective power of the state, or of their despair.[12] The auditors processed between 1,000 and 1,100 petitions for pardon daily for the Supreme Soviet of the USSR alone. The auditors complained that they were overloaded with work and did not have the time to consider the contents of the files.[13] In late 1953, 346,339 applications for pardon were received by the Supreme Soviet from convicts, according to the June 1947 decrees. A special department existed to process them.[14] Two-thirds of the pardons that were granted in the early 1950s were for theft convictions.[15]

Only a minuscule number of supplicants were granted pardons. The Presidium of the Supreme Soviet pardoned several hundred individuals in the late 1940s and several thousand in the early 1950s. The rate of pardons remained at approximately 1 per cent (peaking at 1.6 per cent in 1952) of the total number of petitions received. The rate was nevertheless somewhat more elevated, approximately 4 per cent, if the number of files actually evaluated by the auditors are considered.[16]

Only in a small minority of cases that received favourable responses were the files containing appeals archived and preserved. They contain letters, a copy of the tribunal verdict, administrative forms containing each detainee's identity, history, and behaviour in the camps, and a brief summary of why the pardon was granted. Any letters of support from family members and close friends, the administration, and official documents supporting or verifying prisoners' arguments were appended to detainee letters.

To retrace the "moral economies" of these convicted thieves and understand their relationships to their rights, I examined the social profiles constituted by the archives. An overview of recipients of pardons from the Presidium of the Supreme Soviet of USSR reveals a high level of social diversity, despite a distinct overrepresentation of the "popular classes." The sample of 186 files of those convicted under the June 1947 decree on socialist property selected for the study were divided into broad categories based on Soviet forms identifying the petitioners according to social categories as either peasants, workers, or employees.[17] The sample covers a ten-year period (1947–57) and consists of 4 individuals identified as employees, 64 as workers, and 109 as peasants. Nine files do not identify a social category. Being designated as a peasant did not signify that an individual worked as an agriculturalist, because fewer than ten actually worked in agriculture. Information about their pre-arrest professions provides a portrait of the colourful lives of Soviet working classes, with a high representation of dockers (approximately twenty), mechanics-fitters (ten), port and railway labourers, conductors, machinists, inspectors, wagon couplers, switchmen, signalmen, and mechanics, as well as masons, turners, carpenters, and riggers. The worlds of kitchens, bakeries, and shopkeepers are also well represented, although to a lesser extent. A further fifteen cases concern individuals who were out of work or homeless. The state security apparatus is remarkably well represented, including thirty soldiers and policemen and ten heads of barracks and camp guards. Finally, five adolescents enroled in technical schools are also present in the sample. Generally low literacy levels reflected by the files are indicative of peasant farmers who later worked as labourers, soldiers, artisans, and employees. The sample includes the files of only thirty women who received pardons. In terms of national or ethnic origins, the files mirror the ethnic mosaic of the USSR, with a majority of Russians (125), followed by twenty-six Ukrainians, eight Belarussians, and five Tatars.[18] Most of the pardoned detainees in the sample were single (101), seventy-five were married, and nine had lost their spouses. The overwhelming majority were heads of household, occasionally with children, but more often with elderly parents (except for approximately thirty cases in which family dependents were not mentioned). Family ties are also mentioned in supporting letters from families that are included in the files. Seventy-nine files show no evidence of any family attachments.

Over fifty members of the sample had been awarded medals. Ten belonged to, or were candidates for, the Party, and twenty were Komsomol members. A further twenty files represent disabled (*invalidy*) veterans, fifty-six were wounded during the war, ill, or labelled disabled. A significant number of those pardoned were thus in poor health, medically certified unable to work, qualified only for light work, or were still housed in the infirmary. Being disqualified for work was tied to their calamitous pre-detention histories, often further complicated by experiences in the camps, such as hard labour, malnutrition, illness, or wounds inflicted by camp guards or fellow detainees. Most of these pardoned convicts had been arrested *in flagrante*.

In their applications for pardon, the detainees first described an itinerary or trajectory that attested to their integration into the socialist regime and their right to benefit from state protection. The criminal acts of which they were convicted is often evoked with regret through confession or acknowledgment and a description of the context of the alleged infraction. Biographical half-fictions inspired by canonical Soviet narratives are relatively common, underscoring the fact that these individuals belonged to groups that normally could anticipate some level of protection by the socialist state, such as the poor, veterans, or heads-of-household. In the letters that I analysed, service to the state, particularly through acts of official violence and repression in the army, the police, or the Gulag is often referred to, occasionally with bitterness or as justification for deviant acts or heeding calls to (state-sponsored) violence. Many pardoned detainees in the sample had spent their careers following orders, including policemen, camp guards, and soldiers in special NKVD divisions. They presented themselves as members of social classes that supported and served the regime or had actively participated in it by giving of their youth, their energy, or their blood.

Erroneous Legal Categories

The letters were written in the camps on post-war paper that was of relatively uniform quality, strangely better quality than that used for official copies of the verdicts, which were often recopied in cursive script. The actual handwriting varies widely and includes abundant errors and missing words. Some letters composed in non-Russian languages are summarized succinctly on a page that follows the appeal letter in which the entire letter is reduced to a single Russian-language paragraph. The layout of the text is occasionally from left to right rather than top to bottom, requiring the reader to reorient the page. Cursive script occasionally includes effects such as outsized capital characters to illustrate allegiance to the USSR (particularly in the word "fatherland" [*otechestvo*]), or for placing stress on other important words. The material aspect of letters from friends and family appeal to readers' emotions, such as when children wrote to ask for the return of their mother on tear-streaked paper torn from a ruled school notebook. While they constitute legal supplications intended to persuade high-level state officials, these letters from the prisoners represent above all narratives that describe social and familial trajectories that can be corroborated and completed by referring to the remaining contents of the files.

Numerous letters contain denials of guilt that claim that the writers did not commit the theft, that it was committed on the orders of a superior, or that the author had been under the influence of degenerate comrades.[19] Other letters assert their authors' ignorance of the law, including the letter of Alina Vasilev'va Maslova, who, in the North Caucasus in the fall of 1947, had stolen two kilograms of wheat from a train with fellow sixteen-year-old students, all of them driven by hunger.[20] Another convict defends his theft by arguing that he shared stolen alcohol and assuredly had not denounced his partners in crime, although that he found his "sentence too severe."[21] Bega Aga Megedinovich Kerimov claimed not to have stolen the wooden planks that he was convicted of stealing, but that had simply moved them to a different location.[22]

Ol'ga Ivanovna Karpova argued that her case had been "formally" reviewed by the tribunal. She absconded with several boxes of cookies – five boxes weighing forty-one kilograms – to her home, but her intention was to return them the following day. She acknowledged that she should not have committed the act, adding that she had lost both her son and her husband while interned in the camps.[23] Gennadii Kondrat'evich Emel'ianov argued that he was convicted despite a lack of evidence, that the accusation was illegal, and that he was not even acquainted with the others accused of the same theft.[24] Mariia Grigor'evna Danilova accused a guard of arresting her as she was crossing the potato field in the Siblag camp from which she was accused of removing ten potato sprouts. The special camp tribunal had sentenced her because it was her second theft in a few days.[25]

Forty-year-old Fedor Ivanovich Azhnov asked to be freed several times using legal channels to appeal to the Supreme Court. His first pardon request was sent while he was detained in Moscow in investigating prison no. 4. In addition to his letters, his file included letters from his wife, who was the mother of their four children, the oldest of whom suffered from epilepsy. The story of the theft, discovered in September 1947, resembles descriptions of disproportionately harsh judicial punishment published in internal directives by the public procurator or the Ministry of Justice, or Party to denounce excessive sentences. After his rounds had ended, a railway signal controller in Voskresensk named Azhnov found eleven boxes containing four hundred grams of buckwheat concentrate (*kasha*, an important staple of Russian nutrition) on the railbed. He took them home, unaware that a wagon had been burgled a few days earlier. After discovering that the *kasha* was no longer edible, he used three boxes to feed his cow and attempted to sell the rest at the market, where he was arrested. During the inquest, it was proven that he was working at the time of the burglary, and he was sentenced to seven years in the camps for theft of socialist property. The detainee and his spouse based their appeals for clemency on their worthy backgrounds and their membership in the under-educated working class, as well as a lifetime of faultless labour, their misunderstanding of the fact that their act represented a theft, and finally an error in the qualification of the crime, since he was merely guilty of not returning a found object for which he should normally receive a sentence of up to one month of detention. His explanation that he had found an object presumably authorized him to initiate an appeal, but the argument that an error of legal categorization had occurred could also be included in pardon requests (many of which the auditors forwarded to state procurators or the courts). In addressing the president of the Presidium, Azhnov's wife firmly maintained that "it seems to me that theft and appropriation of found objects (*prisvoenie nakhodki*) are two different things. It is true that I now understand that appropriating found objects is a punishable crime under Soviet law, but I implore you to take into consideration the low value of the found object and the insignificant nature of the category of the crime."[26]

During the inquest, her husband was notified that he was being tried exclusively for this infraction – the non-restitution of a found object – and not for theft because he was working at the time that it took place. The verdict included in the file clearly shows, however, that the conviction for theft was maintained.[27] In Azhnov's case, his appeal for pardon was based in part on evidence of support from his family and the *kolkhoz* and the municipality (*sel'sovet*). His spouse had been the chair of a collective farm and, like her husband, had received awards for her work.[28] He was also recognized for good behaviour in camp. He suffered from sciatica but had recovered enough to fulfil 120 per cent of his quotas, according to the head of the camp. In a shakily written letter full of errors, Azhnov acknowledged his fault in not reporting the boxes that he had found. He fully recognized his mistake and promised to assist in the future in discovering those who were implicated in crimes intended to drain the power of the State.[29] The Supreme Soviet initially declined to free him, but it ultimately justified its decision in favour of pardoning him by citing his need to help his ailing wife and daughter, the satisfaction of the vice-president of the Moscow railways in his past work, and his productivity in the camps. The auditor did not mention the argument concerning legal qualification, however.[30]

Numerous letters thus referred to excessive or disproportionate sentences for the crimes committed, an argument retained by the authors of the pardons. A young girl judged her crime to be minor – she had admittedly taken some sugar, but there was so much of it that she had never in her life seen such a quantity, and the abundance created the temptation to steal for someone for whom this was not her first theft.[31] Anastasiia Filippovna Agofonova claimed that she was unaware that she was stealing in responding to an order from her boss.[32] These individuals were clearly unable to grasp the concept of "socialist property" as conceived by Stalin.

True Criminals?

Arrest and incarceration encouraged awareness that theft was indeed stealing. However, the letters serve as reminders that the petitioners did not experience their act as criminal. The intention was either omitted or effaced. Although prisoners acknowledged their infractions, they explained their motives and insisted on their subjectivity at the moment of their crimes. Roman Nikitovich Eremenko, for example, worked in a bakery. Recently employed, he had not received the ration ticket associated with his new job. He grabbed some bread and was sentenced in Ukraine in July 1947 for twice taking eleven kilograms of bread. As he explained: "I've never been a criminal at heart."

Born in a poor family in 1903, Eremenko had served in the Red Army. He continued, "The crime that I committed is an extraordinary tragedy and a lesson in my life. One must always be attentive. In view of my age, I do not understand how I can be detained for ten years for a tiny little crime."

> I ask you to consider that in committing this crime, it never occurred to me that I could be pursued and classified as an enemy of the people for taking a small roll … such a verdict should be directed at real criminals but classifying me as one of them is not possible. What happened to me could have happened to many people, because at the time it was very difficult to get bread.[33]

By borrowing the authorities' rhetoric, convicts attempted to distinguish themselves from true criminals and "socially harmful" individuals by playing on the contrast between their social belonging and the regime's discourses concerning its "enemies." Some displayed extensive knowledge of the lexicon of the Soviet penal system that had been inherited from the Revolution and Stalin's punitive campaigns. In the legal texts of the 1920s, lawmakers referred to "social defence" measures (or those "within the law") rather than using the customary term of sentences. Such measures allowed a dangerous individual to

170 Juliette Cadiot

be either "mechanically" eliminated or "improved" by forced labour.[34] Detainees defended themselves against being perceived as a danger to society – several openly stated that they were not "socially dangerous."[35] They also claimed that they were neither delinquents (or professional thieves, *vory*) nor bandits, but they could still be transformed by their experience in the camps. Abdurashid Mumilov, who was homeless, wrote "pardon me as an orphan. I am nevertheless not a depraved or dangerous man for society."[36]

Terentii Dmitrievich Sur'ev, a farmer of Chuvash nationality and the orphan of a father who died in the war, had been summoned to replace his father in the army in 1943. At the age of seventeen, he therefore joined the military and, beginning in 1947, had fought Ukrainian nationalists with Ministry of the Interior troops until the time of the theft in 1949. A dog handler, he boasted of having directly participated in the assassinations or arrests of Ukrainian nationalists (UPA/OUN),[37] describing his participation in manhunts with his dog. During his heyday, he had personally liquidated thirteen "detained political elements, without even counting the bandits." Proud of his assassinations and skills as a chekist, he had acted with the certainty that each of these UPA/OUN "bandits" represented a serious menace to the country. He wrote with no sense of guilt, but instead out of pride and satisfaction that each liquidated member represented a "step towards communism." He expressed pride in having combated hate (*s nenavist'iu*) in order to defeat troublemakers in Western Ukraine and encouraging "the local population to live peacefully and to organize the collective economy." In a drunken state, he and his accomplices had stolen a 153-litre keg of beer that they "found" on a railway and buried before consuming it and destroying the evidence. A military trial in open session in the presence of two lawyers sentenced him to fifteen years in the camps, in addition to confiscating his assets "to make an example" of him. He was expelled from the Komsomol and was serving his sentence in the region of Arkhangel'sk, where at the time of his petition he was working as statistician in a camp. Two of his pardon petitions had been rejected but, he benefited from the amnesty decree in March 1953 that reduced his sentence by half. In his pardon letter, he stressed the fact that "Soviet power [*Sovetskaia vlast'*] gave me the possibility of studying in a technical agricultural high school and receiving an education, but that education is going to waste [*kvalifikatsiia propadaet darom*]." He concluded that

> finding myself in a camp is a hard life lesson. I am quite certain that the Soviet government will consider the unique nature of my error, a random thing in my life, my youth, as well as my service with the troops of the Ministry of the

Interior of NKVD-MVD-MGB. If necessary, I am ready to defend my Fatherland at any moment. And I am firmly convinced that the Soviet authorities, as a former chekist, will not offend me and will pardon me.

His mother proposed to help her son directly. Believing her son's infraction to be unimportant, she asserted that she was prepared to reimburse five hundred rubles to the State in order to secure his liberation.[38]

Self-sacrifice in defence of the Fatherland redefined the socio-political hierarchy inflicted on the USSR by the ordeal of the war. Sur'ev did not promote his participation in the fight against the Nazis and his arrival in Warsaw and Berlin, however. Instead of emphasizing his wartime military experiences, he focused on his career as a chekist and his loyalty to the nation, symbolized by participation in killing new citizens in the name of Sovietization. Indeed, the study sample of detainee letters contained a significant number of pardoned prisoners who had been participants and witnesses of state-sponsored violence, including soldiers and members of the political police special forces (twenty-seven cases), camp guards (seven cases), informants (three cases), and a policeman. These close relationships to the state were expressed in ideological and moral terms, occasionally through allusions to killings that were presented as a positive credential, a valuable argument that Sur'ev advanced in support of his cause. His sentence was ultimately commuted under the banal pretext of good behaviour in the camp. A further example was an Armenian named Aram Vartanov who had been a cashier in civilian life as well as in the camp and who recalled the ties between his family and the revolutionary Stalin, Dzhugashvili or "Soso." As a child, his father had taught him that the future Stalin would become a "grand professor of power." While working in a tavern in Tbilisi, he had heard Stalin addressing the crowds and asked for his advice. The family consisted of revolutionary Bolsheviks, a rarity in majority-Menshevik Georgia, and four of the five sons were members of the political police. Vartanov boasted that he and his brothers shared their chekist background. He had been sentenced for cheating during the 1947 monetary reform, but even the chief of police had been astonished by the severity of his sentence.[39] Ivan Egoshkin, a former soldier who stole 120 rubles and received two light wounds and two more serious injuries asked to be freed so that he could resume his position in the army.[40]

Sergei Inchin confessed to theft in his pardon request. He was honestly and even zealously serving his sentence but requested to be freed. He pointed out that he was helping the administration maintain order and discipline among his fellow prisoners by halting escape attempts, a role fulfilled in the camps by snitches and the operational department.

In support of his request, he described how on 18 October 1949, a group of prisoners eager to avenge themselves had attacked him with an axe. He suffered fifteen wounds in the attack and was crippled for life. The penitentiary administration confirmed his exemplary behaviour in the camp where, as a well-behaved prisoner, he had been awarded medals and bonuses. The administration also attested that Inchin had remained in the infirmary for four months due to wounds to his face, skull, left forearm, and femur, as well as a broken jaw. Crippled and permanently disfigured, he explained that he detested the mobsters (*vory*) and had collaborated with the administration to uncover their plans. He was afraid for his life and was liberated three years after the incident in 1951.[41] Murders of informants, who were treated as traitors – "bitches" (*stukachi*) in the language of the camps – has been well documented in Gulag administrative correspondence and the accounts of former detainees.[42] To combat increasingly anti-authoritarian criminal gangs, Gulag officials required operational departments to recruit a network of informers, including incarcerated thieves.[43]

Family Vulnerability

Some pardon applicants tried to appeal to the auditors' emotions. The letters often mentioned deaths in the family since the detainees had been detained, their families' misery, and their own bottomless despair.

Ivan Vasilenko, sixteen, was initially arrested, but because the transit camps were full, he had the good fortune of being released because of his young age. Left alone with little to eat, however, he was starving and, after a few days wandering in search of food, he began to steal before being arrested in a movie theatre. His sisters eventually tracked him down in the Gulag and found him in 1950 after an exhaustive search: "On 14 November 1947, they liberated me for being sick. I wasn't yet 18 at the time. Since my father was killed during dekulakization …, I was raised in an orphanage, and when they liberated me, I didn't have a *kopek* and I was alone and sick. For several days, I didn't commit any crimes, but hunger overtook me. In the train station of Kokand, I broke a hole in the side of a freight car and poured out 12 kilos of wheat and 2 of sugar." He ended his appeal with an homage to the Stalinist socialist state: "I could have approached Soviet institutions and, considering my health, they would have given me a job and I would not have committed a crime. My parents found me. They all have responsibilities. I am only a criminal before the state. After doing time in the camps, I sincerely acknowledge my criminal error, and it will never happen again. I ask the Praesidium of the Soviet Supreme to pardon me [*prostit'*]. It will never be repeated."[44]

One sister invited Kliment Voroshilov, president of the Supreme Soviet, personally to intervene. She provided a more detailed account of their childhood than her younger brother. Their father was a poor peasant (*batrak*) who had been a red partisan during the Civil War in Kuban and on the Don. He died in 1930, but contrary to her brother, she did not mention dekulakization in her account. Her mother died in 1933, and the children were sent to an orphanage, after which the three eldest left for the war, where two of them died. An older sister returned, and the youngest sister was requisitioned to participate in the "liberation" of Ukraine in 1944, leaving her brother behind in a professional school. Ivan Nikolaevich had ended up in the network of factory training schools (FZO, *shkola fabrichno-zavodskogo obusheniia*) in which children stayed for a six-month period. They were exploited under frightening unsanitary conditions and many fled. His sister concluded by arguing that

> if he did commit a crime, it was out of hunger. He is not a bandit or a professional thief. Free him and give him an honest job, because his brothers and sisters defended the Fatherland, his brothers died at the front, and only one sister came back from the War. My sister and I are members of the great Communist Party, and our situation is unacceptable (*i nam eto ne k litsu*), although we are certain that he committed a crime due to hunger. Please allow us to meet our brother soon, because he has not known life and does not know how to live or what life is.[45]

Many of the letters' authors described their thoughts at the time of the theft, which frequently centred on hunger that was afflicting them or their family members. Many petitioners also reported being unaware that they were committing a crime or being convinced that a minor theft would remain unnoticed. Tat'iana Georgievna Gorbatovskaia, for example, worked in the ports, had no husband, and had to provide for an invalid son and mother. As she explained: "On the day of the theft, there was nothing left to eat at home. I couldn't bear my mother and my son's hunger. They did not have even a scrap of food. So, I decided to commit a crime, thinking that no one would ever notice."[46]

At the age of fifty-seven, Evdokiia Orlova (sixty at the time of her appeal) was classified as an *invalid* and unable to work by the camp medical commission. She had stolen seventeen kilograms of fodder beets at a time, as the verdict reflected, when the harvest was not yet complete, and she did not have the right to serve herself in the fields.

Explaining that she had found the beets on the road, she asked for a pardon: "I am asking you to remove this shameful stain from me ... I didn't think I was committing a crime and that I was risking being punished." She asked if she could be granted clemency due to her age and did not think her theft should be considered a crime because the beets were not edible for humans but destined for livestock. She was ashamed of the dishonour that she had brought on her sons, who were former soldiers, and was worried about her husband who remained alone.[47]

Thefts of Misery

Disabled, wounded, unable to work, or ill: fifty-six of the detainees in the study sample were assigned to these categories. Being unable to work was an incentive for Gulag camp directors to free them in order to remove useless inmates. These manoeuvres (*aktirovanie, razgruzka*) could pass through a variety of channels that included camp tribunals following judgments by medical commissions or administrative decisions.[48]

Dmitrii Dmitrievich Kosiachenko maintained his innocence despite a detailed verdict containing accounts of witnesses and his attitude during his trial.[49] Employed as a type of camp guard trained by the prisoners themselves (*samookhrana*), he had fought against the Finns and been awarded medals. An invalid with two missing fingers and a paralysed knee and in poor health, he was granted a pardon in order to help his family.

Most detainees were destitute citizens, many of whom had no home and were out of work. Some referred directly to famine (*golod*) and economic difficulties (nineteen cases) or difficult material situations (thirty-two cases). This Presidium's recognition of prevailing poverty in the republics illustrates a form of clemency extended the underprivileged that is also present in Western legal and philosophical thought, as well as the Soviet promise of universal social protection. Residing in poorhouses, and sometimes in the street, Ol'ga Vasileevna Fomina, sixteen, had stolen thirteen kilograms of salt but was ultimately freed.[50] This was also the case of Aleksandr Ivanovich Bobrov, a rigger in the port of Murmansk who stole two kilograms of meat and could not afford winter clothes that were crucial in northern Siberia.[51]

Many of the narratives concerned the period between 1946 and 1947, when peasant ration cards were reduced or cancelled, families were starving, and there was a proliferation of minor thefts. In September 1946, for economic reasons, the government had implemented sharp reductions of aid to the population. The number of Soviet citizens who were classified as eligible for food ration cards decreased from 87 million to 60 million. In rural areas, dependents were excluded from rations and families were harshly affected by famine. Indeed, most of the citizens deprived of rations by these austerity measures were residents of villages and small rural towns and, as they testified, "to survive we had to steal."[52]

In the city of Gor'kii in August 1947, Gennadii Davydov was charged and convicted of repeatedly stealing firewood from trains to resell it. He was sent to a children's camp where his initial appeal, written with the help of a lawyer like his mother's appeal for pardon, was unsuccessful. His appeal succeeded only after the direct intervention of the chief procurator of the USSR, Grigorii Safonov, who was able to arrange his liberation in 1949. In her letter, his mother described the family's dire situation. An officer's widow who resided in a remote village, she no longer received ration coupons for bread with which to feed her three children. Her oldest son was compelled to walk sixteen kilometres to attend school, where he was experiencing difficulties because of severe hunger and was likely to have to repeat the school year. In April 1947, he had started a new existence, selling cigarettes (*papirosy*) along the railway and collecting a few coins (*milostynia*) by begging in train stations. Until his indictment in July, he left the family home and returned only intermittently. In 1949, seeking to offer a guarantee, his mother informed Soviet officials that because her financial situation had improved and that combined with her pension, she was earning a thousand rubles per month, a very good income.[53] The family's morality thus seeming better ensured, her son was freed.

In 1947, Maria Tokmena, a Siberian peasant who was born in 1920, was sentenced to ten years in the camps. Her father died when she was twelve, and her mother, a widow with five children, sent them to work at a young age. From thirteen to sixteen, Maria worked as a nanny and housekeeper, later working in a *kolkhoz* as a "man of pain," a labourer (chernorabochii). After she was arrested for stealing crops from a field, she was sent to the Gulag, where she was assigned to hard labour cutting wood (which was normally reserved for men).

She described herself as an honest worker in her petition for a pardon, which was written in a mix of first and third person. Despite her arduous labour, she no longer received her portion of bread, however, or sometimes a reduced ration of four hundred grams per day.

"When I came home there was nothing to eat, not a coin in the house. When I went to bed hungry, I couldn't sleep, so I decided to pick potatoes from the kolkhoz." She concluded: "pay attention to me, because I have already been in the North for four years, my health is poor, and I will be unable to complete my sentence. I have brothers and sisters. I will tell everyone not to take what is not theirs [*ni brat' ni chego chuzhogo*]. Forgive my younger years. I can still live free, although I no longer believe in my health. I will no longer take state property or that belonging to others [*chuzhoi*]."

In a later petition, she again called attention to her blameless behaviour in the camp, arguing that she put all her energy into working

> because my health is not important to me. Nevertheless, I suffer because I fulfil or exceed my quota and work all the time felling trees. Citizen Shvernik, I ask you to pardon me and free me.
>
> I would tell all of my comrades and brothers and sisters not to [take] socialist and private property. I swear to you and to the Soviet homeland that in all my life, I will not make a single remark, offense, or crime, and I will live only according to the rules established by our government ... I will go along with other Soviet citizens on the right way of life under communism, and I will work honestly and join the ranks of Soviet citizens, and also with a watchful eye, I will keep the order in the Soviet Union, I swear it.[54]

These narratives and testimonials serve as a reminder that the Soviet Union remained populated by legions of the poor, the marginalized, and the excluded, despite the regime's claims to have eradicated social problems. The vast campaigns of repression in the 1930s linked to industrialization and the impoverishment of rural areas had created a miserable nomadic population and the cataclysm of the Second World War accentuated the situation. The destitute were nevertheless trapped, and their often-agonized testimonies referred to their right to survive and to state protection of the poor, a long Western tradition whose traces remained present in the Soviet Penal Code. It had become difficult to appeal to this tradition, however, due to official denial by the paternalistic State that it was massively betraying its commitment to protecting the poor in giving to the political police the power to "solve" social problems of juveniles, women as disabled, the whole vulnerable population. These letters cast doubt on the capacity for subjectivization when an adolescent has encountered at each step of his trajectory the ambivalent figure of the protective State. If this assistance is offered, it is under the sordid aspect of the re-education colony, the school of apprenticeship, the roundup of street children.[55]

The Experience of the Gulag

The letters in the sample were written in order to petition for pardons, but some of them also revealed their authors' sense of injustice and astonishment that their acts had led to incarceration. Only when they questioned the Soviet penal system did their letters begin to take on a subversive character, particularly when they described the desolation that predominated life in the Gulag. Paradoxically, criticism and zealous ideological support are not mutually contradictory, however. Ivan Sova, who had served as a soldier since 1941 and fought from the Caucasus to Berlin, had been wounded and awarded medals. A year after at last being demobilized in 1947, he and several accomplices had stolen some grain. He was sentenced to eighteen years in the Gulag and in 1952, after four years in a camp, he pleaded for a reduction in his sentence or to be assigned the function of a free camp worker and Gulag employee (*naemnyi*), which would permit him to leave the detention area. He acknowledged his crime, but argued that his sentence was disproportionately severe, explaining:

> Falling into such a community and finding myself in the camp for the first time in my life, it is very hard for me to endure these rules. I cannot survive until the end of my sentence. If it is impossible for the Supreme Soviet to shorten my sentence, give me the death penalty. Shoot me ... I cannot bear to experience what I am living now. My youth is partially gone, but if I stay I will lose my humanity [*chelovechestvo*] and my youth under these conditions. I have already lost half of my health.[56]

Convicted thieves' petitions occasionally openly questioned the penal system and Soviet penal policies or the fact that they were sent to the camps. Their petitions were interspersed with expressions of despair and evocations of the unendurable conditions in the camps and their disproportionate punishments relative to their crimes. Their supplications were in fact not supplications, but efforts to satisfy a craving to express their voices and ensure that they were heard, even if it meant expressing rebellion. In 1948, based on his former Party membership, Timofei A. Saraev accused the procurator of lying in the charges brought against him. He called upon the chief procurator of the USSR, Grigorii Safonov, to come to live in the camp in order to realize what happened when one received a several-year sentence and moved from the bureaucratic side of a sentence to the distant shape of justice amid the scandalous conditions of the concentration camps.[57]

A report to the state procurator field on 18 December 1959, examined the reasons for the increase in the anti-Soviet statements of prisoners' petitions. The report cited detainees' letters and terms in support of its recommendations. For example, in February 1958 in the Krasnodar camp, Vladislav Kliment'evich Bobrovskii, who was serving a sentence for theft of socialist property, explained: "I have become politically bad ... under the difficult conditions of internment, I have doubted the rightness of Soviet policy ... I have become a man who is an enemy of the Soviet Union."[58]

Another detainee sentenced for theft of socialist property was treated with contempt and terrible violence by criminal gangs. Hiding to escape numerous rapes committed by his fellow detainees, Stefanenko, born in 1937, was seventeen in 1956 when he was indicted for theft. Arriving at the camps, he was the victim of multiple rapes and was infected with syphilis. In despair, he attempted to escape. He was advised to write anti-Soviet poems, because anti-Soviet discourse would be referred to a special investigation by the political police (KGB). Detainees who were subjects of these investigations were moved to a different camp and judged and sentenced again for a political crime. Their entire file was also reviewed as part of the process. Stefanenko, like other victims of rape and violence, explicitly invoked this strategy in his petitions.[59] Other cases followed, including a prisoner who had helped the political police prevent an attempted escape. Detainees learned about his intervention and threatened him and, hoping to be expediently liberated, he used the same method of submitting anti-Soviet letters. Despair also led to detainees to use other approaches that involved anti-Soviet statements. A.E. Budanov, who was born in 1930, was illiterate. He was initially sentenced to seven years for stealing socialist property, but his sentence was increased to twenty-five years following two attempted escapes. He hoped for a reduced sentence, but after clashes with camp authorities, his appeals were greeted by with official silence. Following the amnesty laws that liberated over half of the Gulag population after Stalin's death, he was angered by regulations banned the reduction of sentences for detainees with long sentences.[60] In an intense psychological state, he decided to engage in anti-Soviet speech.

L.A. Solodovnikov, who had little formal education, was born in 1936 and was sentenced three times (the most recent sentence for fourteen years in the camps for theft). He proclaimed his innocence, arguing that he was wrongly incarcerated and filing a series of complaints and appeals. Because his earlier letters had received little attention, he began to add anti-Soviet discourse in hopes of a faster response. Addressing the Party committee in Omsk region, he wrote:

> My patience is exhausted ... I refuse Soviet citizenship and I am going to have diarrhea (I have diarrhea) and curse the power of the guards ...

I cannot conceal the fact that in writing this declaration, I have the hope that more insightful organizations will intervene after reading it, in other words, the political police (KGB). I will naturally not be happy with this declaration, but at least it will demonstrate and prove that I am not guilty ... but now, I hope that these anti-Soviet statements will be sufficient to cause the political police to intervene in my affairs.[61]

A trial for anti-Soviet speech was opened that proved that he had in fact been falsely accused of theft, having on the contrary contributed to the discovery of the crime as a police informer.[62]

The paradox is that by engaging in anti-Soviet speech and distancing themselves from professions of allegiance, these detainees ultimately obtained protection and clemency. Indeed, political crimes, such as anti-Soviet speech, were subject to specific procedures, including the departure of the detainee from the camp and the re-examination of their entire penal files by the political police, which thus took the place of the ordinary judicial process and could revise judges' mistakes.

Although anecdotal because they are associated with a new legal process that was not reflected in its results, these cases exemplify the extremes of the Soviet penal and carceral systems and the normative reversal effected by a break with the law and the authorities. The unspeakable conditions of judgment and confinement thus triggered criticism of the regime, which was a risky strategy because political crimes could be far more unforgivingly punished than theft. Ironically, however, this approach provided a solution that allowed some prisoners to escape from the Gulag. Objectively, and subjectively, they were forced to become dissidents to escape the system.

Conclusion

The language of convicted thieves found in the above sample of petitions for clemency offers insights into how Stalinist decrees intended to protect socialist property represented a significant departure from the earlier legal environment. Almost overnight, traditional practices were severely punished as socialist property laws outlawed behaviours that were previously considered to be based on natural laws governing trade and nutrition. Defining property as under socialist ownership, combined with an increasing commodification of everyday objects, radically overturned the long-standing socio-economic and legal role of property. These extraordinary changes affected every social class, forcing a new class of "thieves" to invent a new tradition by affirming allegiance to the new society in their petitions and testimonies, even though they acted in ways that the state no longer deemed acceptable.[63] This dramatic change in the legal environment had significant implications for the ways in which the people thought about and managed commodities, ultimately transforming their relationships with the Soviet state as a protective and even paternalist authority and shaping their perception of shared social norms and values.

To defend themselves, convicted thieves invented a new discourse in which they promoted their roles in society, even when they did not follow, recognize, or even grasp its rules establishing an extreme degree of protection to socialist property. Their partial understandings occasionally led them to express themselves awkwardly about this conception of property and its precise contours and contents.

My initial assumptions were that the new Stalin-era legal environment governing socialist property upended established beliefs and practices. The justifications offered by convicted thieves who requested pardons in effect offer alternative insights into the functioning of the legal system, while also illustrating a strange relationship to equity and justice that could only sound familiar to an early modern historian accustomed to this type of source. In defending themselves, few of these thieves questioned the law itself, with the majority merely claiming that the rules did not apply to their particular case.

The profession of historian sometimes requires us to retrieve sad stories from the archives and stories about oblivion and resuscitate antiheroes and infamous criminals who suffered dreadful punishments at the hands of the State. I have attempted here to allow these Stalin-era thieves to speak once again, even though they left few traces beyond their awkward appeals for pardon. Their collective and individual ability to cope with revolutionary times and with the trauma of war should be understood in light of the right of Soviet citizens to be protected and understood by the State. Their letters define the terms of a social pact with the powerful Soviet State. In coping with new official policy grounded in the Stalinist State's drive to accumulate capital to fuel industrial and military development that somehow became embodied by socialist property, they were proclaiming their rights to a share of this wealth based on their commitments and skills and their status as loyal citizens. By labelling them as criminals and thieves, the Stalin regime dramatically altered the terms of the social agreement and alienated vast swathes of Soviet society. When Stalin died and Beria decided to open the gates of the Gulag and reform the Stalinian penal system, Lazar Kaganovich affirmed, "We were all in favor of releasing these petty thieves [*vorishki*]."[64] A new decree in January 1955 made petty thefts (*mel'koe khishchenie*) punishable whenever possible by labour for

Socialist Property and the Voices of "Thieves"   181

the common good or by light sentences. An internal discussion among judiciary institutions unsuccessfully sought to precisely define petty theft,[65] whereas serious thieves, economic embezzlers, and traffickers remained subject to Stalin's unfamous 1947 decree until a new Penal Code was enacted in 1960.[66]

NOTES

1 Nicolas Werth, *La terreur et le désarroi: Staline et son système* (Paris: Perrin, 2007); Yoram Gorlizki, "Theft under Stalin. A Property Rights Analysis," *Economic History Review* 69, no. 1 (2016): 288–313; Peter H. Solomon, *Soviet Criminal Justice under Stalin* (Cambridge: Cambridge University Press, 1996); Peter H. Solomon, *Soviet Criminologists and Criminal Policy* (New York: Columbia University Press, 1978); Juliette Cadiot, *La Société des voleurs, Socialisme et Propriété sous Stalin* (Paris: Editions de l'EHESS, 2021).
2 The Penal Code distinguished between secret theft (*krazha*), open, non-secret theft (committed with or without violence, *grabezh*), and assault (*razboi*). Simple theft (committed alone and as a first offence) was also distinguished from aggravated theft (such as recidivism or gang theft), including a criterion of need that downgraded simple theft to minor theft if the accused proved that he or she acted out of need due to unemployment, for example, and if the value of the theft corresponded to his and his family's basic needs. Sentences were shortened by three months of corrective labour (for simple theft, it was three months' detention or corrective labour). In addition, the proposed Penal Code of 1903, Penal Codes of 1922, and the edited version in 1926 stipulated that a crime could be committed out of extreme necessity to protect themselves or against another danger that could not be avoided through other means. In analysing the 1926 code, penal expert A.A. Zhizhilenko notes that Article 13–2 disallowed penal responsibility for thefts committed in cases of extreme penury. It offered the example of an individual dying of hunger who could not be sanctioned for stealing bread; Nikola S Timasheff, "The Impact of the Penal Law of Imperial Russia," *American Slavic and East European Review* 12, no. 4 (1953): 441–62. A.A. Zhizhilenko, *Prestupleniia protiv imushchestva i iskliuchitel'nykh prav* (Leningrad: Izdatel'stvo "rabochii sud," 1928), 74–87.
3 As he explained: "Capitalism could not have smashed feudalism. It would not have developed and solidified if it had not declared the principle of private property to be the foundation of capitalist society and it had not made private property sacred property, with any violation of its interests strictly punished and with the creation of its own state to protect it. Socialism will not be able to finish off and bury capitalist elements and

individualistic self-seeking habits, practices and traditions (which are the basis of theft) that shake the foundations of the new society unless it declares public property (belonging to cooperatives, state farms or the State) to be sacred and inviolable." R.W. Davies, *The Stalin-Kaganovich Correspondence, 1931–36* (New Haven, CT: Yale University Press, 2003), 166–7.

4 Iu.N. Afanas'ev and V.P. Kozlov, eds., *Istoriia Stalinskogo Gulaga: Konets 1920-kh-pervaia polovina 1950-kh godov: Sobranie dokumentov v semi tomakh* (Moscow: ROSSPEN, 2004), 641–2. To justify the proposed amnesty of March 1953, Beria cited the presence of 1.25 million thieves of socialist and personal property in the Gulag camps, representing half of the total number of detainees. V. Naumov and Iu. Sigachev, eds., *Lavrentii Beriia, 1953. Stenogramma iiul'skogo plenuma TsK KPSS i drugie dokumenty* (Moscow: Mezhdunarodnyi Fond Demokratiia, 1999), 19–21. Preparatory documents for the amnesty were collected by the Ministry of Justice, the procurator, and the Ministry of the Interior. Gosudarstvennyi arkhiv Rossiiskoi Federatsii (GARF) R-9492/2/127/21–42.

5 The effort to develop a doctrine led to the 1948 publication of a monumental volume by the jurist Anatoli V. Venediktov that provided a coherent vision of the new system of socialist property. A.V. Venediktov, *Gosudarstvenaia Sotsialisticheskaia Sobstvennost'* (Moscow: Izdatel'stvo Akademii Nauk SSSR, 1948).

6 Solomon, *Soviet Criminal Justice under Stalin*; Donald A. Filtzer, **Soviet Workers and Late Stalinism: Labour and the Restoration of the Stalinist System after World War II** (Cambridge: Cambridge University Press, 2002).

7 In his seminal book, *La division du travail*, which discussed the question of law, Emile Durkheim observed: "There are acts that are more severely repressed than they are disapproved of by common opinion ... the subtraction of public items leaves [the people] relatively indifferent but is nevertheless punished by fairly harsh chastisements. At times, the punished act does not violate any common sentiment: there is nothing in us that protests against fishing or hunting out of season." Emile Durkheim, *De la division du travail social* (Paris: PUF, 1998), 49.

8 E.P. Thompson, *Whigs and Hunters: The Origin of the Black Act* (London: Allen Lane, 1975); Edward Palmer Thompson, "The Moral Economy of the English Crowd in the Eighteenth Century," *Past & Present* 50 (February 1971): 76–136.

9 Thompson, "The Moral Economy."

10 James C. Scott, *The Moral Economy of the Peasant: Rebellion and Subsistence in Southeast Asia* (New Haven, CT: Yale University Press, 1976).

11 K. Mirzazhanov, *Amnistiia i pomilovanie v Sovetskoi ugolovnoi politike* (Tashkent: FAN, 1991), 17–18, 20. Miriam Dobson, *Khrushchev's Cold Summer: Gulag Returnees, Crime, and the Fate of Reform after Stalin* (Ithaca, NY: Cornell University Press, 2009); Golfo Alexopoulos, "Exiting the Gulag after War. Women, Invalids, and the Family," *Jahrbücher für Geschichte Osteuropas* 57 (2007): 563–79.
12 GARF R-7523/89s/10/33.
13 GARF R-7523/69s/174/7–11.
14 GARF R-7523/69s/174/8.
15 GARF R-7523/89s/2/1.
16 After Stalin's death, as part of the far-reaching amnesties granted by Beria and his successors, this rate increased from 2.5 per cent for the Supreme Soviet of the USSR in 1954 to 6.2 per cent for the entire country, GARF R-7523/69s/652/124–5.
17 I thank Anna Sventsitskaia from GARF for her help in building the database and Lina Tsrimova for her help in the transcription of cursive letters.
18 Followed by three Armenians, three Azeris, a Georgian, two Chuvashes, a Latvian, a Kalmuk, a Mordvin, an Ingush, a Komi, a Kazakh, a Lezghin, an Uzbek, a Bashkir, a Mari, and a Jew.
19 Antonina Matveevna Simacheva and others stole eight kilograms of wheat at the age of sixteen because "lots of people were taking grain" during this period of famine, GARF R-7863/16/202.
20 GARF R-7863/15/231.
21 GARF R-7863/21/1029.
22 GARF R-7863/21/3065.
23 GARF R-7863/19/1614.
24 GARF R-7863/24/751.
25 GARF R-7863/19/1010.
26 GARF R-7863/15/3/25.
27 GARF R-7863/15/3/10.
28 GARF R-7863/15/3/3–3v.
29 GARF R-7863/15/3/11–12v.
30 GARF R-7863/15/3/2–2v.
31 GARF R-7863/18/2863.
32 GARF R-7863/19/38.
33 GARF R-7863/20/831/3–4.
34 The objective of the RSFSR Penal Code of 1922 is said to be the legal defence (*pravovaia zashchita*) of State workers against crimes and socially dangerous elements. This defence was administered by imposing "social defence" measures to those who infringed upon the revolutionary order, Evgeny B. Pashukanis, *La Théorie Générale Du Droit et Le Marxisme* (Paris: EDI, 1976), 170–3.

35 David R. Shearer, *Policing Stalin's Socialism: Repression and Social Order in the Soviet Union, 1924–1953* (New Haven, CT: Yale University Press, 2009); Paul Hagenloh, *Stalin's Police. Public Order and Mass Repression in the USSR, 1926–1941* (Baltimore: Johns Hopkins University Press, 2009).
36 GARF R-7863/23/1665.
37 The letter referred to the meaning of the acronyms in his letters, to nationalist and guerilla movements who fought against sovietization of western Ukraine during and after the war, the OUN was the Organization of the Ukrainian Nationalists, and UPA, Clandestine Ukrainian Army, its clandestine army branch.
38 GARF R-7863/20/2621.
39 GARF R-7863/19/579.
40 GARF R-7863/22/877.
41 GARF R-7863/18/1054/19ob–20; 44ob–44, 49.
42 Varlam Shalamov, *Récits de la Kolyma* (Paris: Denoël, 1969); Shalamov, *Essais sur le monde du crime* (Paris: Gallimard, 1993); Iu.N. Afanas'ev and V.P. Kozlov, eds., *Istoriia Stalinskogo Gulaga: Konets 1920-kh-pervaia polovina 1950-kh odov: Sobranie dokumentov v semi tomakh. Tom 6. Vosstaniia, bunty i zabakostovki zakliuchennykh* (Moskva: ROSSPEN, 2004).
43 James Heinzen, "Corruption in the Gulag. Dilemmas of Officials and Prisoners," *Comparative Economic Studies* 47, no. 2 (June 2005): 456–75.
44 GARF R-7863/21/1055/2, 5–6.
45 GARF R-7863/21/1055/5–6. The letters date from 1954, the date on which he was ultimately released.
46 GARF R-7863/15/102/16.
47 GARF R-7863/16/163/6, 7–8.
48 Golfo Alexopoulos, *Illness and Inhumanity in Stalin's Gulag* (New Haven, CT: Yale University Press, 2017); Mikhail Nakonechnyi, "Factory of Invalids, Mortality, Disability and Early Release on Medical Grounds in Gulag, 1930–1953," unpublished PhD diss., Oxford University, 2021. See also the chapter by Alan Barenberg in this volume.
49 GARF R-7863/22/1317.
50 GARF R-7863/16/238.
51 GARF R-7863/17/85.
52 Werth, *La terreur et le désarroi*, 411–13.
53 GARF R-7863/16/274/2–2v, 7–7v/12–12v, 18, 22, 24.
54 GARF R-7863/18/2864.
55 Here is the example of Ramazan Kerimovich Azimov, GARF R-7863/23/38. Olga Kucherenko, *Soviet Street Children and the Second World War, Welfare and Social Control Under Stalin* (London: Bloomsbury, 2017). See also the chapter of Immo Rebitschek in this volume.
56 GARF R-7863/21/6671/2ob–4.

57 GARF R-8131/37/4666/81–8.
58 GARF R-8131/32/6327/144.
59 GARF R-8131/32/6327/161–3, 165.
60 Dobson, *Khrushchev's Cold Summer*; Marc Elie, "Rehabilitation in the Soviet Union, 1953–1964: A Policy Unachieved," in *De-Stalinizing Eastern Europe: The Rehabilitation of Stalin's Victims after 1953*, ed. Kevin McDermott and Matthew Stibbe (London: Palgrave-McMillan, 2015), 25–45; Marc Elie, "*Les anciens détenus du Goulag. Libérations massives, réinsertion et réhabilitation dans the USSR post-stalinienne*," unpublished PhD diss., Paris, EHESS, 2007; Jeffrey S. Hardy, *The Gulag after Stalin: Redefining Punishment in Khrushchev's Soviet Union, 1953–64* (Ithaca, NY: Cornell University Press, 2016).
61 GARF R-8131/32/6327/170.
62 GARF R-8131/32/6327/170–2.
63 See Cadiot, *La Société des voleurs*.
64 *Izvestiia TsK KPSS*, 1, no. 312 (January 1991): 192. He accused Beria of also seeking to free recidivist thieves and other hardened criminals, concluding that it was clear that it was to subsequently utilize them in dubious, fascistic affairs.
65 GARF R-9474/16s/545/60–3; Yoram Gorlizki, "De-Stalinization and the Politics of Russian Criminal Justice, 1953–1964," PhD diss., University of Oxford, 1992.

7 "They Are Afraid": Medical Surveillance of Reproduction and Illegal Abortions in the Soviet Union, 1944–1953

AMANDA McNAIR

In April 1951, a people's court in Tbilisi, Georgia, began the trials of M.G. Mikirtichian and A.G. Kazarova, the former on the charge of receiving an illegal abortion and the latter on the charge of performing it. Both women pleaded not guilty. The alleged incident had occurred five months previously. In telling her story, Mikirtichian claimed that her lower back was in pain and she was bleeding from her vaginal area after carrying a large and heavy bundle of firewood into her home, which she shared with her husband, mother-in-law, and young child (although when the incident occurred, she was home alone). Mikirtichian knew that Kazarova, a paramedic, lived on the same street as she did, so she sought her help to stop the bleeding. Kazarova came to Mikirtichian's home and gave her an injection for no charge. The next day, investigators arrived at Mikirtichian's door and interrogated her about the incident that had occurred the previous night. They alleged that she had had an illegal abortion, which she vehemently denied. When the investigators demanded an explanation as to why Kazarova had been over with medical supplies in the night, Mikirtichian gave the story as told above. The interrogators then asked her to sign a statement, seemingly believing her story. However, what Mikirtichian signed held an entirely different statement – one which indicated that she paid Kazarova 300 roubles to perform an illegal abortion. The court records do not say if she was illiterate or not. Although we have no precise timeline for this, soon afterwards Mikirtichian was brought to a clinic for a gynaecological examination by a doctor. The doctor determined that Mikirtichian had not had an abortion (and testified to this effect during the trial). For unknown reasons, the investigators were not satisfied with this answer and so took Mikirtichian to be examined by a different doctor, in this case a forensic expert. However, the expert agreed with the first doctor – no abortion had taken place. Again, the investigators refused to accept this answer. They took Mikirtichian to visit a third doctor, who finally gave the investigators the answer they wanted to hear: yes, an abortion had occurred. However, the doctor could not say how the abortion had been performed, as there was no evidence of forceps, burns, or erosions, which were the main ways to induce an illegal abortion. Further doubt was cast on the allegation when multiple witnesses testified not only to the character of Mikirtichian, but also asserted that she would never ask for an abortion and certainly did not pay Kazarova for one. Despite the distinct lack of physical evidence and the absence of damning testimony against the women, the court in Tbilisi convicted both Mikirtichian and Kazarova on 21 April 1951. Mikirtichian was sentenced to two years in prison and Kazarova to three years.[1]

The case against Mikirtichian and Kazarova was characteristic of how expert medical knowledge intersected with issues of social control and sexual morality in the Soviet Union. In this chapter, I explore how the Soviet state used medical justifications to intervene in the private and intimate lives of its citizens. The state was interested in increasing the birth rate, particularly in light of the staggering demographic imbalance after the Second World War. As such, my chapter will focus largely on the post-war and late Stalinist period. Late Stalinist society as a whole faced stringent measures of social control, as there was a crackdown of theft of state property and corruption as well as several (anti-Semitic) campaigns, targeting the intelligentsia.[2] After the war, efforts were redoubled to make citizens compliant, and physicians and procurators were drawn into these schemes and policies. The trial illustrates the importance that the late Stalinist system put on trying to prosecute and charge those engaged with illegal abortions. Yet the medical surveillance put in place was fundamentally flawed, as both physicians and procurators begrudgingly did the bare minimum to enforce the aggressive pronatalist policies.

The struggle to convict and punish those who had, and especially who performed, abortions was crucial to the aggressive pronatalist policies that were enacted by the Soviet Union beginning in the 1930s. The USSR had originally been the first nation in the world to legalize abortions performed in medical institutions in 1920. These were to be conducted under the strict supervision of the expert of medical professionals. The idea of women deferring to medical personnel led to the medicalization of motherhood and reproduction: women were to be instructed by medical experts on how to take care of themselves, their bodies, and their potential future children properly.[3] This practice of demanding women to submit to the expert care of the doctor persisted throughout the Soviet Union's lifetime. In 1936, the physicians' role and importance grew with the re-criminalization of the abortion procedure and, effectively, many forms of contraception. Many Soviet officials had originally thought that women wanted to have an abortion because they were impoverished and unemployed; and that in time, as Marxist ideology claimed, the need for abortion would be eliminated as women achieved true gender equality and were happy with all the benefits that communism provided.[4] This, however, never occurred. Instead, women clamoured to receive the procedure. In the Russian Soviet Federated Socialist Republic (RSFSR), physicians performed 1,500,000 abortions in 1935 alone.[5] The 1936 ban on abortion was supposed to increase the birth rate. This increased control over reproduction was part of an ideological shift to make the Soviet family become the bedrock of society. Officials assumed that women would accept the ban and have more children. Yet within a year, this proved false as thousands of women simply went through illegal means to have the procedure, typically in far more dangerous conditions. David Hoffmann reports, "Of the 356,200 abortions performed in hospitals in 1937, and 417,000 in 1938, only 10 percent had been authorized, and the rest were incomplete illegal abortions."[6] Women faced two options if they wanted to have an abortion: pay someone to perform the procedure, with the high possibility that they had limited or no medical knowledge; or induce one themselves. As the number of illegal abortions grew, the Soviet government increasingly relied on physicians to whistle-blow on their patients and placed investigative and judicial bodies at the centre of policing and prosecuting women's reproduction.

This story is one largely of the post-war or late Stalinist period from 1944 to 1953, as this was when the Stalinist administration cracked down and actively prosecuted women who had abortions and those accused of performing the procedure illegally. The newfound vigour for the prosecution was likely due to the large demographic crisis that occurred in the post-war period. The Soviet Union lost an unprecedented 27 million citizens in the Second World War, which is not analysed in this chapter. This crisis affected Soviet pronatalist policies until the 1990s. Mie Nakachi provides a perspective on the imbalance: "the sex ratio imbalance deteriorated enormously. The average ratio of men and women of reproductive age reached as low as 19:100 in some rural areas."[7] The state worried about a population decline, which would mean fewer workers for the economy in the future. Before the Second World War was even over, a new family law was passed in 1944. Its ideological aims were similar to the 1936 Family Law – to further strengthen the family and, again, increase the birth rate. The law, however, might have only de-stabilized the family structure by not legally recognizing *de facto* marriages (i.e. cohabitation between partners without formally registering their union as a marriage). The 1944 law further undermined pre-war family structure by not allowing women to claim alimony or child support from male sexual partners. Instead, the state would pay women a fee, which was determined by whether she could work and the number of children she had.[8] As such, this clause allowed men to have sexual freedom while simultaneously restricting women's choices. In addition, both of these clauses were essential in explaining why many women in the post-war era wanted an abortion – unstable partnerships and marriages and the lack of help from partners.

This chapter contributes and builds on the scholarship of reproductive politics and social control in the Soviet Union. Mark Field describes three "points of contact" between a doctor and a patient: the doctor–patient consultation, abortion commissions, and post-abortion emergency care.[9] Additionally, Field called doctors disenfranchised bureaucrats in the Soviet system. While not disagreeing with the principle set out by Field, I echo Christopher Burton's important point: physicians were more than just "points of contact," but were also informants, criminal investigators, and educators.[10] However, I push this description even further: since physicians only half-heartedly complied with the surveillance system the state put in place, they had far more agency than they have previously been given credit for. Donald Filtzer documents how doctors were instrumental to the state's medical surveillance on factory workers and making sure they were attending. Though Filtzer notes, "Doctors were not always as ruthless in this regard as the regime would have liked."[11] This illustrates that physicians chafed under the state's restrictions, whether they were about work attendance or reproductive choices. Peter Solomon Jr. analyses the pressures placed on the Ministry of Justice's judicial officials regarding illegal abortion cases and also demonstrates that the police and procurators also did not fully participate in the Soviet system of medical surveillance and policing. This chapter will be the first to combine the surveillance and policy responsibilities from both the Ministries of Health and Justice.[12] Furthermore, no scholar has focused on how women, physicians' patients, interacted with and negotiated the system to their own advantage or documented their refusal to engage with it. Other scholars, such as Wendy Goldman and Mie Nakachi, have documented the staggering numbers of women who had abortions and examined the top-down political discussions behind the pronatalist policies.[13] However, none of these authors have not included the sources or accounts of "ordinary" Soviet women – though it was not the purpose of their respective works. This chapter also relies on testimony from women and physicians from the Harvard Project on the Soviet Social System (HPSSS), records and meetings from the Ministries of Health and Justice, and court documents as these sources are vital for illustrating the differences between the party-state's policies and the lived experience of not just physicians and procurators, but also Soviet women. As such, I provide an analysis of not just state-oriented views and practices, but also provide an examination and discussion of the struggles women and physicians faced under Stalin's surveillance and control.

This illegal abortion case of Mikirtichian and Kazarova was unusual in many regards; but it nonetheless reflects many of the tensions and inconsistencies that were present within the illegal abortion laws. First and foremost, most illegal abortions came to the attention of the police and procurators when women sought emergency medical treatment after the procedure had gone awry. Legally, the medical officials had to report the abortion, and many of them did. However, Mikirtichian did not go to the hospital, so it is unclear how the investigative bodies found out about the incident. Second, there was no clear evidence that an abortion had even transpired. Two of the three physicians testified that there was no indication of the procedure occurring, and the physician that did testify that Mikirtichian had an abortion claimed there was no sign of forceps or of other indicators (such as burns, cuts, scrapes, etc.) of an abortion. Finally, the case also demonstrates the immense pressure and also the lack of timeliness that many illegal abortion cases faced. The police and procurators needed to fulfil case quotas and convictions, yet were also slow with their paperwork and cases and trials were delayed for weeks, if not months, along with this case.

I will now walk through each of these points and demonstrate how this case illustrates the tensions in the bureaucratic politics between the Ministry of Health and the Ministry of Justice as well as how women attempted to demonstrate their own agency and control of their reproductive capacities. First, I examine the physicians, their legal responsibilities, and what was expected from them. Second, I illustrate the ways in which women attempted to work the system to their advantage. Finally, I investigate the departmental infighting that occurred over reporting, investigating, and prosecuting illegal abortion. The mutual unwillingness of the Ministries of Health and Justice to co-operate spilled over into constant resentment between them, and an institutional blame game ensued. Ultimately, neither side wanted to police illegal abortions – which, therefore, hamstrung from the beginning the punitive surveillance system that the state wanted to implement.

Physicians and Patients

Physicians' responsibilities increased with the aggressive pronatalist policies that the Soviet Union implemented, beginning with the 1936 criminalization of abortion. They were already considered to be the "gatekeepers" to abortion access, not least because they served on the commissions that had been erected in the 1920s to determine if a woman qualified to have an abortion.[14] While the ban severely restricted women's access to the procedure, it did not eliminate it completely, and these commissions remained in place. Instead, the ban restricted the criteria, which now consisted only of forty-nine medical reasons, ranging from heart conditions to blindness.[15] In order to receive a legal abortion, women had to go through masses of bureaucratic red tape. First, a woman needed to confirm her pregnancy with a doctor and request to have an abortion for a medical reason. Then, the physician would perform tests to confirm that the woman had the disease she claimed. If the doctor was satisfied then they would write up a report, detailing the reasons why they felt the woman should have the abortion. The report would then be sent to the abortion commission who would review the woman's case. This reinforced the idea and practice that women needed to comply with the expertise of medical professionals, especially in order to achieve a legal abortion. Abortion commissions consisted of an obstetrician-gynaecologist, a therapist, and a third member who would rotate, being a physician who was a specialist in the particular disease the pregnant woman claimed to have.[16] The result was that women who did not meet the stringent criteria – or who decided to circumvent the lengthy process altogether – sought illegal alternatives, resulting in a significant increase in the number of such abortions. Such women took control of their own reproductive capacities in the best ways they could and, in many cases, abortion was the only way they knew how to terminate a pregnancy.

After the 1936 ban, doctors were supposed to report if women had illegal abortions, but many refused to comply.[17] This practice was forced to change with the issuing of the November 1940 manual *Instructions on the Battle Against Criminal Abortions* issued by the Ministry of Health. This booklet made it crystal clear that physicians would now be the initial investigators and whistle-blowers when a patient was suspected of having an illegal abortion. The instructions contained within were specifically issued to give unambiguous instructions on how illegal abortions were to be reported and investigated. The first step was that medical officials were to notify the local procurators about the suspected illegal abortion within twenty-four hours of the woman being admitted to the medical institution.[18] The doctor would also include their own reports and notes about the situation, which included an explanation as to why they felt the abortion was criminal, a description of the circumstances that led to the abortion, and finally, the results of the woman's gynaecological examination.[19] In order to determine how and by whom the abortion was conducted, there were two approaches doctors used: first, an interrogation of the woman by the physician; second, a gynaecological examination, which provided physical evidence not just as to whether an abortion had occurred but also how it might have occurred. Many common signs of an abortion were included, such as looking for "traumatic damage" to the vagina, cervix, uterus, and/or birth canal; burns or scrapes of the cervix or uterus; the presence of forceps; or even the introduction of substances to induce an abortion, like iodine.[20]

The medical materials provided by the doctor were to be used to help initiate a case against the abortionist or, if the abortionist could not be discovered, the woman herself. These reports also left a paperwork trail, since not just the physician but also the head doctor at the time needed to sign off on the report and make a note of its existence in their record books.[21] This additional step may have been another way to hold multiple physicians accountable for reporting criminal abortions. Even if the woman died, it was still necessary for physicians to notify the procurator's office. The instructions dictated that it was essential for the clothing the woman wore as well as any documents that were collected to be sent to the investigators. In the event of a death, an autopsy and forensic medical examination were to be conducted.[22] Ideally, the materials collected would be enough to create a case against the abortionist.

In addition to these reports, the 1940 instructions detailed ways a physician could get a (potentially deathbed) confession from a patient.[23] Women who went to clinics for post-abortion care were severely sick or near death, and therefore extremely vulnerable. Many women would answer in order to continue receiving help. The interrogation was supposed to lead to a confession that established the circumstances that led the woman to resort to a criminal abortion as well as how and by whom the operation was performed.[24] Interrogation, however, rarely led to information regarding abortionists as women would refuse to name names, claim they performed the abortion themselves, or maintain that they had an accidental miscarriage. One doctor claimed, "women ... categorically deny outside interference when they have had an [illegal] abortion."[25] Although some women would admit to having a criminal abortion, only to successfully retract the statement later.[26] Women were not supposed to be interrogated by the official investigator or procurator without the doctor's permission, but since physicians were the ones at the hospital collecting the initial information, they were the first ones to interrogate the patient.[27]

Medical surveillance was not confined to simply reporting women if they had an illegal abortion, however. Instead, the Ministry of Health devoted large amounts of time and effort to trying to prevent illegal abortions from occurring from the moment women came in to confirm their pregnancy.[28] During the appointment, a one-on-one conversation between the physician and the patient occurred. Doctors were not just to check the woman's blood pressure, urine, and pelvis, but were also to attempt to check that the woman would continue the pregnancy if there were no medical reasons for her to apply for a legal abortion.[29] Despite this conversation being considered the most difficult form of medical education due to its intimate nature, Ministry of Health internal reports and pamphlets issued within the medical field implied the blame was on doctors if the consultation conversation was not carried out correctly.[30] Comrade E. Isaeva, the head of the Administration for Maternity Care, sent updated suggestions and instructions on how doctors should behave when conducting anti-abortion propaganda to the Deputy Minister of Health of the USSR, M.D. Kovrigina. Physicians needed to be sensitive to a woman's needs while also analysing her answers to see if she would request an abortion or keep the pregnancy. The instructions claimed that only if women could trust the physician and medical personnel would they believe that the state would take care of them and the future child.[31] Doctors were ordered to persuade the woman until she accepted that the "reason" for not having a child was insufficient or there could be a change in her personal circumstances.[32] If women were not inclined to listen to the doctor's advice, medical personnel were to remind the woman that motherhood was a noble and respected position in the Soviet Union, that monetary benefits could be received from the state, and that the effects of illegal abortions could be serious, if not fatal.[33]

These internal documents from the Ministry of Health readily assign blame to those who digressed from the state's directives. A 1950 report written by Isaeva and another Ministry of Health official gave directions on how doctors and their assistants should approach, talk to, and persuade a woman and her relatives to keep her pregnancy. This required great sensitivity on the part of the medical official and "an insistent desire to achieve favourable results in their work."[34]

The directive to get women to talk clearly had two reasons. First, for one to be considered a good physician, it was necessary to interrogate the woman and have her reveal these personal reasons. Second, these statements introduce the idea of personal responsibility. If a health professional could not achieve these goals, then he or she failed to cultivate the trust of the patient, to be sensitive enough, or to investigate fully. The public never saw these internal reports, but they were circulated among the general medical community. The Ministry of Health wanted to warn everyday health professionals that they were to be held accountable if they failed to stop criminal abortions or to conduct the necessary health education.

State medical officials, however, also suggested some more subversive ways in which physicians could convince their patient to keep the pregnancy. Women who specifically came to the doctor for a medical referral for a legal abortion were watched, particularly if a patient developed a history of requesting abortions.[35] Since women were legally allowed to have a clinical abortion if they suffered from a detrimental disease, state health professionals were worried that women would attempt to fake illnesses to have an abortion. Therefore, to document this, after a consultation where a woman requested a clinical abortion, the physician had to submit paperwork to the hospital administration documenting the appointment's notes, the reason for the abortion request, and the tests necessary to prove the patient's specified illness. The request created a paper trail as the woman's gynaecologist had to have the head doctor of the hospital or clinic sign and submit the appeal.[36] Abortion commissions would review the documents and reasons for the abortion, return their verdict to the hospital or clinic, and copies of the appeal and decision were to be kept at the medical institution. In keeping these records, hospital administrations were able not just to collect data for Ministry of Health statistics, but closely watch women's medical histories to police their behaviour in the future.[37]

Doctors were specifically instructed to give particular care to the observation of single women, women in *de facto* marriages, and women who had what was referred to as a "nervous condition."[38] The Instructions implied these groups of women were thought to be at particularly high risk for wanting to terminate a pregnancy. For single women, their living or work situations might not have facilitated having a new child, as they would likely be in a hostel, work dormitory, or communal housing. *De facto* marriages were perceived to be unstable, as they were not recognized in the post-war system as being legal due the ironically named 1944 Family Law. As such, if women in these groups were pregnant, their partners would have no legal or financial obligations to them or their children.[39] In the last case, there is no elaboration of what constituted a "nervous condition." One can infer that such a condition would be picked up via body language or responses to questions posed during the consultation. In these cases, if the physician suspected the woman might want an abortion, either legal or illegal, then they would not immediately notify the woman of her pregnancy. Instead, the doctor would recommend the woman come in for a re-examination in a few days. In that time period, the physician would pass the case to social and legal workers so they could find out about the woman's life, her living conditions, her relationship with her family or partner, and determine the "appropriate measures of moral impact" for the patient in order to convince her to keep the pregnancy.[40]

Physicians were not only largely resentful of their new roles, but concerned about what it would mean for women in their communities. Doctors understood that women would remain reluctant to come to the clinics once they figured out physicians' role in the surveillance scheme, and this would lead to larger problems. Women avoided the clinics, particularly if they knew they were pregnant and planned on having an illegal abortion.[41] This could present further issues if a woman had additional medical issues, such as venereal diseases, since they could not be treated because of the woman's refusal to come to the clinic. A doctor in Kyiv noted that this phenomenon meant there was "no complete continuity in the treatment and supervision."[42] A doctor in Russia contended, "If two-thirds of pregnant women avoid maternity clinics, it is because they are afraid that clinics will report their pregnancy."[43] Women clearly adopted this avoidance tactic because they knew they faced surveillance in terms of home visits from medical staff, hospitals routinely checking their medical files, and potentially being detained in maternity clinics until their due date.

Many physicians did seem to sympathize with their patients and would sometimes aid them to avoid being arrested and prosecuted. Women could face serious consequences if they survived their post-abortion care, which included being fined to being sentenced to prison. Some doctors would evade reporting illegal abortions, or at least report that the woman had a miscarriage. One physician who worked in Central Asia, though she does not specify where, explained that in her clinic, "Doctors, as a rule, tried to help these women and always wrote that the woman lifted something heavy … none of my colleagues ever heard anyone say that it was either [a] self-abortion or that it was performed by somebody else either."[44] Referring back to the Georgian case, even after examining the evidence, it is unclear if Mikirtichian's abortion was intentional or not. While she attempted to excuse herself by stating that she was already a mother and had never sought an abortion before, this explanation was problematic for two reasons. The first is that women who sought abortions statistically tended to already be mothers and in the prime of their reproductive years, between twenty and thirty-nine years old.[45] The second is because Mikirtichian claimed to be carrying firewood which was extremely heavy. While this may be factually true, women who induced abortions themselves told doctors and authorities that they had lifted heavy items and therefore it was an accidental miscarriage. This excuse was also very common advice from *babkis* (older women from rural areas who used folk medicine and had no formal medical training), beginning in the 1920s.[46] There were physicians who were certainly willing to help women, though they might not have done so with investigators standing over them and inspecting their reports.

Evidently, though, women did not passively accept the attempted social control via medical surveillance. However, many of the recorded incidents discussed below demonstrate that women relied more on the expertise of the physicians and asked for their help in providing them with an illegal abortion, or how they could safely have one at home; this is a drastic change from the pre-war period when most women, particularly rural ones, distrusted doctors and instead would seek the advice of *babkis*. This may be because doctors and hospitals were more widespread or that the doctors' experiences were mostly in larger cities when they had multitudes of women asking for help. Either way, it is clear that women tried to work the Soviet Union's medical system in their favour by finding doctors who were sympathetic, or ones at least willing to take bribes, in order to have an illegal abortion in relative safety. As one physician described, "Each doctor, every day, is asked by many people to perform abortions. Friends, friends of friends ask, 'help, help.' You have to give advice and this is dangerous."[47] It seemed from interviews, which gives testimony that is largely absent from the medical or legal records, that physicians were, overall, largely sympathetic to the plight of these women. One doctor interviewed said there were certainly some loopholes that could be exploited to help women, such as diagnosing women with certain diseases, like acute anaemia.[48] Another loophole described by another physician was to diagnose a woman with malaria, even though she clearly did not have it.[49] However, this allowed the doctor to legally prescribe her quinine, which was a natural abortifacient. As such, women figured out how to use quinine to their advantage. The only issue was when women ignored the physicians' orders to only use small amounts, which would be enough to induce an abortion; these women, instead, took a much larger dose than what was needed and, therefore, needed to be taken to the hospital to be treated. If another doctor interrogated and reported this woman, then the whole scheme would be revealed.[50] One "ordinary" woman who was interviewed revealed that she made her own contraception with quinine.[51] She mixed her prescription of quinine with a cocoa-butter substance, then let it dry and cut it into small slices and used it as her own prophylactic.

However, many doctors also confessed they were worried about being punished for trying to heavily persuade the abortion commission to allow a legal abortion for women, or for conducting an illegal abortion themselves.[52] Abortionists with medical training who performed illegal abortions were supposed to be sentenced to between five and eight years in prison, and up to ten if a woman died.[53] Soviet press reported that most illegal abortions were conducted in "unsanitary conditions" by medically ignorant people.[54] However, it is also clear from interviews with physicians that some doctors did take the risk for some of their patients, and some without any monetary compensation.[55] One doctor discussed how her friend performed an illegal abortion for a patient in the woman's apartment but was found out because the patient ended up losing too much blood and needed to be transferred to the hospital. While the woman herself never revealed the doctor's name, when the police went to the apartment and interviewed the neighbours, a young boy said that he had seen a woman enter with a medical bag. That testimony alone was enough to sentence the doctor to fifteen years.[56] Other doctors charged exorbitant fees to make the risk worth it to them. Women reported that illegal abortions ranged from 200 to 1,500 roubles. When taking into consideration that the average factory worker made around 300–500 roubles a month, these fees were incredibly steep. This also illustrates that the price of 300 roubles that investigators alleged Mikirtichian paid Kazarova for her illegal abortion was not random. However, this did show the length that women were prepared to go to terminate an unwanted pregnancy.

Policing and Prosecuting

The doctors and procurators were both under immense pressure from the heads of the Ministries of Health and Justice to limit the number of illegal abortions that were occurring. Just as physicians had short deadlines to report their patients, investigative and judicial bodies also had very tight timelines to follow; in which respect, similar to physicians, they often dragged their feet. While I have not found any particular moral objections to banning abortion among procurators in the way that the evidence suggests was the case with doctors, the Ministry of Justice was already under tight deadlines and had to balance these responsibilities with other cases.[57] The intense pressure to meet deadlines and successfully solve cases led to officials not only construing existing data, but also simply fabricating it at times. Since investigators and procurators had to complete a certain number of cases per month, they preferred to avoid illegal abortion cases, as they were not considered "easy."[58] In order to simplify their workload, however, investigators purposefully neglected to look for the abortionist in criminal abortion cases as this was often difficult, especially when women refused to name anyone. However, even when physicians reported their patients, the Ministry of Justice still often failed to meet the stringent deadlines set. When these practices were investigated, the bureaucratic blame game began. Regardless of the political in-fighting, the ministries obeying Stalin's harsh policing had an unintended consequence: restricting women's contraceptive choices forced them to use criminal abortions, as many women did not qualify for a legal abortion under the new restrictive guidelines, which reinforced officials' views that control over women's reproduction needed to be strengthened.

In a meeting in 1945, the future Minister of Health under Nikita Khrushchev, M.D. Kovrigina, illustrated how vital physicians were to the prosecuting process and how the medical community was now an instrument of control for the state, "If we work badly, the judicial and investigative bodies do not work at all."[59] The doctors in the audience, however, had serious contentions with this statement. They all joined together to give variations of how procurators had not or would not investigate the illegal abortion cases that they sent to the procurators. One doctor claimed that he repeatedly visited his procurator's office to follow up on cases and discovered that they had been transferred to different districts and the investigator had already moved on to an entirely separate case.[60] Another physician argued that medical officials were willing to combat abortion, yet the procurator's office treated the cases with little interest. Therefore, physicians were fighting a losing battle without the assistance of investigators and procurators.[61] If investigative bodies were not able to complete their jobs, then trials were delayed or never even brought to court, which allowed the problem to continue to be rampant.

Yet the Ministry of Justice maintained that the lack of abortion cases being prosecuted was the fault of physicians and medical staff. A representative of the state procurator acknowledged the criticisms of the lacklustre performance of some procurators, but he maintained that doctors were to blame for the quality of medical documentation submitted to the procurator.[62] He argued,

"Can we send cases with such [medical records] to the court? No, we cannot, if we do not have objective medical information which demonstrates that there was an abortion as a result of a criminal intervention."[63]

The Ministry of Justice had valid points in that medical personnel were reluctant to report or hand over patient files.

Despite legally only having twenty-four hours to submit their report, procurators' offices throughout the Soviet Union consistently complained and reported that they most often received material regarding illegal abortions between twenty and thirty-five days after the incident had occurred.[64] In a 1950 report, the Chairman of the Sverdlovsk regional court claimed, "In the case of a criminal abortion, it is often not stated under what circumstances and in what condition the pregnant woman was admitted to the hospital and the circumstances that led the health worker to conclude that this case was a criminal abortion."[65] Some physicians only reported if the woman had died, again in the same amount of time.[66] When physicians would report, they would not typically submit the medical file and notes; or if they did submit the file and notes, they would be extremely scant in information.[67] In 1951, a procurator from Leningrad claimed that only 8 per cent of women admitted to hospitals as a result of illegal abortions were ever reported to the prosecution authorities.[68] As such, procurators continued to imply that it was the physicians who impeded their investigations and cases of criminal abortions.

A particularly contentious issue was in the potential confrontations between doctors and patients. While the 1940 instructions state that the questioning of physicians and medical personnel, as well as potentially summoning them to court as witnesses, was only to be done in cases of extreme necessity.[69] The woman who had the abortion could only be interrogated by the procurator or investigator with the permission of the doctor.[70] Yet investigators commonly merged these two functions. Investigators ruthlessly interrogated the victims, regardless of how the women or physicians felt regarding the situation. Absent from the cooperation of the victim, it could be difficult to determine if the abortion was a miscarriage or illegally produced.[71] Even if women, such as Mikirtichian, refused to admit they had an illegal abortion, they would refuse to accept this answer and press further hoping the woman would confess.

As investigators attempted to fill their closed case quota, they did not consider the relationship between the doctor and the woman. Women were continuously humiliated, as they were forced to relive the traumatic experience of a potential botched abortion, and endured invasive medical exams, and intrusive questioning both by medical professionals and investigators as their private lives would be publicly discussed in court. As in the case of Mikirtichian, she had to endure three gynaecological examinations by three different physicians who read their reports to the court, portions of which made it into the record.

Reports from procurators demonstrate that the investigative bodies would fixate on obtaining the confession from women who had an abortion. This is also clear from the Georgian trial: authorities refused to believe Mikirtichian and either falsified her statement or coerced her into signing one that did not relate to the story she described. The authorities would neglect interviewing family members or searching homes or apartments for items that may have indicated an abortion (this included particular instruments, "recipes," etc.). Investigators and procurators focused on simply prosecuting the woman by the easiest means (i.e. the interrogation) instead of focusing on finding an abortionist. As one report describes, "The police and investigating authorities are extremely superficial in investigating ... They do not take all the necessary measures to clarify the persons responsible ... they are satisfied with the allegations that they [the women] performed the abortions themselves."[72] Reports discussed the "significant drawback" of the courts to not prosecute women who are interviewed or are witnesses in illegal abortion cases to have had or performed a criminal abortion themselves.[73] This would involve far more work for the investigative and judicial bodies, which is probably the main reason why they did not pursue these options.

This is not to say that judicial bodies were not immune to issues of time management regarding illegal abortion cases. Despite the 1940 instructions stating that courts needed to have illegal abortion cases no later than ten days from when they were received, the courts simply could not keep up with this demand.[74] In Sverdlovsk *oblast'*[75] in 1949, the courts only reviewed about half of the illegal abortion cases within the mandated ten-day period.[76] In the Molotovsky district of Sverdlovsk, out of 125 cases, 48 per cent were seen in ten days, though most were in court within twenty days, or 83.2 per cent. Despite this, there were still some cases that took over a month to have their day in court.[77]

In 1950, out of 266 reports for which preliminary check was completed in a procurator's office in Leningrad, only sixteen reports, or 6 per cent of all the received reports, were checked within the legally mandated ten-day period.[78] In several cases in Leningrad, it took investigators two months to even initiate the investigation of alleged criminal abortion cases.[79] Of the nearly 200 cases completed between February and April 1951, the abortions had been committed in 1950.[80] As such, the Mikirtichian and Kazarova case was investigated quite quickly in comparison. It seems that the investigation and examination took place within a few days; however, having the trial five months later aligns with these practices. The prosecution office attempted to explain the reason for the amount of time between initiation and completion was due to the lack of cooperation on the part of medical personnel and institutions.

Many courts claimed they could not hold to illegal abortion trials within the deadline since their investigative workload was too much. They referred as well to the difficulties of transferring both prisoners and their case materials. One procurator complained that if he gave all the suspected criminal abortion cases to the investigators, then they would not have had time to complete any of their other work.[81] The chairman of the Sverdlovsk regional court complained that for a number of cases, there were no special circumstances that impeded their trial and delay was through the fault of the courts.[82] In 312 cases for Sverdlovsk *oblast'*, only 66.1 per cent of materials were transferred to the appropriate investigating authorities within three to ten days; however, there were some cases where it took over a month to have the documents transferred. In some cases, its paperwork was filled out incorrectly and could not be determined when it arrived to the correct prosecuting office.[83] In two separate cases, two women who were on trial for illegal abortions were supposed to appear in court on 27 July 1948, but their case was cancelled and transferred to a people's court of the Pervouralsk district, where it was considered only on 24 March 1949.[84] While the report does not say the fate of these two women, this does not appear to be an isolated incident, for the description comes after a report on how judicial bodies routinely failed to meet deadlines for illegal abortion trials.[85] This demonstrates that the investigative and judicial bodies consistently overlooked illegal abortion cases, against both women who had them illegally and the abortionists themselves.

Even when cases made it to court, the prosecuting and sentencing of abortionists was uneven throughout the Soviet Union. The procurator of Krasnodar *krai* (region) reported that in 1950 and the first half of 1951, his department located and closed down twenty-six abortion clinics throughout the city of Krasnodar.[86] During this same period, probably due to the large number of illegal abortion clinics discovered, the percentage of convictions with a sentence of three to ten years nearly doubled from 36 per cent to 63 per cent.[87] Yet, in 1952, a report to the deputy General Procurator of the USSR from the head of the Criminal Judicial Department, reported how investigative authorities lacked initiative in their cases. They often limited themselves to only finding enough evidence to prosecute the woman who had the abortion, not the abortionists themselves.[88] The reason for this has two possible, and related, explanations: the first, procurators needed to reach a certain case quota and they found chasing down abortionists difficult and time consuming; the second, if a procurator needed to fulfil his quota limit, then he would go to the local hospital and search for cases of "self-abortion."[89] However, if the convicted abortionist was a physician, he or she was supposed to be banned from practising for an unspecified period of time. Yet, throughout the entire Soviet Union in 1951, this punishment was applied to only thirty people; of which about 30 per cent of those convicted of providing illegal abortions were doctors or people with at least secondary medical education.[90] Kazarova, who had formal medical knowledge as a paramedic, was sentenced to three years and forbidden from practising for an additional year. While this was only the minimum sentence for an abortionist, her appeal was denied and the Supreme Court of the USSR replied to her, stating, "it is established that you are condemned correctly."[91]

Conclusion

The 1936 criminalization of abortion made it nearly impossible for Soviet women to control their fertility safely. The law took away women's reproductive autonomy in an attempt to raise the birth rate. This only worked temporarily, as it rose from 30.1 in 1935 to 39.6 in 1937 but declined quickly thereafter. By 1940, the fertility level for Russia was below the 1936 level.[92] The Soviet government placed physicians and medical officials in charge of defending and actively endorsing the state's pronatalist agenda. This agenda demanded doctors and medical personnel to not just subject women to "education" about the dangers of abortion, but to coerce and, in some cases, force them to keep their pregnancies. In placing the responsibility of pronatalism in the hands of doctors cultivating relationships with their patients, top governmental officials would blame the physicians if they failed to persuade their patient to not have an abortion. By having the medical community work with law enforcement agencies, in a broader context, the Soviet government used medical justifications to intervene in citizens' private lives in attempts to control them.

The period of late Stalinism saw an increasing desire and attempt to control every corner of society.[93] The increasing implementation of the criminal laws became a critical tool for the advancement of the socialist project, as a criminal conviction meant time spent in prison or labour camps. As Juliene Fürst argues, "Stalinist social control was based on an exclusionary model, which neatly divided society between those who were allowed and expected to participate, and those who were exiled to … Soviet 'non-spaces'… Late Stalinist rule had no time for correcting imperfections."[94] The division between those who were allowed to participate in everyday society and those in "Soviet non-spaces" was in the hands of the medical personnel and legal officials. These latter two groups were therefore further instruments in constructing and implementing social control throughout the Soviet Union. Women, if seeking an illegal abortion, made the implicit decision to not participate in Soviet society, as they had broken the law. Their own fate was decided for them if there was a court case.

As has been demonstrated, physicians and judicial bodies did not always fully comply with Soviet law themselves. Many doctors did not agree with the outright ban, especially as they continued to treat thousands of women who suffered or died due to illegal abortions. Investigators wanted cases that were easier in order to meet their case quotas. Judicial bodies also needed to meet their own successful case quotas and suffered if too many were overturned or acquitted. Furthermore, women often sought medical personnel, especially physicians, who were sympathetic and helped them obtain the safest abortion possible. Several doctors did help their patients in their plight – by circumventing the abortion commission or by performing an illegal abortion themselves. Yet, ultimately, women were far more constrained in their actions. Though they demonstrate how people who did not fully accept the official norms and control of the Soviet system were able to exploit the gaps in its administration and inefficiencies in order to use them to their own advantage.

As the state attempted to increase its hold on society, Soviet citizens found themselves in a double role of being representatives of the state as well as citizens. Individuals could represent state interests officially but privately disagree with them or vice versa.[95] This conundrum can be seen with medical and legal officials in the pursuit of criminal abortions. Physicians and other medical staff were in a paradoxical position, as they were instructed to police their patients and report any illegal abortions, yet privately they sought to increase prophylactics and expand the criteria for the abortion procedure in order to cut down on the number of illegal abortions. Investigative and judicial bodies sought to keep up with Stalin's tightening of criminal law and increased sentences. Procurators and judges balanced the convictions given, often not protesting at or giving the full sentence. Yet these two administrations did not work well together since the officials would blame the other for not being able to perform the job the state assigned them to the fullest. Reproductive politics encapsulates how the post-war period is best understood as a debate between official norms and the people affected by them.

Medical personnel and legal officials promoted the state's pronatalist agenda. With abortion illegal again, the procedure was medicalized. The state attempted to control women's sexuality and reproductive autonomy with both legal punitive administrations and medical institutions. Feeling pressure from Party officials, top medical administrators continued to pressure hospitals to perform and consistently update their duties and variations of health education. With physicians showing movies, reading popular novels and propaganda, as well as hosting lectures, they increased the professional regulation of women's bodies and reproduction by producing and regulating knowledge of the abortion procedure. When they failed to control their patients' decisions, medical officials were to report them to the legal agencies. Investigative bodies and procurators would humiliate women by exposing their private life in court and potentially publishing their crime and verdict. In addition, women's punishments ranged from fines to lengthy jail sentences, which were increased in the post-war period. While policing women's reproduction largely did not work due to departmental in-fighting and lack of resources, the abortion surveillance system that was enacted by the health and legal administrations tied into larger issues of the state's social control of Soviet citizens.

NOTES

1 Gosudarstvennyi arkhiv Rossiiskoi Federatsii (GARF) R-9474/33/375/19–26.
2 James Heinzen claims that, with the exception of 1949, at least five times as many people were convicted of property crimes each year until 1953. See James W. Heinzen, "Informers and the State under Late Stalinism: Informant Networks and Crimes against 'Socialist Property,' 1940–53," *Kritika* 8, no. 4 (2007): 793; Juliane Fürst, "Introduction – Late Stalinist Society: History, Policies and People," in *Late Stalinist Russia: Society between Reconstruction and Reinvention*, ed. Juliane Fürst (London: Routledge, 2006), 9.
3 Tricia Starks, *The Body Soviet: Propaganda, Hygiene, and the Revolutionary State* (Madison: University of Wisconsin Press, 2008), 3–11, 95–161; Elizabeth Waters, "The Modernisation of Russian Motherhood, 1917–1937," *Soviet Studies* 44, no. 1 (1992): 123–35.
4 For more on 1920s reasoning and abortion statistics, see Wendy Goldman, *Women, the State, and Revolution: Soviet Family Policy and Social Life, 1917–1936* (Cambridge: Cambridge University Press, 1994), 254–96.
5 Goldman, *Women, the State, and Revolution*, 289.
6 David Hoffmann, *Cultivating the Masses: Modern State Practices and Soviet Socialism, 1914–1939* (Ithaca, NY: Cornell University Press, 2011), 154–5.

7. Mie Nakachi, "N.S. Khrushchev and the 1944 Soviet Family Law: Politics, Reproduction, and Language," *East European Politics and Societies* 20, no. 1 (2006): 40.
8. Rudolph Schlesinger, *Changing Attitudes in Soviet Russia: The Family in the USSR* (London: Routledge, 1949), 367–77.
9. Mark Field, *Doctor and Patient in Soviet Russia* (Cambridge, MA: Harvard University Press, 1961).
10. Christopher Burton, "Mizdrav, Soviet Doctors, and the Policing of Reproduction in the Late Stalinist Years," *Russian History/Histoire Russe* 27, no. 2 (2000): 199–200.
11. Donald Filtzer, *Soviet Workers and Late Stalinism: Labour and the Restoration of the Stalinist System after World War II* (Cambridge: Cambridge University Press, 2002), 101.
12. Peter Solomon, Jr., *Soviet Criminal Justice under Stalin* (Cambridge: Cambridge University Press, 1996).
13. Goldman, *Women, the State, and Revolution*; Mie Nakachi, *Replacing the Dead: The Politics of Reproduction in the Postwar Soviet Union, 1944–1955* (Oxford: Oxford University Press, 2021). For a broader sense of biopolitics and socialism, see Sergei Prozorov, "Living Ideas and Dead Bodies: The Biopolitics of Stalinism," *Alternatives: Global, Local and Political* 38, no. 2 (2013): 208–27.
14. Hilevych and Sato also use the term "gatekeepers" in discussing intrauterine devices and birth control pills in the 1950s–80s. Yulia Hilevych and Chizu Sato, "Popular Medical Discourses on Birth Control in the Soviet Union during the Cold War," in *Children by Choice? Changing Values, Reproduction, and Family Planning in the 20th Century*, ed. A. Gembries, T. Theuke, and I. Heinemann (Berlin: De Gruyter Oldenbourg, 2018), 99–122, 105–6. On abortion in the 1920s and 1930s, see Goldman, *Women, the State, and Revolution*, 261–2.
15. GARF 8009/22/209/29–33.
16. GARF 8009/22/238/24–5.
17. Nakachi, *Replacing the Dead*, 10.
18. GARF 8009/22/15/9.
19. GARF 8009/22/15/9–10.
20. GARF 8009/22/15/9–10.
21. GARF 8009/22/15/9.
22. GARF 8009/22/15/11.
23. GARF 8009/22/15/10.
24. GARF 8009/22/15/10.
25. GARF 8131/32/54/55.
26. An example of this is GARF 8009/22/53/2ob–2.
27. GARF 8009/22/15/12.

28 GARF 8009/22/209/95.
29 Kyiv State Archive 46/8/2/34–5; Burton, "Mizdrav, Soviet Doctors, and the Policing of Reproduction in the Late Stalinist Years," 198.
30 GARF 8009/22/209/95.
31 GARF 8009/22/209/97.
32 GARF 8009/22/209/97.
33 GARF 8009/22/209/97.
34 GARF 8009/22/209/95.
35 GARF 8009/22/209/96.
36 GARF 8009/22/53/9–11.
37 Medical institutions kept records of the number of abortions, both legal and illegal, performed. They would send these numbers into the Ministry of Health. For examples of these cards from the 1950s, see GARF A-482/50/3297.
38 GARF 8009/22/209/96.
39 Mie Nakachi argues this was one of the most significant post-war creations from Khrushchev's 1944 Family Law. Mie Nakachi, "Population, Politics and Reproduction: Late Stalinism and Its Legacy," in *Late Stalinist Russia: Society between Reconstruction and Reinvention*, ed. Juliane Fürst (London: Routledge, 2006), 25–6.
40 GARF 8009/22/209/95–6.
41 GARF 8009/22/15/4.
42 Kyiv State Archive 46/8/2/28.
43 GARF 8009/22/15/4; Mie Nakachi, "Abortion Is Killing Us: Women's Medicine and the Dilemmas for Postwar Doctors in the Soviet Union, 1944–48," in *Soviet Medicine: Culture, Practice and Science*, ed. Frances L. Bernstein, Christopher Burton, and Dan Healey (London: Routledge, 2006), 201.
44 Harvard Project on the Soviet Social System. Schedule B, Vol. 22, Case 1379 (NY) (interviewer M.F.). Widener Library, Harvard University, 23.
45 For an example, see GARF 9492/1a/648/37–8.
46 Goldman, *Women, the State, and Revolution*, 281.
47 Harvard Project on the Soviet Social System. Schedule B, Vol. 22, Case 1379 (NY) (interviewer M.F.). Widener Library, Harvard University, 25.
48 Harvard Project on the Soviet Social System. Schedule B, Vol. 2, Case 1758 (NY) (interviewer M.F.). Widener Library, Harvard University, 47.
49 Harvard Project on the Soviet Social System. Schedule B, Vol. 22, Case 1379 (NY) (interviewer M.F.). Widener Library, Harvard University, 25.
50 Harvard Project on the Soviet Social System. Schedule B, Vol. 22, Case 1379 (NY) (interviewer M.F.). Widener Library, Harvard University, 25.
51 Harvard Project on the Soviet Social System. Schedule B, Vol. 24, Case 139 (interviewer K.G.). Widener Library, Harvard University, 63–4.

52 Harvard Project on the Soviet Social System. Schedule B, Vol. 21, Case 376 (interviewer M.F.). Widener Library, Harvard University, 12.
53 Harvard Project on the Soviet Social System. Schedule B, Vol. 2, Case 1758 (NY) (interviewer M.F.). Widener Library, Harvard University, 50; Schedule A, Vol. 20, Case 396 (interviewer J.O., type A4). Male, 42, Great Russian, Administrator in economic organization, and engineer. Widener Library, Harvard University, 18.
54 This was not a phenomenon that only occurred in the late Stalinist period, but throughout the Soviet Union's lifetime. For an example, see *The Current Digest of the Soviet Press* Volume VII, Number 38, 1955, 23.
55 Harvard Project on the Soviet Social System. Schedule B, Vol. 22, Case 1379 (NY) (interviewer M.F.). Widener Library, Harvard University, 25; Interview Schedule B, Vol. 22, Case 486 (interviewer M.F.). Widener Library, Harvard University, 9.
56 Harvard Project on the Soviet Social System. Schedule B, Vol. 22, Case 1379 (NY) (interviewer M.F.). Widener Library, Harvard University, 25.
57 Solomon, *Soviet Criminal Justice Under Stalin*, 374.
58 Ibid., 375.
59 GARF 8009/22/53/3.
60 GARF 8009/22/53/3–4.
61 GARF 8009/22/53/4.
62 Nakachi, "Abortion Is Killing Us," 201.
63 GARF 8009/22/15/8–9.
64 GARF 1831/32/54/55, 70.
65 GARF 9492, op 1a/648/49.
66 Solomon, *Soviet Criminal Justice*, 218.
67 GARF 1831/32/54/56.
68 GARF 1831/32/54/56.
69 GARF 8009/22/53, l 12.
70 GARF 8009/22/53/12.
71 Solomon, *Soviet Criminal Justice*, 218.
72 GARF 9492/1a/648/79.
73 GARF 9492/1a/648/50, 80.
74 GARF 9492/1a/648/39
75 "Oblast" refers to a regional administrative unit in the Soviet Union or present-day Russian Federation. "Raion" refers to the smaller district unit.
76 GARF 9492/1a/648/56.
77 GARF 9492/1a/648/39.
78 GARF 1831/32/54/5–6.
79 GARF 8131/32/54/6.
80 GARF 1831/32/54/4.
81 GARF 8131/32/54/57.

82 GARF 9492/1a/648/39.
83 GARF 9492/1a/648/49.
84 GARF 9492/1a/648/39.
85 GARF 9492/1a/648/39.
86 GARF 1831/32/54/60.
87 GARF 1831/32/54/64.
88 GARF 8131/32/1024/9, 18.
89 Solomon, *Soviet Criminal Justice*, 219. For more on the Soviet legal system, see E.L. Johnson, *An Introduction to the Soviet Legal System* (London: Methuen & Co Ltd, 1969).
90 GARF 8131/32/1024/13.
91 Schlesinger, *Changing Attitudes in Soviet Russia*, 271; GARF R-9474/33/375/19zh.
92 Hoffmann, *Cultivating the Masses*, 155.
93 Fürst, "Introduction," 9.
94 Ibid., 10.
95 Ibid., 13.

PART III

Post Stalin: Trajectories of Social Control

8 From the Street to the Court (and Back): Juvenile Delinquency in the 1950s

IMMO REBITSCHEK

In spring 1955, the youth of Berezniki caused a stir. On 2 May a group of at least fifty people, schoolchildren mostly, gathered at Churtensk street. For reasons that remain unclear, the group moved towards apartment building no. 9 and, according to police reports, began to circle the building and smash the windows. Some of the residents left their apartments and confronted the youths. The conflict quickly turned physical. Some of the teens attacked a woman and hit her on the head with a rock and then turned on her husband and son. A little while later, a police car entered the scene, but the police (*militsiia*)[1] were outnumbered and practically helpless. Some of the kids blocked the street and told the *militsiia* that the car "will go through only over our dead bodies." Four hours later the situation was resolved. The *militsiia* most likely had called for reinforcement and arrested some of the teenagers. The procurator of the district (*raion*) then took control of the investigation. Whether and how many of them went to trial is unknown.[2]

The events in this small mining town on the banks of the Kama River were a colourful episode but not the only incident in an extensive report of the Perm' regional procuracy covering "juvenile crime" (*nesovershennoletniaia prestupnost'*), "homelessness" (*bezprizornost'*), and "neglect" (*beznadzornost'*) in this region of the Urals. The different categories of "juvenile issues" (*dela nesovershnnoletnikh*) already reflect the complexity of a problem that authorities in the Soviet 1940s and 1950s tried to grasp. Minors from all backgrounds were drawing institutional attention. Schoolchildren, Komsomol members, and young workers made it into police and other reports: kids were drinking, fighting, and sometimes attacking people and property. Others were simply caught unsupervised. In the cosmos of "homelessness" and "neglect" on Soviet streets one could find kids escaping from the orphanages as well as youth gangs (*khuligany*) robbing adults in broad daylight.[3] The spectrum of undesirable behaviour and crime, as we will see, was wide and its boundaries fluid.

Street children challenging Soviet authorities was by no means a post-Stalinist phenomenon. The confrontation with the state and its institutions were part of the everyday culture in the post-war Soviet Union.[4] In 1956, the number of criminal cases against underage delinquents spiked but still did not yet reach the levels seen in 1945.[5] The Second World War had left an entire generation literally and figuratively displaced, turning the streets into "spaces of social disorder."[6] These children of war struggled not only with material hardships but also with the state authorities and their parents' generation in a "quest for a new post-war identity."[7] Juvenile crime and violent behaviour by underage youth groups in particular shaped the public perception that the country was facing a crime wave after 1945.[8] Before that, unsupervised children and adolescents had posed a distinct target group during the mass operations of the 1930s. One can go back even further and trace the Soviet regime's "youth issue" to its origins, when the Bolsheviks had inherited the burden of million "unsupervised children" in the aftermath of World and Civil War.[9] The kids of Berezniki were definitely not the first to fly in the face of the *militsiia* and surely, they were not the last.

Throughout the decades – through terror and war – the Soviet youth challenged state authorities and their attempts to enforce social control. Post-Stalinist Russia experienced yet another surge of crime rates and non-conformist behaviour among all age groups. The first Gulag amnesty in spring 1953 brought the release of over one million people, which contributed to a sudden spike in property-related delicts and cases of assault that were tried in court.[10] At the same time, the regime prioritized the struggle with social misconduct and violent behaviour and thus drew more attention to these conflicts, and to youth behaviour in particular. Given the long continuity of confrontation between children and state authorities, one must ask what changed since Stalin was gone. To be more exact: to what extent did the state adjust its ways of policing youth after 1953? We know of generational changes, cultural markers among young Soviet citizens who appeared increasingly daring towards the Soviet state. Both "Stalin's Last Generation"[11] and Khrushchev's youth facilitated social and cultural change – but what about the institutional reaction to what I will call "non-conformist behaviour"? What can we learn about post-Stalinist social control over juvenile behaviour when looking through institutional lenses?

Historians have studied the world of Soviet street children. The behaviour and cultures of Soviet *bezprizorniki* are a research topic in their own right.[12] From the revolutionary period to the late Stalinist era, historians have shown the ambivalences of repressive, exclusive, and protective custodial regimes.[13] Olga Kucherenko has debunked the myth of an advanced Soviet childcare program during the war. She pointed to the central government relying on "poor administration," "constantly punitive legislation," and deportations to police millions of displaced children. These policies also included rehabilitation or correctional elements, yet the "warfare state" mainly utilized its repressive tool kit of custodial and penal institutions to combat social disorder.[14] Juliane Fürst also emphasized how the Soviet regimes addressed its non-conformist youth mainly through repression and exclusion in postwar times. The Soviet state did address social needs and also provided protective elements while policing its children yet prioritized the eradication of non-conformist behaviour altogether.[15] During the war, the Soviet Union (as other states) punished and excluded displaced kids as "agents of social disorder," while providing others aid and shelter. This duality is explained on the one hand with the ineffective management of resources. The state appeared as a "hierarchical network" governing scarce resources and leaving kids to the mercy of bureaucratic incompetence.[16] On the other hand, the state categorized its displaced youth as promising (thus eligible to care) or threatening and applied repressive techniques (such as deportations or arrest) as an expedient solution to combat the latter.[17]

Accounts on crime and criminality in the post-Stalin era have drawn our attention to the cultural implications of social deviance. In Brian LaPierre's reading, the post-Stalinist state used its legal resources to contain (and define) social disorder. Legal authorities used the article on "hooliganism" (*khuliganstvo*) to antagonize and frame deviant behaviour as the social and cultural threat to a peaceful socialist community.[18] At the same time, the regime increasingly relied on educational campaigns and facilitated peer pressure in schools, enterprises or the Komsomol, to push children and adolescents into submission. The collective leadership found a new balance between coercion and propaganda when controlling youth behaviour.[19] While this shift is beyond doubt, in all these accounts the state remained a rather monolithic agent that sometimes overstrained its resources and adjusted its tactics towards an ever-growing and complex social (and cultural) spectrum. Research tends to erase this complexity on the side of the state and often does not differentiate within the institutional framework of state power. To regulate behaviour, to enforce social control, the Soviet government operated through a variety of institutional channels and agents: criminal investigations, police controls, court proceedings, orphanages, labour camps, and other penal and custodial institutions. Legal historians have emphasized the efforts of judges, investigators, and procurators to establish a separate procedural framework for juvenile delinquencies yet rarely turned it into a research topic – especially regarding late and post-Stalinism.[20]

On the following pages I would like to shed light on this complexity, asking in what ways juvenile behaviour challenged public authorities or drew the attention of state institutions. What strategies and approaches did these authorities rely on to enforce social control among the Soviet youth? I will give an overview on the ways and policies, the institutions and strategies used from official authorities to respond to juvenile behaviour, considered either "illegal" or at least worth policing in the early 1950s. Instead of building around a watershed of 1953, I will treat the late 1940s and early 1950s as a single coherent period based on consistent crime rates but more importantly, on policing strategies that evolved throughout time. This periodization is also reflected in recent Gulag historiography.[21]

I will give a brief outline on the situation in the Soviet streets in the early 1950s, drawing a short statistical sketch of homelessness, neglect, and crime shortly before and after 1953. This provides us with an image of the "streets," seen through the lens of the state. On this basis, we will follow the children through these lenses from the streets through various institutions to the courts and labour camps – not to portray the Soviet youth but to highlight different strategies and agents of social control: namely the police organs (*militsiia*, MVD officials) and legal institutions (procuracy and judiciary). While the *militsiia* defined the everyday encounter for street children with the state, it was the procuracy that oversaw the legal, administrative, and social implications of juvenile behaviour in the Soviet Union. In 1940, the Procurator General established a specific "Department for Juvenile Issues," rebranded as a "Task Force" (*gruppa*) in 1944 with branches in every region.[22] The Soviet procuracy did not only account for the prosecution in court but also inspected all judicial measures and actions taken by investigators, the police, and the courts. In theory, nearly every step of the way from the streets to the court fell into the procurators' jurisdiction or at least supervision.[23] It was their task and professional conviction to enforce procedural rules either along with or against the resistance and inertia of the *militsiia* and other MVD branches. However, there was no difference in pedagogical viewpoints. The procuracy advocated the same position towards juvenile delinquency and towards punishment as educational means as the other state institutions. All authorities involved (teachers, directors, *militsiia*) were in line with the idea that "repression" – the detention in Correctional Labour Camps – was a legitimate "complementary" tool for the re-education of juvenile offenders.[24] The procuracy and its task force rather sought to enforce a clear differentiation between "negligence" and "crime" and a more precise and elaborate way of investigating, contextualizing, and sentencing juvenile criminality. Based on the files of the regional procuracy of Molotov region (renamed Perm' in 1954), the Procurator General, and the Ministry of Justice, I will shed light on the continuities, changes, and institutional differences in policing Soviet street children before and after 1953.

Dangerous Streets – The "Juvenile Issue" in the Early 1950s

In the 1950s Molotov was a region in transition. The Urals region had been growing swiftly ever since the evacuation of heavy industry into the hinterland during the war. At the same time, administrative reforms had left the newly created region without proper infrastructure while the ever-growing system of penal and POW camps brought a steady influx of prisoners, *spetskontingenty*, deportees, and (underage) refugees.[25] The Urals were a basin for displaced persons of all kinds. Molotov's population grew from 300,000 in 1939 to 1.85 million in 1946, and the permeable borders of the camp and prison system shaped the face of a post-war society in conflict. The campaign against theft in 1947 brought millions of people (and parents) to court and to jail.[26] As the Gulag grew in the late 1940s, so did the crime rates in the region and also the number of underage persons on the radar of Soviet authorities. The first amnesty after Stalin's death in 1953 released yet another wave of underage delinquents into the streets of Molotov.[27] How did Soviet authorities read and quantify this situation?

The state radar for juvenile activities relied on the aforementioned categories of neglect, homelessness, and criminality. The terms stem from pre-revolutionary times. *Bezprizorniki* became a popular catch-all category to identify and describe mostly homeless children, street gangs, and orphans who evaded state custody. There was a rhetorical difference between "homeless" orphans and "neglected" *beznadzorniki* (with parents), yet both the discourse and the administrative framework surrounding it tended to merge them in describing youngsters out of control.[28] Two notorious decrees in spring 1935 established the administrative framework, and subsequent regulations in 1943 and 1952 amended it for years to come. The radar (roughly) distinguished two groups: first, homeless and neglected children, as well as "petty *khuligany*" or criminals too young for prosecution (under twelve), destined for "education" and "help from the state."[29] The other group consisted of juvenile delinquents (between twelve and sixteen),[30] left to the responsibility of law enforcement. The administrative eye thus saw social cases on the one hand and criminal cases on the other. The statistics on juvenile behaviour were kept accordingly. In the early 1950s the *militsiia* biannually detained more than 160,000 "neglected" and between 15,000 and 20,000 "homeless" children. At the same time, the courts tried between 10,000 and 13,000 juveniles.[31] Juvenile delinquency rose steadily since 1940 and peaked in 1945, remaining at a high level until 1947.[32] In that year, nearly 60,000 juvenile offenders received a court sentence. The campaign against theft petered out in 1950, and only 11,000 juvenile cases were registered after that.[33] In 1954, juvenile delinquency rose with regular cases, from 38,529 in 1954 to nearly 50,000 sentences in 1956.[34] Juvenile offences consistently made up 5 per cent of the overall crime rates in the Soviet Union, and also the proportion between "neglected" and "criminal" persons remained relatively stable. In 1954, the *militsiia* in Molotov detained ten times more children than the procuracy brought to court. The same rate applied to the RSFSR, where the *militsiia* detained 246,000 children, and 24,252 were brought to court.[35]

Three things are apparent here. One, in the eyes of legal and police authorities, the "juvenile issue" was most pressing in the late 1940s and, after a brief phase of statistical decrease, was on the rise again and stayed at a high level after 1953. Second, the issue of "negligence" seemed constantly to outweigh the threat of criminality, implying that the country was struggling with bureaucratic weaknesses and heedless parents rather than crime waves. More importantly, the lion's share of street children went through the corridors of the police while only a fraction faced legal charges. These numbers reflect certain social anomalies and shocks (war, legal campaigns, amnesties), but one must question both the numbers and the administrative rigour behind these categories. How came these numbers into existence, how to distinguish social from criminal cases, and what did it mean for juveniles to end up in either of these categories?

MVD Street Work

The practical difference between these categories was determined by the institutions involved. Furthermore, it reflected a particular sphere of influence which since 1935 was claimed by the Ministry of the Interior: "The Struggle with negligence and homelessness is the most important and everyday task of the entire Chekist apparatus." Accordingly, only the NKVD (then MVD) could respond to "thieves, hooligans, bandits and counterrevolutionaries."[36] The rhetoric itself transcended the line between social needs and criminal offenders. "Homelessness" was not an analytic category but the Ministry's label for individuals challenging and escaping social control. Consequently, before and after 1953 a juvenile's first encounter on the streets with the state was with the *militsiia* (as part of the GUM and thus the MVD), and it was the *militsiia* that ultimately defined the situation and the reasons for detention. The procuracy usually had to make sense of it through the police reports. Accordingly, 162,799 minors were detained in the first six months of 1952. The majority of them (77 per cent) were school-aged children. A quarter of them did not attend school – which in itself could be seen as a frequent cause for the police to get custodial institutions involved. However, in the procuracy reports (based on data received by the *militsiia*) it was no significant category of its own. The *militsiia* classified notable juvenile behaviour according to vague (and interchangeable) categories: nearly 10,000 kids were detained for "begging" (*nishchenstvo*), and approximately 19,000 were accused of "street commerce," which usually referred to illegal trade practices. Thus, less than 20 per cent of the detainees were ascribed a concrete economic activity, no matter how petty that might have been. Another 8,000 children and adolescents were considered "criminals" and thus left for the procuracy to sort out. The overwhelming majority of those kids (109,778) simply were taken into police custody for what would translate best as "mischief" (*ozorstvo*).[37] In the early days of Soviet power, the term referred to the psychological remnants of capitalism in the people's consciousness.[38] One generation after the revolution it had become a flexible category that often went together with "petty hooliganism," and in the early 1950s it worked as an umbrella term for behaviour which the *militsiia* and the procuracy deemed either dangerous or provocative but not punishable by law.

For example, a procuracy report in 1954 mentioned how plenty of schoolkids were being detained for "ice skating in the wrong places" and hanging on to driving cars.[39] Other notable incidents were usually related to alcohol. Selling liquor in schools was an often-discussed matter between the *militsiia* and procuracy and was seen as a gateway to more serious crimes like "hooliganism." In December 1952, the district police and procuracy of Molotov held a joint meeting to discuss the state of criminality in the region. To the deputy head of the 10th *militsiia* department, the problems among the youth started with negligence and ended with crime. "Hooliganism is overpowering us, and nobody has talked about the reasons for hooliganist actions ... nobody has talked about child negligence and homelessness, which takes place here, for example: see the Iurkantsev [case]. They sell alcohol in school."[40] Every incident which could not (yet) be qualified as crime was labelled with negligence and homelessness. In many other reports these categories were interchangeable. One procuracy report was listing "mischief, street hooliganism and negligence" as one category in order to describe that the number of detained juveniles had risen by nearly 500 people to 2,800 in the year 1954.[41] Another report on the fluctuation of detainees in the childcare institutions of the MVD revealed that 362 children between the ages of eight and thirteen had been detained in Molotov in the last three months of 1949. Other than "theft" and "violation of transport rules" (usually in reference to children caught wandering the railway lines), the report listed 131 cases with "other reasons" for detention.[42] In the eyes of the procuracy, there was no consistent framework that could distinguish nuances among non-conformist behaviour. A pre-printed form by the procuracy to record the *militsiia*'s detainees in its notorious "Receiver-Distribution Centres" (DPR) even had a column for the "accidently detained."[43]

The discursive intersections are notable but not that surprising, as it did reflect the institutional claim, not a social reality. More importantly, all these incidents – acts of violence and suspect behaviour in general – ended up in the same institutional pool. Detention was often a pre-emptive response to all kinds of non-conformist behaviour, blurring the lines of prosecution and care, especially when the *militsiia* was involved. Detention was supposed to be a sorting act, instead it drained children and adolescents from all backgrounds into an institutional abyss which was hard to escape from.

Child Houses and Receiver-Distribution Centres – Keeping Track of Chaos

Olga Kucherenko and others have written a lot about the clutter of care and penal institutions.[44] While some kids were sent back to their parents and some to the procuracy for criminal investigation, others went through DPR and either stayed there for months or were transported to foster institutions run by the Ministry of Education – so-called child houses (*detskie doma*), schools, and orphanages. The system was established in the 1930s, and since then the procuracy's task force tried to keep track with the often hazardous living conditions in these facilities – or with the sometimes erratic paths detainees were taking afterwards. In 1955, the Molotov *militsiia* repeatedly picked up and detained the fourteen-year-old Valeri Vladimirov. The boy was spending his nights sleeping in boiler rooms of a factory or at train stations. According to the procuracy, his father, an inspector in the local pit, had left Valeri and his mother for another family. Valeri's mother then had left too, and the three kids stayed with their grandmother. Ultimately, Valeri was not released from custody but instead transferred to a penal colony where he was still registered a year later.[45]

Valeri's story was no exception, nor was it new. Once a kid was detained by the *militsiia*, his or her way led to the DPR, which then was supposed to sort out those who were brought together in the first place. Sending him to a correctional labour colony (run by the Gulag) ran counter to what the procuracy actually considered the most urgent issue: keeping "criminals" and others separate. However, the procuracy accounted for control and the improvement of this system but could barely keep up with the pace and the workload. As we have seen, a child's way through detention found expression in various records and statistics of the procuracy. It was only after these details came to light that the task force could intervene if the grounds for detention seemed unreasonable, the living arrangements in the detention facilities were insufficient, or (adult) criminal offenders were detained with neglected children. In some places, the procuracy could respond to these kinds of violations promptly. For example, orphanages (*detskie doma*) were run by the Ministry of Health and Education, and the expanding network of these child houses rarely met the required standards. Since the 1920s, the Soviet state had stipulated guidelines for providing these children with appropriate sanitary conditions, full nutrition, and basic education, yet depending on the place (and the resources available to local authorities), the reality was often different.[46] Until 1953, between 8,000 and 10,000 children were running away from these institutions every year, not least because these facilities rarely could provide basic hygienic needs. The procuracy responded with administrative and legislative measures, prosecuting dozens of directors every few months for "malpractice," theft, and other economic crimes.[47] These efforts may have had a deterring effect but barely prevented further mismanagement. Criminalizing an economy of scarcity ultimately did not improve the children's situation but led merely to more convictions and staff shortages. This trend continued after 1953.

In a similar fashion, DPRs as detention stations but also "child houses" had a notorious reputation as chaotic, overcrowded, and underequipped transit centres for both "neglected" and "criminal" youth.[48] This image was in large part owed to the procuracy, which documented profound violations of hygienic, legal, and administrative standards. More importantly, the uncontrolled mashup of detainees and petty criminals in the aforementioned statistics were a particular thorn in the procuracy's side. For years, the procurator's office in Molotov reported how the DPRs were essentially recruiting stations for criminal gangs. Not only petty criminals but all kinds of (older) offenders often found their way in these facilities and not only undermined what was left from its educational concept but terrorized or pressured other inmates to join them. In war times, the DPR of Chusovoi and Kungur were notorious in that regard.[49] Furthermore, many kids simply ran away and the MVD lost track of them in the system. While the number of escapees dropped in the early 1950s (in 1951, only 4 per cent of Molotov's DPR inmates ran away), it spiked again in 1954. In his annual report, the head of the task force of the RSFSR stated that still many children flew from the DPR because of "inadequate living conditions and bad educational work."[50] For example, in the first nine months of 1954, the thirteen-year-old Vladimir Politov was registered five times in a DPR. Both of his parents were working as train conductors, and every time he was detained he ran away, only to be detained again.[51] Cases like his show that social care facilities were often transitory in character while the procuracy mostly limited itself to document these developments, or sometimes urge superiors to intervene.

In both institutions, the renaissance of the correctional agenda in the Soviet penal system had a positive effect. The educational aspects of Soviet childcare received more political attention from 1954 onwards, securing more resources and allowing more children to benefit from its programs.[52] In conjunction with the political pressure to prosecute or at least punish officials for neglect and mismanagement, the procuracy detected fewer incidents of "malpractice." On the other hand, the system of DPR and child houses made up only a fraction of the task force's supervisory work (not least because it had no permanent official present nor special jurisdiction). The procuracy and its task force had to manage their resources accordingly and directed their efforts there where they had most influence: the investigation, prosecution, and penalizing of juvenile offenders.

Policing Juvenile Crime

Before and after 1953 the overwhelming majority of children who had an encounter with the state did not become subjects to criminal investigation. As we have seen, 90 per cent of the kids detained never met a procurator nor an investigator. While comparably few faced prosecution, this group received considerably more attention, expertise, and effort from the authorities than any other group. While the NKVD and later MVD directed its efforts to simply pull (*iz'iat'*) the kids from the streets, isolate them from society, and thus blurring the lines between care and incarceration, the procuracy and the judiciary aimed to draw these lines more clearly.

In the 1930s the Soviet leadership had put an end to experimental pedagogy and abandoned the idea of rehabilitation without punishment. Since then, the regime has been gradually lowering the age of criminal responsibility (depending on the crime between twelve and fourteen) without introducing a proper code for juvenile delinquency. The decree of 7 April 1935 only gave out the premise to apply "all punitive measures." Procurators, judges, and investigators had no guideline to refer to and were left, in the words of Peter Solomon, to "pick up the pieces."[53] Over the next decades, Soviet jurists and legal practitioners advocated for the establishment of proper legal and technical guidelines and a special procedural legislation for juvenile delinquency: such as the presence of an adult during interrogation; the medical examination to determine a delinquent's age, or not to allow cases against minors to be prosecuted with a procurator's sanction.[54] Early on, legal experts were arguing to introduce separate juvenile court sessions, due to the "specific characteristics" and the delinquent's "dependency (the tendency to imitate others, suggestibility, volatility of will, immature character) and unusual evidence material." This did not mean that the procuracy somehow suggested a more lenient or less strict approach to juvenile delinquency. Procurator General Bochkov personally was among the first in 1940 to push for a lower age of criminal responsibility.[55] In fact, the procuracy and the Ministry of Justice sought to render the entire legal process of investigation, prosecution, and trial more precise and fit to the extraordinary needs of underage delinquents – and since the late 1940s they were increasingly successful with it.

On the one hand, the jurists' struggle for a separate procedural legislation was in vain. Each new code of criminal procedure (1938, 1943, 1952, 1953, 1956) was published without a specific segment for juvenile crimes, although the juvenile cases had been tried in separate chambers since the 1920s.[56] On the other hand, throughout the 1940s and 1950s countless instructions and decrees issued by the Procurator General and the head of the procuracy task force filled this gap, guiding the procurators and investigators in their efforts to adapt their work to the special circumstances of juvenile delinquency. In 1950, the procuracy published an extensive guideline for the interrogation of children, prohibiting psychological manipulation (false promises, verbal threats) as it would only produce "low-grade evidence" and furthermore prove the "interrogator's powerlessness and his incapacity to work with children."[57] Other instructions demanded a thorough medical examination not least to prove that the suspect is in fact underage.

The question now is to what end did these officials pursue this line, and did it make a difference to the children? The goal (as for the system of criminal justice in general) was that every criminal investigation would lead to a conviction. Flimsy evidence and withdrawn testimonies could lead to halted investigations or, worse, acquittals which would fall directly back on the procuracy. This premise applied to all kinds of criminal cases, but in dealing with underage delinquents the procuracy and the judiciary seemed to be particularly successful. Since the end of the Second World War, the procuracy took over more juvenile cases from the *militsiia* and gradually decreased both the rate of cancelled investigations as well as return rates (that is, the number of cases returned by the courts to investigation). In 1945, the *militsiia* was investigating 75 per cent of the cases against juveniles. Seven years later, the procuracy led more than 70 per cent of these investigations.[58] Until 1954, this number rose to more than 90 per cent.[59] The same applied to the courts. In 1949, a procurator was present in 72 per cent of all court proceedings of underage delinquents – compared to 91 per cent in 1953. At the same time, fewer and fewer cases were dismissed, returned, or ended up in acquittals. In 1952, investigations halted before court made up only 1.2 per cent, and between 1948 and 1954 the percentage of cases returned by the courts never exceeded 2 per cent.[60] From a statistical point of view, in the struggle with juvenile delinquency the procuracy was at its most efficient – with very practical consequences for the suspects. The smaller the proportion of case dismissals, the more children have been sorted out during preliminary investigation. More importantly, the investigative procedure itself adapted to the situation of the delinquent and produced more information – including the suspect's personality, his/her social background, and a psychological profile.

In 1956, a fifteen-year-old was accused of raping a five-year-old. The investigator had no doubt about the suspect's guilt and initiated a criminal proceeding. Shortly afterwards, the procurator halted the investigation and called for an additional expert opinion. The expert concluded that the young man was mentally disabled and thus must not be prosecuted in court. The case was rejected, and the investigator was scolded for "not considering the personality of the accused and the reasons[!] for the crime which could have resulted in trying him unjustifiably."[61] Even in the face of grave crimes the prosecution of juveniles was no automatism, as the danger of a returned or halted proceeding was a strong incentive. In other instances, the investigation had also the purpose to unveil if other delinquents were involved and to identify possible (adult) instigators. Often, the parents drew the attention of the legal authorities. Lev Nedopekin was underage and accused of stealing 70 kilograms of flour. The procurator stopped the investigation and instructed the investigators to inquire about Nedopekin's criminal history and his family background, as it was his father's workplace where the flour was stolen. The procurator wanted to know other instigators and "how the son ended up in such a life and how long he has been drinking."[62] Eventually, the father most likely was being fined. Unlike in political cases, these investigations against instigators rarely entailed more prosecutions. Only a couple of hundred cases against "instigation" (*podstrekatel'stvo*) in the entire RSFSR were brought to court in 1954.[63] Still, the investigative inquiries yielded important context that was especially relevant to the judges.

In the Soviet system of criminal justice, acquittals were taken as a sign not only of "legal liberalism" but the ultimate proof for a spoilt and wrongful legal process. Since the late 1940s, leading officials in the procuracy and the judiciary actively campaigned against high acquittal or turnover rates.[64] A low (or better: non-existing) acquittal rate was an important marker, most legal officials (and Party leaders as well) were highly observant of. Proceedings against juvenile offenders were no exception in that regard. Between 1952 and 1954, the acquittal rate in these proceedings in the entire RSFSR varied between 0.7 and 1.5 per cent.[65] The overwhelming majority of cases resulted in a conviction. However, since the late 1940s soviet judges increasingly relied on the information provided by the investigators and took into consideration the age and the psychological and personal background of the defendant when deciding on a suspended sentence. The phenomenon was not new, as Soviet legislation and jurisprudence left a certain scope for the "individualization of punishment" and encouraged "not to incarcerate those who inspire hope of self-correction" – a concession especially to juvenile offenders.[66] The use of either Article 51 (imposing a penalty below the legal limit – non-custodial sentences, e.g.) or Article 53 (suspending the sentence altogether) had often led to conflicts in the judiciary, but a considerable number of judges kept looking for opportunities to spare juvenile offenders from imprisonment – even at the height of the campaign against theft in 1947/8.[67] When the campaign pressure eased, this practice became more common. For example, in 1952 the sixteen-year-old Shagatbudinov and his friend were accused of stealing honey. There were prosecuted under Article 1 of the infamous 1947 decree on theft, but Shagatbudinov at least got away with probation. The judicial administration in Molotov approved of the verdict, considering that his friend was the instigator and he himself "had no previous conviction, good credentials from his *kolkhoz* and only recently had turned 16."[68] Judges always found an angle to justify either Article 51 or 53. Cases like Shagatbudinov's were no exception by the late 1940s and early 1950s but appeared on a regular basis. Even though provincial courts received mixed signals from Moscow about the general use of these articles, they used them rather frequently as far as juvenile offenders were concerned. In summer 1947, the share of suspended sentences issued by Molotov courts was 15 per cent, rising to 34 per cent a year later. By 1952, this share went back to 25 per cent. Still, the higher legal organs and the Supreme Soviet encouraged judges to apply non-custodial sentences for juvenile offenders who were sixteen or younger. In this age group the share of suspended sentences was at 44 per cent in 1952. For certain types of crimes, such as *khuliganstvo* (rape) but also theft, the share was even higher, ranging between 50 and 60 per cent in 1952.[69] Juvenile offenders, especially under the age of sixteen, had in general a higher chance for either non-custodial sentences or a suspended sentence altogether. This trend continued throughout the 1950s and was formalized eventually with the 1958 law, raising the age of criminal responsibility to sixteen for most offences.[70]

Interestingly, while the procuracy still often (unsuccessfully) protested these court decisions, its officials ultimately gave in to the trend. In 1952, the judicial college of the Molotov regional court rejected 95 per cent of the procuracy's protests against verdicts concerning juveniles.[71] In that year, the deputy leader of the juvenile task force Orlov criticized the "mass application of article 51 and 53" as "hardly justifiable."[72] Only one and a half years later, he admitted that the application of these articles (as far as delinquents under the age of sixteen were concerned) "should be accepted as largely correct." Although the Procurator General and the head of the RSFSR procuracy did successfully protest some of these court decisions in 1953, these cases concerned only 243 people countrywide.[73] Overall, in practice but also in theory, the procuracy found consensus with the Supreme Court and the Ministry of Justice that the extraordinary character of juvenile delinquency demanded for a thorough legal process and a verdict fitting the circumstances of the individual delinquent. At a joint meeting of the heads of the procuracy and the judiciary in 1955, the chair of the Supreme Court of the USSR, Anatoli Volin, explained that, as far as juveniles were concerned, "punishment should be strictly individual and neither mild nor excessive."[74]

Clearly, not every investigator or judge was willing or able to guarantee a transparent procedure or was constantly observant of all the guidelines provided. Also, we lack a considerable amount of court statistics to make a more substantiated assessment of the sentencing practices after 1953. However, one can state that unlike the detention system of the MVD the legal machinery for the prosecution of underage delinquents was – before and after 1953 – no unchecked abyss but urged its officials to individualize and regulate the proceeding – even though the courts were enforcing this claim in a different way than the procurators. This claim extended even to the spheres following a conviction. Especially the procuracy's concern for procedural norms did reach through the "revolving door"[75] of the Gulag and it was here that Stalin's death had in fact the most substantial consequences for the institutional framework of policing Soviet children.

Kids in the Camps – before and after Stalin

In late 1953, the parameters for social control within the Soviet penal system shifted considerably. After Beria's downfall, the collective leadership introduced further reforms to reconfigure the Gulag towards a smaller, more efficient, and less cost-intensive correctional system – curbing the MVD's authority as well as strengthening penal before economic logics and rejuvenating the notion of "corrective" labour.[76] Two major steps in this direction were made when the new leadership granted the procuracy and the judiciary long-standing demands. In September 1953, the Supreme Soviet removed low-ranking MVD officials and also "paramilitary guards" from military jurisdiction and allowed conventional ("territorial") procurators to investigate and charge them in regular courts.[77] Even more important, on 26 February 1954 the camp procuracy was first integrated into the territorial procuracy and then dissolved. Instead, in every regional procuracy the "task force for penitentiary supervision" received additional personnel and took on the responsibility to investigate and prosecute crimes and delicts within the Gulag system.[78] The procuracy had now more capacities, direct insight, and legal jurisdiction to enforce procedural norms within the Soviet penal system. This change also affected the Corrective Labour Colonies and Camps for underage delinquents (DTVK/L) and their inmates.

As with other parts of the camp system, for years the Gulag had shielded and essentially jeopardized the procuracy's attempts to enforce procedural norms in the DTVK. Most of the time, procurators could not inspect the juvenile camps without an appointment (and the consent) of the camp administration that had direct control over the camp procurator (being essentially a part of this administration). Most territorial procurators compiled their knowledge about the number of escapes, violent incidents, or the intolerable living conditions from single reports or brief inspection tours. The fact that underage and adult offenders often shared the camp zones was special cause for major concern among procurators. In 1947, 40 per cent of the DTVK Kungur in Molotov were adults.[79] In January 1951, Procurator General Grigori Safonov scolded his subordinates for the devastating situation in the juvenile camps. Mass escapes, murder, and theft were as frequent as the use of "anti-pedagogical measures" (that is, physical violence), while adult criminals were essentially reigning in the camp zones as brigadiers. Safonov instructed local procurators to study camp reports more closely, but he too knew that without legal jurisdiction they had little leverage to enforce a strict division of underage and grown-up inmates or to prosecute illegal actions in the camps in general. As Juliane Fürst had put it: "Camps for juvenile delinquents, while representing the pinnacle of Soviet control, were in fact non-Soviet spaces."[80] This situation was about to change in 1953.

The post-Stalinist reforms granted the procuracy leverage and insights, but they did not instantly improve the situation of juveniles in the DTVK/L. Still, they increased the scope of information gathered from the camps and allowed the procuracy to interfere in camp matters and slow down the local administration for a more thorough and individual procedure. As mentioned earlier, the renaissance of the correctional principle and the overall reform spirit since 1954 enabled the juvenile care and penal facilities to benefit from more financial and other resources. The Party leadership revived the commitment to the ideals of "re-education" in the Gulag. The camp administration was instructed to improve the living conditions in the camp system and to implement programs and allocate resources for re-integration and re-education (without giving up on the notion of retribution and productivity).[81] In 1955, the Kungur colony had a library with over 4,000 books.[82] Instead of guards and inmates, the procuracy reports now differentiated "teachers" and "pupils" (*vospitanniki*). More importantly, the procuracy now had the chance to document violations in these facilities which had been obscure for many years and to sanction those which had not been sanctioned in the first place – by inmates and personnel. In 1947, the inspection report for the Kungur colony registered mostly the number of inmates, including the distribution of age and criminal offence.[83] In contrast, the task force report for the same colony in 1956 listed not only that five out of 349 inmates were over eighteen years old. It also gave detailed information on how often and how many inmates were sent to the "penal room" and on what grounds. In many cases, these measures were considered "unnecessary" and "without reason," as one inmate was punished for ruining his winter boots. Another one, a certain Chernikov, was sent to the "penal room" ten times between July 1955 and February 1956 for "violations of discipline." "Individual talks" and repeated attempts to "sort out the issue at *aktiv* meetings" had no effect. In other cases, inmates had been transferred after the inspection by the procurator had found their rooms not convenient (or simply "too cold"). One "teacher" was arrested and removed from the colony after he had beaten a child with a stool.[84]

The procuracy did not have the capacity to document and punish all violations within the camp system. While the Kungur colony received particular attention by the procuracy for its model character as an educational facility, the task force for penal supervision had also to keep an eye on the rest of the camps in Molotov. In 1954, more than 60,000 inmates spread over three camp complexes (Nyroblag, Usollag, and Kizellag), located within a radius of 700 kilometres. The inspection of a single camp department (Nyroblag consisted of ten) took officials from the procuracy task force between twenty and thirty days.[85] With the exception of the Ministry of Justice's brief interregnum in 1953, the Gulag and its entangled facilities were at the mercy of the MVD/MGB, and the procuracy had to put work and time into enforcing norms. Still, through investigations and prosecutions it created a general sense of legal accountability in these structures. The situation for children in the Gulag improved only slowly. The living conditions were often miserable, and violence and arbitrariness played a major role in the everyday experience of Soviet care. Still, the enforcement of procedural norms contributed to a stronger regulation and individualization of institutional approach towards juvenile delinquency and care. Places like the Kungur colony became increasingly "Soviet" after all.

It would be naïve to take regulation for liberalization. The procuracy and the judiciary rather defused and decelerated proceedings that had been treated as automatisms for years. For example, the so-called Beria-Amnesty in spring 1953 was essentially a blind administrative act to relieve pressure from the camps and help Beria to stage himself as reformer.[86] In contrast, one year later, in April 1954, the Soviet government ordered an "early release of all juvenile delinquents" from the entire TVK/L system who "had proven their betterment with exemplary behaviour and a conscientious relationship with work and learning in the penal facilities." In order to become eligible for release, the delinquents had to have served at least one third (and at least six months) of their prison term.[87] Judges and procurators were together examining each case and weighing prison terms against individual behaviour and the risk to release potential recidivists. The process took several months – and was prone to complications – as both the task force for penal supervision and the task force for juvenile issues were involved. In one case, the local procurator had made eight mistakes in his calculations, which stalled the release of forty-two camp inmates.[88] At the same time, the scope for arbitrary action was smaller than before. The camp administration would make the first character assessment of their inmates together with the camp procuracy and they had to justify and explain their decision for release in court with the particular inmate present. Sometimes, when camp officials tried to spare productive workers from release by referring to their negative behaviour in the camp, the procurator in court could refute the notion by questioning the camp official and referring to the files which did not list a disciplinary offence in this case.[89]

The entire process dragged on for months and most camp procurators, but also the courts in Molotov, were overwhelmed by the workload. Often, they confirmed the release lists without further examination of the case and courts had to make a quick decision. In April 1954, Molotov's TVK/L counted 4,201 inmates under the age of eighteen, of which 2,845 (63 per cent) were considered by the procuracy eligible for amnesty. While the task force for penal supervision registered that the remaining 37 per cent were not to be released, its report did not mention any second case examination or late releases. The entire release procedure was no legal proceeding.[90] The regime had little interest in a close case examination on behalf of the inmates (unsurprisingly, in June 1954 all but 2 per cent of the investigative files of amnestied inmates were to be destroyed). It rather relied on the procuracy and the courts to supervise and slow down a process, to get rid of a part of the camp population that did not pose an imminent social threat (old people, women, juveniles, sick) – yet, unlike in the past, this process was now being more closely observed and its executing organs could be held accountable for mistakes more frequently.

Conclusion

When viewing Soviet street children through institutional lenses in the early 1950s, three aspects become apparent: variety, continuity, and change. The institutional approach towards non-conformist behaviour and juvenile delinquency varied, depending on whether the police or legal organs were involved. Already in the 1930s, the NKVD had set the course to isolate and extract unwanted (juvenile) behaviour from the streets. The ministry had created a vast network of officials and institutions that first defined and then were supposed to differentiate but in practice amalgamated non-conformist behaviour into a singular social threat. Since the 1930s, the *bezprizornik* was very much also an institutional product. Given the sheer number of displaced and homeless children, this blending seemed a logical and logistical consequence. Still, the legal organs, and first and foremost the procuracy, took on the responsibility to differentiate this group, to follow their tracks through the institutional abyss and to distinguish criminal from social cases.

The division of labour and the competing approaches are part of a wider continuity in the history of Soviet statehood. In enforcing social control, it was not operating as a monolith but throughout the 1940s and 1950s, legal organs were struggling and operating to enforce procedural norms within the realm of the police apparatus. The more control and resources the procuracy had at its disposal the higher the chances were for a delinquent to either receive institutional attention, a proper legal process, or to avoid a penal institution altogether. Stalin's death induced change in that regard, as the procuracy and the judiciary gained leverage over low-ranking police officials and insights into the former exclusive domains of the MVD/MGB. This breakthrough increased after 1953 and paved the way to a better division between social care and penal system. As the Soviet leadership shifted its political favour from police to procuracy, it released the political blockage to enforce trends that had been initiated and tested long before: enforcing procedural norms for the sake of precision and predictability in exercising social control.

These trends were also the pillars on which the campaign for "Socialist Legality" rested. Soviet legal professionalism allowed the post-Stalin regime to contain social disorder.[91] At the same time, the revived correctional agenda and Khrushchev's emphasis on including the public as well as the larger shift towards pre-emptive policing strategies[92] led to a certain de-professionalization of youth work in the Soviet Union. After the age of criminal responsibility had been raised in 1958, the government re-introduced juvenile affairs commissions (which drew its members mostly from the Party *aktiv*) as coordinating and supervising bodies for juvenile delinquency prevention with "quasi-judicial function."[93] Under Khrushchev, the procuracy and the judiciary retained and expanded their claim over the juvenile issue, while the new Party leadership sought to mobilize agency (and expertise) from below.

Eventually, neither these commissions, the police nor the procuracy were capable (nor supposed) to compensate for material scarcity and political neglect. Children experienced abuse and arbitrary violence in foster and penal institutions long after Stalin was gone. Procurators sometimes became complicit in covering up the situation in these facilities. Police and procuracy could align in local networks that were difficult to permeate. Eventually, the full separation of penal and foster structures (and practices) remained an ideal rather than reality.

NOTES

1 The Soviet civil police were called "militsiia." Both terms ("police" and "militsiia") will be used interchangeably.
2 Gosudarstvennyi arkhiv Permskogo kraia (GAPK) 1366/1/644/23.
3 Ibid. The term *beznadzornye* can also be translated as "vagabond" children.
4 Juliane Fürst, *Stalin's Last Generation. Soviet Post-war Youth and the Emergence of Mature Socialism* (Oxford: Oxford University Press, 2012).
5 In 1956, courts in the RSFSR tried and convicted over 49,000 juvenile offenders, compared to 52,000 in 1945.
6 Nick Baron, "Violence, Childhood and the State: New Perspectives on Political Practice and Social Experience in the Twentieth Century," in *Displaced Children in Russia and Eastern Europe, 1915–1953. Ideologies, Identities, Experiences*, ed. Nick Baron (Leiden and Boston: Brill, 2017), 280.
7 Juliane Fürst, "The Importance of Being Stylish: Youth, Culture and Identity in Late Stalinism," in *Late Stalinist Russia. Society between Reconstruction and Reinvention*, ed. Juliane Fürst (London: Routledge, 2006), 210.
8 Elena Zubkova, *Poslevoennoe sovetskoe obshchestvo: Politika i povsednevnost'. 1945–1953* (Moscow: ROSSPEN, 2000), 90–1.
9 See Alan M. Ball, *And Now My Soul Is Hardened: Abandoned Children in Soviet Russia, 1918–1930* (Berkeley and Los Angeles: University of Berkeley Press, 1994).
10 Iu. Afanas'ev, ed., *Istoriia stalinskogo Gulaga. Konets 1920-kh – pervaia polovina 1950-kh godov. Tom 1. Massovye repressii v SSSR* (Moscow: Rosspėn, 2004), 613–14.
11 Fürst, *Stalin's Last Generation*.
12 Miriam Galley, '"We Punch Like One Fist": Street Children, Gangs and State Authority in Stalin's Soviet Union," *Jahrbücher für Geschichte Osteuropas* 64, no. 1 (2016): 26–53.
13 For the early Soviet State, see Ball, *And Now*.
14 Olga Kucherenko, *Soviet Street Children and the Second World War: Welfare and Social Control under Stalin* (London: Bloomsbury, 2016).

15 Fürst, *Stalin's Last Generation*, 198.
16 "The mistreatment of displaced children was not a deliberate state policy; rather, the children often became unintended victims of narrow-minded, incompetent, corrupt and indifferent individuals in positions of power." Kucherenko, *Soviet Street Children*, 174.
17 Cathy A. Frierson and Semyon S. Vilensky, *Children of the Gulag* (New Haven, CT: Yale University Press, 2010).
18 Brian LaPierre, *Hooligans in Khrushchev's Russia. Defining, Policing, and Producing Deviance during the Thaw* (Madison: University of Wisconsin Press, 2012).
19 Juliane Fürst, "The Arrival of Spring? Changes and Continuities in Soviet Youth Culture and Policy between Stalin and Khrushchev," in *The Dilemmas of Destalinization: Negotiating Cultural and Social Change in the Khrushchev Era*, ed. Polly Jones (London: Routledge, 2007), 135–53; Elizabeth White, *A Modern History of Russian Childhood: From the Late Imperial Period to the Collapse of the Soviet Union* (London: Bloomsburg, 2020), 125. For the late Soviet Union, see esp. Mirjam Galley, *Building Communism and Policing Deviance in the Soviet Union: Residential Childcare, 1958–1991* (London: Routledge, 2021).
20 Peter H. Solomon, *Soviet Criminal Justice under Stalin* (Cambridge: Cambridge University Press, 1996); Aleksei P. Dyn'ko, "Iuridicheskaia otvetstvennost' nesovershennoletnikh i deiatel'nost' detskikh penitentsiarnykh uchrezhdenii po ee realizatsii v sovetskoi gosudarstve poslevoennogo vremeni (1945–1956 gg.)" (kand. diss., Kuban Gos. Agr. Universitet, 2012).
21 See S.S. Vilenskii et al., eds., *Deti GULAGa. 1918–1956* (Moscow: Mezhdunarodnyi fond Demokratiia, 2002), 11.
22 Vilenskii, *Deti GULAGa*, 401.
23 Immo Rebitschek, *Die disziplinierte Diktatur: Stalinismus und Justiz in der sowjetischen Provinz* (Cologne: Boehlau Verlag, 2018), 45–55.
24 See the elaborate discussion of the head of the Task Force Vramshapu Tadevosian on juvenile delinquency and homelessness. V.S. Tadevosian, "Bor'ba s detskoi prestupnost'iu v SSSR (k piatiletiu zakona 7 aprelia 1935)," *Sovetskoe Gosudarstvo i Pravo* 4 (1940): 61–80.
25 Oleg Leibovich, *V gorode M. Ocherki sotsial'noi povsednevnosti sovetskoi provintsii* (Moscow: ROSSPEN, 2008); M. Emelin, "Bor'ba s detskoi besprizornost'iu i beznadzornost'iu v gody Velikoi Otechestvennoi Voiny (1941–1945 gg.)," *Voprosy iuvenal'noi iustitsii* 2 (2010).
26 Yoram Gorlizki, "Theft under Stalin: A Property Rights Analysis," *Economic History Review* 69, no. 1 (2016): 288–313.
27 Andrei S. Berkutov, "Bor'ba s ugolovnoi prestupnosti v Molotovskoi oblasti v poslevoennye gody (1945–1953 gg.)" (kand. diss., Permskii Gosudarstvennyi Universitet, 2004).

28 Vilenskii, *Deti GULAGa*, 182–7.
29 Ibid., 383, 496.
30 Already in 1918, the Bolshevik government considered offenders less than seventeen years of age as "juvenile" cases, but the implementation of this threshold varied throughout times. Ball, *And Now*, 95.
31 Gosudarstvennyi arkhiv Rossiiskoi Federatsii (GARF) R-8131/ 32/ 3176/24–8.
32 Fürst, *Stalin's Last Generation*, 169.
33 Vilenskii, *Deti GULAGa*, 480.
34 Ibid., 554.
35 GAPK 1366/1/646/9; GARF R-8131/32/4559/37–46.
36 Vilenskii, *Deti GULAGa*, 187–91.
37 GARF R-8131/ 32/3176/24–5.
38 LaPierre, *Hooligans*, 29; B. Shaver, "Bor'ba s khuliganstvom i s khuliganami," *Sotsialisticheskaia zakonnost'* 1 (1940): 12–14.
39 GAPK 1366/1/645/28.
40 GAPK 1366/3/53/ 3.
41 GAPK 1366/1/644/22.
42 GAPK 1366/1/638/41.
43 Ibid.
44 Kucherenko, *Soviet Street Children*; Rebitschek, *Die diszipliniere Diktatur*, 151–74.
45 GAPK 1366/1/646/41.
46 Catriona Kelly, *Children's World. Growing Up in Russia, 1890–1991* (New Haven, CT: Yale University Press, 2007), 248–9.
47 In the first quarter of 1953, the task force with the Procurator General reported the prosecution of 400 employees of the Ministry of Health and Education for these very reasons. GARF R-8131/32/3176/100.
48 Kucherenko, *Soviet Street Children*, 125–9.
49 GAPK 1366/1/633/2.
50 GARF R-8131/32/4559/22.
51 Permskii Gosudarstvennyi arkhiv noveishei istorii (PermGANI) 105/21/310/5.
52 Kelly, *Children's World*, 258.
53 Solomon, *Soviet Criminal Justice under Stalin*, 203.
54 See the joint draft between NKIu, NKVD, and the procuracy in 1940, GARF 9492/1/52/3–4.
55 Rossiiskii gosudarstvennyi arkhiv sotsial'no-politicheskoi istorii (RGASPI) 82/2/884/172–3.
56 See NKIu RSFSR, ed., Ugolovno-protsessual'nyi kodeks. S izmeneniiami na 1 dekabria 1938 g. (Moscow: Iuridicheskoe Izdatel'stvo NKIu SSSR, 1938) and the following versions until: Ministerstvo Iustitsii RSFSR, Ugolovno-protsessual'nyi kodeks. Ofitsial'nyi tekst s izmeneniiami na 1

fevralia 1956 i s prilozheniem postateino-sistematizirovannkyh materialov (Moscow: GosIzdat Iuridicheskoi Literatury, 1956).
57 Vilenskii, *Deti GULAGa*, 417.
58 GARF R-8131/38/486/59; GARF R-8131/32/3176/27. Back in 1944/5 the proportions were reverse, when 75 per cent of the investigations were being carried out by the *militsiia*. GARF A-461/8/844/134.
59 GARF R-8131/32/4559/48–9. On 5 April 1954, the Procurator General instructed his procurators not to leave a single juvenile case to the *militsiia* for investigation.
60 GARF R-8131/32/3176/27; GARF R-8131/32/4559/49.
61 GAPK 1366/1/646/10.
62 Ibid.
63 In 1954, courts in the entire RSFSR tried only 354 cases against "instigators." See GARF R-8131/32/4559/49.
64 This campaign was rather short-lived but led to a lasting stigmatization of acquittals or returns of cases. Peter H. Solomon, "The Case of the Vanishing Acquittal: Informal Norms and the Practice of Soviet Criminal Justice," *Soviet Studies* 39, no. 4 (1987): 531–55.
65 GARF R-8131/ 32/4559/49; GARF R-8131/32/3176/27; 113.
66 D. Gorvits, "Uslovnoe osuzhdenie nesovershennoletnikh," *Sotsialisticheskaia zakonnost'* 10 (1946): 22–4.
67 Gorlizki, "Theft under Stalin," 288–313.
68 Solomon, *Soviet Criminal Justice*, 388–9; GAPK 1461/1/201/11.
69 N.K. Morozov, ed., *Sbornik deistvuiushchikh postanovlenii plenuma Verkhovnogo Soveta SSSR. 1924–1957 gg.* (Moscow: GosIzdat Iuridicheskoi Literatury, 1958), 17–19.
70 Peter H. Solomon, *Soviet Criminologists and Criminal Policy. Specialists in Policy-Making* (New York: Columbia University Press, 1978), 71, 191.
71 GAPK 1461/2/201/12.
72 GARF R-8131/32/3176/29.
73 Ibid., 114.
74 GARF R-8131/32/4014/101.
75 Golfo Alexopoulos, "Amnesty 1945: The Revolving Door of Stalin's Gulag," *Slavic Review* 64, no. 2 (2005): 274–306.
76 Jeffrey S. Hardy, *The Gulag after Stalin: Redefining Punishment in Khrushchev's Soviet Union* (Ithaca, NY: Cornell University Press, 2016), 72; Nanci Adler, *The Gulag Survivor: Beyond the Soviet System* (New Brunswick, NJ: Transaction Publisher, 2004), 83; See also the Statute on Corrective Labour from 10 July 1954 in Nikita Petrov and A.I. Kokurin, eds., *GULAG (glavnoe upravlenie lagerei) 1917–1960. Rossiia XX Vek: Dokumenty* (Moscow: Mezhdunarodnyi fond Demokratiia, 2000), 151–60.
77 GARF R-8131/32/2229/110.

78 GARF R-8131/32/3284/20; GAPK 1366/3/5/38. The Molotov procuracy hired three new procurators and a secretary for this purpose.
79 GAPK 1366/1/636/15.
80 Fürst, *Stalin's Last Generation*, 179.
81 Hardy, *The Gulag*, 77–81. This development corresponded with a shift in custodial practice (such as orphanages), where the regime also "became less punitive in certain aspects." Kelly, *Children's World*, 260.
82 Kelly, *Children's World*, 258.
83 GAPK 1366/1/636/15.
84 GAPK 1366/1/646/21.
85 GAPK 1366/1/673/7; GAPK 1366/1/305/127–9.
86 Marc Elie, "Khrushchev's Gulag: The Soviet Penitentiary System after Stalin's Death, 1953–1964," in *The Thaw. Soviet Society and Culture during the 1950s and 1960s*, ed. Denis Kozlov and Eleonory Gilburd (Toronto: University of Toronto Press, 2013), 109–42.
87 GAPK 1366/3/55/106–7.
88 GAPK 1366/1/643/82.
89 GAPK 1366/1/673/33.
90 Ibid./31–2. Amnesties in this case were administrative procedures without any legal implications. Albert P. van Goudoever, *The Limits of Destalinization in the Soviet Union: Political Rehabilitations in the Soviet Union Since Stalin* (London: Croom Helm, 1986), 40.
91 See Yoram Gorlizki's article in this volume.
92 See also Evgenia Lezina's article in this volume.
93 Solomon, *Soviet Criminologists*, 72.

9 After the XXth Congress: Liberalization and the Problem of Social Order

YORAM GORLIZKI

The year 1956, when Nikita Khrushchev gave his secret speech, was a watershed in the history of the Soviet Union. Much of the year's significance stemmed from the speech itself. Within weeks of Khrushchev's oration in late February, extracts were read out to stunned audiences at closed Party and Komsomol meetings across the country. Aside from the revelations about Stalin himself, the effects of the speech went further, sowing doubts about the reliability of the Soviet press, about the culpability of members of Stalin's ruling group, and about the fallibility of the Party.[1] In early March tens of thousands took to the streets in demonstrations in Tbilisi and other Georgian cities in protest at Khrushchev's perceived slurs on Joseph Stalin as a Georgian; the protests were eventually put down, with much bloodshed, through military force.[2] One of the problems presented by the speech was that it was never publicly acknowledged, so that as news of it spread, the lingering questions it raised could not be openly addressed. Towards the end of October, the post-Stalin leadership faced its first full-blown crisis in the form of a popular uprising in Hungary, which was also suppressed by the military. The Hungarian rebellion found echoes in the Soviet Union as small groups of sympathizers assembled in public spaces, distributed leaflets, and disseminated anonymous letters. To stall the rising tide of internal dissent the Soviet regime launched a crackdown, albeit one implemented not by the military but by a joint action of the security police and the ordinary justice agencies. This campaign in late 1956 came to serve as a litmus test of how far the regime had come since Stalin's death in reining in the security police and in protecting the integrity of the judicial system. The moment would mark, according to Hornsby, a "key turning point in efforts to establish a more effective system of social control without recourse to terror."[3]

This new system of social control was shaped by two factors. The first was an ensemble of policies linked to a campaign for "socialist legality." Despite its roots in the mid-1930s, the notion of socialist legality had gained traction in the months after Stalin's death. After March 1953 it would come to have two meanings. The first, with a provenance going back to 1930s, placed emphasis on the observance of legal rules and procedural norms. While this aspect of socialist legality had been elaborated by the legal agencies in the late 1940s, it was only with the dictator's death that it would reach a mass audience. By contrast, the second meaning of socialist legality, which was largely put forward by politicians, was entirely novel. This centred on the containment and delegitimization of extra-judicial forms of repression, a position that could not have been entertained while Stalin was alive. As the Soviet leadership came to grips with its first major post-Stalin crisis at the end of 1956, it may have been tempted to row back on its commitment to socialist legality; indeed, it is in testing the robustness of this commitment that the months following the Hungarian crisis would prove to be decisive.

The idea of socialist legality was nurtured by a small band of legal theorists and justice officials and implemented by the country's elite justice institutions. But there was also a second vector framing the regime's approach to social control, and this would have deeper social roots. The release of over a million ex-convicts from the Gulag in the spring and summer of 1953 unleashed a major crime wave which sent the numbers of violent attacks, murders, rapes, thefts of personal property, and cases of hooliganism spiralling upwards. As Miriam Dobson has shown, many ordinary citizens were unable to make sense of this upsurge of violence other than by resorting to stock Stalinist images of "enemies," "degenerates," and "parasites."[4] Memories of the summer of 1953 would reverberate across the following decade and inform later public and government reactions to outbreaks of crime and collective violence.

Achieving social control entailed containing social disorder while keeping within the bounds of socialist legality. This task was made more difficult by the fact that many of the state's own officials had only a primitive grasp of the values of rule-adherence and restraint that the state was now proclaiming. Of no organization was this more true than the civic police (*militsiia*), whose ranks dwarfed those of other justice and law-enforcement institutions. In a direct carry-over of police practices from the Stalin era, the *militsiia* in the mid- and late 1950s were regularly rebuked for their own "violations of socialist legality."[5]

The two poles of this historical process are mirrored in the structure of this chapter. In the first part we look at how a set of ideas centred on socialist legality became institutionalized as bureaucratic practices. The significance of these ideas is that they enabled an alliance of justice officials and legal theorists to curb the worst excesses of Soviet dictatorship. Beyond their instrumental avowal of these norms in the immediate post-Stalin succession, however, it was an open question how deep the commitment of Soviet politicians would be to these principles.

In the second part we see how in the late 1950s the institutions of socialist legality confronted a fast-changing social reality. Nowhere was this social transformation more acutely reflected than in the high levels of geographic mobility. In addition to the release of hundreds of thousands of ex-convicts from the camps, and the return of deported peoples to their homelands, the revoking of Stalin's labour decrees, especially on unlawful quitting, led to soaring levels of labour turnover and interregional migration. The return of former convicts and deported ethnic groups to their homelands led to inevitable conflict with those who had in their absence taken over their homes and laid claim to their property.[6] Restrictions on entry to Soviet capitals through the *propiska* system pushed large numbers of economic migrants to the margins of the country's largest cities, fomenting hotspots of social discontent.[7] Khrushchev's Virgin Lands campaign, launched in 1954, which saw the resettlement of 300,000 young labourers in the arid steppes of Northern Kazakhstan and Altai Krai, also triggered riots as large contingents of young men were herded into remote locations poorly provided for in terms of food, water, and basic amenities.[8] Such flashes of instability strengthened the growing chorus for a reimposition of law and order.

While the culture of "socialist legality" was fostered by elite jurists, it was not widely shared among officials from the country's mass law-enforcement agency, the *militsiia*, for whom the overriding social task was the preservation of public order. The chapter closes by showing how, at the end of Khrushchev's tenure, the tension between justice agencies proclaiming the values of socialist legality and law-enforcement agencies promoting the protection of public order would find a new resolution.

Contribution

The literature on the law and justice reforms in the Soviet Union in mid-late 1950s has tended to gravitate towards one of two broad interpretations. Some contemporary observers such as Harold Berman saw this as a time of liberalization. Exemplified by new laws on petty theft and petty hooliganism, on the repeal of Stalin's draconian labour laws, and on the relegalization of abortion, the new legislation of these years was seen as broadly consistent with the anti-Stalinist thrust of the secret speech.[9] A second perspective focuses on Khrushchev's impulse to reshape society in a new socialist image. The rise of comrades' courts and of anti-parasite tribunals, and the growing accent on hooliganism offences in domestic as opposed to public settings suggests increasing state intrusion into the personal domain. According to Lapierre, this was "a time of repressive social discipline in which the state sought to expand its policing power to the most mundane aspects of everyday life."[10] Far from being instances of liberalization, these were all examples of a state intent on refashioning human nature by penetrating and reordering the domestic realm.

There are difficulties with both approaches. The first ignores a countercurrent of harsh laws on social order issues that enjoyed popular support. As the decade wore on this position was anchored in a conservative jurisprudence on the need to protect public order and social cohesion.[11] In order to understand the flaws of the second position we need to begin by acknowledging its strengths. It has two signal advantages. First, in giving pride of place to the role of ideology it points to an important element of ideological continuity between Stalin and Khrushchev, a continuity that helps explain Khrushchev's political triumphs.[12] Second, it shows how the Khrushchev administration reverted to Stalin-era strategies, most notably the adoption of unregulated fast-track procedures in the decree on petty theft of December 1956.[13] Where this approach stands on less firm ground is that it pays insufficient attention to the Soviet state, to its institutions and to its ideas. Somewhat paradoxically, although it accords great importance to the role of ideology it has only a thin understanding of the power of ideas in coordinating the activities of state actors. And in the realm of law and justice, no idea loomed larger than that of socialist legality.

Socialist Legality

"Of all the banners that were waved in the rhetorical winds of the XXth Congress," noted one contemporary Western observer, "the banner of 'socialist legality' was one of the largest and bravest."[14] Although the slogan of socialist legality had shot to prominence in the months after Stalin's death, it had a long pre-history which stretched back to the 1930s. The term had first entered the Soviet lexicon early in that decade as a replacement for "revolutionary legality," a concept which had come into use in the aftermath of the October Revolution but which had been tarnished by close association with the violent and arbitrary campaigns for collectivization, grain requisitioning, and class war of the late 1920s and early 1930s.[15] The term "socialist legality" was supposed to exemplify the regime's newfound commitment to legal rules, procedural norms, and to the stability of laws and, by implication, to its rejection of simplification, flexibility, and arbitrary rule in law. In institutional terms "socialist legality" was closely tied to the all-union Procuracy and its first head, Andrei Vyshinskii.[16] Yet as a concept socialist legality was only properly elaborated in the late 1940s when justice officials and legal theorists began to explore in concrete detail what it might mean for the administration of justice.[17] It was in this period that socialist legality became closely associated with a major campaign against "unfounded prosecutions."[18]

After Stalin's death the concept of "socialist legality" branched off in two directions. The first, which was articulated by the same justice officials who had spearheaded the debates of the late 1940s, tended to focus on the themes they had championed under Stalin, such as the need to ensure that Soviet citizens were protected from "unfounded prosecutions."[19] But there was also a second meaning, in whose elaboration it was the politicians who took the lead. Its first use in this latter sense was in an editorial in *Pravda* on 6 April 1953, which took aim at Lavrentii Beria's adversaries in the Ministry of State Security, Mikhail Riumin and Semen Ignat'ev, for "gross violations of socialist legality" in prosecuting the Doctors' Plot.[20] After Beria's removal, Khrushchev ploughed the same furrow, except that now he targeted not Riumin and Ignat'ev but "Beria and his gang." "The despicable Beria gang" ran one editorial, "tried to remove the state security agencies from the control of the Party and of the Soviet state ... and to create within these agencies an atmosphere of lawlessness and arbitrariness." Prime among Beria's misdeeds was the "creation of an extrajudicial body ... to deal summarily with innocent persons." One of Khrushchev's most important steps in the summer and autumn of 1953, well before XXth Congress, was a restructuring of the Ministry of Internal Affairs and a purge of its personnel. It was in this context that the abolition on 1 September 1953 of the Special Board, the extra-judicial tribunal which had tried hundreds of thousands of Soviet citizens in summary procedures without the presentation of evidence or the presence of the accused was hailed as "of great significance in strengthening socialist legality."[21]

In the months after Stalin's death socialist legality ran along two channels. The first, promoted by justice officials and legal scholars, focused on the importance of legal rules and procedural norms. Although these jurists were pursuing the same policies they had argued for under Stalin, they took advantage of the post-Stalin campaign to make them more accessible to a wider public. By contrast the second channel of socialist legality was pursued by politicians and involved removing one of Stalin's most cherished forms of rule, the apparatus of extra-judicial repression. As Khrushchev and those around him knew full well, this was something that neither he nor any other politician could have done while Stalin was alive. At the same time, once this principle was introduced, it was quickly cloaked in the mantle of the 1936 Constitution.[22]

It was one thing to talk up these principles when the going was good, as it had been in the first two years after Stalin's death, but it was quite another to stand by them in a moment of crisis. The eighteen months after the XXth Congress would see the two pillars of socialist legality put under great stress. The first line of attack concerned the principle that law be applied in accordance with procedural norms. After the uptick in "anti-Soviet" sentiments within the Soviet Union in the immediate aftermath of the Hungarian uprising, the Central Committee issued a closed letter on 19 December 1956 encouraging more prolific use of political charges by the security police, the KGB. According to Hornsby, from the end of 1956 to 1958 a total of 3,764 citizens were convicted of anti-Soviet activity in cases investigated by the security police, "a figure comfortably exceeding that of any subsequent period during the entire post-Stalin era."[23] While Hornsby rightly points to the sharp rise in the volume of convictions for political crimes, especially after the de-escalation of the preceding years, when set against earlier trends the figures remain modest: less than a decade earlier the convictions for counter-revolutionary crimes had been, for the years 1949–52, 76,689, 53,179, 47,613, and 27,098, respectively.[24]

Two factors appear to have played a role in reining in the security police. First, the reforms of the Procuracy, especially the new statute on procuratorial supervision of 24 May 1955, had strengthened its monitoring of KGB investigations. In fact procuracy officials, and especially the Procurator General, Roman Rudenko, played a key role in muting the language of the closed letter of 19 December.[25] Second, the USSR Supreme Court intervened to ensure that regional courts and, indirectly, investigators of the KGB, exercised restraint.[26] A first draft Supreme Court resolution in January 1957 coupled attacks on "anti-Soviet elements" with warnings about the "impermissibility of unfounded prosecutions."[27] An even more guarded draft resolution of 7 July 1957 called for great care by the justice agencies in implementing laws on anti-Soviet activity.[28] Further, a key Supreme Court report on this subject of early 1958 took care not to dramatize the rise of counter-revolutionary activity; to distinguish genuine, deep-seated counter-revolutionary orientations from occasional, flippant, and "every-day" (*obyvatel'skykh*) utterances; and to qualify the latter accordingly.

Although the July draft was never formally adopted nor the Supreme Court report ever published, they were widely distributed and discussed at the highest levels of the Supreme Court as well as within the security agencies. In these discussions the chair of the Supreme Court, Aleksandr Gorkin, took a firm line, sometimes against the direct opposition of the KGB. "Counter-revolutionary intent is an obligatory element of counter-revolutionary crimes and without evidence of its presence actions which 'outwardly' appear to be anti-Soviet are not in fact counter-revolutionary crimes," he argued.[29] In fact, the Supreme Court report noted that the application of Article 58–10 fell sharply in the second half of 1957. Notwithstanding the allure of political repression in a time of crisis, arrests by the KGB in total numbered less than 3,000 in 1957, followed by a drop in 1958.[30] This was a small fraction of the volumes of the late 1940s and suggests that the post-Stalin provisions on socialist legality were holding firm.

The second test of socialist legality concerned the constitutional monopoly of the courts on the application of criminal punishments. From April 1957 draft legislation appeared in each republic of the Soviet Union envisaging a punishment of exile on "parasites" which was to be levied not by the courts, but by anti-parasite tribunals which consisted, in effect, of working collectives.[31] The outstanding feature of the draft laws was the authorization for a "general meeting" (*obshchee sobranie*) within residential units to constitute itself as a trial organ for adoption of a penalty against residents deemed to be "anti-social parasite elements." The only punitive measure available was exile, a quintessentially criminal punishment, of a period from two to five years.[32] This contravened the second pillar of socialist legality, which had come into prominence after Stalin's death, that only properly constituted courts could administer criminal punishments.

The main proponent of the draft legislation on "parasites" was Khrushchev himself. It was Khrushchev who came out strongly in favour of the anti-parasite legislation in a speech in Minsk, published in *Izvestiia* on 25 January 1958.[33] In addition, the language of the drafts, with their reference to "spongers" (*tuneiadtsy*), "parasitic elements," and "unearned income," was a remarkably close echo of an earlier initiative which Khrushchev had launched as First Secretary of Ukraine in 1948.[34] Although a union-wide decree drafted by Khrushchev had eventually been passed on 2 June 1948, widespread abuse of its provisions, including their wrongful application to youths, war veterans, and pensioners, meant that its application fell from 27,335 cases in its first year to 4,756 in 1949, and by 1951 it had been completely replaced by an amendment to the labour decrees.[35]

By the time the RSFSR draft law on parasites was published on 21 August 1957, a number of republics, such as Uzbekistan and Turkmenistan, which had published their drafts in April, had already adopted anti-parasite laws, and some others, such as Latvia, Tajikistan, Kazakhstan, and Armenia, were to go ahead with their own laws in the coming months. Yet the Russian draft was given a rough ride in the central press, especially among jurists.[36] They argued that the notion of liability was very vague, with public meetings left to draw their own inferences, and that the procedures were poorly defined. More significantly, the penalties envisaged appeared to endow a noncourt institution with the right to impose criminal punishments. In the two weeks following publication of the draft A. Vasil'ev, writing in *Sovetskaia Rossiia* on 30 August, and Krozkhin (no initials), writing in the same paper on 3 September, noted that exile was a form of criminal punishment and that the only branch of government empowered to impose criminal sanctions was the judiciary. The greatest blow to the draft came from those who criticized it on the grounds that in assigning authority to detain and arrest offenders the draft law contravened the 1936 USSR Constitution. On 12 October, also in *Sovetskaia Rossiia*, G.Z. Anashkin, the deputy chair of the RSFSR Supreme Court, argued that the draft law violated Article 127 of the USSR Constitution and Article 131 of the RSFSR Constitution, which stated that "no person may be placed under arrest except by sanction of the court or the procurator."[37]

On the strength of these objections, the draft laws on parasitism were never passed in the RSFSR or in five of the other union republics, including the Slavic republics of Ukraine and Belorussia, while in the eight republics where it had been adopted it fell into disuse. Instead, the regime persisted, as a backstop, with the old legislation of 21 July 1951. While not all justice officials were happy with this development and some, such as the procurator of the Sverdlovsk region, Klinov, at a conference in spring 1959, urged that the draft be put into law so that "we can purge (*ochistit'*) our cities and industrial districts of persons leading a parasitic way of life" objections from the legal community in the RSFSR were to prove insurmountable.[38] Although on 4 May 1961 a separate anti-parasite law would eventually be adopted in the RSFSR, its provisions were telling precisely because "parasites" were now to be tried in the ordinary courts, in effect bringing the legislation into line with the Constitution. Despite an explicit endorsement from the leader of the Soviet Union the anti-parasite legislation as originally envisaged was blocked on the grounds that it violated the second principle of socialist legality.

Although it had benefited from the early post-Stalin campaign, one reason why the first principle of socialist legality, on the observance of procedural norms, was to prove robust in the mid-1950s is that it was grounded in bureaucratic norms that had been inculcated in justice officials since the mid-1940s. The assimilation of these norms ran in parallel with other institutional continuities that crossed the Stalin–post-Stalin divide.[39] There were two sides to this coin. From an external perspective these norms appeared as "indicators" or "bureaucratic targets." In the case of the procuracy, they consisted of a fixation on acquittals and supplementary investigations and in the case of the courts as a preoccupation with *stabil'nost'*, the proportion of verdicts overturned by a higher court following a cassational appeal.[40] The decline in all three indicators that had begun in the late 1940s was entirely unaffected by the change of administration in the Kremlin in 1953.[41]

From an internal psychological perspective, these indicators were taken seriously as evidence of "unfounded prosecutions," which is to say prosecutions which violated the constitutional rights of Soviet citizens. What we find in the period after XXth Congress is that senior justice officials continue to take these indicators seriously and they carry on linking this concern with the issue of unfounded prosecutions.

An abiding theme of the legal press for much of 1957 and 1958 was the concern of judges, not only at the regional but also at the district courts, to avoid *otmeny*, that is, cases vacated by higher-standing courts. The problem with *otmeny* is that they appeared to represent a breach of the constitutional right of a defendant as embodied in the rules on criminal procedure. A lead article in the journal *Sovetskaia iustitsiia* in 1958 reported that approximately half of the reversals of verdicts originally passed by the people's courts occurred on the grounds that they violated procedural rules intended to ensure constitutional safeguards for the defendant, such as Article 111, which provided for an open trial and for the right to a defence.[42] Similarly, an overriding theme of a procuracy conference held in Moscow on 8–9 April 1957 was the condemnation of the ongoing practice of groundless arrests and arraignments.[43] The following year attacks on such practices came from highly placed functionaries, such as the RSFSR minister of justice, Boldyrev, and the deputy Procurator General, A.N. Mishutin.[44]

One notable feature of the period after the XXth Congress is that by the mid-1950s concern over "unfounded arrests" and "unfounded prosecutions" was such that not only the procuracy but also the agencies it supervised, most notably the KGB, were subject to the same rules and expectations. Through institutional inertia, the procuracy's aversion to "unfounded arrests and prosecutions" was extended to the agency it now supervised. Hence, at the all-union conference of investigators of the agencies of state security from 9 to 13 June 1958, the deputy head of the KGB, P.I. Ivashutin, after acknowledging that there had been "certain instances" of unfounded arrests declared: "All our operational staff should know that ... the time has come, at last, to understand, that every unfounded arrest brings not only serious trauma to the person ... but often also exerts a serious influence on his official and public standing."[45]

Our examination of the draft anti-parasite legislation of the spring of 1957 and of the campaign against anti-Soviet activity of December 1956 suggests that the two key pillars of socialist legality, that criminal penalties were the exclusive prerogative of the courts, and that the operations of the justice agencies adhere to the procedural codes, counted for something. In the first case an attempt by Khrushchev to have popular assemblies levy criminal sanctions was successfully rebuffed by justice officials who cited key provisions in the constitution to bolster their position; in the second a powerful campaign launched by a leadership unnerved by the uprisings in Eastern Europe was held in check by the justice agencies and in particular by the USSR Supreme Court, on the grounds that investigations should not involve violations of citizens' rights or breaches of key procedural norms.

Social Order

In summer 1956 reports reached the Central Committee of a terrible case of murder and gang rape of a Russian female engineer, T.M. Bulokhova, on her way to a seismic station near Kirovobad in Azerbaijan on 16 July 1956. A high-level delegation led by the USSR minister of internal affairs, Nikolai Dudorov, was despatched to the region and submitted a report to the Presidium of the Central Committee on 1 October 1956. The report described the city of Kirovobad, and in particular its main textile factory, as in effect under siege from rapists, murderers, thieves, and hooligans such that "female workers are afraid to go out of their living quarters in the evenings." The city park was virtually deserted from mid-evening, and nearly all dwellings had iron grilles on the windows. "The more than 4,000 female workers at the plant, most of whom are Russian, told us that as a result of the impunity of hooligans and other criminals, around 1,000 workers a year leave the plant." "As a result of the bribery, speculation, and mutual favours (*krugovaia poruka*) the population does not feel that Soviet power as such exists in the city."[46]

The following week, on 10 October, a commission headed by Anastas Mikoian submitted a draft resolution to the Presidium entitled "On shortcomings in the work of the USSR Ministry of Internal Affairs and on measures for their elimination."[47] The draft recognized the need to balance socialist legality against the goal of preserving public order. "The Central Committee and the Council of Ministers note that over the last few years much work has been done to strengthen socialist legality in the country. Measures have been adopted to ensure the protection of the rights of citizens as guaranteed by the USSR Constitution." Achieving socialist legality was not the regime's only concern, however. Anxiety over public order, already ramped up by the crime wave of 1953, also needed to be addressed. "In consolidating socialist legality and in strengthening the defense of public order we attach great significance to the need for a marked improvement in the work of the USSR Ministry of Internal Affairs."[48] Accusing local organs of the MVD of a deliberate non-reporting of crimes and of a refusal to start criminal cases, the draft claimed that up to 30 per cent of dangerous crimes, such as murder, robberies, and thefts of state and personal property, went unsolved. It went on to list, as its first recommendation, that the USSR Ministry of Internal Affairs "strengthen public order and ensure the security of its citizens" and that achieving this required "a fundamental improvement in the struggle with criminality … especially murders, rapes, thefts and hooliganism."[49]

In the course of 1956, the need to observe socialist legality evolved in tension with the goal of protecting social order. Deepening public unease over public disorder was refracted through two policy issues, that of "hooliganism" and the regime's response to first-degree murder. In considering the first of these issues we should recall that while in English "hooliganism" is a "quaint and slightly archaic term of admonition" with no formal status in law, the Soviet system was unusual in treating hooliganism itself as a crime.[50] While the Soviet state had initially defined the crime of hooliganism in sweeping terms as "any act of violence, damage or destruction of property in a public place," that definition had over the 1940s and early 1950s been relaxed to encompass any act that expressed "disrespect for the Soviet social collective and its values."[51] Framed along these lines, convictions for hooliganism had crept up in the late 1940s, rising from 45,024 in 1948 to 126,772 in 1955. However, it was in 1956, the year of the secret speech, that the fastest rise, of over 55 per cent, was recorded, taking the figure to 196,558. At the same time successful prosecutions for lesser crimes of violence, such as "blows" and "light blows" "leading to bodily harm," had also been on the rise in the early 1950s so that, as a share of all convictions in the USSR, these crimes, along with hooliganism, had grown from 8.6 per cent in 1950 to 32 per cent in 1956.[52]

By 1956 two currents of opinion had formed on social order issues. Among jurists the new debate on the Fundamental Principles of Criminal Legislation which had commenced early in 1956 revealed a cleavage between one group of lawyers who vowed to uphold legal and procedural norms and who argued that a crime was a crime, irrespective of its perpetrator, methods, or object, and another which laid particular stress on the "struggle with crime," especially the crimes of murder, rape, assault, embezzlement, and hooliganism.[53] This reflected a growing concern among the latter group with what were known as "crimes against the person" and "crimes against personal property," which they viewed in the first instance not in terms of individual rights but as infringements of public order.[54]

The fruits of Mikoian's commission were a key Central Committee resolution of 25 October 1956 entitled "On shortcomings in the work of the Ministry of Internal Affairs and on measures for their elimination," which served as a signal for regional Party committees to issue their own directives. On 5 November the *biuro* of the Briansk *obkom* passed a resolution condemning all the justice agencies for their "liberal attitude towards violators of social order," while a meeting of the Penza regional *aktiv* the following month, on 12 December, decried the "liberalism of the administrative agencies [i.e. the justice and law enforcement agencies] towards criminals."[55] Justice officials themselves began to speak more openly in the press about the need to deal with violations of public order.[56] That autumn a review of public meetings ahead of the new elections of people's judges noted popular dissatisfaction with how crimes of violence were dealt with. "Widely discussed," observed one report, "is the need to raise criminal punishment for hooliganism, physical harm, attacks and robbery [*telesnoe povrezhdenie, razboi i grabezh*]."[57]

Public anger converged on two issues. The first was hooliganism. As we have seen, hooliganism was an elastic legal category unique to the Soviet justice system that was viewed, precisely because of its poorly defined boundaries, with disfavour by many Soviet jurists. This lack of precision had made it an attractive dumping ground for a host of miscellaneous rule violations so that by the mid-1950s the scope of offences covered by the term had become very broad. At the same time the tariff of available punishments for hooliganism was exceedingly narrow, leaving judges with little room for manoeuvre. To afford them greater discretion on 20 December 1956 the RSFSR Supreme Soviet adopted a decree on "Petty hooliganism" for minor violations such as spitting, swearing, pestering, and causing a commotion in a public space. Petty hooliganism cases were heard before judges in fast-track procedures and could carry a punishment of three to fifteen days in pre-trial detention cells. Lapierre is right to argue that in envisaging custodial punishments in unregulated and accelerated hearings without the benefit of procuratorial oversight the decree ran counter to a central tenet of socialist legality, and some jurists voiced their concern on these grounds.[58] At the same time jurists were at pains to emphasize that this was an "administrative" rather than a "criminal procedure" and that it treated "misdemeanours" rather than "criminal offenses." Moreover, and in this respect it was quite different from the anti-parasite legislation, the decree amounted, in effect, to a Faustian bargain: jurists accepted it because it unburdened the main justice system of a huge volume of trivial cases precisely so that they could bestow their attention on mainstream criminal cases and offer defendants the full panoply of constitutional protections under the mantle of socialist legality.[59]

Arguably the chief significance of hooliganism lay not in the realm of workload management or administrative efficiency but of ideology. As Miriam Dobson has rightly observed, "for many citizens heroes and enemies were central components of the political language they had learned over preceding decades and Khrushchev's renunciation of the notion of "enemies of the people" had wrongfooted them."[60] It was in this context that "hooligans" and "hooligan criminals" became an attractive alternative to the classic Stalinist formulations. On 5 October 1958 *Komsomol'skaia pravda* published an article, "Etogo proshchat' nel'zia" (This we shall not forgive) on a case of aggravated hooliganism that had led to the murder of a military cadet. The article sparked a debate and elicited a wave of letters to the paper.[61] It is in the letters, some of which were unpublished but which were passed on to the Central Committee and the Supreme Soviet, that we see a subtle restyling of the language and concepts of the Stalin era. Consider the following letter from "Petrov, a worker from Moscow": "Hooligans and murderers are enemies of the people. That is a noble motto (*blagorodnyi deviz*), a sound slogan which reflects our epoch. We must tear out this 'cancerous tumour' (*vyrezat' 'rakovuiu opukhol'*), and we must do so soon."[62] Public concern over hooliganism was such that *Literaturnaia gazeta* received up to a thousand letters on each article it published on the topic. It is in one such article, by V. Soloukhin, on 13 January 1959, that we see the hooligan – the subject of the article – folded into the subject of the "criminal" in terms that resonated strongly with the Stalin era.

> We should understand that criminals are our political enemies. We are progressing to communism, but they are getting in our way and hindering our advance. They draw honest young workers into their orbit. It is appropriate to recall that during the counter-revolutionary rising in Hungary,

not the least important part was played by criminal elements. If a criminal murders, robs or cripples a Soviet worker, or morally corrupts a young lad, in what way is he not a saboteur? Is not an attack on the life of a citizen a diversion? A criminal despises our society, is hostile to it. He is our most real enemy. That means we must treat him as a saboteur, as a political enemy.[63]

In the emerging debate among jurists, one group, which focused on the "struggle with crime" began to present "hooligans" and others who committed "crimes against the person" not as a threat to individual rights but as a challenge to social order. In an article in *Sotsialisticheskaia zakonnost'* early in 1959, the procurator of the RSFSR, A.A. Kruglov, wrote: "Recently in the press particular attention has been paid to the need to increase the struggle with crimes against the person. The Soviet people justifiably demand that an end be put to all mould [*plesen'*] and scum [*nechist'*] which impedes our movement forwards. No mercy should be given to the hooligans and robbers [*grabiteli*] who violate our social order. The parasites who lodge themselves in the healthy body of our society should be severely punished – so demand the workers."[64]

There was also a second social order issue which stirred public concern: the regime's policy response to cases of first-degree murder.[65] In the Russian Federation, after the law on aggravated murder of 25 April 1954, many death sentences originally passed at regional courts had been appealed and commuted by the RSFSR Supreme Court. These decisions stoked public indignation, but they also angered regional Party bosses who believed that the regime was losing a grip on social order and who saw in executions an effective remedy. One natural focal point for lobbying by regional Party leaders was the administrative organs (AO) department of the newly established RSFSR *biuro* of the Central Committee. Shortly after its formation in March 1956, the RSFSR AO department was showered with notes from regional committees complaining of the RSFSR court's perceived "liberalism" in its application of the death penalty. According to one letter from a secretary at the Kirov *obkom*, almost half the death sentences passed at the regional court in the three years since the April law had been commuted by the RSFSR court.[66] A similar communique from the Gor'kii *obkom* related that despite the "widespread approval" with which the local population had greeted the original death warrants in their region, the RSFSR court had replaced over two fifths with custodial sentences. "Such a practice does not help in the struggle with serious crimes," the report argued.[67] Similar protests hailed from other regional Party committees.[68] "Many voters have raised the question," one report in October 1957 commented, "of strengthening the struggle with murderers, and have expressed the wish that those guilty of pre-meditated murder should in all cases be executed."[69]

Certain regional Party committees assumed that they could ply the RSFSR court as they did their own regional courts. One letter, from the Taganrog *gorkom* to the RSFSR Party secretary, Beliaev, in March 1957 expressed dismay that the republican court had failed to sanction the execution of an alleged murderer of two girls. "The community of Taganrog," it said, "is deeply indignant at such an outcome. The city Party committee considers that the RSFSR Supreme Court has ruled incorrectly on the guilt of [the defendant]. We ask you to interfere in this case so that the criminal gets his just deserts."[70] Although such appeals rarely brought immediate results, the collected pressures of the regional committees, the provincial procuracies, and occasionally, the corresponding regional courts, did eventually rise up through the capillaries of the Party hierarchy. Members of the RSFSR court recalled being invited to the RSFSR AO department and told to take a tougher line.[71] Nonetheless, despite a wholesale purge of the leadership of the RSFSR court in spring 1957, liberal-minded judges such as S.V. Borodin and the first deputy, F.L.Tokarev, continued to apply downward pressures on sentencing.[72]

To Western eyes this might appear as illicit interference by politicians in the judicial process. Yet what is most striking about these cases is that in sharp contrast to the situation that had obtained twenty years earlier, decision-making authority over the death penalty was now insulated from the machinations of local politicians. No matter how strongly regional Party leaders felt about the punishment of individual crimes, they were constrained to operate through clearly defined channels and through a decision-making structure which vested the power of capital punishment in a central institution to which they had no direct access. Regional leaders had no option but to observe the new protocols and to apply pressure on the RSFSR Supreme Court through the only route that was open to them, the administrative agencies department of the Central Committee, whose own authority to interfere in individual decisions was sharply circumscribed.

In the late 1950s hooliganism and murder had become touchstone issues for the Soviet public. Earlier we saw that the justice agency most closely associated with the campaign for socialist legality from late 1930s had been the procuracy. The procuracy was a small, elite organization consisting of around 23,000 officials, most of whom were trained jurists with a higher legal education.[73] In the mid-1950s the procuracy was very much in the ascendancy, benefiting from a high-profile statute on procuratorial supervision of 24 May 1955, which set out the organization's powers, and from its leader, Roman Rudenko's, close personal ties to Khrushchev. And yet the institution most plainly on the front line in the battle for public order was not the procuracy but the *militsiia*. By contrast with the procuracy, the *militsiia* was a mass organization with over a quarter of a million officials, 46 per cent of whom had no more than a primary education and 42 per cent of whom had an incomplete secondary education. "That means," observed the minister of internal affairs, Nikolai Dudorov, in 1956, "that about half our force is virtually illiterate while most of the other half doesn't have a secondary education ... Comrade Bulganin is right, we need to lift the *militsiia* up from the dirt and to put it on its feet."[74] The pool of recruits for positions in the organization was so shallow that it often had no choice but to recruit candidates with questionable records.

A great difficulty for the regime in the mid-1950s was that the *militsiia* appeared unable to shake off many of the practices of the Stalin era. *Militsiia* officials were regularly rebuked for abuse, negligence, drunkenness on the job, and amoral misdeeds, but also for unfounded arrests, assaults, beatings, and even in some cases for the unauthorized killing of Soviet citizens. In the language of the time the *militsiia* were said to be "violating socialist legality." "In the organs of the *militsiia*," noted Dudorov in March 1956, "many crimes are committed by the officials themselves. This is a most serious misfortune."[75] There were reports of unfounded arrests and of beatings by *militsiia* officials. "Arbitrary rule and lawlessness," observed a report on the state of discipline and criminality within the *militsiia* submitted to the collegium of the MVD of 25 June 1956, "find expression in the use of force against Soviet citizens, in injuries, and in killings. There are still many cases of *militsiia* officials taunting and mocking our citizens."[76] While it was practices of this kind that had prompted the Central Committee resolution of October 1956 cited earlier, a year later the *militsiia* had made little progress. On 29 January 1958 the Central Committee issued another resolution, entitled "On violations of legality by the *militsiia*," which lamented the spread of unfounded detentions. On 24 February Rudenko called for criminal cases to be started against those *militsiia* officials who wilfully falsified the materials of the inquiry or who were found guilty of illegal detentions. A month later P. Kudriavtsev, the acting Procurator General, wrote to Dudorov complaining of the "crude violations of the law on the inviolability of the citizen" by *militsiia* officials.[77]

Khrushchev's approach to the problem was two-fold. First, he initiated one of his trademark administrative reforms. On 15 August 1958 he dismissed Dudorov and began to cut the USSR Ministry of Internal

Affairs down to size.[78] Over 1958 and 1959 the Russian *militsiia* was forced to shed 12 per cent of its workforce, and the following year the all-union ministry was closed down and jurisdiction over its activities, including the administration of the *militsiia*, was handed over to its republican counterparts.[79] The other side of Khrushchev's pincer movement was a campaign to transfer social control functions from state organizations such as the courts and the *militsiia* to non-state agencies, such as the comrades' courts and the people's guards, the *druzhiny*. As he launched the campaign at the beginning of 1959, Khrushchev invoked a heightened, rarefied rhetoric of a world in which the social and economic bases of crime would wither away and the remaining infractions of public morality would be handled informally.[80]

All Khrushchev succeeded in doing, however, was to store up problems for the future. These would resurface with a vengeance in a series of riots and public disturbances in the early 1960s.[81] As far as we can tell, most of these mass disorders appear to have had no explicit political content. Far from being anti-regime, anti-Stalinist, or anti-communist, they were conservative in nature and were directed not against the system as such but against local injustices or the disruptions caused by Khrushchev's destabilizing reforms.[82] It is in this context that the Novocherkassk massacre of June 1962 had a particular salience. The political leadership in Moscow recognized that unless it acted swiftly by sending in troops it was unclear how quickly or how far the demonstrations in Novocherkassk might spread. Now there was a real threat that the problem of social control might mutate into a problem of authoritarian control, in which the dictator faces a real threat of popular rebellion.[83] It was in order to forestall such an eventuality that the country's political elite lurched towards a new formula for social control which rested on organizational stability, a new prophylactic approach to repression, a major investment in agriculture, and in October 1964, the removal of the country's leader.

Conclusion

The emergence of a new template for social control after Stalin rested on the interplay of two forces. The first was a concern with socialist legality. Although it had received a major boost after 1953, the idea of socialist legality had been elaborated in some detail in the late 1940s and was wedded to institutional practices that also date from that period.[84] After 1953 this combined with a second strand of socialist legality which centred on the containment and delegitimization of extra-judicial forms of repression. By 1956 these ideas had become sufficiently institutionalized to withstand significant political pressures, including Khrushchev's proposal on "parasites" and the potentially destabilizing crackdown of late 1956 on "anti-Soviet elements."

The second force was the need to maintain social order. The social transformation of the Soviet Union in the late 1920s and early 1930s had been reinforced by a suite of coercive policies, including mass killings, the resettlement of social and ethnic groups, and draconian punishments for minor offences. Stalin's successors recognized the benefit of moderating and reversing many of these policies. Notwithstanding their intentions, however, even mild correctives, such as the Amnesty of 1953, the return of deported peoples, and the abolition of the labour decrees, would prove to be tripwires for new bouts of social disorder. To this the justice and law-enforcement agencies offered two divergent responses. Officials from the core justice institutions, such as the courts and the procuracy, espoused the virtues of what we might think of as a "Soviet rule of law." This, however, would prove to be a much harder ask for the poorly trained and under-educated *militsiia*. While police forces over the world are prone to break rules and violate the rights of citizens, the Soviet *militsiia* of the 1950s inherited a particular legacy and working culture from the Stalin era, one that would prove hard to shake off.

Khrushchev's challenge was to achieve social order within the bounds of socialist legality. His last throw of the dice was the campaign in 1959 to mobilize non-state, non-coercive, "voluntary" institutions in the cause of the self-administration of Soviet society. Yet in launching these policies Khrushchev was merely pursuing a mirage. From summer 1962 the country's political elite realized as much and began to reach out for a new formula of social control. Khrushchev's relentless administrative reorganizations were one factor that turned bureaucratic elites against him. Yet the bout of major social disturbances, including strikes, demonstrations, and a major crime wave at the turn of the 1960s, may have alarmed them, and many ordinary citizens, even more. What they showed was that Khrushchev was unable to secure one of the key functions of any state, namely the preservation of public order. Brezhnev's approach would be altogether different. To the administrative elites he offered bureaucratic stability and to ordinary citizens the balm of social stability. There were to be no wild promises, nor any hint of liberalization. Instead, Brezhnev provided a steady improvement in the standard of living underpinned by a system of low-key coercion. What his administration showed was that withstanding the stresses and strains of the last months of 1956 had been no fluke; by this stage, three years after Stalin's death, the practices of socialist legality had been firmly woven into the fabric of the Soviet state and would henceforth serve as a foundation for the legal ideology of the post-Khrushchev era.

NOTES

For helpful comments on an earlier version of this paper my thanks go to Peter Solomon, Immo Rebitschek, Alexandra Oberländer, Tatiana Borisova, and Vera Tolz.

1. For discussions, see Polly Jones, "From the Secret Speech to the Burial of Stalin: Real and Ideal Responses to de-Stalinization," in *The Dilemmas of De-Stalinization: Negotiating Cultural and Social Change in the Khrushchev Era*, ed. Polly Jones (Abingdon: Routledge, 2006), 41–63; and Robert Hornsby, *Protest, Reform and Repression in Khrushchev's Soviet Union* (Cambridge: Cambridge University Press, 2013), 31–44. For a recent microhistory of the year 1956, albeit from a Moscow perspective, see Kathleen E. Smith, *Moscow 1956: The Silenced Spring* (Cambridge, MA: Harvard University Press, 2017).
2. On this, see the essays in the recent collection edited by Timothy K. Blauvelt and Jeremy Smith, eds., *Georgia after Stalin: Nationalism and Soviet Power* (Abingdon: Routledge, 2016).
3. Hornsby, *Protest*, 108.
4. Miriam Dobson, "'Show the Bandit-Enemies No Mercy!' Amnesty, Criminality and Public Response in 1953," in *The Dilemmas of De-Stalinization*, ed. Polly Jones, 25–6, 30–1.
5. For the best account of police practices in the Stalin era, see David R. Shearer's seminal *Policing Stalin's Socialism: Repression and Social Order in the Soviet Union, 1924–1953* (New Haven, CT: Yale University Press, 2009).
6. Vladimir A. Kozlov, *Mass Uprisings in the USSR: Protest and Rebellion in the Post-Stalin Years*, ed. and trans. E.A. MacKinnon (Armonk, NY: M.E. Sharpe, 2002), chapters 3 and 4.
7. On the use of the *propiska* system which regulated access of economic migrants to large Soviet cities, see Victor Zaslavsky, *The Neo-Stalinist State: Class, Ethnicity, and Consensus in Soviet Society* (Armonk, NY: M.E. Sharpe, 1982), chapter 6. On the resulting disorders in settlements on the boundaries of the large cities, see Kozlov, *Mass Uprisings*, chapters 8–10.
8. Kozlov, *Mass Uprisings*, 27–43, 74–7.
9. Harold J. Berman, *Soviet Criminal Law and Procedure. The RSFSR Codes*, trans. Harold J. Berman and James W. Spindler (Cambridge, MA: Harvard University Press, 1966), 46–7. Note that Berman specifically uses the term "liberalization."
10. Brian LaPierre, *Hooligans in Khrushchev's Russia: Defining, Policing, and Producing Deviance during the Thaw* (Madison: University of Wisconsin Press, 2012), 130. This approach also draws on Oleg Kharkhordin,

The Collective and the Individual in Russia: A Study in Practices (Berkeley: University of California Press, 1999).

11 One writer who rightly draws attention to a "conservative shift" but who places it in the early 1960s is Marc Elie. Elie makes the important point that the "counter-reform" was never intended as "a return to the Stalinist system." See Marc Elie, "Khrushchev's Gulag: The Soviet Penitentiary System after Stalin's Death, 1953–1964," in *The Thaw: Soviet Society and Culture during the 1950s and 1960s*, ed. Denis Kozlov and Eleonory Gilburd (Toronto: University of Toronto Press, 2013), 127. Another writer who dates this shift, as do I, to the mid–late 1950s, is Jeffrey S. Hardy, *The Gulag after Stalin: Redefining Punishment in Khrushchev's Soviet Union, 1953–1964* (Ithaca, NY: Cornell University Press, 2017), 131–6; 140–2.

12 On this, see Yoram Gorlizki, "Party Revivalism and the Death of Stalin," *Slavic Review* 54, no. 1 (1995): 1–24.

13 Lapierre, *Hooligans*, chapter 3.

14 Leon Lipson, "'The New Face of 'Socialist Legality,'" *Problems of Communism* 7, no. 4 (1958): 22. Also see George Ginsburgs, "'Socialist Legality' in the USSR since the XXth Party Congress," *The American Journal of Comparative Law* 6, no. 4 (1957): 546–59; George Ginsburgs, "The Soviet Procuracy and Forty Years of Socialist Legality," *The American Slavic and East European Review* 18, no. 1 (1959): 34–62.

15 Efforts to breathe new life into the term "revolutionary legality" and to make it stand for greater predictability in law had included the joint decree of 25 June 1932 entitled "O revolutsionnoi zakonnosti" and Vyshinskii's article in *Pravda* three days later entitled "Revoliutsionnaia zakonnost' i nashi zadachi." Yet while Vyshinskii's article was ostensibly intended as a repudiation of the nihilist strain in Soviet law, it is notable that even here Vyshinskii described revolutionary legality as "a weapon of proletarian struggle against class enemies." The June decree was in any case soon superseded by Stalin's infamous Theft Law of August 1932, in which he had stipulated in bleakly utilitarian terms that "the main concern of revolutionary legality at present must be the protection of public property and nothing else." See Eugene Huskey, "Vyshinskii, Krylenko, and the Shaping of the Soviet Legal Order," *Slavic Review* 46, nos. 3–4 (1987): 416–17; Peter Solomon, *Soviet Criminal Justice under Stalin* (New York: Cambridge University Press, 1996), 158–61; Yoram Gorlizki, "Theft under Stalin: A Property Rights Analysis," *Economic History Review* 69, no. 1 (2016): 297.

16 The Procuracy's monthly journal, which began publishing in 1934 and was edited by Vyshinskii, was first called *Za sotsialisticheskuiu zakonnost'*, only to be renamed *Sotsialisticheskaia zakonnonost'* (i.e., socialist legality) the following year. Huskey, "Vyshinky," 418. Also see A. Vyshinskii, "Novyi

izbiratel'nyii zakon i sotsialisticheskaia zakonnost': Rech' prokurora SSSR na 4-i sessii TsIK SSSR VII sozyva" (Moscow: Partizdat TsK VKP(b), 1937), and "Prokuror i sotsialisticheskaia zakonnost'," *Izvestiia* 28 May 1938, 1.

17 K.P. Gorshenin, *Sotsialisticheskaia zakonnost' na sovremmenom etape* (Moscow: Pravda, 1948); S. Studenikin, ed., *Sotsialisticheskaia zakonnost' v sovetskom gosudarstvennom upravlenii* (Moscow: Pravda, 1948); G.N. Safonov, "Vsemerno ukrepliat' sotsialisticheskuiu zakonnost'," *Pravda*, 20 June 1948, 2.

18 The relationship between the concept of socialist legality and these campaigns in the late 1940s is explored at length in chapter two of my book manuscript "Taking Dictatorship Seriously: Justice and the Constitution in Soviet Russia."

19 K.P. Gorshenin, "Sotsialisticheskaia zakonnost' na strazhe interesov naroda," *Pravda* 17 April 1953, 2; "Sotsialisticheskaia zakonnost' i okhrana prav sovetskikh grazhdan – vazhneishaia osnova dal'neishego razvitiia i ukrepleniia sovetskogo gosudarstva," *Sovetskoe gosudarstvo i pravo*, nos. 2–3 (1953); R. Rudenko, "Neustanno ukrepliat' socialisticheskuiu zakonnost'," *Pravda*, 4 January 1954, 2. For a discussion of the use of socialist legality in this period that comes to a somewhat different view, see Immo Rebitschek, *Die disziplinierte Diktatur: Stalinismus und Justiz in der Sowjetischen Provinz, 1938 bis 1956* (Vienna: Böhlau Verlag, 2018), 332–9.

20 "Sovetskaia sotsialisticheskaia zakonnost' neprikosnovenna," *Pravda*, 6 April 1953, 1. The editorial was preceded by an MVD communique two days earlier and by an accompanying internal order, signed by Beria, "On forbidding the application of any force or physical influence against those held in custody (k arestovannym)," Gosudarstvennyi arkhiv Rossisskoi Federatsii (GARF) R-9401/1a/509/90–1.

21 Editorial, *Sovetskoe gosudarstvo i pravo*, 2 (1956): 2 (source of the quotations); and "Sotslialisticheskaia zakonnost' na strazhe interesov naroda," *Kommunist* 6 (1953).

22 For a different reading, that one cannot separate these channels, as both the rejection of extra-judicial measures and the focus on the importance of procedural norms are parts of an underlying professional ethos of legal specialists, see Rebitschek, *Die disziplinierte Diktatur*.

23 Hornsby, *Protest*, 108.

24 GARF, R-9492/6s/14/8. These figures are for the higher courts, line courts, transport courts, and military tribunals. They do not include figures for the Special Board of the MVD.

25 Papovian and Papovian argue that the final version was substantially milder than the first version and imply that this was due to the intervention of Rudenko. See Elena Papovian and Aleksandr Papovian, "Uchastie verkkhovnogo suda SSSR v vyrabotke repressivnoi politiki.

1957–1958 gg." In *Korni travy. Sbornik statei molodykh istorikov*, ed. A.S. Eremina and E.B. Zhemkova (Moscow: Zven'ia, 1996), 57–8. A draft of 21 November can be found in *Prezidium TsK KPSS 1954–1964*, t. 2, ed. A.A. Fursenko (Moscow: ROSSPEN, 2006), 494–507. The final version is in *Reabilitatsiia: kak eto bylo. Fevral' 1956-nachalo 80-kh godov*, t. 2, ed. and comp. by A. Artizov et al. (Moscow: Materik, 2003), 208–14.

26 Control over state crimes was progressively decentralized after the XXth Party Congress. On 27 July 1956 state crimes, with the exception of espionage, were transferred to republican and oblast' courts from the all-union court; on 29 March 1957 state crimes and large-scale thefts were transferred to the regional courts. See George Ginsburgs, "Soviet Court Reform, 1956–1958," in *Soviet Law after Stalin. Vol. 2*, ed. Donald D. Barry et al. (Alphen aan den Rijn: Sijthoff and Nordhoff, 1984), 83, 89–90.

27 Papovian and Papovian, "Uchastie," 60.

28 Ibid., 62.

29 Elena Papovian, "Primenenie stati 58–10 UK RSFSR v 1956–1958 gg," in Eremina and Zhemkova, *Korni travy*, 83. Note that the emphasis on counter-revolutionary intent was a feature of policy on state crime already in the mid-1950s (ibid., 74). Also see Papovian and Papovian, "Uchastie," 62–7.

30 Papovian, "Primenenie stati," 80–2; Papovian and Papovian, "Uchastie," 61, 68.

31 The draft law on anti-social, parasitic elements was first published in Estonia on 3 April 1957 and then in Latvia, Azerbaijan, Lithuania, and the Kirgiz and Uzbek SSSRs on 11, 17, 18, 23, and 26 April 1957, and subsequently in the Kazakh, Tadjik, and Turkmen SSRs on 5, 10, and 19 May; in Armenia on 30 July; and Georgia on 18 August 1957. The RSFSR was the penultimate republic to propose a draft law, on 21 August.

32 See Albert Boiter, "Social Courts in the USSR" (PhD diss., University of Columbia, 1965), 125–9.

33 Support for the anti-parasite tribunals is also attributed to Khrushchev in *Pravda*, 18 October 1960 (Boiter, "Social Courts," 134).

34 On the close parallels, see "Neizvestnaia initsiativa Khrushcheva," *Otechestvennye arkhivy* 2 (1993): 34–5.

35 "Neizvestnaia," 38.

36 This argument was made in Boiter, "Social Courts," 155–72.

37 Cited in Boiter, "Social Courts," 155, 157–8, 172.

38 GARF R-353/13/ 286/66.

39 For more on this line of argument, see Yoram Gorlizki and Oleg Khlevniuk, *Substate Dictatorship: Networks, Loyalty, and Institutional Change in the Soviet Union* (New Haven, CT: Yale University Press, 2020) chapters 2 and 3.

40 The pioneer in the study of this topic is Peter Solomon, who first addressed it in his classic article, "The Case of the Vanishing Acquittal: Informal Norms and the Practice of Soviet Criminal Justice," *Soviet Studies* 37, no. 4 (1987): 531–55, and then later in *Soviet Criminal Justice after Stalin* (New York: Cambridge University Press, 1996), chapter 11. For the best summary of the different forms of appeal in the Soviet courts, including the so-called cassational appeal, see Harold J. Berman, *Soviet Criminal Law and Procedure: The RSFSR Codes*, trans. Harold J. Berman and James W. Spindler (Cambridge, MA: Harvard University Press, 1966), 87–90.
41 Solomon, "Vanishing Acquittal," 541; *Effektivnost' pravosudiia i problema ustranenii sudebnykh oshibok*, ed. V.N. Kudriavtsev (Moscow: Akademiia Nauk, 1975) t.1: 9, 178–9, 190.
42 See the issues of *Sovetskaia iustitsiia*, 1957 no. 6: 8, 20, 49; 10: 4, 61; and GARF 353/13/ 197/79; f.353/13/287/49.
43 This was discussed in *Sotsialiticheskaia zakonnost'* 1957 no. 6: 56–8.
44 Boldyrev in *Sovetskaia iustitsiia*, 1958 no. 12: 1–5; Mishutin, *Sotsialiticheskaia zaknonost'* 1958 no. 8: 3–8. Both these cases are cited in John Gorgone, "The Legislative Process in the USSR: Soviet Jurists and the Reform of Criminal Procedure, 1956–1958" (PhD diss., Indiana University, 1984), 33.
45 Papovian, "Primenenie," 83.
46 Fursenko, *Prezidium TsK*, 2, 435–6.
47 The resolution is in Fursenko, *Prezidium TsK*, 2, 456–62.
48 Ibid., 456.
49 Ibid., 456–8.
50 Lapierre, *Hooligans*, 3–4.
51 Lapierre, *Hooligans*, 62–3.
52 GARF R-9492/6/14/14–16; and see Yoram Gorlizki, "Delegalization in Russia: Soviet Comrades' Courts in Retrospect," *American Journal of Comparative Law* 46, no. 3 (1998): 411.
53 Gorgone, "Legislative Process," 17–18.
54 In this respect Berman's argument that the new order of chapters in the 1960 RSFSR Criminal Code reflected a changed balance between the state and the individual (Berman, *Soviet Criminal Law*, 55–6) may have been misconceived. For conservative jurists the new emphasis on "crimes against the person" and "crimes against personal property" was important precisely because it was expressed not as a concern for the individual *per se* but as a bulwark for the protection of public order.
55 Letter 16 November, Rossiiskii gosudarstvennyi arkhiv sotsial'no-politicheskoi istorii (RGASPI) 556/23/8 and letter of 19 January 1957, RGASPI 556/23/26.
56 For example, in the article by the senior MVD official Barsukov in *Sovetskoe gosudarstvo i pravo* 2 (1957): 23–33.

57 GARF 353/3/901/50.
58 Lapierre, *Hooligans*, 97, 101–2, 114–15, 129–30.
59 On this, see Gorlizki, "De-Legalization," 412–13.
60 Dobson, *Khrushchev's Cold Summer*, 102, and see 166–7; also see Lapierre, *Hooligans*, 186–7.
61 The debate centred on a number of articles that were published in quick succession: "khuligan – vrag obshchestva," *Leningradskaia Pravda*, 10 October 1958; "Prestuplenie i nakazanie" in *Literaturnaia gazeta*, 14 October 1958; a piece by the chair of the Moscow City Court, L. Gromov in the 19 October 1958 issue of *Leningradskaia pravda*; "O podlinnom gumanizme," *Pravda*, 1 December 1958. There was also an important follow-up piece in the 13 January 1959 issue of *Literaturnaia gazeta*, by V. Soloukhin, which is discussed below.
62 GARF R-9474/10/197a/30.
63 *Literaturnaia Gazeta*, 13 January 1959; also see the review piece, "Hooligans Are Politics," *Radio Free Europe Research Bulletin*, 27 January 1959.
64 A.A. Kruglov, "Uchastie obschestvennosti v ukreplenii sovetskogo pravoporiadka," *Sotsialisticheskaia zakonnost'*2 (1959): 8.
65 The following passage draws on Yoram Gorlizki, "Political Reform and Local Party Interventions Under Khrushchev," in *Reforming Justice in Russia, 1864–1994: Power, Culture and the Limits of Legal Order*, ed. Peter Solomon (Armonk, NY: M.E. Sharpe, 1997), 267–9. On attitudes to capital punishment in this period, see Yana Skorobogatov, "Killing the Soviet Man: The Death Penalty in the Soviet Union, 1954–1991" (PhD diss., University of California, Berkeley, 2018).
66 RGASPI 556/23/85/78.
67 RGASPI 556/23/58/43–4.
68 See letter of 14 May 1957 from Drozdov in RGASPI 556/23/33.
69 GARF R-353/3/901/50.
70 Letter from S. Bitkin to N.I. Beliaev, 8 March 1957, in RGASPI 556/23/32.
71 Interview with S.V. Borodin, the former deputy chair of the RSFSR Supreme Court, 3 June 1991.
72 See the report on a legal conference held in June 1957, and especially comments from the heads of the Ivanov, Rostov, Stavropol, Kursk, and Belgorod courts. *Sovetskaia iustitsiia* 6 (1957): 50, 52; and Gorlizki, "Political Reform," 268–9.
73 Rebitschek, *Die disziplinierte Diktatur*, 344–5.
74 Yoram Gorlizki, "Policing Post-Stalin Society: The *Militsiia* and Public Order under Khrushchev," *Cahiers du Monde russe* 44, nos. 2–3 (2003): 472. Also see Rebitschek, who suggests that the militia carried out nine out of every ten arrests. *Die disziplinierte Diktatur*, 387, 396.
75 Vladimir Nekrasov, "Nikolai Dudorov," *Sovetskaia militsiia* 6 (1990): 18.

76 Cited in Vladimir Kozlov, *Massovye besporiadki: kriminologicheskoe, ugolovno-pravovoe, ugolovno-protsessual'noe i kriminalisticheskoe protivodeistvie* (Moscow: Izdat. Iurlitinform, 2013), 201–2; RGASPI 556/23/8.
77 Kozlov, *Massovye besporiadki*, 206; and Kozlov, *Mass Uprisings*, 148, 153.
78 See in particular *Prezidium TsK KPSS 1954–1964. T. 1. Chernovye protokoly zapisi zasedanii, stenogrammy*, ed. A.A. Fursenko (Moscow: ROSSPEN, 2006), 333.
79 V.F. Nekrasov, "Nikolai Stakhanov," *Sovetskaia militsiia* 7 (1990): 26.
80 *Vneocherednoi XXI s'ezd kommunistichesoi partii sovetskogo soiuza. Stenograficheskii otchet*. T. 2 (Moscow: Gosud. Izdat. Lit., 1959), 445. On Khrushchev's speeches on this theme, see Dobson, *Khrushchev's Cold Summer*, 146; and Lapierre, *Hooligans*, 133, 170–1.
81 See Kozlov, *Mass Uprisings*, chapters 9–13; and Samuel Baron, *Bloody Saturday in the Soviet Union: Novocherkassk, 1962* (Stanford, CA: Stanford University Press, 2001).
82 Kozlov, *Mass Uprisings*, xii, 24–5.
83 On this, see Gorlizki and Khlevniuk, *Substate Dictatorship*, 2, 255; and Milan Svolik, *The Politics of Authoritarian Rule* (New York: Cambridge University Press, 2012).
84 This is discussed at greater length in Gorlizki, "Taking Dictatorship Seriously."

10 From Mass Terror to Mass Social Control: The Soviet Secret Police's New Roles and Functions in the Early Post-Stalin Era*

EVGENIA LEZINA

The young Muscovite Sergei Sytov, an officially unemployed man in his early twenties, bought goods from foreigners for resale. Eventually, he was summoned to the Moscow KGB Directorate, and in January 1959 the newspaper *Komsomol'skaia pravda* published a feuilleton on him based on the data provided by the secret police.[1] Sytov was then warned by the *militsiia* that if he did not find a permanent job within three weeks, he would be expelled from Moscow under the anti-parasite law. Informed by the KGB of Sytov's misconduct, the Party, Komsomol, and the procurator's office jointly decided to bring him to administrative responsibility and try his case before the people's court visiting session, a form of show trial.[2] Sytov was then detained by the *militsiia*. On the procurator's order, his fitness for work was determined by the Serbskii Institute, later ill-famed for its abuse of psychiatry. Finally, in January 1962 the Baumann district people's court decided to evict the young man from Moscow for five years and confiscate his property. The case garnered extensive media coverage.[3]

This story, which appeared in the in-house journal of Soviet counterintelligence *KGB Sbornik*, reflects a new approach to ensuring state security and social control that emerged in the USSR after the death of Joseph Stalin and reached full swing in the late 1950s and early 1960s.[4] During this period, as Oleg Kharkhordin has argued, "chaotic and punitive terror of the Stalinist years" gave way to "a relentless and rational system of preventive surveillance."[5] Generally, this approach was based on a comprehensive and multichannel social control associated with a return of mutual surveillance practices in new forms and the congruent transformation of the secret police's ideological tenets and working methods.[6] The emphasis was now placed on preventing crime and strengthening secrecy, with novel tacit forms of control and manipulation being introduced. Although, as the above case shows, the new system relied on multiple actors, state security agencies were assigned an orchestrating role in it.

This chapter will look at how the transformation of the Soviet political regime in the post-Stalin era affected the work of its political police, focusing on the newly emerging priorities, practices, and social control mechanisms designed to ensure preservation of a single-party rule and maintaining a grip over society in new conditions.

After Stalin's death in March 1953, the leadership of the Communist Party of the Soviet Union (CPSU) proclaimed a return to "socialist legality," abandoning extrajudicial repression and cancelling most draconian acts. Other indicators of change were a series of amnesty decrees, subsequent release, and partial rehabilitation of political prisoners, as well as a reorganization of the Gulag.[7]

As noted in earlier studies, the renunciation of mass violence and placing state security agencies under collective control of the Politburo was driven by the CPSU leadership's urge for self-preservation and their fear of the return of the Great Terror when many Party functionaries fell under the wheel of repression.[8] Yet, the change of strategy could likewise have been determined by the fact that social and political forces inherited by the USSR and potentially capable of challenging Soviet rule had largely been destroyed by the time of Stalin's death – from political opposition and the nationalist underground to private entrepreneurs and peasant owners. Therefore, in the post-Stalin era, the technology of suppression was altered accordingly: providing general control over the population, the instruments of repression were now more precisely targeted at certain groups within society.

The Central Party Committee set up the Committee for State Security (KGB) under the Council of Ministers of the USSR in its decree of 12 March 1954. The decree announced the directions of internal security that defined the structure and functions of the KGB Fourth (Secret-Political) Directorate.[9] State security agencies were now tasked with: "fighting against the anti-Soviet underground and nationalist formations; eliminating the remnants of armed gangs in the western regions of Ukraine and Belarus, in Lithuania, Latvia, Estonia; timely disclosing hostile activities of bourgeois nationalists, Trotskyists, rightists, former members of anti-Soviet political parties and organizations, churchmen, sectarians and individual anti-Soviet elements; suppressing of subversive activities of emigrant centers abroad."[10]

Given that the major declared threats were mainly residual phenomena from the past and were largely confined to the western frontier, the Soviet people's "moral and political unity" could generally be counted upon. It is no coincidence that at the Twentieth Party Congress in

February 1956, First Secretary Nikita Khrushchev instructed the Central Committee to develop a new Party Program that took into account the proximate embarking on the construction of communism.[11]

However, new anxieties were not long in coming. The authorities feared that political, nationalist, and religious activists would resume their activities after returning from exile or the Gulag.[12] The aftermath of Khrushchev's secret speech was indeed marked by growing unrest and the emergence of anti-Soviet groups and student circles not only in the border western regions, but also in central Russia. In response to these movements, as well as to the upheaval in Hungary and Poland which partially triggered them, the Central Committee on 19 December sharply retorted with a closed letter entitled "On strengthening the political work of Party organizations among the masses and suppressing attacks by anti-Soviet, hostile elements," sent to Party organizations countrywide. This was followed by ordering a new round of arrests in 1957–8, mainly among the youth and intelligentsia.[13] The clampdown largely wiped out the nascent activism, but repression then gave way to a new mode of ensuring state security. Although the secret police still relied on targeted suppression of what it considered as threats to the public order and political unity, its priority was now the prevention of anti-Soviet acts as well as the re-education and reintegration of offenders. As the confrontation with the West intensified, the main foe of the Soviet regime was believed to reside outside the USSR, while inside the country a threat of "ideological subversion" was expected to emanate from "individual anti-Soviet elements" whose anti-Soviet stance was allegedly foreign inspired.[14]

From the 1950s on, the KGB primarily targeted representatives of the "Soviet intelligentsia," who were potentially capable of dissent, and young people who were influenced by Western radio broadcasts and fashion, religious beliefs, nationalist sentiments, etc.[15] In the eyes of the regime, non-conformist religious communities in particular were impeding the achievements of complete social cohesion. They were targeted by Khrushchev's anti-religious campaign.

At the same time, the CPSU renewed its focus from before the war on social engineering. As it was pointed out in one of the brochures of the period, "along with the creation of a highly developed economy, communism presupposes the formation of a new person."[16] Adopted at the Twenty-Second Party Congress, the 1961 Party Program not only promised the advent of communism in twenty years, but also proclaimed the emergence of "a state of the entire people" (*obshenarodnoe gosudarstvo*). Accordingly, it introduced a twelve-point Moral Code of the Builder of Communism listing the new Soviet man's "essential characteristics."[17]

In this context, the education of masses and the prevention of crimes within widely formulated and implemented preventive measures (*profilaktika*) gained particular importance progressively coming to replace arrests.[18]

Not only did excessive repression violate the underlying premise of the "moral and political unity of the Soviet people," the state leaders acknowledged it to be insufficient to terminate undesirable activities (primarily, of autonomous religious communities and nationalist groups). Therefore, increasing energies of the Party, KGB, and their auxiliaries – labour collectives, people's patrols, comrades' and people's courts, media, etc. – were expended in re-educating those citizens who fell under alien influences, behind which loomed various lifestyles and ideas not fitting into the Soviet ideological canon and undermining the unity of the "builders of communism."

The Sytov case showed that the justice system and state security agencies considered the unemployed as "parasites" (*tundeiadtsy*), but this term also included those not involved in "socially useful labour."[19] The "stylish youth" (*stiliagi*), which tended to form "antisocial" groups, exasperated the authorities with their excessive longing for attributes of Western life – music, fashion, dancing, goods, etc. – as well as frequent smuggling.[20] As this longing was deemed as potential disloyalty, the authorities feared that "antisocial" behaviour could easily develop into "anti-Soviet."[21] The "guilt" of non-conformist religious communities, labelled as "churchmen and sectarians" (*tserkovniki i sektanty*), came from their reluctance to participate in activities of Soviet collectives, avoidance of voting and enrolment in the Komsomol, alleged detachment from "socially useful labour," and occasionally refusing to take up arms.[22] Consequently, within broadly defined *profilaktika*, the KGB strived to warn the "honest, but temporarily unhinged," as well as "unstable, wandering and alienated Soviet people," and "help them recover and atone for their guilt with honest labour." The KGB focused on co-opting and assimilating them and helping them return to the bosom of collectives.[23]

Profilaktika in chekist theory was preventive action "taking place before the initiation of criminal activity" that "should pre-empt the occurrence of criminal intent and its transformation into specific socially dangerous acts."[24] But in reality, *profilaktika* was something much more than that. It was perceived by the KGB "not only as a measure of warning and suppressing the hostile activities," but also as that "of shaping the Soviet worldview among those citizens who, for reasons beyond their control, took a hostile path."[25] While scholars have addressed various aspects of *profilaktika*, including its educational impact, the fact that it represented one of the forms of the secret police's upgraded operational agent activities (*agenturno-operativnaia deiatel'nost'*) has largely been overlooked.[26] Additionally sources show that *profilaktika* relied on a greater variety of actors than scholars have believed. *Profilaktika* could imply an almost unlimited set of sanctions aimed at solving multiple tasks – from re-education to disruption, from undermining reputation to changing public opinion, from suppressing "hostile activities" of individual transgressors to the liquidation or disintegration of entire groups and communities.

Most importantly, the KGB became a leading force in the mutual surveillance structures. It was one of the many actors involved in widespread rituals of re-education (*perevospitanie*) and public shaming (*prorabotka*) engulfing workplaces, colleges, and schools throughout the Soviet Union, and one of the central agencies of this new social reality, performing as a chief organizer and arranger of various public shaming and re-education campaigns under its domain.[27] The latter were determined by the plans of operational agent activities developed by state security agencies in agreement with the Party.

The first part of this chapter will address the newly emerging principles of the KGB operational agent work linked with tools of surveillance, including agent networks, trusted persons, and *profilaktika*. In the latter case the focus will be on *profilaktika* of group members and on sessions carried out by collectives, including Party, Komsomol, or public organizations, assemblies at places of work or study, etc. I will then explore the secret police's reliance on the public's help in preventing ideological and antisocial deviations, especially the bodies entitled to impose penalties and sanction offenders, such as people's patrols, labour collectives, comrades' and people's courts. The third part of this contribution will examine the KGB's struggle with the major perceived organized threats to the regime through the so-called disruption measures (*mery razlozheniia*), highlighting the clampdown on unregistered religious communities under Khrushchev.

Upgrading KGB Practices: Agents, Trusted Persons, and *Profilaktika*

In the post-Stalin era, the preservation of a single-party system based on a rigid ideological doctrine required new mechanisms for maintaining social unity and loyalty to the regime. In this context, the announced return to socialist legality, the reported rejection of physical violence and mass terror was part of a drive to re-legitimize the Soviet system and restore confidence in its institutions, including state security agencies. As Julie Fedor has shown, this campaign, clothed in the idea of returning to Leninist norms and reviving the "glorious chekist traditions," turned out to be a success, leading to almost a complete rehabilitation of the Soviet secret police by the end of the 1950s.[28]

Since its founding, the KGB combined propaganda efforts with greater secrecy, moving under various "covers," both internal and external. From the late 1950s, the Committee's focus on enhancing secrecy (*konspiratsiia*) and on covert work was embodied, among other things, in the figure of a KGB active reserve officer working undercover in civilian organizations and enterprises. The above tendency was also manifested in a proliferation of various special checks, performed by the political police, but not linked with it formally: security clearances to classified works and documents, and later – admissions to communications with foreigners and travels abroad.[29] Additionally, the KGB worked to improve its outdoor surveillance and postal control (PK).[30]

Gradually, as the rehabilitation of the secret police proceeded, it received more powers and its tasks became more ambitious: the KGB leadership now regarded ensuring state security as everyone's business (*obshenarodnoe delo*) and implied engaging citizens in mutual surveillance.[31] "Links with the people" (*sviaz' s narodom*) was also premised on increased interaction of the security officers with the population – either through lecturing on political vigilance in labour collectives across the country or recruiting volunteers as secret assistants.[32] This growth of contacts was supposed to stimulate feedback and indeed by 1960 "the receipt of signals from workers about the facts of suspicious behaviours" was said to be on the rise.[33]

Mobilization of the population in information gathering was accompanied by attempts to improve work with agents, traditionally the political police's main instrument in the fight against the regime's "enemies." Notably, however, already in 1952, Stalin had demanded a significant overhaul of agent networks and the number of agents was reduced twice or thrice, while the category of informants (*osvedomiteli*), the basis of a mass agent-informant network (*agenturno-osvedomitel'naia set'*), was abolished.[34] As a result, the agent network of the Ukrainian SSR Ministry for State Security shrank almost fourfold: the number of agents dropped from almost 209,000 in 1951 to 137,300 in 1952 and just around 54,000 in 1953.[35] This indicates that a change in the secret police's roles occurred well before Khrushchev's reforms, being apparently linked with the reshaping of social structure and elimination of "hostile" classes in the USSR under Stalin.[36]

Nevertheless, after the establishment of the KGB, the Party set out to reduce the agent network further, transforming its functions and composition. In the Central Committee March 1954 resolution, it was ordained to create a "quantitatively small, but qualitatively good" agent apparatus and to clear it of "double-dealers, disinformers and provocateurs, as well as persons unable to benefit the KGB organs."[37] As a result, the number of agents in the KGB of Ukraine was again reduced by more than half: from 57,500 in 1954 to almost 25,000 in 1956.[38] Likewise, the KGB staff numbers countrywide were cut in half in 1953–5.[39] The Central Committee additionally ordered to review operational cultivation files (*dela agenturnoi razrabotki*) and clear operational records of such cases that relied on "unjustified data and thereby compromised honest people."[40]

Khrushchev himself expanded on the new requirements for agents at the first all-union meeting of KGB officers held in June 1954. He insisted on increasing agents' education levels, underscoring that an agent must "be more cultured than those whom he cultivates" so that he could "subordinate them morally," and emphasizing that "the overwhelming majority of agents must be honest, our people."[41] Hence, from now on, priority was given to voluntary recruitments on the so-called patriotic/ideological-political basis, while recruitments based on compromising information were allowed in exceptional cases only.[42]

Generally, the Central Committee attempted to oblige state security bodies to turn agents into major means of operational work, making them fight real "foreign agents" or true "enemies" of the Soviet state, and not persecuting "honest Soviet people."[43] In ensuring internal security, agents' main tasks were penetrating the ranks of religious, nationalist, and other organizations; participating in cultivations of "anti-Soviet groups" and disruptions of undesirable structures; "ideologically disarming of those under cultivation"; taking part in *profilaktika*; and monitoring its targets.[44]

Simultaneously, a significant part of agents' functions was to be taken over by a new category of secret assistants – trusted persons or proxies (*doverennye litsa*) – that embodied a discursive development of the "link with the people" concept. They were to be recruited on a voluntary and free basis and provide the security officers with the "signals," or information deserving their attention.[45] Although the need to engage such assistants was noted already in the July 1954 KGB Chairman's order no. 00405, it provided for their recruitment only for short-term assignments.[46] For a few years trusted persons were rarely employed. Their widespread use was encouraged by the order no. 00225 of July 1959, announcing proxies as "the asset/active of state security agencies, an important means of strengthening their ties with the population," which coincided with the unwinding of Khrushchev's campaign to mobilize the public (*obshchestvennost'*) and proliferation of prophylactic activities.[47]

According to the 1961 KGB review, trusted persons were by then widely employed in preventing emergencies and accidents at defence, industrial, and transport facilities; in helping investigate incidents and guard state secrets; in searching for state criminals; and in protecting national borders. The secret police also engaged them in counter-intelligence work on tourist groups and delegations travelling abroad, as well as foreigners from capitalist states residing in the USSR.[48] Along the lines of the Fourth Directorate, security operatives acquired proxies for "the timely receipt of signals at higher educational institutions, research institutes, creative organizations, theaters, medical institutions, in work on churchmen and sectarians, for searches of the authors of anti-Soviet anonymous documents."[49] The KGB also reportedly took advantage of trusted persons in *profilaktika*, making them "actively influence" the offenders, "explain the public danger and harmfulness of their actions," and monitor their behaviour after *profilaktika* sessions.[50]

Despite the obvious parallels between trusted persons and former informants, the KGB leadership emphasized the differences between these categories. In particular, they underlined the publicity of cooperation (the facts of cooperation themselves, in contrast to the content, theoretically should not have been classified), the lack of formalities in contacts with trusted persons (there were neither collaboration subscriptions [*podpiska o sotrudnichestve*] nor pseudonyms) and differing instructions given to the former and new assistants. The cooperation with the KGB allegedly did not exclude trusted persons "from active participation in public and political life, as was the case with many informants."[51]

Although agents, alongside residents and safe apartment owners, belonged to tacit assistants who worked in full secret and largely provided cooperation subscriptions, they were apparently in many ways also similar to proxies and informants in the past.[52] The above-mentioned KGB order no. 00225, in particular, indicated a high turnover of agents, an excessively large volume of the agent apparatus and its misuse.[53] At a meeting of the heads of the Ukrainian KGB regional branches held in October 1959, the delegates recognized that more than half of the agents in the secret networks of the Ukrainian eastern regions were not involved in operational cultivations (that is: comprehensive and organized counterintelligence work).[54] They basically performed

The Soviet Secret Police's New Roles in the Post-Stalin Era   271

Table 10.1. Agents' networks of the KGB of Ukraine during the late Stalinist and Khrushchev periods[55]

	Agents and residents	Safe apartment owners
1951	208,753	–
1952	137,270	–
1953	53,902	–
1954	57,430	4,828
1955	28,489	3,173
1956	24,894	3,436
1957	27,021	3,723
1958	32,770	3,948
1959	40,398	4,751
1960	25,709	3,603
1961	23,682	3,280
1962	21,632	2,804
1963	21,145	2,730
1964	21,856	2,657

surveillance. By 1959, the agent network also swelled from recruitments (see Table 10.1).[56]

It can be therefore argued that agents and trusted persons combined still represented a mass surveillance network.[57] Besides, two acting categories of covert assistants were characterized by a mutual overflow: operatives could develop trust with individuals to recruit them later as formal agents or reconnect retired ("archival") agents by establishing trust relationships with them.[58] Along with providing information to the KGB, state security agencies also used trusted persons in operations.[59] Given these similarities, chekists themselves had at times admitted that proxies and former informants were twin-brothers.

Other types of secret police assistants emerged as well. At high-security defence facilities, industrial and transport enterprises, in addition to agents, residents, and trusted persons, voluntary members of standing commissions rendering assistance in safeguarding state secrets and ensuring facilities' protection provided support to state security agencies. Created under Party committees, such commissions and assistance groups worked closely with KGB operatives. The latter participated in commissions' meetings, "openly and systematically" met with members to "develop practical measures," "increase their vigilance," and "direct their work in the interests of protecting state security."[60] Members of commissions and assistance groups were also instrumental in carrying out educational and preventive work among the personnel admitted to secret works and documents and in increasing political vigilance both at facilities and their surroundings.[61] It was also common practice to include KGB reserve officers working at enterprises as commission members.[62]

During the analysed period, assistance groups could also be formed on a temporary basis from among the patrolmen, Komsomol, and trade union activists to "monitor foreigners, suppress their attempts to penetrate areas of especially important objects, collect intelligence information, etc."[63]

Furthermore, since the early 1960s the secret police at industrial enterprises relied on supernumerary or freelance KGB operational officers (*vneshtatnye operativnye sotrudniki*). Acquired from among reserve KGB and Army officers, earmarked to work in state security agencies in an emergency, they represented an additional level of police control in industry.[64] Supernumerary officers were entitled to work with agents, acquire and work with trusted persons, assist in safeguarding state secrets and implementation of general control at enterprises, etc.[65]

Thus, despite the dissolution of a mass-informant network and decrease in the surveillance apparatus based on misinformation and all-encompassing controls, the secret police secured itself a plethora of new collaborators who made a KGB bidding on a voluntary basis.

Evidently, social surveillance based on wide-spread information gathering was no less important for the post-Stalinist state security agencies than for their predecessors.[66] As Mark Harrison has argued, surveillance was at the heart of *profilaktika*, the major innovation of the KGB destined to serve as "an effective link between state security agencies and the people."[67] Although the need for preventive measures was part of early KGB instructions, *profilaktika* became widely employed only after 1958, when the number of arrests on political charges decreased and the strengthening of ties with the masses became a priority.[68]

As noted earlier, *profilaktika* was part and parcel to secret police agents' activities. KGB order no. 00225 stressed that *profilaktika* should be equated in its importance "with serious operational measures" and that "work of those operatives who, through agents or other means, were able to put a Soviet person on the right path" should be "highly appreciated."[69] Crime prevention, it was emphasized, was to be combined with well-organized operational agent activities, for, in order to choose between arrest and *profilaktika*, one needed "to know the true intentions of those being cultivated and the reasons that pushed them on a criminal path."[70]

Before applying *profilaktika* to anti-Soviet or antisocial misconduct, KGB officers normally initiated operational check files (*dela operativnoi proverki*) to examine the evidence with the help of operational agent procedures.[71] Yet, the very opening of such files could entail tangible consequences for victims and affect their career prospects, as material from operational reviews were taken into account when granting permissions to travel abroad and admissions to top secret work and documents.[72]

The secret (*neglasnaia*) *profilaktika* included talks or chats (*besedy*) with KGB officers or other state officials.[73] In addition to prophylactic talks in the premises of the secret police (by way of official summons or the secret "taking off" [*s'emka*], namely the temporary abduction of a person and his or her delivery to the KGB office), the *profilaktika* targets could also be called up for conversations with representatives of Party, Komsomol, or public organizations, or alternatively managers at their workplaces.[74]

Exerting influence through agents and trusted persons constituted another form of secret *profilaktika*. "A smart agent can actively influence a *profilaktika* object, explain all the harmfulness of his judgments, use concrete examples to convincingly show their inconsistency, dissuade and ideologically disarm him and, finally, persuade him, if necessary, to show up in state security organs with confession of guilt," pointed out order no. 00225.[75] In practice, however, this form of *profilaktika*, at least initially, was used quite rarely due to fears of losing valuable sources in case of their probable unmasking.[76]

By the end of the 1950s, which coincided with the deployment of the campaign to mobilize the public, a substantial part of *profilaktika* was held publicly (*glasnaia*) through shaming meetings carried out with the help of Party, Komsomol, or trade union bodies at places of work or study, etc. These actors could also hold *profilaktika* meetings on their own, without KGB officers' direct involvement.[77] As will be shown below, *profilaktika* was also effectuated through other public structures, including comrades' courts, though less frequently. In Leningrad, where students and other young people became targets of about 30 per cent of all *profilaktika* in 1956–8, the local KGB Directorate influenced deviants "through parents, relatives, teachers, and school management" as well as by summoning them "for interrogations as witnesses and conducting with them substantive talks based on the obtained testimony."[78] The "hostile activities of Ukrainian nationalists" were often "discussed" at so-called "themed evenings" or public gatherings that brought together former nationalists and their victims, KGB officers and local activists to solve multiple tasks from self-exposing and denouncing nationalists and their views to increasing political vigilance.[79]

274 Evgenia Lezina

Figure 10.1 Distribution of different forms of *profilaktika* conducted by the KGB in the Ukrainian SSR, 1960

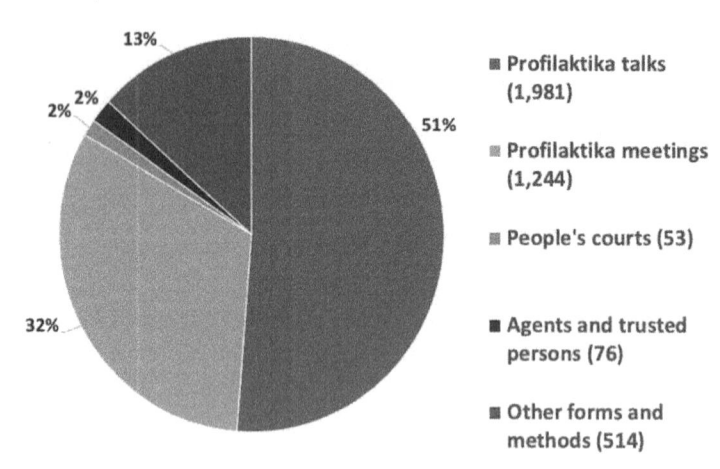

- Profilaktika talks (1,981) — 51%
- Profilaktika meetings (1,244) — 32%
- People's courts (53) — 2%
- Agents and trusted persons (76) — 2%
- Other forms and methods (514) — 13%

Exerting influence through print, radio, and television, which, alongside meetings, constituted public *profilaktika*, was widely employed by the KGB.[80] This included denunciations of one's anti-Soviet or antisocial misconduct, public confessions by offenders or more general exposures of "undesirable phenomena" (parasitism, sectarianism, nationalism, etc.) in the media. The secret police directives insisted on combining open and secret *profilaktika*.[81]

While the countrywide statistics for the analysed period are unavailable, according to the existing data, from the mid-1960s onwards, the KGB conducted an average of 15,000 *profilaktika* per year.[82] In Ukraine out of the total 3,871 persons subjected to *profilaktika* in 1960, 34 per cent were influenced with the public's help – 1,244 by meetings at places of work or study and fifty-three by public courts. Another seventy-six targets were approached by agents and trusted persons. Half of all cases (1,981) were talks with KGB officers, while 514 *profilaktika* relied on "other forms and methods" (although not specified, this, at least partially, refers to using the media to pressure people)[83] (Figure 10.1).

Profilaktika in any format presupposed mandatory confessions of "guilt" by offenders. Failure to do so almost invariably generated continued pressure from the secret police or tougher sanctions, including criminal penalties. Confessions of errors during prophylactic chats (often in writing), in turn, frequently entailed an additional price: culprits either had to appear at public shaming meetings, or act as witnesses in criminal cases, or condemn one's behaviour (group, fellow believers) in the media.

Whenever a person had to undergo a prophylactic talk at the local KGB office, a public shaming meeting at his or her workplace, a comrades' court trial, or exposure in the media, it became "a life-changing moment."[84] Citing fear as an intimate companion of *profilaktika*, Harrison pointed to both the egregious reputation of the Soviet state security and the breadth of sanctions in its arsenal, including arrests. Apparently, the threat of arrest was the major "argument" of operatives in trying to extract confessions or promises to cease misconduct out of offenders.[85]

Edward Cohn likewise has underscored the power of pressure, pointing to "sinister realities behind *profilaktika*" and citing an example of a tenth grader from Pagėgiai in southwestern Lithuania who committed suicide the day after his prophylactic chat in 1955.[86] Another reported suicide occurred in the Karelian town of Segezha in 1959, where the locksmith Timofeev took his life because he was suspected of having authored an anti-Soviet leaflet and forced to confess this during a series of prophylactic talks that lasted seven hours a day for three consecutive days.[87] The ominous circumstances looming behind a benevolent term are revealed with even greater clarity in the case with a Lithuanian Catholic priest Shamshonas, who, against his beliefs, committed suicide in 1961 after a "conversation" with KGB officers who not only asked him "inappropriate and insulting questions" but tried to recruit him as an agent despite his categorical refusal.[88]

As already noted, prophylactic talks often preceded public exposures. The combination of these measures was viewed as most effective, for, as the head of the KGB Directorate for the Kharkiv region pointed out during the 1959 meeting, the public discussion of "political delusions and perversions" made culprits "feel their full responsibility to the collective and subsequently take measures to wash away the shameful stain in front of it."[89] The secret police also viewed public shaming meetings as a way of fixing (*zakreplenie*) *profilaktika* results.[90] The chekists tended to underline the educational value of such gatherings not only for its immediate objects, but for everyone involved. In fact, public meetings could gather between several dozen and several hundred participants, which not only significantly expanded *profilaktika* audiences and turned collectives into its indirect objects, but also spawned joint liability, making everyone responsible for everyone else.[91]

State security officers took great care to ensure that *profilaktika* meetings under their charge went off without a hitch.[92] In public sessions invariably coordinated with the Party bodies, KGB operatives or investigators either openly served as the main denouncers or worked behind the scenes providing the Party or Komsomol secretaries with relevant material for denunciations.[93] Chekists also prepared and guided other sessions' participants, among whom could be their agents and trusted persons. The script included a confession by the offender, usually agreed upon during a prophylactic chat. The punishment demanded by the collective was, as a rule, also inspired by the secret police. The consequences for individuals subjected to *profilaktika* varied depending on the severity of the ideological offence and the culprit's degree of remorse. The outcome could be an official reprimand or warning, placing a wrongdoer under the guardianship (*poruka*) of the collective, transferring the case to a comrades' or people's court, ousting from the Party or Komsomol, demotion or dismissal from work, expulsion from university, college, school, etc. For young men, such expulsion meant an almost automatic draft into the army. However, in relation to students, it was also common to transfer deviants to work in collective farms or factories with a trial period.

Profilaktika that targeted groups usually dealt with youths, intelligentsia groups, or religious communities. In general, any group that did not fit into the ideological Soviet canon was viewed as an alien element in the "people's" state.

The youth groups which came in the KGB's view were of several types. First, mostly in the national republics of the USSR, the late 1950s were marked by the emergence of "groups of nationalist character," often created under the influence of former independence fighters, priests, and other activists, many of whom were returnees from exile or the Gulag. In Ukraine and the Baltic republics, the majority of protest groups during this period were inspired by ideas of national independence. These were mainly groups of students distributing handwritten or photocopied leaflets, such as the underground youth religious-nationalist *Laisves Kovunai* organization, created in August 1954 in Panevėžys, "Kaunas Underground Youth Organization of 16 February," founded in late 1955, and the "Freedom for Lithuania" group set up in late 1957 at Kaunas Polytechnic Institute.[94]

In total, twenty-five anti-Soviet organizations and groups with 129 members claimed by the KGB to be "anti-Soviet" were disbanded by the Lithuanian KGB in 1956–7.[95] According to other data, in 1957–8, state security agencies identified thirty-eight "nationalist" groups with 180 participants mostly created in schools due to "negative attitudes to the collective farm system, idealization of bourgeois Lithuania and nationalist leaders, anti-Russian sentiments, etc."[96]

In Ukraine, between 1954 and mid-1964, i.e. over the decade of the "Khrushchev thaw," the secret police disbanded seventy-seven nationalist organizations and groups with a total of 602 participants (of which about 70 per cent were in the western regions).[97] Also, in 1954–8, the Ukrainian KGB liquidated fifty youth groups with almost

Table 10.2. "Anti-Soviet" groups disbanded in the Ukrainian SSR, 1954–8

Year	Youth groups			Intelligentsia groups		
	Number of groups (participants)	Among them		Number of groups	Among them	
		Arrests	Profilaktika		Arrests	Profilaktika
1954	9 (63)	27	36	–	–	–
1955	8 (39)	17	22	–	–	–
1956	9 (57)	14	28	–	–	–
1957	9 (43)	15	28	1	2	–
1958	15 (93)	13	75	3	3	8
Total	50 (295)	86	189	4	5	8

three hundred participants, of whom about a third were arrested and two thirds subjected to *profilaktika* (Table 10.2).[98]

The second type of organizations likewise labelled as "anti-Soviet" were groups pursuing a return to Leninist principles. Most of the groups created in Russian cities in 1956–7 fit under this label, including the Moscow-based "Union of Patriots," founded at Moscow State University (Krasnopevtsev–Rendel's group), the "Russian Democratic Party" (Sitovenko–Efremov–Kriuchkov's group), and the "Union of Revolutionary Leninists" (Solov'iev–Lukin–Sidorov's group); the Leningrad-based "Union of Communists–Leninists" (Trofimov–Pustyntsev's group) and Pimenov–Vail's group at Library Institute; the "Revolutionary Communist Circle" at Rostov State University (Anikushkin's group); Pirogov's group in Arkhangelsk; the "Socialist Union of the Struggle for Freedom" in Kyiv (Feldman–Partashnikov's group), and others.[99]

Groups united around ideas of promoting artistic freedom and self-expression constituted a third type of informal activity targeted by the secret police in the late 1950s and early 1960s. These included the "Club of Music Lovers" created in 1957 in Kharkiv, the "VSKHNIT" ("Great Sons Willing to Find the Truth of Mysteries") society founded the same year at Mykolaiv Shipbuilding Institute, the *Green Noise* journal issued at Kyiv State Conservatory in 1958–9, or the *Syntax samizdat* poetry journal published in Moscow in 1959–60.[100]

Finally, the KGB's attention was drawn by the "antisocial" groups of *stiliagi*, who organized parties accompanied by what the KGB reported as, "stylish 'rock-n-roll' and 'boogie-woogie' dances," "vulgar, often anti-Soviet jokes," as well as invariable "drunkenness and sexual debauchery."[101] Among them were the Kyiv-based "Submarine" and

"Kino" groups, "Blue Horse" in Kharkiv, "Pornoratsiia" in Vinnytsia, and a student group in Odessa, all active in 1958.[102]

Except for communities of the *stiliagi*, that could number more than a hundred participants, youth groups generally consisted of no more than several dozen members. Having a diffuse structure, they were overwhelmingly disclosed through "signals" received from agents, trusted persons, or other activists. Subsequently, agents were recruited inside these groups to conduct their operational cultivation. With regard to both alleged "anti-Soviet" and "antisocial" structures, the KGB, as a rule, combined arrests of leaders with *profilaktika* of rank-and-file members, after which groups predominantly ceased to exist.[103] However, the severity of sanctions also correlated with the degree of remorse of offenders during prophylactic talks or public meetings held at places of their work or study.

A differentiated approach to *profilaktika* outcomes can be traced in the case of a school group in the Lithuanian town, Kapsukas, organized by a few schoolmates in 1957 to mostly distribute nationalist leaflets. After its post factum disclosure, six of its former members were subjected to *profilaktika* in December 1959. Three students were expelled from universities and sent to work either on collective farms or on construction sites, one was arrested and two technical college students were placed under the guardianship of their colleges' collectives.[104]

In the *profilaktika*'s aftermath, its targets were routinely placed under surveillance by KGB agents or trusted persons.[105] If groups' ex-participants continued their "hostile activities," they could be subjected to operational cultivation or recruited as agents or proxies.[106]

How broadly *profilaktika* could actually be interpreted demonstrates the case with the central Kaunas cemetery, which for several years in a row became the site of spontaneous protests on the All-Souls' Day, the traditional day of commemoration of the dead. On 2 November 1956 an estimated crowd of 1,400, mostly students and teenagers, gathered there near the monuments to the fallen Lithuanian soldiers and legendary pilots Darius and Girenas, and sang national hymns.[107] Consequently, eighty-five persons were detained, four of them convicted, over a hundred were subjected to *profilaktika*, and more than a dozen of those interrogated were recruited as agents and proxies.[108] In 1957 an attempt at a spontaneous protest at the cemetery was repeated on All Souls' Day. This time about 2,000 people gathered there, of whom 105 were detained and 102 subsequently convicted.[109] But not only the wrongdoers were sanctioned. To prevent further incident, the authorities decided to liquidate the central Kaunas cemetery itself. It was demolished by orders of the KGB and turned into a recreational park in 1959.[110]

The KGB in the Shadow of the Public: Surveillance and *Profilaktika* with the Help of "Voluntary" Institutions

Public shaming meetings were the most common, but not the only, form of the KGB's appeal for the public's help. The secret police took advantage of other forces reactivated under Khrushchev's campaign to mobilize "voluntary" institutions, such as people's patrols, assistance groups, comrades' courts, and people's courts.[111] Notably, in contrast to the collectives that carried out *profilaktika* meetings, the above structures were entitled to subject culprits to stricter sanctions and legal penalties. Relying on their help, chekists unfailingly coordinated their action with the Party organs and were assisted by the *militsiia* and the procuracy. Thereby, the KGB partially transferred some of its surveillance and repressive functions to other actors, while maintaining its full control and organizing role.

Generally, the secret police turned to the public in cases of either more serious misconduct, or unrepentance of offenders, or when they found it necessary to publicly condemn "undesirable phenomena" (parasitism, speculation, sectarianism, nationalism, etc.), or when they possessed reliable connections with local activists. Importantly, however, the KGB enjoyed extensive latitude to enact these "forms of surveillance, admonition and control" flourishing in the USSR since the late 1950s.[112]

To illustrate, state security agencies could either penetrate or fully subordinate people's patrols (*narodnye druzhiny*), voluntary detachments for maintaining public order, fighting delinquencies and "the vestiges of capitalism," entitled, among other things, to detain offenders.[113] Although people's patrols formally acted under the control of local Party bodies, the secret police kept a watch on patrolmen's "political vigilance" and occasionally involved them in their own activities, such as monitoring foreigners and identifying their "links" with Soviet citizens;[114] fighting speculators (*fartsovshchiki*), "parasites," *stiliagi* and other non-conformist youth;[115] struggling with autonomous religious communities;[116] assisting in the elimination of riots;[117] and patrolling border areas.[118]

Simultaneously, local branches of the state security could set up special patrols and detachments under their full control to curb citizens' contacts with foreigners, prevent smuggling, or promote Soviet propaganda among foreign visitors. For example, by the early 1960s such patrols were created at the Komsomol city committee in Odessa and among service personnel of hotels and restaurants visited by foreigners in Moscow.[119]

In border areas security officers and representatives of the border troops normally became part of the people's patrols' district headquarters. They lectured patrolmen on political vigilance and set them tasks for protecting the state border. By mid-1963, there were about seven hundred voluntary people's patrols in the Ukrainian frontier regions, consisting of 23,000 Komsomol members and activists, as well as many pioneer groups named "Young Friends of the Border Guards."[120]

A prominent Ukrainian dissident, Leonid Plyushch, recalled how, as a high school student in 1954–5, he joined a "Brigade of Assistance to Border Guards" in Odessa, sharing the belief of other youngsters that their "prime mission was to help catch spies."[121] Since the border troops were part of the KGB, such brigades were operated by the Committee. Odessa was a port city and traditionally had a lot of foreigners. According to Plyushch, the brigadiers "were instructed in the use of firearms, trained to catch spies, and sent out to patrol the border at night."[122] Later, Plyushch joined the Komsomol detachment that students nicknamed the "Light Cavalry." "Made up of students and young workers," explained Plyushch, "the Cavalry was assigned to catch prostitutes, thieves, and currency speculators. It was particularly persistent in hunting *stiliagi*, young men with long hair, loud shirts, tight trousers, and thick-soled shoes. When they stopped a *stiliaga* on the street, the cavalrymen would appeal to his conscience. If this didn't work, his hair would be cut, and his trousers slit."[123]

Offenders caught by *druzhinniki* during raids or patrols could be subjected to further *profilaktika* with the other public forces' assistance. According to anti-parasite laws introduced in the union republics since the late 1950s, working collectives and people's courts were authorized to evict the so-called *tuneiadtsy*, "persons evading socially useful work and leading an antisocial parasitic way of life," for a period of two to five years.[124]

The collaboration of various bodies and the KGB's behind-the-scenes role in the anti-parasite campaign is well documented in the case with a construction technician of the Moscow health district department Iakov Kats. Having changed nine jobs in three years, he allegedly got a job just "for appearance's sake," but, as was evidenced through KGB agents and outdoor surveillance, used to meet with foreigners during working hours "for speculative purposes."[125] Security officers predictably reported him to the secretary of the Party district committee who instructed the people's patrol to collect "materials exposing Kats' parasitic lifestyle." Having collected compromising data, the patrol's headquarters handed them over to the district procurator. The latter, in turn, issued an opinion stating that Kats' co-workers should decide on his fate. The public meeting organized in early 1962 in the Central

Telegraph club in which patrolmen also took part, passed a verdict to evict the twenty-seven-year-old from Moscow for a period of five years. This public verdict was then approved by the executive committee of the district Council of People's Deputies.[126] Just like with another *stiliaga* Sytov, whose case was considered by the district court in the same month, Kats' case received wide media coverage.[127]

During Khrushchev's anti-religious campaign, the anti-parasite legislation was widely employed against religious ministers and activists with more than four hundred evangelicals being exiled in the early 1960s.[128] The secret police was apparently behind these evictions, as well as other persecutions of believers. The KGB Directorate for the Orenburg region, for instance, organized a whole series of deportations of the Mennonite communities' leaders, evicting around twenty persons with families in 1961–4.[129] In one case, local chekists sent materials "about reactionary activities" of two Mennonite preachers Hermann Herzen and Hannah Bergmann from Sorochinsky district to the procurator, who handed them over to the local public. The residents' assemblies then passed a sentence for a five-year eviction to each, approved in March 1963 by the executive committees of the local Soviets.[130] In another case, the decision to expel the Mennonite leader and father of twelve children Pankrats was made by a village assembly (*sel'skii skhod*). Notably, according to the 1961 decree, meetings of local residents were not entitled to consider cases on evictions at all.[131] Other Mennonite preachers Keller and Classen from Novosergievsk district were sentenced to five-year evictions by a district people's court in February 1963 after the KGB had sent relevant data to the regional procurator, who handed them over to the court.[132]

In certain *profilaktika* cases, state security agencies took advantage of comrades' courts (*tovarishcheskie sudy*): elected public bodies were likewise designed to prevent crimes and educate Soviet citizens through persuasion.[133] As usual, when providing information and preparing court sessions, chekists predominantly chose to act indirectly, relying on the intermediaries, including people's patrols or assemblies of activists. There is evidence of the KGB's resorting to this form of public influence when dealing with speculators,[134] authors of anti-Soviet inscriptions or "politically harmful statements,"[135] border regime violators,[136] participants in mass riots,[137] Ukrainian nationalists,[138] religious believers,[139] and other wrongdoers.

This approach is exemplified in the following case narrated in the *KGB Sbornik*. Aleksandr Zakharov-Greben', a nineteen-year-old research institute employee, was repeatedly detained by people's patrols for alleged speculation with tourists from capitalist states.

In February 1960 he was summoned together with his mother to the Moscow KGB Directorate for a prophylactic chat, where he "behaved insincerely, didn't draw any conclusions and continued to meet with foreigners."[140] Once the KGB informed the secretary of the Party district committee about this case, a comrades' court session was organized by the local people's patrol in agreement with the Party bodies. As it was discovered that Zakharov-Greben' had recently entered the Moscow Pedagogical Institute of Foreign Languages, the young man was refused admission. A comrades' court session organized in September 1960 was attended by the patrolmen, over seven hundred of Zakharov-Greben's former and current co-workers, and the *Moskovskii komsomolets* correspondent who later reported on the proceedings. The ensuing article, entitled "Renegade on Trial," is striking in its emotionally aggressive language. The author expressed doubt whether there was at least something human left in the young man and cited one of the denouncers who branded him as a "black sheep" whose "soul has grown like bark from mud."[141] The patrolmen acting as public procurators "sharply condemned Zakharov-Greben's antisocial behaviour," so the court decided to petition the authorities to deprive him of his residence permit (*propiska*). The offender wrote an open letter announcing a beginning of "an honest life" and "encouraging his former 'cronies' to model themselves on him." This was followed up by another prophylactic talk. Zakharov-Greben' then reportedly learnt a lesson and "frankly spoke about people who systematically used their meetings with foreigners for speculative purposes."[142]

Comrades' courts were also widely employed by the secret police to publicly condemn believers of non-Orthodox Christian communities. Court verdicts were occasionally instigated to remove children from believers' families, a common practice during the anti-religious campaign.[143]

Conducting open-court trials over unwanted "elements" to enhance educational impacts on broader audiences was another mainstream practice of the period. Such open sessions, including visiting sessions of the people's courts, pertained to cases under the KGB's purview, including treason, speculation, currency rules' violations, anti-Soviet leaflets' distribution, etc.[144] Open hearings also became pervasive under the anti-parasite campaign, an infamous trial of the future Nobel Prize winner for Literature, poet Joseph Brodsky, expelled from Leningrad by the district people's court in March 1964, representing just one of numerous instances.[145] Other popular targets of open trials masterminded and directed by the KGB were former members in the Ukrainian nationalist underground. Amir Weiner cited the 1959 Party Central

Committee in Kyiv report telling about fourteen public trials staged in Western Ukraine over the past few years with some fifty-one former "OUN bandits" having been tried and twenty-four sentenced to death.[146] By 1962 the number of such trials exceeded twenty, according to the KGB's own data.[147]

Open criminal trials of religious ministers and activists likewise became a token of time, marked by a tightening of anti-religious legislation.[148] A show trial held in Drezna near Moscow in April 1961, in which six Pentecostal ministers were sentenced to terms between two and ten years in prison on trumped-up charges of "fanaticism," was widely publicized.[149] Similar sessions were held elsewhere.[150] In July 1959 Jehovah Witnesses' leaders were convicted in Ukrainian Pervomaisk,[151] in January 1960 the leaders of two Pentecostal groups were subject to an open trial in Mykolaiv,[152] in 1961 Pentecostal preachers were openly tried in Saratov[153] and in Nakhodka,[154] while the Uniate priests were sentenced in Lviv in October 1962.[155] As will be shown in the following section, demonstrative trials of believers alongside extensive media coverage that they garnered were part of a broader KGB strategy of disrupting non-Orthodox communities during Khrushchev's anti-religious campaign.

Between *Profilaktika* and *Razlozhenie*: Disruption of Unregistered Religious Communities

Generally, *profilaktika* and other secret police operational agent measures targeting individual offenders and groups proved effective, almost invariably leading to a complete cessation of "hostile activities."[156] The suppression of organized action by nationalist groups, religious communities, and anti-Soviet organizations abroad, though, required effort of a different sort, and the results were not as obvious. To terminate such activities, the KGB reanimated its tactic of "decomposition" or "disruption" (*razlozhenie*). It dated back to the early 1920s and was based on psychological techniques of manipulation, provocation, and other covert methods employed to halt unwanted collective action through splits, discreditations, and other means of "operational psychology."[157]

The KGB Counterintelligence Dictionary defined "disruption" of anti-Soviet organizations and groups as "a method of operationally cutting short the enemy's organized subversive activity," the essence of which was the destruction "of the structural links between the members," in order to "disrupt them from within."[158] This could be achieved "by introducing or exacerbating ideological disputes between members of the organization (group), discrediting the aims of the organization in the eyes of rank-and-file members, intensifying conflicts between the leadership and rank-and-file members, arousing mutual mistrust amongst the leadership, intensifying their rivalries, etc." Such processes could be engendered or augmented through "feeding" certain information to several group members and playing upon differences between them. The term "disruption" could also cover "ideological work carried out with the help of mass media, the public exposure of the leaders, and individual preventive measures against errant members of anti-Soviet groups, etc."[159]

Major targets of "disruption" inside the Soviet Union during the late 1950s and early 1960s were nationalist groups as well as unregistered religious communities.[160] In total, almost half (3,649) of 7,430 non-Orthodox Christian communities in the USSR remained unlegalized by the late 1960s.[161] Struggle with religious groups that refused to register under repressive Soviet legislation was one of the main KGB's tasks since its inception. Such communities were labelled as "illegal groups carrying out anti-Soviet activities under religious cover" and were severely persecuted.[162] However, their liquidation remained elusive. The meeting of the KGB local branches' leaders held in March 1957 recognized that arrests alone had not eliminated Jehovah's Witnesses structures. Thus, along with "isolating Jehovah's leaders by arresting and compromising them," a stake was made on "promoting proven agents of state security agencies as substitutes for arrested ministers into illegal Jehovah's structures for their disruption."[163] At another meeting of senior officials, held at the KGB central office in March 1959, the agents infiltrated directly into the Jehovah's Steering Committee and other units were tasked with "identifying hostile elements from among Jehovah's Witnesses and conducting their operational cultivation," taking measures "to deactivate or to compromise reactionary Jehovah's leaders," "to reduce organizational links" of the movement, etc.[164]

A 1959 *KGB Sbornik* article reports on the influence exerted through KGB agents on the then-head of Jehovah's Steering Committee Pavlo Ziatek, resulting in the adoption of several decisions beneficial for the KGB. One of them was a resolution to stop printing Jehovah's literature in an illegal printing house. Furthermore, under the agents' influence, Ziatek reportedly allowed Jehovah's Witnesses "to take part in elections to local bodies of Soviet power, join trade unions, and celebrate public holidays" and removed women from leadership positions (women traditionally played more active roles in the movement).[165] These activities eventually caused a split in the ranks of the Jehovah's Witnesses.[166]

According to the KGB review on disruption of "illegal church-sectarian groups" issued in 1958, a similar approach of combining arrests with covert decomposition was applied to other non-Orthodox religious communities, including Pentecostals, Baptists, True Orthodox Christians, Inochentists, and Khlysts. The review proposed to continue "separating believers from the hostile influences of the church-sectarian activists," taking more active measures "through agents and other means" "to compromise the church-sectarian authorities and weaken their influence on believers" to eventually "achieve complete disintegration of illegal groups."[167]

Alongside covert measures undermining faith communities from within, the KGB employed propaganda to discredit their activities publicly. In consultation with the Party, the secret police published articles and feuilletons in the all-union and local press and participated in the preparation of documentaries and feature films, books, and brochures "exposing the hostile activities" and "reactionary nature" of the "sectarian underground."[168] According to incomplete data, more than 550 of such publications appeared in 1958 alone.[169]

The KGB Directorate for the Primorsky Territory managed to issue over thirty "anti-sectarian" materials in the regional and local press in 1958. One of the articles about a self-exposure by a former Baptist was even selected by the Press Bureau of *Pravda* to be published in regional newspapers countrywide and was included in a collection by *Glavpolitizdat*.[170] Another reported "achievement" was issuing 30,000 copies of the denunciation by former Pentecostal preacher Fedor Miachin. There is evidence, however, that this self-disclosure was made in exchange for a promise by local chekists to terminate a criminal prosecution of Miachin for a car accident that he was involved in.[171]

It is noteworthy that the KGB also used "disruption" methods on individual groups as well. Thus, members of the Muslim murid communities in several Dagestan villages became targets of extensive "operational agent preventive measures with the help of the public," as a *KGB Sbornik* article detailed.[172] The followers of sheikh Amai (Arslanukai Khiderlezov), himself arrested and exiled in the 1930s, resumed their activities in 1960, causing KGB officers great alarm. The republic's Committee decided to "organizationally disintegrate the sect, tear its members away from reactionary activities and involve them in socially useful labour." They started with *profilaktika* of individual murids, persuading them to condemn "the sect's harmful activities" in public. One of the sheikh's grandsons was forced "under threat of criminal prosecution" to "accept the KGB's offer" to issue an open letter condemning the leaders and active community's members. Once it appeared, more letters of condemnation and self-renunciations were broadcast on the republic's radio and television stations.[173]

The murids were denounced by several village assemblies, which the media covered. In the sheikh Amai's home village of Germenchik, chekists sought to demolish the prayer house (*ziiarat*), erected on the sheikh's grave that became a place of pilgrimage for murids from all over the republic. They also tried to discredit the sheikh's daughter, who enjoyed authority among villagers. Another of the sheikh's grandsons "was recommended" to come up with a public proposal "to take down the *ziiarat* from his grandfather's grave and stop the pilgrimage." After such a letter appeared in the local newspaper, the secretary of the district Party committee, the chairman of the district executive committee, and a KGB operative arrived in Germenchik and organized a meeting of the local activists, which was also attended by the village elders. The meeting agreed "to convene a village assembly and discuss an antisocial behaviour of the sheikh Amai murids." The village gathering met on the same day and the Party secretary and security officer addressed it, followed by more than twenty participants condemning the murids and demanding confession by the sheikh's relatives. The next day, believers themselves demolished the prayer house at the cemetery in the presence of the whole village. Detailed reports of the gatherings appeared in the local newspapers, and a film produced by the republican television was screened several times allegedly "at the viewers' request." Similar assembly held in Verkhneie Kazanishche village demanded criminal prosecution of one of the murid leaders, and an open trial was later organized on the spot.[174]

By combining arrests with *profilaktika* and disruption measures, the secret police, according to their own data, managed to liquidate 175 "church-sectarian groups" in 1958 alone and "to tear away about 9,000 believers" from the activists' influence, "involving them in socially useful labour" in just thirty country's regions.[175] Nevertheless, the KGB was never able to get rid of non-conformist religious communities or force them to register. Furthermore, Committee's efforts actually prompted more illegal religious activities. The anti-religious campaign in fact generated the Baptist church's massive split in the early 1960s, when the Initiative or Reform Baptists (*initsiativkniki*) formed an illegal community in protest against spiritual restrictiveness imposed by official membership.[176] Jehovah's Witnesses, Pentecostals, and other non-Orthodox confessions continued to pose problems for the Party and KGB until the end of Soviet rule.[177] Nonetheless, disruption techniques elaborated during the anti-religious campaign were subsequently widely employed by the political police against dissident groups during the 1970s and 1980s as well as informal public associations and movements during *perestroika*.[178]

Conclusion

The period of the late 1950s and early 1960s was marked by a propensity of the Soviet authorities to sit on two chairs. The Party leadership took pains to demonstrate the popular, benevolent nature of the regime, while ensuring preservation of a single-party dictatorship and non-market economy. Having abandoned mass arrests and executions, the secret police in the post-Stalin era resorted to new methods of suppressing potentially disloyal citizens and groups. Importantly, a new approach to ensuring state security took root after the phase of direct terror and mass violence, which had effectively eliminated the possibility of meaningful organized resistance. The Soviet authorities fairly calculated that the residual phenomena in the form of nationalist, religious, and political "undergrounds" would soon be done away with, and lesser means would suffice to suppress the remaining or re-emerging "anti-Soviet" or "antisocial" "elements." Hence, the reduction of chekist cadre and agent networks should not have constituted a serious problem for state security bodies operating under these new conditions.

Since the classes and social groups inherited from the previous epochs no longer existed, the major menace was now associated with groups potentially capable to challenge Soviet rule. Dissident intelligentsia and youth were inclined to fall under diverse "bourgeois" influences like fashion, radio broadcasts, nationalist ideas, and religion. These new targets determined the requirements for KGB agents and personnel, especially the recurrent demands to increase their education levels.

Additionally, the state compensated for the greater complexity of society and greater openness of the regime in the post-Stalin era by maintaining the country's isolation with closed borders, stricter censorship, and the jamming of foreign radio broadcasts. It also engaged in sophisticated mass controls through various systems of admissions and privileges, timely suppression of ideological deviations, tough and quick isolation of dissidents, and exerting educational and *profilaktika* measures on broad audiences.

Despite the declared dissolution of a mass-informant network in 1952 and the further downsizing of the agent apparatus under Khrushchev, the secret police's surveillance networks appear to have survived and became an important part of the emerging social control system. Although in fighting dissent state security agencies no longer relied on wide-scale disinformation and falsified informants' reports, the emphasis was still placed on both overt and covert preventive measures rooted in mass surveillance. Comprehensive social controls through networks of agents and trusted persons turned into the basis of

288 Evgenia Lezina

prophylactic policing, as well as reliance on other structures of mutual surveillance that proliferated under Khrushchev's campaign to mobilize the public: labour collectives, Party and Komsomol bodies, comrades' and people's courts, people's voluntary patrols, commissions, and assistance groups at industrial facilities, etc. Undesirable structures, such as non-conformist religious communities and "anti-Soviet" groups capable of steady collective action, were subjected to more stiff disruption techniques. Conducting *profilaktika* and *razlozhenie* with the public's help allowed the KGB to remain in the shadows, delegating some of its "dirty work" to other bodies, they also helped the Committee expand its own surveillance networks and enhance its standing within society.

NOTES

* This chapter was prepared as part of a research project funded by the German Research Foundation (DFG), project no. 403506742. The author's special gratitude goes to the archivists of the Lithuanian Special Archives in Vilnius, the Archives of the Security Service of Ukraine, and personally to the SBU Archives director Andriy Kohut for their assistance and support.
1 I. Shatunovskii, "Pechal'nyie rytsari zhevatel'noi rezinki. Fel'eton," *Komsomol'skaia pravda* 14, 17 January 1959, 4.
2 Peter Juviler, "Mass Education and Justice in Soviet Courts: The Visiting Sessions," *Soviet Studies* 18, no. 4 (1967): 494–510.
3 V. Noskov and Iu. Uryvaiev, "Strozhe podkhodit'k tuneiadtsam," *Sbornik KGB SSSR* 17 (1962): 121–3. Earlier on Sytov's case see, S. Marfunin et al., "O praktike raboty po provedeniiu profilakticheskikh meropriiatii," *Sbornik KGB SSSR* 1 (1959): 52–3. See also Yuri Feofanov, "Pora podvesti chertu," *Izvestia* 11, 12 January 1962, 4.
4 *Sbornik KGB SSSR* (USSR KGB Review) was a quarterly journal (bimonthly since 1985 and monthly since 1989) issued between 1959 and 1991. It served as a major platform for exchange of experience between the KGB counterintelligence branches. It can be found in collection (*fond*) 13 of the Haluzevii derzhavnyi arkhiv Sluzhbi bezpeki Ukraini (HDASBU).
5 Oleg Kharkhordin, *The Collective and the Individual in Russia: A Study of Practices* (Berkeley: University of California Press, 1999), 299.
6 On the post-Stalinist secret police, see Amy Knight, *The KGB: Police and Politics in the Soviet Union* (Boston: Unwin Hyman, 1988), chapter 2; Julie Fedor, *Russia and the Cult of State Security: The Chekist Tradition, from Lenin to Putin* (London and New York: Routledge, 2011), chapter 2; Edward Cohn, "Coercion, Reeducation, and the Prophylactic Chat: *Profilaktika* and

the KGB's Struggle with Political Unrest in Lithuania," *The Russian Review* 76, no. 2 (2017): 272–93; Idem, "A Soviet Theory of Broken Windows: Prophylactic Policing and the KGB's Struggle with Political Unrest in the Baltic Republics," *Kritika* 19, no. 4 (2018): 769–92; Mark Harrison, *One Day We Will Live without Fear: Everyday Lives under the Soviet Police State* (Stanford, CA: Hoover Institution Press, 2016); Idem, "If You Do Not Change Your Behaviour: Managing Threats to State Security in Lithuania under Soviet Rule," *Working Paper* 247 (2015); Jens Gieseke, "The Post-Stalinist Mode of Chekism," *Securitas Imperii* 37, no. 2 (2020): 16–37.

7 Miriam Dobson, *Khrushchev's Cold Summer: Gulag Returnees, Crime, and the Fate of Reform after Stalin* (Ithaca, NY: Cornell University Press, 2009), 109–54; See also Yoram Gorlizki's contribution to this volume.

8 Nikita Petrov, *Pervyi predsedatel' KGB Ivan Serov* (Moscow: Materik, 2005), 163–7; Knight, *The KGB*, 51.

9 Viktor Chebrikov, ed., *Istoriia sovetskikh organov gosbezopasnosti. Uchebnik* (Moscow: Vysshaia Krasnoznamennaia Shkola Komiteta Gosudarstvennoi Bezopasnosti pri Sovete Ministrov SSSR imeni F. E. Dzerzhinskogo [VKSh], 1977), 497–8. On the Fourth Directorate's structure, see Nikita Petrov, "Spetsial'nye struktury KGB SSSR po bor'be s inakomysliem v SSSR, 1954–1989," in *Trudy Obshchestva izucheniia istorii otechestvennykh spetssluzhb. Tom 3*, red. V.K. Bylinin (Moscow: Kuchkovo Pole, 2007), 306–7.

10 Prikaz KGB pri SM SSSR no. 00630 ot 27.09.1954 "Ob organizatsii agenturno-operativnoi raboty 4 Upravleniia KGB SSSR i sootvetstvuiushchikh otdelov periferiinykh organov' (1954–00630): HDASBU 9/248-sp/88ob–88.

11 *XX s'ezd KPSS. 14–25.2.1956. Stenograficheskii otchet. Tom 1* (Moscow: PolitIzDat, 1956), 118.

12 One of the 1955 KGB directives ordered to intensify work on "persons who served sentences for espionage, sabotage and terrorist actions, Trotskyist, nationalist and other anti-Soviet activities." Ukazanie KGB SSSR pri SM SSSR no. 161ss ot 27.12.1955 "O svoievremennom vyiavlenii prestupnykh namerenii vrazhdebno nastroiennykh lits i presecheniia liuboi popytki s ikh storony pereiti k organizovannym aktivnym deistviiam protiv SSSR': HDASBU 9/254/145ob–145.

13 Vladimir Kozlov et al., eds., *Sedition: Everyday Resistance in the Soviet Union under Khrushchev and Brezhnev* (New Haven, CT: Yale University Press, 2011), 45; Nikita Petrov, "KGB i XX s'ezd KPSS (1954–1960)," *Rossiia i sovremennyi mir* 91, no. 2 (2016): 136–54. On the turbulences in the western borders, see Amir Weiner, "The Empires Pay a Visit: Gulag Returnees, East European Rebellions, and Soviet Frontier Politics," *Journal of Modern History* 78, no. 2 (2006): 333–76. For the text

of the letter, see Rossiiskii gosudarstvennyi arkhiv noveishei istorii (RGANI), 89/6/2/1–12. Based on the Central Committee letter on 29 December 1956 the KGB order no. 165ss was issued, obliging local branches "strengthen operational agent work to identify and remove the organizers and inspirers of anti-Soviet activities from among the bourgeois nationalists, Trotskyists, terrorists and other hostile elements." HDASBU, 9/258-sp/233–40.

14 Filipp Bobkov, "Ideologicheskaia diversiia imperializma protiv SSSR i deiatel'nost' organov KGB po bor'be s nei," 1963: Lietuvos Ypatingasis Archyvas (LYA), K-1/10/325/25.

15 Ukazanie KGB pri SM SSSR no. 72ss ot 31.05.1955 "O napravlenii oriientirovki ob agenturno-operativnoi rabote po vyiavleniiu i presecheniiu vrazhdebnoi deiatel'nosti antisovetskikh elementov sredi molodezhi': HDASBU 9/253-sp/140–8.

16 Antonina Shchedrina, *Bor'ba s tuneiadtsami* (Moscow: Iuridicheskaia literatura, 1965).

17 Dobson, *Khrushchev's Cold Summer*, 210–11. Programme of the Communist Party of the Soviet Union, adopted by the 22nd Congress of the CPSU, 31 October 1961 (Moscow: Foreign Languages Publishing House, 1961).

18 "Doklad N. Khrushcheva na Vneocherednom XXI s'ezde KPSS," *Pravda* 28, 28 January 1959, 9.

19 Sheila Fitzpatrick, "Social Parasites: How Tramps, Idle Youth, and Busy Entrepreneurs Impeded the Soviet March to Communism," *Cahiers du monde russe* 47, nos. 1–2 (2006): 393.

20 Ukazanie KGB pri SM SSSR no. 105ss ot 24.07.1958 "O rabote organov gosbezopasnosti po vyiavleniiu i presecheniiu antisovetskoi deiatel'nosti sredi molodezhi': HDASBU 9/270-sp/1ob–2.

21 Cohn, *A Soviet Theory*, 778, 784.

22 Vladimir Fitsev, ed., *Bor'ba organov gosbezopasnosti s podryvnoi deiatel'nost'iu tserkovnikov i sektantov: Uchebnoe posobie* (Moscow: VKSh, 1976), 63; HDASBU 1/1/1097/186.

23 Nikolai Mironov, *Programma KPSS i voprosy dal'neishego ukrepleniia zakonnosti i pravoporiadka* (Moscow: Iuridicheskaia literatura, 1962), 17.

24 Vasili Mitrokhin and Jeff Kingston, *KGB Lexicon: The Soviet Intelligence Officers Handbook* (Abingdon, UK: Routledge, 2002), 39.

25 HDASBU 1/1/1093/197.

26 On *profilaktika*, see Cohn, "Coercion"; Idem, "A Soviet Theory"; Harrison, *One Day*, chapter 5; Fedor, *Russia and the Cult*, 51–6.

27 On *prorabotka*, see Svetlana Stephenson, "A Ritual Civil Execution": Public Shaming Meetings in the Post-Stalin Soviet Union," *Journal of Applied Social Theory* 3, no. 1 (2021): 112–33.

28 Fedor, *Russia and the Cult*, 30–2. Also see Knight, *The KGB*, 63.

29 Evgenia Lezina, "The Soviet State Security and the Regime of Secrecy: Guarding State Secrets and Political Control of Industrial Enterprises and Institutions in the Post-Stalin Era," *Securitas Imperii* 37, no. 2 (2020): 38–69.
30 Chebrikov, ed., *Istoriia*, 509–10.
31 Nikolai Mironov, *Ukreplenie zakonnosti i pravoporiadka v obshchenarodnom gosudarstve* (Moscow: Iuridicheskaia literatura, 1969), 66–73.
32 Fedor, *Russia and the Cult*, 45–51; Chebrikov, ed., *Istoriia*, 503; I. Laptev "Iz praktiki raboty po povysheniiu bditel'nosti trudiashchikhsia," *Sbornik KGB SSSR* 5 (1960): 60–2.
33 A. Tishkov, "Leninskii printsip opory na massy v deiatel'nosti organov gosbezopasnosti," *Sbornik KGB SSSR* 5 (1960): 34–5.
34 Chebrikov, *Istoriia*, 460–1. Amir Weiner and Aigi Rahi-Tamm, "Getting to Know You: The Soviet Surveillance System, 1939–1957," *Kritika* 13, no. 1 (2012): 43–4.
35 HDASBU 42/1/127/4; 42/1/138/3; 42/1/144/2.
36 Petrov, *Pervyi predsedatel*, 105, 131.
37 HDASBU 16/1/921/192.
38 HDASBU 42/1/155/3; 42/1/167/4.
39 Petrov, "KGB i XX s'ezd," 145.
40 Chebrikov, *Istoriia*, 498.
41 Natal'ia Tomilina, ed., *Nikita Khrushchev. Dva tsveta vremeni. Tom 1* (Moscow: Demokratiia, 2009), 522.
42 Prikaz KGB pri SM SSSR No. 00405 ot 26.07.1954 "O zadachakh organov gosudarstvennoi bezopasnosti' (1954–00405): HDASBU 9/248-sp/28ob–28. Prikaz KGB pri SM SSSR no. 00225 ot 15.07.1959 (1959–00225): HDASBU 9/273-sp/56ob–56; Prikaz KGB pri SM SSSR no. 00430 ot 01.12.1960 (1960–00430): HDASBU 9/280-sp/192ob–192.
43 1954–00405: HDASBU 9/248-sp/28ob–28, 31ob–31; 1959–00225: HDASBU 9/273-sp/52ob–52; 1960–00430: HDASBU 9/280-sp/192ob–192.
44 1954–00405: HDASBU 9/248-sp/28ob–9; 1959–00225: HDASBU 9/273-sp/59ob–59; HDASBU: 16/1/922/40–1, 225.
45 On the use of proxies, see Fedor, *Russia and the Cult*, 48–51.
46 1954–00405: HDASBU 9/248-sp/29.
47 1959–00225: HDASBU 9/273-sp/60ob–1; 1960–00430: HDASBU 9/280-sp/194ob–194.
48 Ukazanie KGB pri SM SSSR no. 6ss ot 12.1.1961 (1961–6ss): HDASBU 9/62-sp/233. Ukazanie KGB pri SM SSSR no. 100ss ot 31.10.1961 "O napravlenii Obzora osnovnykh nedostatkov v profilakticheskoi rabote organov KGB' (1961–100ss): HDASBU 9/289-sp/21ob–36.
49 E. Pitovranov and F. Bobkov, "O doverennykh litsakh," *Sbornik KGB SSSR* 2 (1959): 51–2.
50 1961–6ss: HDASBU 9/62-sp/241ob–3.
51 Pitovranov and Bobkov, "O doverennykh litsakh," 53; HDASBU 16/1/922/204–5.

52 Residents and safe apartment owners, alongside agents, were part of the KGB agent network. According to the "Counterintelligence Dictionary," a "resident" (*rezident*) was recruited by the secret police to direct "a group of agents or cooptees," while a "keeper of rendezvous premises" (*soderzhatel' iavochnoi kvartiry*) is "someone who cooperates secretly with the state security agencies and makes living or working premises for which he is responsible available to operational officers for the purpose of receiving agents (or residents)." See Mitrokhin and Kingston, *KGB Lexicon*, 345, 377–8.
53 1959–00225: HDASBU 9/273-sp/52ob–3, 56.
54 "Razrabotka operativnaia" is defined in the Counterintelligence Dictionary in two ways: "In the broader sense, it is a process of covert and comprehensive study, for intelligence and counter-intelligence purposes ... In a narrower sense, it is a form of operational activity, carried out against particular individuals (or groups) suspected of involvement in the preparation or commission of crimes against the state." See Mitrokhin and Kingston, *KGB Lexicon*, 83, 276.
55 HDASBU 42/1/127/4; 42/1/138/3; 42/1/144/2; 42/1/155/3; 42/1/161/3; 42/1/167/4; 42/1/172/1; 42/1/176/1; 42/1/181/1; 42/1/185/2; 42/1/191/2; 42/1/195/2; 42/1/199/2; 42/1/203/1.
56 Ensuing criticism of the agent apparatus's swelling by the KGB leadership led to its reduction in the Ukrainian SSR by 36 per cent in 1960. HDASBU 16/1/922/82–3, 282. After 1964, the intelligence apparatus grew steadily, reaching almost 80,000 agents and safe apartment owners by the end of the 1980s. HDASBU 42/1/342/2.
57 Although there was no centralized registry of proxies, according to some data, their number could reach half of the agent network, equal it, and even exceed it twice. See HDASBU 16/1/922/18, 32; B. Luginin, "Nazrevshii vopros," *Sbornik KGB SSSR* 4 (1960): 11.
58 1960–00430: HDASBU 9/280-sp/190ob–190; HDASBU 16/1/922/23–4, 143–4, 152, 182, 207, 220, 232, 286–7, 309, 337.
59 1960–00430, HDASBU 9/280-sp/194ob–5; 1961–6ss, HDASBU 9/62-sp /241ob–3; Pitovranov and Bobkov, "O doverennykh litsakh," 53.
60 HDASBU 16/1/940/83.
61 Ibid., 86.
62 I. Golovchenko, "Komissii sodeistviia na osobo rezhimnykh predpriiatiiakh," *Sbornik KGB SSSR* 10 (1961): 34.
63 HDASBU 16/1/940/87.
64 Mitrokhin and Kingston, *KGB Lexicon*, 181.
65 HDASBU 16/1/940/95–9; A. Riabchikov and V. Solodovnikov, "Iz praktiki raboty s vneshtatnymi operativnymi sotrudnikami," *Sbornik KGB SSSR* 19 (1963): 61–3.
66 On the Stalin-era surveillance practices, see David Shearer, *Policing Stalin's Socialism: Repression and Social Order in the Soviet Union, 1924–1953* (New

Haven, CT: Yale University Press, 2009); Weiner and Rahi-Tamm, "Getting to Know You."
67 Harrison, *One Day*, 129–30; Chebrikov, *Istoriia*, 503.
68 For example, 1954–00630: HDASBU 9/248-sp/87ob–8, 90ob–90; 1954–00405: HDASBU 9/248-sp/30ob–30.
69 1959–00225: HDASBU 9/273-sp/59ob–59.
70 Ibid.
71 Mitrokhin and Kingston, *KGB Lexicon*, 195.
72 1959–00225: HDASBU 9/273-sp/58; I. Gudkov and I. Kulikov, "Za dal'neisheie ukreplenie sotsialisticheskoi zakonnosti v agenturno-operativnoi rabote," *Sbornik KGB SSSR* 24 (1964): 62.
73 Fedor, *Russia and the Cult*, 51; Cohn, "Coercion," 273–4; Chebrikov, *Istoriia*, 583–4.
74 Ibid.; HDASBU 16/1/922/102–4.
75 1959–00225: HDASBU 9/273-sp/59ob–59.
76 HDASBU 16/1/922/103.
77 HDASBU 16/1/922/103.
78 Nikolai Mironov, "Za smeloe primenenie profilakticheskikh, preduprediteľnykh mer i usilenie sviazi s narodom," *Sbornik KGB SSSR* 1 (1959): 59–60.
79 Boris Shul'zhenko et al., *Ukrainskie burzhuaznyie natsionalisty* (Moscow: VKSh, 1963), 265–6.
80 Chebrikov, *Istoriia*, 583.
81 1961–100ss: HDASBU 9/289-sp/34ob–34.
82 Harrison, "If You Do Not Change," 3.
83 HDASBU 42/1/186/1.
84 Harrison, *One Day*, 135–8.
85 Ibid.
86 Cohn, "Coercion," 282.
87 Prikaz KGB pri SM SSSR no. 00488 ot 19.12.1959 "O bezotvetstvennom otnoshenii nekotorykh sotrudnikov KGB pri SM Karel'skoi ASSR i podgotovke k provedeniiu profilakticheskikh meropriiatii": HDASBU 9/273-sp/164–5.
88 LYA K-51/1/301/52.
89 HDASBU 16/1/922/35. The names of Ukrainian cities follow Ukrainian spelling, rather than the spelling imposed by the Soviet government.
90 Ia. Yeremin, "Iz opyta raboty po razlozheniiu iegovistkogo podpol'ia," Sbornik KGB SSSR 5 (1960): 91.
91 Harrison, "If You Do Not Change," 11–12.
92 1961–100ss: HDASBU 9/289-sp/29ob–30.
93 D. Shchebetenko and A. Verdiev, "Profilaktika–vazhnaia chast' raboty sledovatelia," *Sbornik KGB SSSR* 29 (1965): 75–6.
94 LYA K-18/1/579/27–31; K-18/1/115/61–9; HDASBU 1/1/1083/104–23.
95 LYA 1771/190/11/14.

96 LYAK-51/1/253/244.
97 HDASBU 16/1/940/37.
98 HDASBU 1/1/1093/211–13.
99 Ukazanie KGB SSSR no. 41ss ot 12.03.1958 (1958–41ss) "O napravlenii Obzora nekotorykh realizovannykh del agenturnoi razrabotki antisovetskikh elementov iz chisla molodezhi": HDASBU 9/269-sp/90–110; S.Rozhdestvenskii, "Materialy k istorii samodeiatelnykh politicheskikh ob'iedinenii v SSSR posle 1945 goda," *Pamiat': Istoricheskii sbornik* 5 (1981/1982): 249–61; Vladimir Kozlov et al., *Sedition*, chapter 8; Ludmilla Alexeyeva, *Soviet Dissent: Contemporary Movements for National, Religious, and Human Rights*, trans. Carol Pearce and John Glad (Middletown, CT: Wesleyan University Press, 1987), 273, 295, 421; Marfunin et al., "O praktike raboty," 48–9; HDASBU 1/1/1095/1–14.
100 HDASBU 1/1/1432/69–70, 152, 158; 1/1/1096/181–4, 230–3; 16/1/922/99–101; 1/1/1093/114–20.
101 HDASBU 1/1/1432/153–7.
102 Ibid.
103 1958–41ss, HDASBU 9/269-sp/90–110.
104 LYA K-51/1/250/25–34.
105 Ibid., 34.
106 HDASBU 1/1/1093/166; LYA K-18/1/579/27–31.
107 LYA K-18/1/115/157–8.
108 Ibid., 180–3; K-41/1/509/245.
109 LYA K-51/1/198/90.
110 LYA K-18/1/122/66–9.
111 On the mobilization campaign, see Brian LaPierre, *Hooligans in Khrushchev's Russia: Defining, Policing, and Producing Deviance during the Thaw* (Madison, WI: University of Wisconsin Press, 2012), chapter 4; Dobson, *Khrushchev's Cold Summer*, chapter 5; Kharkhordin, *The Collective*, chapter 7.
112 Kharkhordin, *The Collective*, 282.
113 Their number swelled from 80,000 patrols with 2.5 million members in 1960 to 130,000 patrols with 4.5 million members in 1965. Ibid., 286.
114 HDASBU 16/1/936/78–81.
115 V. Noskov et al., "V tesnom kontakte s druzhinnikami," *Sbornik KGB SSSR* 10 (1961): 100–8; A. Kuvarzin, "Moguchii istochnik tvorcheskikh sil," *Sbornik KGB SSSR* 12 (1961): 36–43.
116 G. Chernikov, "Trudiashchiesia aktivno pomogaiut chekistam," *Sbornik KGB SSSR* 8 (1960): 43–9.
117 A. Komissarov, *Rassledovanie massovykh besporiadkov* (Moscow, 1962), 8.
118 HDASBU 16/1/936/100–5; I. Demshin, "Sil'noie oruzhie v okhrane gosudarstvennoi granitsy," *Sbornik KGB SSSR* 5 (1960): 49–53; Yu. Benn

and S. Karakozov, "Narodnyie druzhiny v pogranichnom raione," *Sbornik KGB SSSR* 5 (1960): 53–7; Chernikov, "Trudiashchiesia," 43–9; Luginin, "Nazrevshii vopros," 8–14.

119 HDASBU 16/1/933/54–5. Noskov at al., "V tesnom kontakte," 100–8.
120 HDASBU 16/1/936/101–2.
121 Leonid Plyushch, *History's Carnival: A Dissident's Autobiography* (New York and London: Harcourt, Brace, Jovanovich, 1979), 11.
122 Ibid., 11–12.
123 Ibid., 14–15.
124 Shchedrina, *Bor'ba*, 6. On the anti-parasite campaign, see Fitzpatrick, *Social Parasites*, 377–408; Dobson, *Khrushchev's Cold Summer:* 178–85; Yoram Gorlizki's contribution to this volume.
125 Noskov and Uryvaiev, "Strozhe podkhodit," 121–3.
126 Ibid.
127 Yuri Feofanov, "Pora podvesti chertu," *Izvestia* 11, 12 January 1962, 4. See also a fragment of the Kats show trial, https://youtu.be/p9q5p38sUJQ (accessed 4 October 2022).
128 Tatiana Nikol'skaia, *Russkii protestantizm i gosudarstvennaia vlast' v 1905–1991 godakh* (St. Petersburg: European University, 2009), 186–8; Andrei Dementiev, *Aven-Ezer: Evangel'skoie dvizhenie v Primor'e, 1898–1990 gody* (Vladivostok: Russkii ostrov, 2011), 167–72.
129 Gosudarstvennyi arkhiv Rossiiskoi Federatsii (GARF) R-6991/4/173/38–41, 221.
130 V. Lisitsyn and I. Tarasov, "Iz praktiki presecheniia antiobshchestvennoi deiatel'nosti sektantov," *Sbornik KGB SSSR* 20 (1963): 38; This decision was overturned as a result of a public procurator's protest in October 1965. See GARF P6991/4/173/39, 88.
131 Shchedrina, *Bor'ba*, 25. As the authors of the *KGB Sbornik* article explained it, there was no necessary premise for holding a meeting of collective farmers authorized to resolve issues of eviction. The meeting of *kolkhozniki* "could not be held, because out of 900 able-bodied collective farmers it was necessary to gather at least two-thirds, and the collective farm club could accommodate only 450 people." Therefore, "instead of a meeting, it was decided to hold a gathering of residents of the Zhdanovsky village council, ensuring the attendance of rural intelligentsia and collective farm activists." See Lisitsyn and Tarasov, "Iz praktiki presecheniia," 41.
132 Ibid., 39; GARF R-6991/4/173/39, 220.
133 On comrades' courts, see Yoram Gorlizki, "Delegalization in Russia: Soviet Comrades' Courts in Retrospect," *AJCL* 46, no. 3 (1998): 403–25; Kharkhordin, *The Collective*, 282–5; LaPierre, *Hooligans*, 147–50; Maria Starun's contribution to this volume.

134 Noskov at al., "V tesnom kontakte," 103.
135 V. Ianin, "Opyt provedeniia profilaktiki cherez tovarishcheskie sudy," *Sbornik KGB SSSR* 10 (1961): 53–4.
136 LYA K-18/1/134/10–13.
137 Komissarov, *Rassledovanie*, 21.
138 HDASBU 16/1/936/119–20.
139 Ibid., 150–1.
140 Noskov et al., "V tesnom kontakte", 103–4.
141 B. Ievseiev, "Otshchepenets pered sudom," *Moskovskii komsomolets* 204, 12 October 1960, 2.
142 Ibid.
143 Nikol'skaia, *Russkii protestantizm*, 190–7; "Ob ispol'zovanii agentury v presechenii ideologicheskoi diversii tserkovnikov i sektantov," *Sbornik KGB SSSR* 22 (1964): 41.
144 Shchebetenko and Verdiev, *Profilaktika*, 77–8.
145 Dobson, *Khrushchev's Cold Summer*, 228–36; Noskov at al., "V tesnom kontakte," 100–8; HDASBU 16/1/922/130.
146 Weiner, "The Empires Pay a Visit," 369–70.
147 HDASBU 16/1/936/145–50. Boris Shul'zhenko et al., Op. cit., 265–6.
148 Nikol'skaia. *Russkii protestantizm*, 188–90.
149 Ibid., 178–9.
150 HDASBU 16/1/936/145–50.
151 HDASBU 1/1/1506/21.
152 Derzhavnyi arkhiv Mykolayivs'koi oblasti (DAMO) 7/8/969/93–105.
153 Sud nad veruiushchimi, https://youtu.be/j4sF0oLO-_4 (accessed 4 October 2022).
154 Dementiev, *Aven-Ezer*, 202.
155 HDASBU 16/1/936/145–7.
156 Harrison, "If You Do Not Change," 2.
157 On the use of "disruption" against believers in the 1920s, see Dementiev, Aven-Ezer, 77–9; Andrei Savin, "'Razdeliai i vlastvui': religioznaia politika sovetskogo gosudarstva i evangel'skiie tserkvi v 1920-e gody," *Vestnik TvGU*, no. 1 (2008): 3–23.
158 Mitrokhin and Kingston, *KGB Lexicon*, 345.
159 Ibid.
160 Outside the USSR disruption was employed against "anti-Soviet nationalist organizations." See I. Khamazyuk and A. Komlev, *Razlozhenie zarubezhnykh antisovetskikh organizatsii* (Moscow: VKSh, 1962); A. Bykov, ed., *Nekotorye voprosy teorii i praktiki organov gosudarstvennoi bezopasnosti SSSR* (Moscow: VKSh, 1971), 62–81.
161 RGANI 5/62/38/49. The Orthodox Church also got affected by the anti-religious campaign, as half of its parishes in the country were closed then by the government. See Nathaniel Davis, "The Number of Orthodox

Churches before and after the Khrushchev Antireligious Drive," *Slavic Review* 50, no. 3 (Autumn 1991): 614.
162 Ukazanie KGB pri SM SSSR no. 39ss ot 15.03.1958 "O napravlenii Obzora materialov o provedennykh organami gosbezopasnosti nekotorykh meropriiatiiakh po razlozheniiu nelegal'nykh tserkovno-sektantskikh grupp i otryvu veruiushchikh ot vrazhdebnogo vliianiia tserkovno-sektantskogo aktiva' (1958–39ss): HDASBU 9/269-sp/82. On antireligious campaign, see Miriam Dobson, "Child Sacrifice in the Soviet Press: Sensationalism and the 'Sectarian' in the Post-Stalin Era," *The Russian Review* 73, no. 2 (2014): 237–59; Nikol'skaia, *Russkii protestantizm*, 172–215; Alexeyeva, *Soviet Dissent*, 201–64.
163 V. Izmailov and V. Titov, "Iz opyta bor'by s antisovetskoi deiatel'nost'iu iegovistov," *Sbornik KGB SSSR* 1 (1959): 80.
164 Ibid., 85.
165 Ibid., 81.
166 I. Khamaziuk, ed., *Podryvnaia deiatel'nost' zarubezhnykh religioznykh tsentrov* (Moscow: VKSh, 1972), 45–6.
167 1958–39ss, HDASBU 9/269-sp/81ob–2.
168 HDASBU 1/1/1097/215.
169 Marfunin et al., "O praktike raboty," 44.
170 Dementiev, *Aven-Ezer*, 158–9.
171 Ibid., 178.
172 O. Murtazaliev and Kh. Israpov, "Sel'skie skhody pomogli profilaktirovat' religioznykh musul'man," *Sbornik KGB SSSR* 29 (1965): 70–4.
173 Ibid., 71–2.
174 Ibid., 72–4.
175 Marfunin et al., "O praktike raboty," 44.
176 Nikol'skaia, *Russkii protestantizm*, 201–15; Dementiev, *Aven-Ezer*, 180–97.
177 For example, in a 1974 note to the CPSU Central Committee the KGB stated that despite counter-measures Jehovah's Witnesses annually increased by about 300–500 people. RGANI 5/67/971/1–2; 5/94/147/23–100.
178 Evgenia Lezina, "The KGB's Handling of Informal Activity and Publicity during *Perestroika*: A Tentative Study Based on New Sources," Paper presented at the 2020 ASEEES Virtual Convention, 7 November 2020.

11 Social Control in Post-Stalinist Courts: Housing Disputes and Citizen Demand of Legality

DINA MOYAL

This chapter examines the relationship between the Soviet state and its citizens in the post-Stalin era. Like the other chapters in this section, it explores the changes that occurred in the way the state exercised its control over the population after Stalin's death, at a time when it promoted the principles of legality and participation, in place of terror. Using court records from former Soviet archives, the article explores how ordinary citizens reacted to the newly defined relations with the state and how this influenced their ability to defend their interests and rights. Specifically, this study dwells on housing disputes that reached the USSR Supreme Court, thus turning the judiciary not only into an institute of conflict resolution, but also to an arena where a dialogue took place between the state and the people over social benefits, distribution of wealth, and moral norms under communism.[1]

To be sure, the ability to turn to courts for help was not a post-Stalinist phenomenon. As the works of Aaron Retish and Maria Starun demonstrate, it was common for Soviet workers and peasants in the 1920s and 1930s to approach the courts and semi-judicial bodies with requests to resolve disputes or defend monetary rights. Moreover, these works show that the state used judicial forums to promote state goals and advance socialist norms, which more often than not converged with citizens' interests. The chapter below continues to follow the dynamic between citizens and courts, but it does so against the backdrop of the discourse of legality and the promotion of "everyday life," which emerged following Stalin's death. These ideas, I argue, introduced a new set of principles and considerations, parallel to socialist ones, which the state could use to achieve social control. At the same time, the new discourse armed the citizens with tools they could use to protect their own rights.

Housing and the Socialist Order

Right to housing was by far the most important property right for Soviet citizens. In the absence of a free market and private ownership of land, in a country where all natural and economic resources officially belonged to the state, Soviet citizens were entirely dependent on the governing system to house them in public apartments, supply them with a job, and to take care of their education, health, and old age. From the state's perspective, command over housing resources (particularly in cities) allowed it to monitor population movement, control the labour force, and supervise urban development. In fact, management of housing space became one of the most effective ways of building a socialist society and manifesting the new revolutionary order: transition from privately owned homes to state-owned housing was an indicator of the Sovietization process and of the extent to which the socialist state spread its power over land and people.[2] After appropriating privately owned buildings and estates during the first decade of the revolution, the late 1920s and 1930s saw a building rush of state-owned communal apartments, which had been part of the industrialization and urbanization campaigns and a symbol of instilling new social norms.[3] Although these new policies had not solved the grave housing shortages in the USSR, 80 per cent of newly built housing space belonged to the state by the eve of the Great Patriotic War.[4]

The Second World War shuffled the cards, however. The war left millions of Soviet citizens without a roof over their heads, adding to the already existing shortage of apartments before the war.[5] The post-war period was one of devastation, want, and extremely hard labour as a result of the loss of a big portion of the productive male population and the enormous number of wounded veterans.[6] To this we must add the mass number of orphans and homeless and uncared for children who challenged the Soviet regime.[7] Hence, in post-Stalinist USSR, the issue of housing represented for many the yearning for normalcy – for the calm everyday life people wanted to have when the war was over. This was particularly true for the younger generation, which was full of expectations of the future.[8] This longing converged with the deep sense of entitlement returning soldiers developed, believing that the state should support them after they had sacrificed their best years for their country.[9] Under these circumstances, housing space no longer epitomized the coercive Soviet order, but turned into a reward the state could offer its citizens. At the same time, years of collective and household self-help during the war led people to regard property they managed as their own, expecting the state to acknowledge their contribution.[10] The reluctance of the Stalinist regime to recognize the needs of the population and prioritize living conditions, however, led to a massive disappointment in the late 1940s and early 1950s.[11] As a result, civil unrest, corruption, rising crime and juvenile delinquency rates ensued, leading in turn to even greater repressions and attempts to restore social control.[12]

After Joseph Stalin's death in March 1953, the new leadership realized that if it wanted to win the support of the population and protect the Party from yet more waves of terror, it should curb coercion and prioritize "everyday life." A series of measures were taken to revitalize society and economy, and to show that the state was "working for the people": releases from the Gulag, rehabilitation of convicts along with the promotion of the light industry at the expense of the heavy one, and softer policies in the countryside are some of the examples. In the second half of the 1950s two major steps were initiated by Nikita Khrushchev to ameliorate living conditions and enhance citizen participation in the construction process: the first was the mass construction of fast-built apartment buildings with separate apartments – nicknamed later *Khrushchevki*; the other was housing cooperatives which enabled citizens to obtain their own apartments.[13]

While for the people this was the compensation they were expecting after a long and turbulent period, for Stalin's successors, as Steven Harris put it, "the everyday was the chief site where they would discover whether or not the communist experiment had worked, and whether their society's sacrifices under Stalin and in World War II had been worth it all along."[14] The goal of the USSR "to catch and overtake" the West was central to Khrushchev's policy, which aimed to prove the superiority of Communist ideology by peaceful means.[15] A careful reading of the utterances of the new collective leadership indicates that the "Thaw" and condemnation of Stalin's "cult of personality" were not designed to undermine the revolutionary efforts. On the contrary: Khrushchev's goal, which he had stated clearly in his Secret Speech at the XXth Party Congress, remained the building of communism, albeit through less coercive means.[16]

The banner of "socialist legality," which had been redefined and lifted shortly after Stalin's death, reflected the same dual goal. On the one hand, it signified the end of arbitrary measures against Soviet citizens and the orderly work of its institutions – the "legality" component; on the other, it also reflected the goal of a social order – the "socialist" component, to be achieved through law obedience by citizens and state officials.[17] Thus, the challenges to "social control without terror," which Yoram Gorlizki and Evgenia Lezina discuss in their chapters, emerged not only because Soviet post-Stalinist reality clashed with the quest of legality or liberalization, but because the regime promised to create an order that would do both: be revolutionary and legal at the same time. Drawing on the promise of legality and return to Leninist norms, the post-Stalinist regime developed a plethora of public mechanisms based on participation and popularization, which were designed to instil socialist order through monitoring of the population.[18] From a (Stalinist) model of state repression of the personal sphere, there was a shift towards a model of policing and intrusion.[19] The vision of the post-Stalinist leadership was that inculcating in the population true communist norms – a true "revolutionary consciousness" of the Leninist courts, if you will – would make repression redundant and would bring about a true socialist and just society. This idea eventually found its official expression in the new Communist Party Program of 1961, which laid out a twelve-point Moral Code for the Soviet Man and stressed collectivism, comradely attitude, humane relations, decency, and intolerance towards injustice and violations of collective interests as essential character traits for builders of communism.[20] As the chapter will further show, these moral demands played a role in court and served as a tool in the hands of citizens who strove for socialist justice.

The housing construction projects Khrushchev launched in the second half of the 1950s were not only a way to appease the public, but also a central site for creating a new "communist way of life" – *kommunisticheskii byt*.[21] Soviet housing, communal and separate, was an arena where Soviet citizens were to realize socialist norms, both from the material and spatial aspects (how the apartment was organized) and from the social perspective (interaction with family members or fellow neighbours who share the apartment).[22] The private home was in this sense a collective arena, subject to communist norms.[23] Moreover, at the very outset, distribution of housing reflected basic prioritization in Soviet society and the long lists of people waiting for their turn to improve living conditions mirrored those preferences.

In practice, however, promises of abundance were not realized overnight. First, it took almost a decade for Khrushchev's housing initiatives to pick up speed, due to delays in legislation and economic adjustments.[24] In the meantime, communal apartments, shared by several families were widespread, and young couples and their children continued living in the same room with their elderly parents, joining long waiting lists for separate apartments. The Soviet system under Khrushchev still created tremendous difficulties for those who wanted to move to another city, maintain permanent housing space, or simply find better living conditions. Citizens could be deprived of their housing space if they lost their job or if their marital or family status changed: divorce, death of parents, and marriage of children all influenced one's right to a housing space. These problems were particularly grave in big metropolitans such as Moscow, Leningrad, and the capitals of the Union Republics, which attracted workers due to their better infrastructure, supply of goods, and job variety.

The situation prompted citizens to take measures into their own hands, elbow their way through housing authorities, and approach the courts to fight for their own housing space. The following pages discuss a number of housing cases that reached the USSR Supreme Court between 1953 and 1964 in the process of appeal in supervision (*nadzor*), an appeal upon permission to a higher court. The files contain lower courts' decisions, along with appeals, letters, and complaints, which brought the case to the highest court in Moscow, as well as the final judgment of the USSR Supreme Court.[25] Unlike criminal cases, where citizens faced the all-powerful state, in civil/housing cases both sides had an equal standing, with the judge serving as a moderator together with the procuracy who represented the owner of the housing space – the state. Moreover, appeals, and particularly overturned decisions, are unique in the opportunity they give us to examine how the legal system works and where and how exactly it is corrected.

Under these conditions the courtroom was no longer a plain coercive mechanism, but an arena where a dialogue took place between the citizens and the state regarding acute questions in society: How should housing space be distributed? Who should benefit from this state resource? What norms should prevail over these disputes? What was a legitimate demand by a Soviet citizen? Examining first the strategies Soviet citizens used in order to approach the court, the text then demonstrates how Soviet citizens interpreted the norms set by the post-Stalinist era and how they used them to promote their interests in the housing sphere. Finally, the chapter shows the influence of the new policies of "socialist legality" on social control and the relationship between state and citizens.

Who Is Entitled to a Housing Space? Demand of Socialist Justice

On 25 January 1953, an article entitled "Actor M. without Make-Up" had been published in the newspaper *Leningradskaia pravda*.[26] The article opened with the following words:

> M., of the Leningrad Theatre of Musical Comedy, is considered to be a rising, if not a leading star. It is claimed that this is a man of talent, who has a

taste for novelty and takes the road of daring creativity … It is particularly regrettable that in his private life M. strictly abides by this same principle … He does not have a family, at least not in the higher sense that Soviet people often attributed to this term. He has a heart that is too 'loving,' and can heat up as easily as it can cool down. Due to these temperature changes, M. builds his relationships with women according to the scheme: 1. attraction. 2. disappointment 3. rupture.[27]

The article subsequently describes how M., a famous Leningrad actor, seduces women in various locations across the USSR and then leaves them when they are about to have his baby. Among those women, the article mentions Sh. and K. [only initials in the article – D.M.], whom M. plays one against the other to evade responsibility or any obligations to them. The author of the article concludes: "He [M.] is confident to this day that one can enter and leave marriage relationships as easily as one unties a tie … But he is wrong. The moral character of a Soviet actor is not the personal matter of M. that one can be indifferent to or close one's eyes to. This is a big and principled question that is inseparable from the actor's creativity, a matter of the honor of the entire theatrical collective."[28] What appears at first glance as a piece of gossip, or at best as a moral-ideological propaganda piece designed to educate Soviet men, a careful reading of one of the USSR Supreme Court files reveals a more mundane part of the story: a dispute over housing rights. It turns out that Vera K., K. in the article, has filed a suit against M. demanding housing space in his Leningrad apartment. According to the article, Vera K. was one of the first victims of M.'s behaviour – she married him in Minsk, gave birth to a daughter, but could not follow him to Leningrad. Later, M. invited her to Leningrad in order to convince another woman he had already been married, but soon afterword he divorced her and kicked her out of the apartment. He let the daughter stay with him but refused to share his two-room space with Vera.

Vera filed a suit demanding the court to allocate to her half of M.'s housing space – 11.7 square metres of his 22.2 square metre room. While the people's court decided in favour of Vera and even ordered to register 5.85 square metres under the name of their four-year-old daughter,[29] the Leningrad City Court annulled this decision upon request of M., and Vera decided to appeal to a higher court. In her letter to the USSR Supreme Court of 24 November 1953, Vera brings forth a number of arguments, which to her understanding are decisive. First, she explains that M. and his neighbour deceived the court into thinking they only owned two rooms in the apartment, while in reality M. enjoyed a second room, formerly belonging to his mother. Hence, an attempt to keep an extra room to himself, not sharing it with Vera, and separating her from her daughter, amounted to "throwing her to the winter streets of Leningrad."[30] Vera added that she had also asked for the help of the "party collective" (*k partiinoi obshchestvenosti*), and this is when *Leningradskaia pravda* published the article mentioned above, supporting her claim.

Vera's claims seem at first glance to repeat the same language of lament and assumptions of a moral economy as did the women demanding alimony payments in Aaron Retish's contribution. She resorts to the arsenal of values and principles the Soviet state offers her and uses those to promote her interests (and official norms): she demands equal and fair distribution of housing space, honest and caring relations a Soviet man should have with the mother of his child, and decent living conditions. Moreover, as the article in *Leningradskaia pravda* stated, M.'s behaviour was not only his and Vera's concern. It was a matter for the entire society. Hence, in the context of building a true socialist society, M.'s behaviour and the rooms he occupied could be interpreted as "bourgeois" and his attitude towards women could be read as an assault towards women workers. In this sense, Vera's claims, and her fight for housing space in the name of Soviet norms, in fact assisted in strengthening the normative order of the Soviet state.

A closer look at Vera's letter of November 1953 (as opposed to the newspaper article of January of that year) also reflects the adoption of certain legal claims which became popular in the early 1950s and in particular during that year: "I trust Soviet laws, I live in a Soviet state, and I am positive that these laws would not separate a four-year-old child from her mother, who due to artificial conditions cannot share the housing space of her child."[31] While educating people about their rights began already in the 1920s and intensified in the 1930s, as Retish shows, the idea that "the Soviet court is a people's court" was propagated intensively after the Second World War, and in particular in 1948 and 1951, the first years since the enactment of the 1936 Constitution that people's judges were elected by the citizens themselves.[32] In addition, as Gorlizki explains, the late 1940s and early 1950s saw the activity of legal officials in strengthening legal norms. All these factors made Vera's statement hardly extraordinary: this was a typical appeal which followed socialist norms and gave its author an advantage in court.

It is therefore particularly interesting to examine M.'s defence, despite his "ideological" and "moral" disadvantage. Staying away from ideological arguments, he focused on the wording of the law: Vera K., he claimed, could not join the daughter's housing space, since the daughter, who was a minor, could not have a separate housing account. In addition, M. asserted that one of the conditions for Vera's moving into the apartment was the consent of his neighbour, Ms. R., who actually refused to this arrangement using the legal argumentation: "The court's decision harmed my interests and infringed my housing rights and the rights of my family members."[33] The court of appeals of the City of Leningrad, and then the USSR Supreme Court, both accepted those claims and decided in favour of M. Although we could claim that unknown factors, such as a possible bribe or the famous name of the actor helped him out in this case, it is nevertheless significant that plain legal arguments were enough to justify the decision in M.'s favour.

In despair and as a last resort, Vera turned to the chairman of the Supreme Soviet of the Soviet Union, Klement Voroshilov, and wrote him a twenty-page letter, which reveals another interesting aspect of the problem. The letter starts with a personal plea for help: "a simple Soviet person who has so much sorrow that only belief in the justice of Soviet laws and in the Communist Party gives her strength to fight this distress."[34] After expressing trust in the system the letter gives away a core reason for the appeal: "Am I to blame that I do not have housing space? ... If I'm not a born 'Leningrader' can't I live in Leningrad? – I am a Soviet person too ... Help me get a place of my own on this earth, so I can live together with my child."[35] The rest of the letter continues with an autobiographical description of the dire conditions she lived in due to the war and the loss of her loved ones. Vera's cry reflected the great shortage in housing and the attempt of many to reach the big cities, where work, food, and consumer goods were more plentiful. However, housing "registration" (*propiska*) was a chief tool for controlling the movement of citizens, and Soviet regulations restricted the assignment of housing space only to workers who lived in the same area and vice-versa.[36] Thus, like many others, Vera was caught in a vicious circle where she could not move to a different city and live with her daughter until she was offered a job there, and she could not find a new workplace in a city where she did not have formal registration. For Vera, this was a fight between a poor working woman and a loving mother and a greedy, bourgeois father who refused to share his housing space. "A Soviet court would not let the stronger and richer side win," she concluded. Voroshilov, however, decided not to intervene in the court's decision, and Vera was left without a housing space in Leningrad.[37]

The policy of housing distribution was particularly sharp in the dispute between Anna A. and Praskovia D. of the city of Voroshilovgrad. The affair started with Praskovia's request that the people's court order Anna to leave the house she lived in and return it to the plaintiff. The people's court ruled in Praskovia's favour, leading Anna to appeal. In its decision of March 1954, the Voroshilovgrad regional court determined the following: In 1945 Praskovia bought a house in the city. Three years later, in 1948, she had been convicted of a crime and sent to a correction camp in the Baku region. When she had been away, her stepson falsified a power-of-attorney and sold her house to Anna A. for 14,000 rubles. In 1953, Praskovia had been amnestied, returned to her city, and demanded her property be returned to her. The regional court decided that the agreement should be annulled: the house should go back to the original owner, who did not give consent to selling the house, and Agabek, the stepson who fabricated the authorization, should return the money to the buyer.[38] A subsequent ruling of the Ukrainian Supreme Court confirmed the lower court's decision, and Anna then turned to the USSR Supreme Court for help.

Trying to convince the court to reconsider her case, Anna revealed the newly available information on Agabek, namely, that he had been stopped at the Russian–Turkish border when crossing it illegally into Turkey and was held behind bars, without any ability or intent to return the 14,000 rubles. After unmasking Agabek, she expressed her opinion that all his actions, in the past and present, were known and supported by Praskovia.[39] Writing to every possible institution that could interfere on her behalf, including Procurator General of the USSR, Roman Rudenko, and the first secretary of the Communist Party of the Soviet Union, Khrushchev, Anna based her demands on moral-political grounds rather than on legal arguments. The letters told the story of a good, hardworking woman who was fighting the injustice and deceit of two speculators – Praskovia, an illegal producer of baked goods and former convict, and her son Agabek, a "swindler," "crook," and "speculator." Finally, Anna stated that the lower court's ruling left her without a house and without money.

Beyond the negative portrayal of the plaintiff and her son, the case of Praskovia and Anna had a wide political dimension: it reflected the situation whereby following the 1953 amnesty hundreds of thousands of Gulag returnees were looking for housing, often trying to get hold of their pre-detention property. The case demonstrated the reaction of the Soviet population to the rehabilitations and their influence on the housing issue. While the new leadership justified the releases by claiming that there was no more threat coming from those people, the case shows the clash between the free population and the ex-convicts.[40] In the minds of ordinary Soviet people, who came to support socialist norms of behaviour, the image of the returnee was still of a criminal. As Miriam Dobson shows in her book on Gulag returnees, expressions such as "there's been too much humaneness shown towards these weeds" or "only the grave can correct thieves and recidivists" were quite common.[41] Moreover, it was very difficult to rehabilitate the released and reinstate them in society, let alone return to them what they owned prior to their conviction. In this case, the situation was particularly complex, as it was not the state who took the property of Praskovia, but her stepson, and it was a fellow citizen who enjoyed it.

Even though Soviet courts were not bound by precedents, the decision could have implications beyond the case in question destabilizing the entire housing distribution policy. It was a competition between two groups over one of the major resources the state provided – housing. As Anna wrote in her letter to Khrushchev, she believed that Praskovia and Agabek abused their status as former prisoners, and knowing they would not be sent to prison again, they gave false statements in court.[42] Praskovia, apparently, was not willing to give up easily either, and she accused Anna of anti-social behaviour as well: according to her story, Anna was involved with "speculative elements" too. Her husband was associated with an illegal wine producer.

The case was discussed by the USSR Supreme Court twice. First, following an appeal from the chairman of the Voroshilovgrad regional court, and then as an appeal from the chairman of the USSR Supreme Court. At first, the deputy chairman of the USSR Supreme Court, P. Bardin, refused to decide in Anna's favour and instead returned the case to the lower court for a more thorough examination of the ownership status of the house prior to the purchasing contract. The examination revealed that, in fact, the house should have been confiscated following the arrest. Furthermore, it turned out that in an attempt to evade confiscation, the house had been sold. Praskovia, it was established, knew about her son's attempts to sell the property, even though she did not give specific consent and instructions on this agreement.[43] When Anna turned out to be an "innocent buyer" according to the law, the USSR Supreme Court decided to accept Anna's appeal, protest the lower courts' decisions, and rule in her favour. While Bardin's first decision was concise and professional, and based strictly on legal arguments, the final decision, written again by Bardin on behalf of the court on 13 August 1955, criticized Praskovia's behaviour while underscoring Anna's actions as an honest buyer.[44] Anna got her house back, and Praskovia had been advised to sue Agabek for the 14,000 rubles.

From the legal perspective, the story is a classic case of a clash between private property rights, which the law should be able to solve. However, in the Soviet reality socialist norms intervene with the decision. As Anna herself asserted in her appeal – law in the Soviet Union should not be used in a "formal way."[45] Anna echoed here a belief that socialist justice should win, and this is apparently determined by a myriad of factors, which include the character of the sides, their social background, matters of social justice, etc. All those factors stood this time on the side of Anna A.

Law as a Form of Criticism from Below

The pattern above, where plaintiffs often followed "socialist" arguments, experienced an interesting development as the principle of socialist legality gained importance starting in the mid-1950s. The discourse of legality, which emerged parallel to the promise of a better life, prompted people to use legal means to achieve the alleged "justice and fairness" under socialism. Newspapers and legal publications of the 1950s and 1960s emphasized the importance of law in a socialist state. Contrary to official declarations of the 1930s and 1940s that emphasized the beneficial content of Soviet law or demand citizen obedience, post-Stalinist newspapers, journals, and books stressed the orderly functioning of both state and society as essential for the defence of citizen rights.[46] Already a few months after Stalin's death, alongside the usual articles blaming thieves, pilferers of public property, and morally corrupt elements, texts criticizing Party and state officials for disregarding the law appeared in the newspapers.[47] In June 1953, for example, a *Literaturnaia gazeta* article discussed the case of a schoolteacher from Rostov na Donu, who had been ordered to vacate her temporary apartment for Party offices. The case would not have had to reach the USSR Supreme Court, established the newspaper, "had socialist legality been observed and Soviet citizen rights defended."[48] Another typical publication of those years established that "All these organs [i.e. state institutions], must be active and resourceful in defending the rights and legal interests of citizens, and take measures to stop breaches of socialist legality and breaches of rights and interest of citizens."[49]

To be sure, the primary motive behind the idea of legality was not citizen rights. The latter were rather the outcome of the orderly work of state institutions and the building of socialism; part of a deal between the state and the people.[50] Moreover, as discussed in other chapters of this section, the state was struggling in those years to overcome a wave of crime, corruption, hooliganism, and red tape. The idea was that bottom-up criticism of state institutions and citizen access to courts would serve as better supervision than other coercive methods. This was "popularization of justice" in practice. And while the main supervisory power over legality had been entrusted in the hands of the USSR Procuracy, the new statute of 1955 gave this body a very wide authority to act upon any complaint regarding legality which reaches its desk.[51]

Thus, socialist legality was not necessarily perceived as the impediment to control but as a tool to achieving it. As Immo Rebitschek shows in his chapter, the broader authority that had been given to the Procuracy to supervise other bodies as part of the legality campaign, in fact assisted the state in achieving better social control.

The fact that all state and public institutions were called to strictly follow the law, stimulated citizens to try and defend their interests through the use of legal proceedings. And indeed, the access Soviet citizens had to the courts had been quite phenomenal. The popularization and participation trends of the 1950s and 1960s made admittance to court quite simple and cheap for Soviet citizens. Very low court fees, relatively swift legal procedures, and limited advocates' fees (though many paid additional unofficial sums) encouraged citizens to turn to the court for help. In addition, the ability to meet with judges in person, even those of USSR and Republican Supreme Courts in capital cities, created a feeling the system was closer to the people than before.[52]

The complaint of one Mikhail B. about the fact he had to settle for a meeting with the deputy chairman instead of Chairman A.F. Gorkin of the USSR Supreme Court only strengthens the impression of the openness of the court: "Believing that this case should be discussed at the USSR Supreme Court, I tried to meet with the Chairman Comrade Gorkin, but was not admitted. I was received instead by the Head of the Judicial Division for Civil Cases of the USSR Supreme Court, Comrade Bardin. He said: 'I remember your case very well, since I did not agree with the protest of the former Chairman, Comrade Volin. Your case is completely just.'"[53] Mikhail B. was not an exception. Similarly, citizen V.E. from Baku described in her letter to Chairman Gorkin in 1964, how she had been summoned to a meeting with the deputy chairman of the Azerbaijan Supreme Court, Barykin, who examined her case and agreed with her that her demands were just. Although Chairman Gorkin eventually did not agree to protest the lower court's decision, her meeting with Barykin was an opportunity to state her arguments.[54] In the case of Tatiana A. vs. Sergei K., the latter complained that the plaintiff succeeded in overturning the lower courts' decisions by "disappearing" from Tbilisi and going to Moscow, "where she worked her way to the Supreme Court of the USSR, achieved the halting of the housing exchange process, and in obscure ways obtained a copy of an order signed by Deputy Chairman of the Supreme Court, Comrade Bardin, which she then brought to Tbilisi."[55] Indeed, the paperwork in the appeal files of the USSR Supreme Court collection confirm this general "accessibility" pattern: the files show that court administrators were careful to forward letters to the judges no matter who the appellant was and where s/he came from – all union republics and different social groups were represented in the court collection, and all received a reply in a timely manner.

By granting Soviet citizens free access to Soviet legal institutions, better supervision of courts and legal institutions could be attained. Intrusion, which was originally designed to supervise private citizens, could be useful in this case as a means for monitoring the work of law officials.[56] This "criticism from below," was not entirely new. Denunciations of the Stalinist period rested on the notion that supervision could be best executed through internal information.[57] However, in the 1950s this internal criticism was meant to help the legal system not to repress its workers but to achieve its new goal: "To see to it that not a single innocent citizen is wrongfully arrested and arraigned, and not a single criminal escaped his justly deserved punishment."[58] In this context, appeals were seen not as a destabilizing event, but as an opportunity to amend the wrongdoing of the system, assuming naturally that a "legal" decision was the one which best served the socialist order.

While such an approach to appeals was originally designed to assist the authorities in convicting and punishing criminals, in the post-Stalinist years this policy came to serve the citizens as well: the system allowed an endless number of appeals, often preferring "correct" decisions to stability and predictability.[59] Furthermore, there were no limitations on the issues which could be reopened, and the appeal in the form of supervision could be filed by a long list of officials: from chairmen of Supreme Courts (of a Union Republic or the all-Union one) to procurators of republics or the procurator general himself, and even the Supreme Soviet of the USSR.[60] Hence, citizens approached whomever they could in an attempt to convince those in power to reconsider a case.[61] This put an enormous burden on judges and courts that were subjected to an endless number of cases moving back and forth between courts.

In his letters to Khrushchev and Voroshilov (as chairman of the Supreme Soviet) in 1957, citizen Mikhail B., whose housing appeal had gone through several actions of appeal-in-supervision but had thus far been rejected, complained about the uncertainty the Soviet legal system created for him. His case concerned the request of his daughter-in-law, Valentina B., a music teacher from Moscow who had already separated from his son, to continue living in her in-laws' apartment after her divorce. Valentina married Igor and departed with him to Kuibyshev shortly thereafter. However, after some time, they separated, and she decided to return to the big city. Claiming that the months she lived in Kuibyshev did not undermine her right to keep her housing space in Moscow, she filed a civil housing suit.[62] Trying to defend his rights using the new arsenal of legitimate legal claims, Mikhail B. complained that two high courts had ruled differently on his case and failed to reach one final decision grounded in law, as was expected in a socialist system governed by law: "How can it be that on the eve of the 40th anniversary of the Great October Revolution in the USSR where exploiting classes were liquidated and all citizens are equally responsible before the law, three High Institutions of Justice and Supervision decide the case in such different manner, insisting that each of them is basing its decision on law?"[63] In his letter to Gorkin (the new chairman of the Supreme Court, to replace Justice Anatolii Volin in 1957), Mikhail B. demanded a ruling that would be based on legal argumentation: "In these times, when the Party and government push forward every day the issue of strengthening socialist legality, such a difference in opinions about the case evokes understandable alarm and requires a full study of the case and the issue of one correct decision."[64]

Demanding Socialist Legality

Reaching one unequivocal decision was not simple, however. As a matter of fact, despite the efforts to present socialist legality as a clear and unambiguous term, with time it seemed that the two components inside it, the "socialist" and the "legal" started to pull in different directions. By the early and mid-1960s there emerged two sets of norms which appeared to exist side by side in the legal system. Parallel to the well-known socialist set of values, a new collection of legal considerations surfaced, which gained more significance with the advent of socialist legality.

By the early 1960s, so the files indicate, Soviet citizens became accustomed to the new discourse on law, which emphasized socialist legality, rights, and a promise of justice for the people, and started using it when turning to the authorities for help: "With this complaint I turn to you for the restoration of legality and defense of my citizen rights guaranteed by the Soviet constitution, which were encroached on by the courts of Georgia," wrote Antonina B. in her complaint in 1964.[65] Insisting that her share of housing space should not be given to her stepson following his father's death, Antonina ended her letter with the words "I believe in the humaneness of the Soviet government, which will not allow that I will be thrown to the street."[66]

Nazik N., an old lady from Armenia, who wrote in 1963 to the USSR Supreme Court on behalf of her son, opened her appeal with reference to the significance of the Russian revolution and its goals: "I am an old woman; [I] remember well the tsarist times, the justice officers, the village constables, the mediators of the *mir*, and other representatives of the state; [I] tasted enough of the lawlessness of those times. [I] Also survived the short-lived rule of the Dashnaks, when the power of law was on the side of whoever held the Mauzer. Finally, the Soviet rule was established and with it legality and order. I write to you about this only because I am stunned at the lawlessness that is allowed in our times with regard to our family."[67] After invoking the revolution in order to ask for justice, Nazik moved to the heart of her claim: the Armenian Supreme Court was wrong to decide to take one of her and her husband's rooms following their son's divorce. Nazik and her husband (the official tenants of the two rooms) had given one room for the use of their son and his wife, but now that the couple divorced, the Armenian Supreme Court decided to give it to the former daughter-in-law. While Nazik agreed that kicking the wife and grand-daughter out of the room would be cruel, she maintained that it was equally wrong to give the entire room to the former wife and force her son to return to his parents' room and share their housing space.[68] Nazik asked the Supreme Court to reaffirm a decision of the lower court that the son's room should be split or shared by him and his former wife (regardless of the divorce), as such a decision would answer both the "legal rights of the mother and the child and those of a grown up man, who will no doubt marry again." "My entire request is legality and legality," she wrote at the end of her letter.[69]

In his own letter to Chairman Gorkin, Zhora, Nazik's son, explained that giving the entire room to his former wife and placing him in his parents' room would mean encroaching on his parents' rights twice: first, as they lost one of their original rooms in the communal apartment and second, as they were forced to share their space with their son. "Where are logic and justice?" asks the appellant.[70] Chairman Gorkin decided to approve the appeal and revive a past decision of the City Court,[71] which stated that since the wife has been registered in the room together with her husband, then upon divorce the division of housing rights is done according to this agreement and not based on general housing space allowances.[72] The final decision represented, then, a compromise between the rights of the parents to keep their housing space, and the state's general preference to divide housing according to the needs of the growing population, and in this case the young mother, who was looking for a separate room. The idea of giving the couple shared rights in their 18 square metre room, is that they can then exchange it for two separate smaller rooms.

Whether Soviet citizens believed in the narrative of a just Soviet law or not, they were definitely aware of the slogan of socialist legality and called on the state to keep it by correcting mistakes, misunderstandings, or corruption in lower courts. In 1964 V.E. from Baku (mentioned above) opened her letter to the chairman of the USSR Supreme Court, Alexander Gorkin, with the following words:

> It has been eight years already since I first turned to the judicial institutions of Azerbaijan and the Supreme Court of the USSR, and we still cannot restore our rights. Illegally, under the order of a number of former officials, who abused their positions, the Soviet court was pressured, and therefore our sacred rights were encroached ... I will say frankly that the blame lies with the high-ranking echelons that are indifferent to the complaints of the workers. Couldn't they look into the matter during the last eight years, help us restore our rights and punish the perpetrators, so that others learn a lesson?[73]

Turning to higher authority was not novel in Russia. A long tradition to turn to the tsar with the request to correct the abuses of local authorities existed in the empire.[74] However, the ability to defend workers' rights against encroachments of the system using official legal guarantees strengthened the Soviet citizen. Unlike the cases of the 1920s and 1930s, the appeal above used legal slogans not only to speak for citizens' rights but also to raise claims against the system itself. In the 1950s and 1960s citizens could approach the courts armed with both socialist and legal arguments.

Interestingly, it was not always clear which would win. A perfect example of such controversy can be found in the Mikhail B. case already mentioned above. The plaintiff maintained that his daughter-in-law's lengthy stay in Kuibyshev (more than six months), caused her to forfeit her right to a housing space in his apartment. Valentina B., for her part, recruited to her defence the parents of children she taught at a Moscow music school, all claiming she was an excellent teacher and an asset to the school. These latter social considerations seemed to prevail when Chairman Volin considered her plea. Volin established that the formal annulment of Valentina's housing registration was the result of deceit carried out by her husband and should not be used against his wife. Volin then stated that the lower RSFSR Supreme Court did not take into account "the moral aspects of the case," in effect supporting people who did not act in good faith and leaving Valentina without a shelter in Moscow.[75]

The invocation of morality in a legal discussion opened the door for injecting different revolutionary norms into legal decisions, turning every decision, whether it concerned property, labour, or family, into a political one. The case itself in fact concerned the distribution of wealth (housing space) in society, involved questions of population control (if denied housing, Valentina would have to return to Kuibyshev), matters of collective action (the students at the school demanded Valentina's return), and prompted punishment of immoral behaviour (the husband should learn a lesson). While every law by its definition sets in motion certain moral policies, the socialist moral code emphasized certain distributive values and social behaviour, which allowed simple people to have a stronger standing in court and left much more room for social activism on behalf of the judges. The civil dispute allowed Valentina to promote her interests using social principles.

Interestingly, in this particular case the presence of legal norms pushed forward by the father-in-law, could be observed in a dissenting opinion of Judge Genrikh Fiofilovich Dobrovol'ski, which had been filed alongside the official court decision. Dobrovol'ski expressed his view that "the protest of the Chairman of the USSR Supreme Court in this case should be rejected" since Valentina did not have the right to reside in the apartment in the first place as she only lived there for one month prior to leaving for Kuibyshev. Dobrovol'ski then concluded:

> Despite my announcement at the meeting of the Division [Judicial Division for Civil Cases at the USSR Supreme Court – D.M.] and a similar announcement by Assistant USSR Procurator, Com. Gurevich, the Judicial Division decided contrary to law, and chose to consider the protest for its content.
>
> The decision of the Division contradicts the law and is wrong in essence, and this is why I do not agree with it.[76]

The existence of an official dissenting opinion was a rare occasion in the Soviet system (as opposed to the adversarial Anglo-American law). Though Soviet law allowed for a dissenting opinion to be expressed and written, and filed in the dossier for future use if needed, this was very rarely practised.[77] However, the fact that in this case Dobrovol'ski's position reached the defendant and was copied and sent with his appeal to Voroshilov at the Supreme Soviet is highly important. Not only does it demonstrate existing differences of opinion among high-level legal officials in the Soviet Union, but it also reveals that opinions which were based entirely on legal grounds were possible. Finally, it is significant that eventually it was Chairman Volin who had been released of his post in 1957, while Dobrovol'ski continued serving as a Supreme Court judge under the leadership of the next chairman, Comrade A.P. Gorkin.

Conclusion

The Soviet courtroom, just like its Western counterpart, was a unique place where law met reality, where theory and practice intersected, and where discourse was most clearly articulated. The dialogue which took place inside the courtroom was constructed from the building blocks provided by the socialist discourse and reflected, therefore, the values, norms, and practices of Soviet society, as well as the changes it went through over the years. The need to adhere to particular conventions taught Soviet citizens how to use the system in a way that would serve their own personal needs. They learned very well the claims that could work in their favour, the rights they were promised and the norms the state wished to strengthen – and they did their best to use them to advance their goals. Housing, as a central state benefit, stood at the centre of those disputes, and while the state tried to control population movement and instil socialist values, citizens attempted to improve their living conditions by using the tools the state gave them. In this sense Soviet citizens were players in the legal game.

As the files show, Soviet citizen–state relations experienced a shift in the post-Stalinist period as Khrushchev lifted the banner of socialist legality. The demand that not only citizens but state institutions too follow legal norms allowed citizens to fight for their cause in court more forcefully. At the same time, the norms governing the housing sphere were still subject to ideology and politics, thus expecting the courts not only to settle disputes but to distribute housing space fairly, taking into account social, political, and class consideration. For the courts, the state's ambition to supply every citizen with a job and housing space according to a particular norm forced judges to constantly move citizens around and adjust their housing privileges to their workplace, and their living space to their marital status, their children's age, not to mention to losses in their family or departures due to detention. The courts appear here not only as institutes for dispute resolution, but as state housing agencies, which are committed to providing citizens with roofs over their heads.

In addition, the post-Stalinist quest for participation and popularization of state functions signified that the citizens too were recruited to assist the court and the legal system in strengthening socialist norms. By calling Soviet institutions to keep the housing laws, and by taking people who deviated from socialist norms to court, citizens de-facto participated in supervising and monitoring the behaviour of their fellow neighbours, family members, co-workers, and even law officials. This model shook the traditional top-down character of Soviet law

Social Control in Post-Stalinist Courts 317

and allowed justice to work horizontally (facing fellow citizens) and even vertically, bottom-up, when suing state institutions. Whether they believed it or not, their actions strengthened the regime and helped the state supervise its officials.

NOTES

1 Support of this study has been provided by the Center for Russian, East European and Eurasian Studies at Stanford University. Preliminary research has been conducted at the Hoover Institution at Stanford University.
2 Statistical data indicate that over the years the Soviet state gradually increased its share of investment in the construction of housing (and consequently its ownership of housing space) from 10 per cent in the 1920s, to about 30 per cent in the 1930s, and to roughly 55 per cent just before the Great Patriotic War. By 1955 the Soviet state was responsible for 82 per cent of house-building investments across urban areas of the USSR. See *Narodnoe khoziaistvo SSSR 1922–1972: Iubileinyi statisticheskii ezhegodnik* (Moscow: Statistika, 1972), 333.
3 See Paola Messana, *Soviet Communal Living: An Oral History of the Kommunalka* (New York: Palgrave Macmillan, 2011); Lynne Attwood, *Gender and Housing in Soviet Russia: Private Life in a Public Space* (Manchester: Manchester University Press, 2010).
4 *Narodnoe khoziaistvo SSSR za 1913–1956: Kratkii statisticheskii sbornik* (Moscow: Statistika, 1956). Rossiiski gosudarstvennyi arkhiv ekonomiki (RGAE) 1562/33/2310/1–250.
5 According to a report sent to L.M. Kaganovich in August 1953, the average housing space per person in the Soviet Union was between 5 and 6 square metres. See Spravka TsSU SSSR L.M. Kaganovichu o sostoianii gorodskogo zhilishchnogo fonda v 1940–1952 gg. ot 18 avgusta 1953. RGAE 1562/33/1682/88–99. On the housing problems in the USSR after the war, see also Rebecca Manley, "'Where Should We Resettle the Comrades Next?' The Adjudication of Housing Claims and the Construction of the Post-war Order," in *Late Stalinist Russia: Society between Reconstruction and Reinvention*, ed. Juliane Fürst (New York: Routledge, 2006), 233–46.
6 Elena Zubkova, *Russia after the War: Hopes, Illusions, and Disappointments, 1945–1957*, trans. and ed. Hugh Ragsdale (Armonk, New York: M.E. Sharpe, 1998).
7 As Immo Rebitschek points out in his chapter, in the 1940s and 1950s a whole array of "juvenile issues" (*dela nesovershennoletnikh*) challenged the social order of post-war Soviet society.

8 Donald Filtzer, *Soviet Workers and Late Stalinism: Labor and the Restoration of the Stalinist System after WWII* (Cambridge: Cambridge University Press, 2002).
9 Ibid. See also Amir Weiner, "The Making of a Dominant Myth: The Second World War and the Construction of Political Identities within the Soviet Polity," *Russian Review* 55, no. 4 (October 1996): 638–60; Mark Edele, "More than Just Stalinists: The Political Sentiments of Victors 1945–1953," in *Late Stalinist Russia*, ed. Fürst, 167–91.
10 See Charles Hachten, "Separate yet Governed: The Representation of Soviet Property Relations in Civil Law and Public Discourse," in *Borders of Socialism: Private Spheres of Soviet Russia*, ed. Lewis H. Siegelbaum (New York: Palgrave Macmillan, 2006). On Soviet people's attitude towards property, see also the discussion in Juliette Cadiot's chapter where she uses the term "moral economy" to explain the feeling of entitlement to the state's property.
11 After the war, for example, the USSR channelled a significant share of its economic resources to the support of the new socialist regimes of Eastern Europe in order to enhance its political influence. See Mark Kramer, "The Early Post-Stalin Succession Struggle and Upheavals in East-Central Europe: Internal-External Linkages in Soviet Policy Making," *Journal of Cold War Studies* 1, no. 3 (Spring 1999): 3.
12 James Heinzen, *The Art of the Bribe: Corruption under Stalin, 1943–1953* (New Haven, CT: Yale University Press, 2016); Cynthia Hooper, "A Darker 'Big Deal': Concealing Party Crimes in the Post-Second World War Era," in *Late Stalinist Russia*, ed. Fürst, 142–63.
13 "O razvitii zhilishchnogo stroitel'stva v SSSR," 31 July 1957, st. 102, *Sobranie postanovlenii pravitel'stva SSSR*, no.9 (1957).
14 Steven E. Harris, "Soviet Mass Housing and the Communist Way of Life," in *Everyday Life in Russia: Past and Present*, ed. C. Chatterjee et al. (Bloomington: Indiana University Press, 2015), 181–202.
15 The USSR's participation in numerous exhibitions and staged events outside the Soviet Union were an attempt to demonstrate its achievements: from agriculture to kitchen supplies to cars. Lewis Siegelbaum, "Sputnik Goes to Brussels: The Exhibition of a Soviet Technological Wonder," *Journal of Contemporary History* 47, no. 1 (January 2012): 120–36.
16 Nikita Sergeevich Khrushchev, *Doklad na zakrytom zasedanii 20go sezda KPSS: "O kul'te lichnosti i ego posledstviiakh"* (Moscow: Gospolitizdat, 1959). Robert Hornsby's claim that the state wished to achieve "social control without terror" stems clearly from Khrushchev's speech. See Hornsby, *Protest, Reform and Repression in Khrushchev' s Soviet Union* (New York: Cambridge University Press, 2013).

17 The "legality" component I use here contains both aspects of post-Stalinist socialist legality Yoram Gorlizki discusses in his chapter: the delegitimization of extra-judicial repression and the observance of laws, which he traces back to the late 1940s. In my dissertation *Did Law Matter? Law, State and Individual in the Soviet Union 1953–1982*, I trace the shift that occurred in the meaning of the term "socialist legality" after Stalin's death to the tension between law and revolution originally to appear in the term "revolutionary legality." Hence, while I concur with Gorlizki on the central role of the term in post-Stalinist policies, I claim that the challenge of "social control" was not "outside" the term socialist legality, but internal to it. That is, legality posed a challenge not only because it forced the regime to loosen its control over the population, but because socialist legality was to bring socialist order through law.
18 Evgenia Lezina's chapter, as well as the works of Oleg Kharkhordin and Robert Hornsby, show how different mechanisms, from workers' organizations, housing committees, and comrade's courts to volunteer people's patrol units (*druzhiny*) and new methods of the KGB, assisted in instilling social order by new means. Oleg Kharkhordin, *The Collective and the Individual in Russia: A Study of Practices* (Berkeley: University of California Press, 1999).
19 See Lewis Siegelbaum, *Borders of Socialism: Private Spheres of Soviet Russia* (New York: Palgrave Macmillan, 2006); Deborah A. Field, "Everyday Life and the Problem of Conceptualizing Public and Private during the Khrushchev Era," in *Everyday Life in Russia*, ed. Chatterjee et al., 163–80.
20 See Miriam Dobson, *Khrushchev's Cold Summer: Gulag Returnees, Crime and the Fate of Reform after Stalin* (Ithaca, NY: Cornell University Press, 2009), 210–11. See also Lezina's chapter in this volume.
21 Christine Varga-Harris, *Stories of House and Home: Soviet Apartment Life during the Khrushchev Years* (Ithaca, NY: Cornell University Press, 2015).
22 Suzan E. Reid, "Communist Comfort: Socialist Modernism and the Making of Cozy Homes in the Khrushchev Era," *Gender & History* 21, no. 3 (November 2009): 465–98.
23 Field, "Everyday Life."164–5, 171–2.
24 While the CPSU Central Committee and the Council of Ministers decrees were issued in 1958, in practice the laws that established suitable legal and monetary mechanisms were enacted in 1962 and 1964. Postanovlenie TsK KPSS i Soveta Ministrov SSSR ot 1 iiunia 1962g. "Ob individual'nom i kooperativnom zhilishchnom stroitel'stve" (*Sobranie postanovlenii Pravitel'stva SSSR*, 1962, No.12, st.93) and *Postanovlenie Soveta Ministrov SSSR* ot 19 noiabria 1964g. "O dal'neishem razvitii kooperativnogo zhilishchnogo stroitel'stva" (*Sobranie postanovlenii SSSR*, 1964, No.25, st. 147).

25 According to the introduction to the collection of civil cases covering the years 1953–77, out of all the cases considered by the USSR Supreme Court from its inception, the archival committee selected for preservation only those files where judgment had been reversed or cancelled. All in all this collection consists of about five thousand files, with roughly two thousand reversed cases between 1953 and 1982. Out of those about a third were housing disputes. See the introduction to the USSR Supreme Court Civil Cases collection GARF R-9474, op.5 and 5(2). This article is based on a very limited number of cases from this collection, while in my forthcoming manuscript I analyse a broader selection of files. Interestingly, the number of cases reviewed and reversed by the US Supreme Court in the last fifteen years is quite similar and reaches four or five dozen every year. See https://ballotpedia.org/SCOTUS_case_reversal_rates_(2007_-_Present) (accessed 1 November 2022).
26 For privacy reasons, I have decided to give only the initials or first names of the subjects of the files.
27 Editorial, "Actor M. without make-up," *Leningradskaia pravda* (25 January 1953). A copy of the article is filed in the court case file. GARF R-9474/5/4589/10.
28 GARF R-9474/5/4589
29 Ibid., l.6–7.
30 Ibid., l.11–12.
31 Ibid., l.12.
32 Michael Kogan, "Shaping Soviet Justice: Popular Responses to the Election of People's Courts, 1948–1954," *Caheirs du monde russe* 53, no. 1 (January–March 2012): 121–39. See also the discussion of the "uniqueness of the Soviet court" in V. Ivanov and Iu. Todorovskii, *Na strazhe Sovetskogo zakona* (Moscow: Gospolitizdat, 1952). A number of posters with this slogan had been printed on the occasions of the election.
33 GARF R-9474/5/4589/1.
34 Ibid., l.21.
35 Ibid., l.29.
36 See, for example, correspondence between the Juridical Committee and the RSFSR Ministry of Public Order on the need to align housing registration and work assignments. GARF A-577/1/205, l.1–4.
37 Here the Procuracy was on the side of M. and R. GARF R-9474/5/4589/9–10. What the Supreme Court did was cancel the decision of the RSFSR Supreme Court on the basis of the legal arguments mentioned and return the case to the people's court.
38 GARF R-9474/5/4749/15–18.
39 Ibid., l. 25.
40 On the discussion of releases from the Gulag and their implication on society, see Miriam Dobson, *Khrushchev's Cold Summer*; and Brian LaPierre,

Hooligans in Khrushchev's Russia: Defining, Policing, and Producing Deviance during the Thaw (Madison: University of Wisconsin Press, 2012).
41 See Dobson, *Khrushchev's Cold Summer*, 42.
42 GARF R-9474/5/4749/25.
43 Ibid, l.63–4.
44 While we do not know whether Bardin genuinely changed his mind or was forced to agree with Volin, it is worth noting that two years later, in 1957, Volin, who served as chairman of the USSR Supreme Court since 1948, had been replaced with Alexander Gorkin, and Bardin admitted in other cases that he disagreed with Volin on a number of occasions.
45 GARF R-9474/5/4749/25. The allegation of "formalism" was often used to characterize bourgeois-like decisions, which allegedly followed positive law rather than natural law. For more on Soviet discussions of formalism and positive law vs. natural law, see Petry Zoltan, "O nekotorykh chertakh doktriny "vozrozhdennogo" estestvennogo prava," in *Kritika sovremennoi burzhuaznoi teorii prava*, ed. K. Kul'char et al. (Moscow: Progress, 1969), 118–64.
46 See, for example, Valentin Nikolaevich Ivanov, *Chelovek i zakon* (Izdatel'stvo TsKVLKSM "Molodaia gvardiia," 1960); V. Korotkov, M. Gol'dshtein, *Chto nuzhno znat' rabochim i sluzhashchim o trudovom zakonodatel'stve* (Moscow: VTsSPS Profizdat, 1960).
47 On the special status of corruption inside the Party, see Juliette Cadiot and John Angell, "Equal Before the Law? Soviet Justice, Criminal Proceedings against Communist Party Members, and the Legal Landscape in the USSR from 1945 to 1953," *Jahrbücher für Geschichte Osteuropas* 61, no. 2 (June 2013): 249–69.
48 Vl. Ponedel'nik (reporter in Rostov na Donu), "Shame," *Literaturnaia gazeta* (18 June 1953).
49 See P.P. Gureev, *Zashchita lichnykh i imushchestvennykh prav* (Moscow: Izdatel'stvo "Nauka," 1964), 3.
50 According to Christopher Osakwe, Soviet law contained a Greco-Hobbesian element that regards citizen rights not as a natural phenomenon but as a product of agreement in society. Hence, this is the outcome of social relations, which are in this case moderated by the state. Christopher Osakwe, "The Four Images of Soviet Law: A Philosophical Analysis of the Soviet Legal System," *Texas International Law Journal* 21, no. 1 (Winter 1985); 1–38.
51 A special Statute on Procuracy Supervision in the USSR, enacted in May 1955, gave the USSR Procuracy a wide supervisory authority over legality in all state institutions (including justice administration) and allowed it to act upon citizen complaints and press charges against Soviet officials who deviated from the law. W.E. Butler, *Soviet Law* (London: Butterworths, 1988).

52 See, for example, Nikolai Stepanovich Prusakov, *Narodnyi sud'ia* (Moscow: Iuridicheskaia literatura, 1965). Prusakov was at the time deputy chair of the RSFSR Supreme Court and he visited the city of Gor'kii to inspect the work of the local court. The book describes the deep involvement of the judge with his community.
53 GARF R-9474/5/4862/55–7.
54 GARF R-9474/5/5014/1–3.
55 GARF R-9474/5/4790/63.
56 The practice of denunciations was the more cruel expression of this horizontal or bottom-up use of the system, which worked in the criminal sphere and allowed people to subject their fellow citizens to the tough hand of the Soviet law and penal system.
57 Wendy Z. Goldman, *Inventing the Enemy: Denunciation and Terror in Stalin's Russia* (Cambridge: Cambridge University Press, 2011).
58 In M. Topuridze, "Guarding socialist Justice," *Zaria vostoka* (31 March 1956). A similar wording appears in a *Pravda* editorial of 1955: "The agencies of the court, of investigation and of supervision by the Procurator's Office, must organize their work in such a way that not a single genuine criminal may evade deserved punishment and at the same time completely eliminate unfounded indictments or arrest of citizens." See editorial, "For further strengthening socialist law," *Pravda* (12 April 1955).
59 The abovementioned goal assumed that every case had only one correct decision, which could be attained through a proper fact-finding process and professional knowledge of the law.
60 Section four of the *Fundamental Principles of Civil Procedure Legislation of the USSR and Union Republics* in *Konstitutsiia i zakony soiuza SSR*, ed. P.P. Gureev et al. (Moscow: Izvestiia sovetov narodnykh deputatov SSSR, 1983), 514–17; and Butler, *Soviet Law*, 334, 362–4.
61 It is worth noting that as much as it was common practice for citizens to write to high-instance officials outside of the legal system, such as the CPSU secretary or the chairman of the Supreme Soviet, with requests to intervene in a case, in all these events the memos in the files indicate that the pleas were forwarded directly to the examination of the Supreme Court.
62 According to Soviet housing laws the house committee could strike a citizen off the housing book if one did not live there for more than six months.
63 GARF R-9474/5/4862/47.
64 Ibid., l.47.
65 GARF R-9474/5/5001/21.
66 Ibid., l.25.
67 GARF R-9474/5/4994/5.

68 Ibid.
69 Ibid., l.6.
70 Ibid., l.1.
71 Although, officially, in the Soviet system, court judgments were not considered to be source of law, "judicial practice" was not ignored, and it did play a role in the development of law. This was done through publication of certain Supreme Court decisions and through guiding explanations (*rukovodiashchie raz'iasneniia*), which the Plenum of the USSR, Union Republic, and autonomous republic Supreme Courts were empowered to issue. Butler, *Soviet Law*, 51–2.
72 GARF R-9474/5/4994/23–5.
73 GARF R-9474/5/5014/1.
74 Aleksander W. Rudzinski, "Soviet-Type Audit Proceedings and Their Western Counterparts," in *Legal Controls in the Soviet Union. Law in Eastern Europe*, vol. 13, ed. Leon Boim et al. (Leyden: A.W. Sijthoff, 1966), 301–4.
75 GARF R-9474/5/4862/15–16.
76 Ibid., l.22.
77 A.D. Kucheruk, *Zapiski narodnogo sud'ii* (Barnaul, Russia: Altaiskoe Knizhnoe izdatel'stvo, 1976), 37.

12 Soviet Socialisms: From Stalin to Khrushchev

DAVID SHEARER

It is a truism that all states, regardless of ideological principles, attempt to exert some kind of social control over their societies; to impose some kind of social and public order, either in indirect or direct forms: whether through policies of taxation, social welfare policies, education, legal structures, or outright coercion. Three aspects distinguished the Stalinist regime in this regard: first, the degree to which policies and institutions of public order became militarized, that is, taken out of the jurisdiction of civil institutions and placed under administrative control of the police and security organs. This approach arose not just because of Stalin's habit to resolve issues by violence, but also out of necessity – that is, the significant under-development of Soviet state institutions, in general, and the scarcity of other social surveillance resources, specifically. In addition to militarization, Stalinist practices were also characterized by the degree to which all state organs, especially the police, approached issues of social order through what may be called a categorical imperative – policies based not on individual behaviour but on the ascribed status of segments or categories of the population. This aspect had an ideological basis, but it arose mainly as a strategy to compensate for the state's underdeveloped policing system. This characteristic also shaped the regime's practices of social surveillance and control. The third characteristic of the Soviet social order practices of the 1930s was the degree to which the state's approach to social order and control, in fact, exaggerated the problems they were supposed to resolve.

These three aspects of Stalinist practice during the 1930s became integral parts of the evolution of a kind of militarized or martial-law socialism during these years That particular type of militarized or war socialism began in the last two years of the 1920s with what was essentially a war crisis, in fact, a two-front war crises, first against Poland and a second domestic war, or return to war, against the country's peasantry.

The threat from Poland was, most likely, not a real threat, but Stalin genuinely believed it was, especially after the rise to power, again, of Józef Piłsudski in Poland in 1926. And it was that concern that turned him so dramatically from NEP to the militarized methods of grain procurement that began in 1928, then to the massive industrial-military buildup of the first Five-Year Plan and, finally, to the war-like measures of collectivization.[1]

Regime officials described collectivization as a narrative of spontaneous revolutionary class struggle in rural areas. In fact, collectivization amounted to a brutal war by the state to subjugate the country's peasantry and to extend state control into the countryside. Stalin needed control over the country's food supplies in case of war, and he cared little how many people had to suffer to achieve that goal. From 1929 through early 1933, Stalin waged a harsh war against the peasantry that left millions dispossessed and millions more dead from famine or deportation or outright murder.

Stalin succeeded in his goal. By early 1933, he declared that the "victory" of socialism had been achieved in the countryside. Most of the arable lands and country's livestock farming had been forcibly taken out of the hands of private peasant farmers and reorganized under state and Party control in the form of large corporate-type farms. These so-called collective or state farms consolidated land, equipment, and animals under supervision of Party and police officials. In a second kind of serfdom, peasants were tied to their villages and farms and denied the right to travel or leave the farms.

Despite the declaration of victory, Stalin's war against the peasantry, combined with the chaos of industrialization during the first Five-Year Plan, created tidal waves of multiple catastrophes – displacement, forced migration, famine, and accompanying criminality – that reverberated across the country, not just in rural areas, but in cities as well. These social catastrophes created disorder on a scale that even Stalin described as a threat. This was Stalin's assessment at the January 1933 plenary meeting of the Central Committee. That plenum is known mostly for Stalin's declaration about the victory of socialism in the countryside – through collectivization and dekulakization. Most accounts stop there, but Stalin went on and, in fact, warned that, despite the victory of socialism, the country still faced its greatest threat yet, which he said were the waves of social disorder that were sweeping the Soviet Union. And in Stalin's perception, that disorder did not arise from the regime's own brutal policies. Social disorder reflected the activities of the state's enemies as they dispersed into the cities and throughout the rest of the country after the great victory of collectivization. Of course, the populations that Stalin referred to as enemies consisted mainly of hundreds of thousands if not millions of homeless, often hungry, displaced people, including some 1.5 million orphans or unsupervised children. These groups moved across the Soviet landscape on a near biblical scale in one of the greatest migrations of the twentieth century. They inundated cities and industrial sites, and they populated the penal colonies and special settlements scattered throughout the Urals, Western Siberia, and Central Asia.

Stalin chose his words deliberately at the January 1933 plenum. He did not refer to social disorder as a threat to Soviet society, or even as a threat to the Soviet economy. He described social disorder, first and foremost, as a threat to Soviet power – *sovetskaia vlast'*. Those are the words he chose, and they reveal that, in Stalin's view, the problem for the regime was not just the waves of disorder created by indigent, displaced people, or even malign criminals. In his reading, waves of disorder created by anti-Soviet elements threatened the very existence of the Soviet state, and those dangerous elements now contaminated the whole of society. No one could be trusted, so it is no surprise that the actions of the regime to deal with this threat took on the characteristics of an occupying or colonial power trying to control a potentially hostile population.

The metaphor of internal colonization has been used by a number of historians and sociologists to describe Stalin's repressive policies. Alvin Gouldner used it in 1975 in his famous article in the journal *Telos*, entitled "Stalinism: A Study in Internal Colonization."[2] Moshe Lewin also used it to describe the differences between Bolshevik and peasant culture, and Lynne Viola expanded its use in her book *Peasant Rebels*.[3] More recently, Alexander Etkind stresses that the Tsarist government used the phrase "internal colonization" – *vnutrennaia kolonizatsiia* – to describe policies designed, not to Russify non-Russian populations in the empire, but primarily to "civilize" and "domesticate" what were considered backward Russian peasants.[4] The early Soviet regime continued to use that phrase. The Soviet voluntary resettlement agency used the word *kolonizatsiia* right up until 1930, when the Stalinist regime shifted the language of modernization from colonization to the language of collectivization and dekulakization. Stalinist officials understood that they could not use the language of colonization, but colonization – or socialist colonization, or socialist occupation – are appropriate terms to describe Stalinist approaches to social order during the 1930s, not just in rural areas, but for the regime's approach to the entire population.

Stalin's comments about social disorder at the January 1933 Central Committee plenum remain an important but still underappreciated historical moment. By declaring social disorder the most serious threat to Soviet power, Stalin dramatically changed both the strategic direction of Soviet policing and the definition of state security. Following the plenum, all the state's judicial, police, and procuracy organs echoed Stalin's declarations about social order being tied to state security. Social order became the central priority of all policing work, both of the civil and political police. Stalin's phrases were codified word for word in the 1934 and 1935 yearly reports of the Supreme Court and the Procuracy to the government, each repeating Stalin's phrases that petty crime and social deviance defined the most dangerous of all threats against the state. Political police were involved in social policing throughout the 1920s, especially against banditry, contraband activities, and even hooliganism, but during that decade criminality and disorder were still regarded as social anomalies, not as threats to the very survival of the regime.[5] Stalin's comments in 1933 transformed public order and social control into a matter of state security and therefore the central business of the political police and, after 1934, the state's security organs. As Yoram Gorlizki points out in his essay, it was only in 1958 that the procuracy and judicial system once again codified criminality as a social danger rather than as a threat to state security. This reordering of criminality returned Soviet law to its status in the 1920s, which corresponded to the social understanding of crime in most countries.

It was at that same plenum meeting in January 1933 that we see the origin of what James Harris calls the "Great Fear" of the 1930s – of enemies masking in the form of loyal workers or collective farmers, or soviet *apparatchiki*.[6] While Soviet power remained strong in centralized Party and state institutions, Soviet order in many places, especially provincial areas, was much more difficult to impose. In many areas of the country, Soviet power looked more like that of a colonial outpost, spread thin and surrounded by hostile natives. Samantha Lomb's essay in this collection highlights this in vivid detail and shows the value of reading local against central archives. Lomb examines records from the Kirov region in central Russia. As she demonstrates, letters from local administrators to regional and district[7] offices during the 1930s reads like reports of colonial officials in other European empires – hostile natives, too few resources, too few people they can rely on, etc. Open hatred of Soviet power, beating of officials if caught alone, even murder, were not uncommon hazards for many local officials.[8]

For Stalin, the answer to this threat to Soviet power was to create his own kind of martial law socialism. This kind of martial law or colonial socialism developed in an ad hoc fashion, piecemeal, as the regime reacted to one social crisis after another, each one of which the regime itself created by its own policies. Passportization, of course, was a key part of the effort to impose social order and keep enemies at bay, as were urban police sweeps, expansion of the number of regime cities and zones, creation of youth detention colonies, forced displacement and deportation, exclusion zones, development of card catalogs for surveillance systems, and other such measures. Each response initially included civil institutions of governance, but then quickly gave way to militarization through intrusive police takeover.

There was, of course, a practical logic to the involvement of the police and security organs in issues of social control, especially given the under-governed character of the civil state. Social institutions were simply overwhelmed by the waves of social unrest and dislocation created by Stalin's revolutionary war from above. Still, Stalin resorted to militarization by inclination, as well. Given that he perceived social disorder as a threat to Soviet power, it is not surprising that Stalin also believed that the political police and security organs were the most appropriate institutions to respond to it. As the state extended its monopoly over all trade and economic activity in the country, almost all social deviance became, by definition, a threat to state power.

In her book *Stalin's Outcasts*, Golfo Alexopoulos noted that, during the 1920s, social marginals were identified by community organizations and even by vigilante consent.[9] Maria Starun's essay follows very much in this vein, given its focus on the different disciplinary frameworks in enterprises during the 1920s, none of which involved the political police, and with little discussion of sabotage or enemy aliens. This changed in the 1930s. Passportization shifted who did the defining of social outcasts – from social and Party-based institutions to police jurisdictions and criteria.

Passportization, of course, had a dual function: to separate out, or isolate, harmful elements, but also as a means of general social surveillance through registration of information in card catalogs, the *kartoteka* system. Similar processes of militarization occurred in dealing with the massive problems of orphans and unsupervised youth during the early and mid-1930s, as well as with the increasing criminalization of indigence and other kinds of social marginality.[10]

Social segregation was not just a matter of inclusion or exclusion. As I have noted elsewhere, there were degrees of exclusion, and these corresponded to geographic spaces. There was, in other words, a spatial dimension to Stalin's kind of colonial, or war, socialism.[11] Regime cities and areas were the most sacred of socialist spaces. These could be strategic areas, such as border zones, or privileged urban and industrial areas, or elite resorts. These were to be protected at all costs by passportization and regular police sweeps. Then there were the social dumping grounds that included whole regions: the Urals, Siberia, and Central Asia, especially. Such spatial divides were not simply dichotomous – between inclusion or exclusion, or between the western vs. eastern areas of the country. Peripheral areas near regime zones also collected the outcasts of Stalin's socialism, especially since many people were not exiled to faraway places but to exclusion zones 30–60 kilometers from urban areas. So, Stalin's was a militarized socialism, but one characterized by an increasingly complex mosaic of more or less socialist spaces. Residency restrictions placed on different populations created a complex mosaic of what officials described as near and alien elements and distant and near spaces. Passportization, in other words, was tied to a particular vision of internal colonization as well as to a corporate ordering of the state and society. That ordering was a geographic as well as a social, ethnic, and occupational construct. And the spatial as well as social segregation had to be policed by an occupying army constantly on guard for violation of social and spatial boundaries. It is no wonder that this kind of militarization was closely associated with the techniques of administrative or police repression, and the withering of civil and judicial processes.

There were, of course, many in the procuracy and judicial systems who loathed police methods and police intrusion into the civil administration of Soviet society. Aaron Sol'ts, for example, a deputy state procurator, wanted to see the political police restricted, even abolished, and more attention given to the civic aspects of socialism. Sol'ts championed legal process over arbitrary police power. Vyshinskii, the country's chief procurator, also defended legal process, but not because Vyshinskii cared about legal rights of citizens. Vyshinskii's ongoing arguments with Iagoda and the police were not about reducing repression but about the function of repression, how it was carried out. The chief procurator believed that repression should be carried out within the legal and court system, in open sight, as a didactic instrument for social disciplining. Iagoda did not care about social disciplining. As a policeman, his job was to ensure the removal of social danger as quickly and as effectively as possible.

This difference of views between Iagoda and Vyshinskii over the function of repression was at the heart of many disputes between the procuracy and the NKVD. One of the most absurd examples of this difference arose in 1936 over the issue of whether to allow the repetition in open court of anecdotes, comic verses, and slanderous epithets about Soviet power or the country's leaders. Iagoda wished these to be suppressed for reasons of security and so as not to turn the courts into a forum for the spread of anti-Soviet slander. Vyshinskii argued that they should be allowed under rules for presenting evidence, but also, and mainly, in order to educate listeners in the unforgiving ways that the state deals with those who slander it. In the end, *sovnarkom*, the Council of People's Commissars, resolved the matter by ordering that the content of slanderous remarks be entered into the court record, but recited only in closed sessions of courts.[12]

This distinction between the didactic and strategic functions of repression mirrors the way Stalin, throughout his rule, played the procuracy, the Party, and police against each other. During the 1930s, it was generally police that had the upper hand in Stalin's martial law socialism. As Immo Rebitschek has shown, that balance of power shifted more to the state's legal institutions after Stalin's death.[13]

Campaigns such as passportization, police sweeps, deportations and displacements, and police-run youth colonies were often referred to collectively as measures of social defence – *mery obshestvennoi zashchity* – and they were designed to protect socialist areas of the country from contamination by anti-Soviet elements. And according to the head of the political police, Genryk Iagoda, they worked. In his 1936 report on the NKVD to the *sovnarkom*, Iagoda declared, confidently, that the problem of social disorder had been largely resolved. The NKVD's three-year effort to identify and contain anti-Soviet and dangerous social "elements" had been a success.[14]

And then, suddenly, came order 00447 from July 1937, the NKVD order that launched the mass repressions of 1937 and 1938 against the very social categories that had supposedly been successfully neutralized. Of course, by early 1937, Iagoda had been replaced by Nikolai Ezhov and arrested. So, it is understandable that Ezhov attempted to discredit Iagoda's policies. But, still, the suddenness and violence of the mass operations has never been definitively explained. Some argue that the mass purges arose out of fears about enfranchising anti-Soviet groups in the 1936 Constitution. Others argue that they were prophylactic measures to purge fifth-column groups in case of war. Still others see the mass purges as a logical and extreme culmination of proactive policies of social shaping that reached back into the 1920s, and even before.[15] Scholars such as Peter Holquist and Amir Weiner highlighted this idea in several groundbreaking articles from the 1990s and early 2000s about violence and modernity in Russia and the Soviet Union. As Holquist wrote in 2003, "Soviet state violence was not simply repressive. It was employed as a tool for fashioning an idealized image of a better, purer society."[16]

More recently, Marc Junge has picked up this theme, arguing that a direct line can be traced from proactive social engineering policies during the 1920s to their logical and ultimate consummation in the mass operations of the late 1930s. As Junge writes: "the Great Terror [sic] was not primarily an exceptional treatment or reaction to external and internal problems. Instead, the Great Terror [sic] of 1937–1938 should be seen in the longer term as a cumulative consequence and peak of a specifically Soviet system of social disciplining that acted, proactively in the sense of political and social engineering."[17]

Such arguments are true to an extent, but only to a limited extent. Certainly, the mass purges of the late 1930s were connected to the previous policies of social control. The Soviet regime had been dealing with huge problems of social displacement and marginal populations since its inception. These problems resulted from the years of war and revolution, and they became exacerbated by the massive dislocations of the first Five-Year Plans in the early 1930s. There certainly was a connection between social marginals and the mass operations of 1937 and 1938. Ezhov made this connection clear at the beginning of the 00447 order, which was designed to resolve ongoing threats of social disorder "once and for all time [*raz i na vsegda*]." So, as Junge and others argue, the mass operations were connected to previous problems of social disorder.[18] This provides a larger context in which to understand the mass purges of the late 1930s, but it does not explain those purges. The cumulative social engineering argument leaves two key questions unanswered: why the mass operations came when they did, in the summer of 1937, and why they shifted policies of social order so dramatically from containment to extermination. The idea of cumulative social engineering explains neither of these historical moments.

The policies of social control of the mid-1930s were not part of some ongoing dynamic of social engineering. Documents about the origin of these policies make clear that they were as much reactive as proactive. True, officials hoped that passportization would catch undesirables before they could disrupt public order. But passportization also originated as a circumstantial response by officials to unanticipated waves of social disruption, mass migration, and the beginnings of famine. The essay by Aaron Retish captures well this dual character of social control policies. Strengthening and enforcement of the state's alimony laws during the 1930s arose as a result of a perceived crisis – the increasing burden on the state having to support women and children whose husbands and fathers had left them. At the same time, As Retish shows, officials hoped that renewed enforcement of alimony payments would act as a social defence against indigent children becoming vagrants and criminals. Retish refers to the latter as a prophylactic measure, but the campaign was both prophylactic and reactive.

Whether proactive, prophylactic, or reactive, campaigns of social defence were instituted to consolidate and defend the gains of the state after its costly but victorious revolutionary war, from 1929 to 1933, to conquer the economy and society. This consolidation was not the revolutionary retreat that Nicholas Timasheff identified in his famous 1946 book *The Great Retreat*.[19] It was not a retreat from revolution, but more a consolidation of state power, the consolidation of an occupying or colonizing force. To use the Bolshevik's own metaphor, in 1929 and 1930, the Bolshevik regime, under Stalin's command, came down from the famous commanding heights of NEP and conquered the economic and social valleys below. This they accomplished at tremendous cost by early 1933. The period of the mid-1930s, then, was a period of occupation and consolidation of that victory. This understanding also makes sense of why, particularly in the summer of 1934, the regime abolished the OGPU, the unified political directorate. A political police was no longer sufficient to protect the state's new monopolies of power. In its place, Stalin's regime created a Chief Directorate for State Security, the GUGB, housed as the main administration within a full-blown Commissariat of Interior, the NKVD.

In her contribution, Amanda McNair reminds us that this new state system was not just a police state. She raises the ghost of Foucault by diving below the level of police administration, down into the micro-level to analyse the role that professionals were forced to play, in this case doctors, as agents of social control. After the anti-abortion law of 1936 came into effect, doctors were, of course, held criminally accountable for performing the procedure. Even more, Williams shows, officials pressured doctors to act as informants, criminal investigators, and educators, all in their capacity to police women's bodies for the state. Whatever policies and campaigns we discuss – outright policing or stricter abortion and alimony laws, they all amounted to greater state control over bodies. They fit within an interpretive framework of consolidation or colonization.

Colonization was not just imposed by police methods, of course. As Samantha Lomb shows in her contribution, tax policies served as a powerful, if often contradictory, means to promote the regime's goals. Her essay shows, especially, the complexity of policies of exclusion or inclusion. As Lomb shows, the central regime acted in rather contradictory ways towards the *edinolichniki*, single-hold farmers who refused to join collectives. Central officials often reprimanded local officials for taxing *edinolichniki* too heavily. Local officials, in contrast, generally pressed for higher taxes and fines that would eliminate any and all private holdings. Lomb's essay also demonstrates, as noted above, the extent to which Soviet power was a colonial power in many of the rural areas of the country.

In his discussion, Timothy Blauvelt shows that the regime's values, culture, and ability to control was not just imposed through colonizing policies, but were internalized by many, especially police agents. As Blauvelt's interesting paper demonstrates, the police agent Sergo Davlianidze's views and acceptance of violence was not so much shaped by a background of war or Civil War, but by the regime's own discourse and by a kind of crowd mentality akin to "crowd violence in slow motion." Blauvelt rejects the notion that Stalinism created an inescapable world view encompassing all Soviet subjects, but he argues that, given the culture of the police, it would have been very difficult, if not impossible, for somebody like Davlianidze in his situation to think outside of the official discourse.

The violence that caught up to people such as Davlianidze was, of course, the mass purges of 1937–8. As we know, the single most deadly campaign of that particularly brutal kind of social control was the NKVD special order 00447 from July 1937. That order, and the operations it launched, were the ultimate in proactive or prophylactic social control, as well as the ultimate measure of state defence. At the same time, viewing this order only as the ultimate response to a host of accumulating social problems falls short of answering two key questions – why it came when it did, and why it so dramatically changed policies towards social marginals from containment to extermination.

To answer these questions, we must consider this order, as well as other campaigns of mass repression, as part of Stalin's mobilization against foreign threat. There were, of course, a number of factors that brought about the cataclysm of the Great Purges of the late 1930s, but it was that circumstance – mobilization for possible war – more than any other single cause that explains the sudden radicalization of social control policies in the summer of 1937 from reaction and containment to prophylactic extermination. Other factors certainly played a role in bringing about the mass operations of the late 1930s. Yes, local officials were worried about being besieged by hostile populations, especially given a new constitution that seemed to give licence to anti-Soviet elements. Local and regional officials expressed alarm about hostile populations in the context of elections to the new Supreme Soviet coming in 1937 and 1938.[20] In the absence of direct documentation, however, we should rely, again, on context and language. Mass social purging as part of war mobilization is consistent with the other mass operations launched during the same period for the same reason, especially the nationality operations and the so-called *kharbintsy* operation against workers that had previously worked on the Chinese–Soviet railroad that cut across parts of Mongolia and Manchuria. Also, and important, the dominant language of the mass operations in 1937 and 1938, and of the purges, was, in general, not about elections to the Supreme Soviet, not really about the new Constitution of 1936, nor about creating a perfect society; it was the language of preventing insurrection and insurgency in the event of war. Even the very pattern of the operations – where they were most intense – also points to vulnerable border regions or lines of communication.[21]

The change in language from containment to extermination occurred suddenly, and that change in language was no accident. It was sudden and it was perpetrated by officials at all levels. We see it not only in social order policies but in the language of the major show trials as well. The August 1936 Trial of the Sixteen, still under Iagoda, was full of Zinovievists and Trotskyists plotting to destroy the Soviet Union, but not of foreign spies and governments plotting invasion. It was the second major show trial, in January 1937, this one under Ezhov, that connected these groups specifically to foreign governments, sabotage, and insurrection. Stalin's speech to the February–March plenum in 1937 was also full of the same language. Whether realistic or not, the dominant narrative in the mass operations and the purges of 1937 and 1938 was about war, sabotage, and insurgency.

So, if we read the historical evidence forward, not in hindsight, what we see during the 1930s is a regime lurching, in an ad hoc fashion, from one crisis to another, each one of which was unanticipated and each one the regime itself created by its own policies. I see the 1930s, therefore, unfolding in several phases, each interrelated but also different. The first phase involved a colonial-revolutionary war from 1928 to early 1933, a costly but victorious war to subdue the economy and society below. Stalinist policies of social control during the middle part of the decade were designed to consolidate the gains of the state after that war and, as I have described, to deal with the waves of social crisis that resulted from it. Late 1936 brought a new crisis, the renewed threat of war, not with Poland this time, but with Japan and Germany. The extraordinary violence of the Great Purges was the regime's reactionary and prophylactic attempt to secure the homeland in case of invasion. Social order policies were certainly connected across these periods, but in applying policies of mass police repression, whether containment or extermination, Stalin and other Soviet leaders were not acting simply or only on ideological impulses to create an idealized body politic. Stalinist leaders used mass forms of repression and violence in response to a specific sequence of crises.

Of course, few of the campaigns of social control put in place by the Stalinist regime achieved their goals. On the contrary, they tended to exacerbate the problems they were designed to resolve. Passportization created a huge reserve of undesirables, which required even more resources to police. The number of regime cities and zones increased several fold over the 1930s, and then became so numerous they were divided into different gradations of "regime-ness." Even the mass operations failed to achieve their goals. Police and official memorandums from the last two years of the 1930s were filled with just as many complaints about petty crime, marginals, etc., as before 1937. Also, and importantly, the decimation of police and procuracy ranks by the purges only made the problems of social order more acute.

Public and social order became even more difficult to enforce during and immediately after the chaos of the war years. Passport and residence regulations were already quite complex, even arcane, by the time the Great Patriotic War began in June 1941. To this complexity the war added anywhere from 17 to 25 million evacuees and displaced people from western areas to cities and towns in the Urals, Central Asia, and western Siberia. And then came whole groups of deported ethnic communities. How were these populations to be accommodated, especially given the shortages and haste of the war years? What kind of documents would they have? What kind of rations, or housing? And what exactly was their status in comparison to local populations who had to absorb the newcomers or live near deported groups? In recent years, a number of studies have appeared depicting the chaos that accompanied attempts to maintain some kind of social order during and just after the war. As Larry Holmes shows in his excellent study of Kirov, local populations at first welcomed evacuees but soon resented their intrusion as the war deepened the crises of food supply and shelter.[22] The hyper-centralization of the war years affected mainly the military effort, supplying war-oriented factory areas with supplies and equipment. Analogously, war conditions exacerbated the kind of militarization that had characterized the 1930s in certain areas of social policy. Care of homeless children, for example, became even more draconian in the 1940s than in the 1930s as custodial institutions became little more than prisons for child labour. In Olga Kucherenko's memorable phrase, Stalinist social policies during the war can be described more as a form of warfare socialism than welfare socialism.[23]

War-time militarization affected many aspects of Soviet life, but other aspects, and even whole areas of the country, were left to their own devices. Mechanisms of social control broke down. Black and gray markets flourished. Migrants, refugees, former convicts, demobilized soldiers, and others flooded, often unchecked, into and through cities and industrial areas and even across borders. Many police officials acknowledged that they could not enforce residence or registration rules. The very inaccuracy of evacuation numbers is evidence of the lack of organization and the chaos of social life in the Soviet Union during and just after the war years.[24]

As is often noted, the Gulag system operated as a microcosm of Soviet society more broadly and, in his essay on *katorga* policies, Alan Barenberg depicts the disruptions and confusion that characterized the Soviet camp system during and after the war. As Barenberg notes, *katorga* was the ad hoc system that arose inside the Gulag administration for cataloguing and handling wartime and immediate post-war categories of prisoners convicted of collaboration with German occupation forces. These were not traditional camp inmates, as Barenberg explains, and camp administrators devised on-the-spot measures to deal with these new groups. In his essay, Barenberg examines the various proposals put forward to standardize these ad hoc measures. He shows how these proposals reflected the confusion and cross-purposes that existed within and between the judicial and police bureaucracies. Gulag administrators tended to see *katorga* inmates as expendable exploitative labour, while judicial officials argued that their level of isolation and punishment should accord to the degree and kinds of crimes they committed; in other words, to the degree they represented a social danger. Interestingly, and as Barenberg notes, this confusion did not just reflect chaotic temporary wartime conditions but also long-standing differences in institutional functions between the judiciary and police: social (punitive) ordering based on perceived threat to society vs. maximization of productive exploitation. Barenberg concludes that policies tended to represent a contradictory combination of both these functions, and his essay reminds us to be careful about attributing a single, totalizing organizational principle to population management and social control. As Barenberg writes, we should not lose sight of the "multiple logics" animating the operations of different state institutions and policies.

Militarization and violence marked much of the Stalinist approach to social order, but Barenberg's essay provides a thoughtful corrective to oversimplification. Barenberg's essay fits well with the complex jurisdictional and functional analysis offered in other contributions to this collection, such as the essays by Juliette Cadiot, for example, on theft laws, and Immo Rebitschek on juvenile policies in the late 1940s and 1950s. Barenberg's analysis of debates over policies and purposes of social control also reminds of the conflicts noted above from the 1930s between Genryk Iagoda, head of the NKVD, and Andrei Vyshinskii, the country's chief procurator, over the socially didactic vs. state security functions of repression. These essays and examples speak to a certain institutional continuity in Soviet history despite dramatic changes in the political and social order from the 1930s to the 1950s.

Ad hoc policies, contradiction, and confusion marked the Stalinist state's policies of social control, especially in the wake of four years of annihilating war. The complexity of regulations, along with the massive displacements caused by the conflict, made any kind of social control difficult, if not impossible. In the post-war period, many officials, even in the state's policing agencies, understood this and attempted to dismantle some of the complexity. Numerous proposals circulated within civil and even police administrations with suggestions to simplify the passport regime, even to passportize rural inhabitants or to eliminate entirely the different gradations of regime cities. Of course, simplification and uniformity of passport regulations or eliminating the status of regime cities, for example, were not motivated so much by sudden concerns about "socialist legality," but about the infeasibility to enforce the complex and cumbersome system of Stalin's militarized socialism. Such attempts made some headway but were not systemic until after the dictator's death. Still, as the essays in this collection show, the regime's struggle for social order did take two radically different and contradictory directions in the post-war years. The first trend was towards demilitarization; taking policing and issues of social control out of the hands of the security organs and returning them to the sphere of the civil police, the courts, and social agencies, at least within the 1939 borders of the country. Following the war, Stalin seemed to have made his peace with the Soviet population, and the depoliticization of criminality and marginality followed rather quickly after 1945. At the same time, the shift towards legal structures placed an enormous burden on civil institutions to enforce laws and maintain order. Immo Rebitschek's essay on juvenile misbehaviour shows this trend especially well. While policing of youth crime during the 1930s had been militarized, Rebitschek traces the transfer of that jurisdiction back mainly to the prosecutorial branches of civil government and the civil police (the *militsiia*), but also to an increasingly complex number of social and state institutions, none of which involved the security organs. What occurred as the regime attempted to take a more nuanced or more humane approach to juvenile delinquency, was that it resulted in a more chaotic way of dealing with juvenile misbehaviour.

The essay by Yoram Gorlizki dovetails nicely with Rebitschek's piece and with the work of Miriam Dobson. Gorlizki emphasizes the tension that arose in the 1950s between reformers' drive for the establishment of regularized legal procedure on the one hand and, on the other hand, the mostly public demand to take decisive action against the perception of rampant public disorder. What an irony that state officials finally gained the power to try to establish legal procedures to protect citizens against arbitrary police authority when those very citizens seemed to yearn for the forceful hand of the regime.[25]

Stalin, of course, did not retreat entirely from his pre-war regime of militarized social control. He never reversed his deportation orders, especially for ethnic groups, and the ethnicization of repression and control is a topic that has once again drawn interest in recent years.[26] Similarly, Stalin reinstituted harsh and large-scale campaigns against theft of state property. As Juliette Cadiot shows, the regime reasserted the state's control over social and economic transactions through those campaigns. The 1947 reassertion of these laws, first promulgated in 1932, were followed by a series of harsh campaigns in the 1950s. As the petitions for lenience demonstrate, those convicted under these laws recognized their violation of law but pleaded that they were not really criminals. Many argued that they had done what they did in order to survive, and they begged consideration of harsh circumstances, due to the war, or shortages, or famine conditions. In a sign of the waning of class categories, those convicted of theft also appealed to special service to the state (as police officials or soldiers) in order to mitigate their sentences. Cadiot shows that, in their petitions, they appealed to a pre-modern kind of moral economy to justify their actions. In drawing these distinctions, Cadiot shows that the 1947 laws and anti-theft campaigns served not so such to prevent theft as to lay down a blueprint for new social relations, or rather an assertion of social norms imposed by the Stalinist state. As Yoram Gorlizki points out, socialist property laws often backfired, or were not enforced stringently since they clashed with more traditional norms that accepted petty theft for the sake of survival. Those charged with enforcing the state's harsh theft laws did not share the underlying values of the sanctity of property, whether state or private. This is very much in keeping with Cadiot's reformulation of that argument as a clash between modern (socialist) property laws and a pre-modern kind of moral economy largely accepted by much of the population, including those charged with enforcing the new property and moral norms.[27]

The promulgation of the 1947 property laws, however, was much more than just a reassertion of the 1932 laws. The difference lay in that, after the war, Stalin enforced those laws through the legal structures of the courts and procuracy rather than through the militarized extra-judicial tribunals of the political police and state security agency. Transition to the codified laws of an emerging civic state in the post-war era, in itself, signified a major change from the ad hoc occupation policies of the Stalinist militarized or colonial state of the 1930s.[28]

Stalin's death on 5 March 1953 accelerated the transition of the Soviet Union away from the emergency war state of the 1930s and 1940s. As some authors suggest, however, and as the previous discussion shows, the transition was not as abrupt as historians previously described, nor as welcome by Soviet citizens as many have assumed. Many citizens, in fact, resented, or at least were confused by, the de-Stalinization campaigns of the new General Secretary, Nikita Khrushchev. The new leaders aimed to dismantle the harsher aspects of the Stalinist regime, but less repression seemed to translate into greater lawlessness. Many longed for a return to the heavy hand of authority to suppress the perceived increase in public disorder that characterized much of the 1950s. Although citizens had been subject to arbitrary, especially repressive, treatment under Stalin's regime, by the mid- and late 1950s, they were hemmed in and subject to an increasingly bewildering web of laws, regulations, and state interference in their lives. If the Stalinist state could be characterized as a militarized kind of socialism, the Soviet Union of his successors came more to resemble something of an authoritarian civic state.

Still, despite some remaining Stalinist sentiments and institutions, things changed, and for the better. Mass murderous repression ceased to exist. The regime opened most if not all of the labour camps. Though clumsy and often in contradictory ways, Soviet institutions, especially the power institutions, began to adhere to constituted legal procedures. And Soviet citizens adapted, as always. Many Soviet citizens may have resented the welter of norms and rules imposed by socialist property laws, for example, but as Dinal Moyal shows, they also learned to use the state's post-war and post-Stalinist norms to defend their own interests. Moyal's contribution explores the ways Soviet citizens turned the tables and used the banner of socialist legality to flood civic courts with complaints against officials and courts. During the Khrushchev period, she notes, the state used the promise of housing to monitor, gain popular support, and prioritize privilege among different social classes. Citizens, however, used the law and notions of social justice to defend their own interests in housing disputes. Citizens internalized quite well the new discourse on law, which emphasized "socialist legality," "rights," and a promise of "justice" and morality for the people, rather than just obedience to law on the part of citizens. As a result, while the state tried to use housing to control population movement and instil socialist values, citizens turned the legal process to their own advantage and, in this sense, became players in the legal game.[29]

As the examples above show, if one post-war trend involved the demilitarization of social control, either by design or by default, the other trend went in a different direction. As responsibility for social control passed from the security sate to the civil state, it, oddly, created a greater degree of legal and judicial intrusion into the daily lives of Soviet citizens. During the 1930s, Soviet citizens might be subject to arbitrary repression under an occupying power; now they were increasingly subject to a complexity of fines, arrests, and imprisonment for an increasingly complex list of civil violations. Harsh labour laws were the most famous example, but only the tip of the iceberg, and this was a trend that continued into the post-Stalin period. As Dinal Moyal writes in her essay: "under Khrushchev, the relations between the private and the public spheres were redefined: from a model of repression of the private by the state ... [to] a model of intrusion – the development of plethora of public mechanism designed to police and monitor the population to ensure socialist norms were properly followed in the private sphere."

This post-war order involved a different kind of socialism, not the militarized or colonial socialism of the 1930s, but something more like a civic authoritarianism. Allen Kassof hinted at this in his groundbreaking 1964 article "The Administered Society," describing post-Stalinist society as totalitarianism without the terror.[30] We may have jettisoned the term "totalitarianism," but work of scholars such as Brian Lapierre, Immo Rebitschek, and Yoram Gorlizki point in this direction. Enforcing social order was a large and increasingly complex problem, but it was no longer tied to the security of the state. And even the role of the state's "security" organs began to change. Evgenia Lezina's richly sourced paper follows very much in this vein, detailing the revived and central role of the state security agency in an increasingly complex web of social surveillance and preventative control. Renouncing mass repression, the post-Stalinist KGB nonetheless assumed an "orchestrating" role in tracking dissidents, religious groups, students, disaffected youth, and others. No longer a state unto itself, this new KGB relied more on increasingly sophisticated methods, civilian cooperation, and collective work with Party and other social organizations to identify, isolate and punish, shame, or re-educate offenders. By the end of the 1950s, as Lezina shows, the new KGB had rehabilitated its reputation not as an organ of terror but as a pillar of the new order of socialist legality.

As the contributions in this collection show, after 1945, the Soviet regime was shifting away from the kind of colonial and martial-law socialism of the 1930s. Social order became increasingly the business of the civil state and codified in an increasingly intricate web of laws, social practice, and judicial and corrective institutions. The police and security organs played a significant enforcement role in this authoritarian social system, but they no longer possessed the arbitrary power they wielded in the 1930s.

NOTES

1 For one of the most articulate statements of Stalin's martial law socialism, see Olga Velikanova, "The First Stalin Mass Operation (1927)," *The Soviet and Post-Soviet Review* 40 (2013): 64–89, especially 78–9. See my own formulation of Stalin's "war socialism" in Stalinskii voennyi sotsializm: Repressia i sotsial'nyi poriadok pri Staline, 1924–1953 (Moscow: Rosspen, 2014) and "Stalin at War 1918–1953: Patterns of Violence and External Threat," *Jahrbücher für Geschichte Osteuropas* 66, no. 2 (2018): 188–217.
2 Alvin Gouldner, "Stalinism: A Study in Internal Colonization," *Telos: Critical Theory of the Contemporary* 34 (December 1977): 5–48.
3 Lynne Viola, *Peasant Rebels under Stalin: Collectivization and the Culture of Resistance* (New York: Oxford University Press, 1996).
4 Alexander Etkind, *Internal Colonization: Russia's Imperial Experience* (Cambridge: Polity, 2011).
5 Stuart Finkel, "An Intensification of Vigilance: Recent Perspectives on the Institutional History of the Soviet Security Apparatus in the 1920s," *Kritika: Explorations in Russian and Eurasian History* 5, no. 2 (Spring 2004): 299–320; Paul Hagenloh, *Stalin's Police: Public Order and Mass Repression in the USSR, 1926–1941* (Washington, DC: Johns Hopkins University Press, 2009); David Shearer, *Policing Stalin's Socialism: Repression and Social Order in the Soviet Union, 1924–1953* (New Haven, CT: Yale University Press, 2009).
6 James Harris, *The Great Fear: Stalin's Terror of the 1930s* (Oxford: Oxford University Press, 2016).
7 "Regional" and "district" refer to the Russian administrative units "oblasti" and "raiony."
8 Lomb's descriptions of conditions in the Kirov district strongly resonate with my own reading in western Siberia archives. See David Shearer, "Modernity and Backwardness on the Soviet Frontier: Western Siberia during the 1930s," in *Provincial Landscapes: Local Dimensions of Soviet Power, 1917–1953*, ed. Donald Raleigh (Pittsburgh: University of Pittsburgh Press, 2001), 194–216.
9 Golfo Alexopoulos, *Stalin's Outcasts: Citizens and the Soviet State, 1926–1936* (New Haven, CT: Yale University Press, 2003).
10 Hagenloh, *Stalin's Police*; and David Shearer, *Policing*.

11 Shearer, *Policing*, 244.
12 Gosudarstvennyi arkhiv Rossiskoi Federatsii (GARF) R-5446/18a/849/1–4. Shearer, *Policing*.
13 Immo Rebitschek, *Die disziplinierte Diktatur: Stalinismus und Justiz in der sowjetischen Provinz, 1938 bis 1956* (Köln/Weimar/Wien: Bohlau Verlag, 2018).
14 Shearer, *Policing*, 285.
15 See especially Peter Holquist, "To Count, to Extract, to Eliminate: Population Politics in Late Imperial and Soviet Russia," in *A State of Nations: Empire and Nation Making in the Age of Lenin and Stalin*, ed. Ronald Suny and Terry Martin (Oxford: Oxford University Press, 2001), 111–44.
16 Peter Holquist, "State Violence as Technique: The Logic of Violence in Soviet Totalitarianism," in *Landscaping the Human Garden: Twentieth-Century Population Management in Comparative Framework*, ed. Amir Weiner (Stanford, CA: Stanford University Press, 2003), 19–45. At the same time, other scholars presented powerful arguments linking modernity with schemes of population management, often with disastrous, totalitarian consequences: Zygmunt Bauman, *Modernity and the Holocaust* (Cambridge: Polity Press, 1991); James C. Scott, *Seeing Like a State: How Certain Schemes to Improve the Human Condition Have Failed* (New Haven, CT: Yale University Press, 1998).
17 Forthcoming, Marc Junge, Andrei Savin, Aleksei Tepliakov, "The Origins of Stalin's Mass Operations. The Extra-Judicial Special Assembly, 1922–1953," *The Secret Police and the Soviet System: New Archival Investigations*, ed. Michael David-Fox and Phil Kiffer (Pittsburgh: University of Pittsburgh Press, 2023).
18 In addition to Junge, see Hagenloh, *Stalin's Police*; and Shearer, *Policing*.
19 Nicholas Timasheff, *The Great Retreat: The Growth and Decline of Communism in Russia* (Boston: E.P. Dutton & Co., 1946).
20 See the essay by Samantha Lomb in this collection. See also Shearer, note 8, above; J. Arch Getty, "Pre-election Fever: The Origins of the 1937 Mass Operations," in *The Anatomy of Terror: Political Violence under Stalin*, ed. James Harris (London: Oxford University Press, 2013), 216–35; Olga Velikanova, "The Myth of the "Besieged Fortress: Soviet Mass Perception in the 1920s–1930s" (Toronto: Centre for Russian and East European Studies, University of Toronto, Munk Centre for International Studies, 2002).
21 Mark Iunge and Rol'f Binner, *Kak terror stal "bol'shim": Sekretnyi prikaz No. 00447 i tekhnologiia ego ispolneniia* (Moskva: AIRO-XX, 2003).
22 Larry E. Holmes, *Stalin's World War II Evacuations: Triumph and Troubles in Kirov* (Lawrence: University Press of Kansas, 2017).
23 Olga Kucherenko, *Soviet Street Children and the Second World War: Welfare and Social Control under Stalin* (London: Bloomsbury, 2016).

24 Shearer, *Policing*, 402–3.
25 Miriam Dobson, *Khrushchev's Cold Summer: Gulag Returnees, Crime, and the Fate of Reform after Stalin* (New Haven, CT: Yale University Press, 2009).
26 See, for example, the collection edited by Andrej Kotljarchuk and Olle Sundström, *Ethnic and Religious Minorities in Stalin's Soviet Union: New Dimensions of Research* (Stockholm: Södertörn Academic Studies 72, 2017), especially the essay by Andrey Savin, "Ethnification of Stalinism? Ethnic Cleansings and the NKVD Order № 00447 in a Comparative Perspective," 47–66.
27 Yoram Gorlizki, "Theft under Stalin: A Property Rights Analysis," *The Economic History Review* 69, no. 1 (2016): 288–313.
28 Gorlizki refers to this civil authoritarianism as a "proprietary" state and identifies its emergence even in the 1930s. This essay stresses the postwar emergence. Gorlizki also notes that, after Stalin's death, the "absolute priority" of socialist property laws unravelled quickly.
29 Moyal parallels Gorlizki's argument, above, about the unravelling of the Stalinist "absolute" conception of socialist legality after Stalin's death. As Moyal writes: "Contrary to official declarations of the 1930s and 1940s that demanded legality mainly of the citizens, post-Stalinist newspapers, journals and books stressed the centrality of law for the orderly functioning of both state and society, and in defense of citizen rights. Already a few months after Stalin's death, a shift could be observed in newspaper articles, where the focus changed from blaming thieves, pilferers of public property, morally corrupt elements, and foreign intelligence services, to examining and criticizing the work of Party and state officials in general and workers of the law system in particular."
30 Allen Kassof, "The Administered Society: Totalitarianism without Terror," *World Politics* 16, no. 4 (July 1964): 558–75.

Contributors

Alan Barenberg is the Buena Vista Foundation Associate Professor of History at Texas Tech University. He is the author of *Gulag Town, Company Town: Forced Labor and Its Legacy in Vorkuta* (2014) and co-editor (with Emily D. Johnson) of *Rethinking the Gulag: Identities, Sources, Legacies* (2022).

Timothy K. Blauvelt is Professor of Soviet and Post-Soviet Studies at Ilia State University in Tbilisi, Georgia, and is also Regional Director for the South Caucasus for American Councils for International Education. He has published several dozen peer-reviewed articles and book chapters. His co-edited volume (with Jeremy Smith) *Georgia after Stalin: Nationalism and Soviet Power* was published by Routledge in 2016, and his co-edited volume (with Adrian Brisku) *The Transcaucasian Democratic Federative Republic of 1918: Federal Aspirations, Geopolitics and National Projects* was published by Routledge in 2021. His monograph *Clientelism and Nationality in an Early Soviet Fiefdom: The Trials of Nestor Lakoba* was also published by Routledge in 2021.

Juliette Cadiot is Professor of modern Russian and Soviet history at the EHESS, Paris, with a particular focus on the history of the social sciences, political history, and the socio-history of law and justice. She authored *Hors Plan: L'économie informelle en URSS* (2018) and most recently *La société des voleurs – Propriété et socialisme sous Stalin* (2021).

Yoram Gorlizki is Professor and Head of Politics at the University of Manchester. His most recent book, co-authored with Oleg Khlevniuk, is *Substate Dictatorship: Networks, Loyalty, and Institutional Change in the Soviet Union* (Yale, 2020). He is currently completing a book on the Soviet justice system.

Contributors

Evgenia Lezina is research associate at the Leibniz Centre for Contemporary History Potsdam, and Senior Research Fellow for the Levada Center in Moscow. She received her PhD in Political Systems and Institutional Change in 2010 at the ITM Institute for Advanced Studies Lucca, where she completed her dissertation on *Transformations of Political Culture in Post-Totalitarian Societies: Post–World War II West Germany and Post-Soviet Russia in Comparative Perspective*. She is currently conducting research on the history of the Soviet state security agencies after Stalin.

Samantha Lomb is Assistant Professor in the Department of Foreign Languages at Vyatka State University in Kirov, Russia, where she has been teaching since 2012. She completed her PhD in History at the University of Pittsburgh in 2014. Her book, *Stalin's Constitution: Soviet Participatory Politics and the Discussion of the 1936 Draft Constitution*, was published in November 2017 by Routledge press. She is currently conducting research for a future book manuscript on daily life on the collective farms and the day-to-day relationships between collective farmers and local officials.

Amanda McNair is a PhD Candidate at the University of Leeds. She received her MA in history from the University of Mississippi in 2016. He dissertation project is entitled "Materials for Maternity: The Abortion Procedure, Communist Morality, and Urbanisation in Soviet Russia, 1944–1968."

Dina Moyal (LLB, PhD) is a legal historian of the Soviet Union. She teaches Modern Russian History at Tel Aviv University. Dina's research focuses on Russian/Soviet legal culture and the role of legal mechanisms in realizing and sustaining social and political goals in Russia.

Immo Rebitschek is Assistant Professor at Friedrich Schiller University Jena. In 2018, he published his monograph on the history of the Soviet procuracy under Stalin: *Die disziplinierte Diktatur: Stalinismus und Justiz in der sowjetischen Provinz, 1938 bis 1956*. He is currently writing a history of famine relief in Late Imperial Russia.

Aaron B. Retish is a Professor at Wayne State University. He authored *Russia's Peasants in Revolution and Civil War: Citizenship, Identity, and the Creation of the Soviet State, 1914–1922*. He has worked extensively on violence in the revolutionary era, local courts, and penal reform, and he is co-editor of *Revolutionary Russia*. His current project is entitled "In the People's Court: Judges, Peasants, and Soviet Justice in the Rural Courtroom, 1917–1939."

David Shearer is a Professor at the University of Delaware. He published several books on the history of Stalinism, social structures, and the political polices in Stalin's Russia: e.g. *Industry, State, and Society in Stalin's Russia, 1926–1934* (1997) and *Policing Stalin's Socialism: Repression and Social Order in the Soviet Union, 1924–1953* (2009). Together with Vladimir Khaustov he published *Stalin and the Lubianka: A Documentary History of the Political Police and Security Organs in the Soviet Union, 1922–1953* (2015).

Maria Starun is a PhD student at Higher School of Economics in St. Petersburg and a scholar of Soviet jurisprudence and legal practice. She received her MA in history at Saint Petersburg State University in 2017.

Index

Abakumov, Viktor S., 112, 117
abortion, 6, 12, 26, 33–5, 41, 74n85, 83, 187–209, 239, 333
appeals, 10, 13, 29, 32, 36, 92, 98, 107–10, 112, 118–20, 141, 164, 166–8, 172–3, 175–6, 178, 180, 195, 203, 245, 250–1, 259n40, 303–6, 308–15, 339
acquittals, 204, 224–5, 235n64
alimony, 7, 10, 25–48, 71n20, 79, 190, 305, 332
All-Union Central Council of Trade Unions (VTsSPS), 80, 84–6, 88, 92
amnesty of 1953, 170, 178, 182n4, 214, 217, 229–30, 254, 264, 307
article 58, 67, 243
Azerbaijan, 246, 258n31, 310, 314

Beria, Lavrentii, 110–8, 122–3, 126, 127n2, 128n17, 128n19, 130n71, 135, 138, 143, 180, 182n4, 183n16, 185n63, 227, 229, 241, 257n20
Brezhnev, Leonid I., 254
Bulganin, Nikolai A., 112, 252

capital punishment, 135, 251, 260n65. *See also* death penalty
Central Asia, 43n7, 196, 327, 330

Cheka (state security police in 1920s), 109, 158n8; *see also* OGPU; NKVD; KGB
Chernyshev, Vasilii V., 135–7, 141–3
children: homeless, 130, 170, 217–8, 231, 300, 327, 336; care of, 12, 26, 34, 36, 46n59, 93, 215, 220, 222–3, 228–9, 231, 300, 336; and crime. *See under* juvenile crime; *see also* corrective labour colonies and camps for underage delinquents (DTVK/L)
Civil War, 58, 62, 80, 99n1, 108–9, 122, 173, 214, 334
codes: of criminal procedure, 223, 246, 259n54; criminal/penal, 36, 67, 103n67, 157n6, 161, 176, 181, 181n2, 183n33; family, 26, 28, 34–6, 41, 45n44, 46n59, 47n74; 74n85; tax, 52–3; labour, 85
collective farms, 3, 10, 27, 30–2, 34–5, 38–9, 43, 49–57, 59–65, 67–8, 70–73n75, 109, 168, 276, 278, 295n131. See also *kolkhoz*
collectivization, 5, 10, 30, 31–2, 34, 43n8, 46n46, 49–51, 53–6, 59, 62–4, 73n58, 240, 326, 327
Communist Party of the Soviet Union (CPSU), 8, 10, 113–4, 119, 173, 264,

350 Index

Communist Party of the Soviet Union (*continued*)
302, 306, 307; Central Committee of, 67, 85, 99n1, 118–20, 135, 242, 246–52, 265, 269, 290n13, 297n177, 319n24, 326–7; Presidium of, 246. *See also* Twentieth Party Congress.
constitution of 1936, 34–5, 52, 60, 63–4, 74n85, 161, 242, 244, 246–7, 305, 312, 331, 334–5
corrective labour colonies and camps for underage delinquents (DTVK/L), 227–8. *See also* Gulag
Council of Ministers, 247, 264, 319n24
Council of People's Commissars (Sovnarkom), 54, 58, 67, 85, 247
courts: comrades' courts, 10, 77–91, 93, 95–8, 101n13, 101n19, 102n24, 103n56, 103n58, 240, 253, 273, 279, 281–2, 295n133; people's courts, 26, 31, 33–7, 41, 42n4, 43n7, 80, 81, 85, 89, 91, 245, 266–7, 279–80, 282, 288; regional courts, 35–6, 200, 202, 226, 242, 250–1, 258n26, 306; Supreme Court (USSR) 19n3092, 35–36, 99, 167, 203, 226, 242–3, 246, 299, 303–12, 314–5, 320n25, 320n37, 321n44, 328; Supreme Court (RSFSR), 33, 37, 46n56, 250–1, 260n71, 314, 320n37, 322n52, Supreme Court (Ukraine), 307; Supreme Court (Azerbaijan), 310; Supreme Court (Armenia), 313. *See also* judges

death penalty, 114, 161, 177, 250–1. *See also* capital punishment
de-stalinization, 107, 117, 126, 340
divorce, 7, 25–6, 29, 33, 38–40, 47n71, 303–4, 311, 313

Estonia, 258n31, 264
Ezhov, Nikolai I., 113, 120, 331–2, 335

Five-Year Plan (First), 5, 77–80, 85–6, 88–90, 97, 100n3, 103n56, 326, 332
Foucault, Michel, 5, 100n3, 333

Georgia, 33, 107–130, 171, 183n17, 187, 196, 201, 237, 258n31, 312
Germany (Nazi), 14, 107, 137, 335
Gulag, 3–4, 6, 8, 11, 19nn28–29, 135–60, 161–2, 166, 172, 174–5, 177, 179–80, 214, 216–7, 221, 227–9, 238, 264–5, 276, 301, 307, 320n40, 337 *see also* prisons

hooliganism, 8, 34, 82, 215, 219–20, 238–40, 247–9, 251, 309, 328
housing, 5, 13, 195, 299–322, 336, 340
Hungary, 237, 249, 265

judges, 7, 28–9, 31–2, 34–42, 80, 87, 94, 161, 179, 204, 216, 223, 225–6, 229, 245, 248, 251, 305, 310–1, 315–6
juvenile crime/delinquency, 8, 12, 19n30, 30, 34, 176, 213–235, 301, 317n7, 338

Kaganovich, Lazar M., 55, 180, 317n5
katorga, 11, 135–60, 337
Khrushchev, Nikita S., 3–4, 6, 8–9, 14–5, 112, 118, 135–6, 155, 199, 207n39, 214, 231, 237, 239–43, 246, 249, 252–4, 258n33, 261n80, 265, 267–71, 276, 279, 281, 283, 287–8, 301–2, 307–8, 311, 316, 318n16, 340–1
Kiev/Kyiv, 196, 277, 283
Kirov region and city, 10, 25, 34, 46n59, 49–52, 56, 62, 66, 70n11, 71n32, 72n42, 73n73, 75n109, 250, 328, 336, 342n8
kolkhoz, 31, 32, 38, 42, 47n59, 168, 175, 226. *See also* collective farms

Index 351

Komsomol, 60, 77, 87, 98, 109–10, 165, 170, 213, 215, 237, 263, 266–7, 272–3, 275–6, 279–80, 282

labour, 11, 25, 30, 39, 55, 59, 64, 67, 77–99, 135–57, 160n35, 165–6, 168, 170, 175, 180–1n2, 203, 215–17, 221, 227, 231, 239, 243, 254, 266–78, 285–8, 300, 314, 336–7, 341.
See also katorga and corrective labour colonies and camps for underage delinquents (DTVK/L)
Latvia, 183n17, 244, 258n31, 264
law, 4, 9, 12–15, 27, 77–81, 93–4, 123, 126, 162, 180, 241–4, 309–13, 315, 328, 331, 339–42; civil, 7, 26, 29–30, 33, 35–42, 52, 55, 189–90, 195, 252–4, 305–6, 308, 332–3; criminal, 7, 88, 161, 168–9, 191, 203–4, 226, 228, 239–40, 244, 250, 263, 280, 337. *See also* socialist legality
lawyer, 8, 92, 114, 118, 141, 170, 175, 248, 310
Leningrad, 34, 80, 93, 103, 200, 201, 273, 276, 282, 303–06
Lithuania, 258n31, 264, 275–8

marriage 26–33, 38, 47n71, 165 190, 195, 303–4, 311, 313. *See also* divorce
mass operations, 3, 6–7, 15, 19n29, 214, 332, 334–6
Mikoian, Anastas I., 246, 248
Militsiia, 7, 12, 30, 213–14, 216, 218–221, 224, 232n1, 235n58, 235m59, 238–9, 252–4, 263, 279, 338. *See also* police.
Ministry for Internal Affairs (MVD), 145, 155, 160n36, 171, 216, 218–22, 227–9, 231, 247, 252, 257n20, 257n24

Ministry of Justice, 80, 167, 182n4, 190–1, 199–200, 217, 223, 226, 229.
See also People's Commissariat of Justice
Ministry of State Security (MGB), 111–12, 118, 171, 229, 231
Molotov, Viacheslav M., 55
Molotov region and city, 139, 145, 148, 150, 152, 154, 158n22, 217–20, 222, 225–30, 236n78
Moscow, 37, 49, 52, 54, 67, 69, 79–80, 84, 96, 112, 115, 118–20, 136, 167, 168, 226, 243, 249, 253, 260n61, 263, 277, 279–83, 303, 310–12, 314

New Economic Policy (NEP), 25, 30, 43n6, 80, 89–90, 97, 326, 333

Odessa, 278–80
OGPU, 110, 333

Party Congress, 20th, 107, 118, 237–54, 301. *See also* secret speech
peasant, 3, 10, 25–41, 49–68, 165, 174–5, 264, 299, 325–7; kolkhoznik, 32; kulak, 31, 50–1, 53, 56, 60, 63–67, 83; poor, 25, 28–9, 53–57, 75, 108, 165, 173; smallholder, 10, 49–69, 326
People's Commissariat of Agriculture (Narkomzem), 51, 56, 59, 67
People's Commissariat of Internal Affairs (NKVD), 7, 10–11, 19n29, 25, 27, 35, 42, 74n106, 107–8, 110–28, 130n71, 135, 142, 155, 158, 160n40, 166, 171, 218, 222, 230, 330–1, 333–4, 337, 344n26
People's Commissariat of Justice (Narkomiust or NKIu), 31–32, 80, 94, 88. *See also* Ministry of Justice

People's Commissariat of State Security (NKGB), 9, 13, 107, 111, 113, 1778–9, 242–3, 245–6, 264–88, 292n52, 319n18, 341
people's courts, 25–27, 29, 31–42, 46n59, 80–81, 85, 89, 98, 187, 202, 245, 263, 266–7, 276, 280–2, 288, 304–5
physicians, 12, 183, 189–205
Poland, 140, 265, 325–6, 335
police (civil), 3–15, 35, 41–42, 166, 171, 190–1, 195, 198, 201, 204, 213, 215–16, 218–19, 230–2, 237, 254, 325–6, 329–38, 342. *See also* militsiia
police (political), 6–7, 11, 13, 15, 17n11, 107–18, 122, 125, 129n17, 171, 176, 178–9, 238, 242, 263–87, 328–35, 342. *See also* KGB, NKVD, NKGB and MVD
prison, 3, 12, 135, 138, 188, 196, 198, 337
prisoners: 135–52, 153–57, 162–64, 167, 169, 171–72, 194, 177–79, 202, 217, 225, 264, 308, 337
prisoners of war (POWs), 135, 137, 140, 217
procuracy. *See* procurator
procurator, 3, 6, 7–8, 12, 19n29, 25, 52, 66–67, 115, 121, 126, 167–8, 175, 177, 182n4, 188, 190–3, 198–205, 213, 216–32, 241–5, 249–54, 263, 280–82, 303, 307, 309–11, 315, 320n37, 321n51, 328, 330–1, 336, 338–9
profilaktika, 266–7, 269–81, 285–8
Prosecutor General, 202, 216, 217, 223, 228, 242, 245, 252, 307, 311

rates and conflicts commissions (RKK), 77–79, 90–98
receiver distribution centres (DPK), 220–2

release: of Gulag prisoners, 136, 140–1, 145–7, 149–51, 154–56, 172, 214, 217, 238–9, 264, 301, 307–8
Rudenko, Roman A., 242, 252, 307
Russian Revolution, 80, 122, 312

Second World War, 11, 141, 144–5, 154, 158n14, 162, 176, 188, 189, 214, 224, 300–1, 305
secret speech, 237, 240, 243, 247, 265, 301. *See also* Party Congress, 20th
socialist legality, 12, 15, 78–9, 123, 127n2, 238–54, 256n16, 257n18, 267, 301–3, 309–16, 319n17, 338, 340–1
social control, 3–15, 25, 27, 38–39, 42, 52, 59, 68, 77–8, 82–3, 90, 92, 99, 108, 136–7, 155–6, 190–1, 197, 203–5, 214, 216, 219, 227, 231, 238, 253–4, 263–4, 272, 287, 299, 301–3, 310, 319n17, 325–41
social disorder, 3, 4, 12–14, 25, 88, 214–4, 231, 238, 253–4, 326–32, 339
Special Board of the NKVD (OSO), 142, 158n14
Stalin, Joseph V., 3–15, 30, 107, 140, 155, 161–2, 169, 171, 180–1, 199, 231–2, 237–52, 263, 268, 301, 325–42
Stalinism, 3–15, 77, 79, 107–8, 119–20, 124–6, 188–9, 203, 214–16, 240, 299–302, 325, 327, 334–42
Supreme Soviet of the USSR, 35–36; 68, 92, 99, 137, 141, 163–4, 167–8, 173, 203, 226, 242–3, 246, 249, 300–17, 320n25, 321n44, 328; of the RSFSR, 33, 37, 46n56, 244, 248, 250–1, 322n52
surveillance, 12–13, 41, 190–1, 196–7, 205, 263, 271–2, 278–83, 287–8, 325, 329, 341

taxes, 39, 49–59, 64, 68, 72n42, 75n111, 333
terror. *See* mass operations
Thaw, the, 113, 276, 301
theft, 8, 11–2, 81, 88–9, 161–74, 178–82n3, 188, 217–8, 220–1, 225–6, 228, 238–40, 247, 256n15, 258n26, 337, 339. *See also* criminal law
Tiflis/Tbilisi, 109

Ukraine, 49, 107, 169–70, 173, 194, 243–4, 264, 269, 271, 274, 276, 283
Uzbekistan, 244

Volin, Anatolii A., 226, 312, 314–15, 321n44
Vorkuta, 140. *See* Vorkutlag
Vorkutlag, 136, 139–44, 147–54, 158n11, 160n36
Voroshilov, Kliment, 173, 306, 311, 315
Vyshinskii, Andrei Ia., 330, 337

women, 10–14, 25–35, 38–42, 83, 93, 165, 176, 187–205, 284, 304–5, 332–3

youth. *See* children

Milton Keynes UK
Ingram Content Group UK Ltd.
UKHW011430250124
436693UK00009B/140/J